UNIVERSITY ~~EGE~~ ~~ER~~
KT-146-706

Martial Rose Library
Tel: 01962 827306

SEVEN DAY LOAN ITEM
To be returned on or before the day marked above, subject to recall.

Lyotard

While analytical philosophers of education have largely disregarded Lyotard, others have linked his work to "education as liberatory discourse." Against these inadequate responses, *Lyotard: just education* fills an important gap in the existing literature on Lyotard in general. This lively series of essays provides a timely exploration of the recurrent theme of education in his work, and brings to a wider audience the significance of this body of thought about education that is subtle, profound and largely unexplored.

The authors argue that Lyotard, following Wittgenstein and broader currents in the Western tradition, did not make a distinction between philosophy and the philosophy of education. This is not only an aspect of Lyotard's work which has been largely neglected until now, but it is also one which raises questions for the discipline of philosophy itself. Contributors to this volume come from a wide range of disciplines: education, French and philosophy; and each chapter extends the scholarship on Lyotard in relation to education, underlining the importance of his work to a wider academic audience. *Lyotard: just education* makes an important and timely contribution to contemporary debates on postmodernism and education.

The contributors: Gordon Bearn, Nicholas Burbules, Nigel Blake, Jan Masschelein and Paul Smeyers, Lynda Stone, Michael Peters, Richard Smith, James Williams, David Palumbo-Liu, A. Tuan Nuyen, J. M. Fritzman.

The editors: **Pradeep A. Dhillon** is Assistant Professor in the College of Education at the University of Illinois, Urbana-Champaign. In addition to her book, *Multiple Identities*, her articles have appeared in journals of philosophy and the philosophy of education. **Paul Standish** is a lecturer in the philosophy of education at the University of Dundee. His books include *Beyond the Self: Wittgenstein, Heidegger and the Limits of Language*, and *Thinking Again: Education after Postmodernism*, which he co-authored.

Routledge International Studies in the Philosophy of Education

Lyotard

Just education

Edited by
Pradeep A. Dhillon and Paul Standish

London and New York

First published 2000 by Routledge
11 New Fetter Lane, London EC4P 4EE

Simultaneously published in the USA and Canada
by Routledge
29 West 35th Street, New York, NY 10001

Routledge is an imprint of the Taylor & Francis Group

Typeset in Baskerville
by Curran Publishing Services Ltd, Norwich
Printed and bound in Great Britain
by MPG Books Ltd, Bodmin

British Library Cataloguing in Publication Data
A catalogue record for this book is available
from the British Library.

Library of Congress Cataloging in Publication Data
Lyotard : just education / edited by Pradeep A. Dhillon and Paul
Standish.
    p. cm.
Includes bibliographical references (p.) and index.
1. Lyotard, Jean François–Contributions in education. 2.
Education–Philosophy. 3. Postmodernism and education. I.
Dhillon, Pradeep Ajit. II. Standish, Paul, 1949–

LB880.L92 L96 2000
370'.1–dc21   00–032830

ISBN 0–415–21547–1

Contents

Contributors

Gordon C. F. Bearn is Selfridge Associate Professor of Philosophy at Lehigh University where he is chair of the department. Since publishing *Waking to Wonder: Wittgenstein's Existential Investigations* (SUNY, 1997), he has been raising Derridean problems for Wittgenstein and Deleuzian problems for Derrida. He is currently following pointlessness and beauty into the manuscript of a book to be called *Life Drawing: An Aesthetics Of Existence.*

Nigel Blake works at the Open University, UK. He is currently Chair of the Philosophy of Education Society of Great Britain. He writes on topics in critical theory and poststructuralism, with a particular interest in higher education, identity and pluralism, electronic media in education, and connections between education and economics. Much of his work is done in collaboration with Paul Smeyers, Richard Smith, and Paul Standish, including *Thinking Again: Education after Postmodernism* (Bergin and Garvey, 1998) and the forthcoming *Education in an Age of Nihilism* (Falmer, 2000).

Nicholas C. Burbules is Professor of Educational Policy Studies at the University of Illinois, Urbana-Champaign. His primary areas of interest are philosophy of education, educational policy, critical social and political theory, and educational technology. His most recent books include *Watch IT: The Promises and Risks of New Information Technologies for Education*, with Thomas A. Callister, Jr. (Westview Press, forthcoming) and *Globalization and Education: Critical Perspectives*, edited with Carlos Torres (Routledge, forthcoming). He is also the current editor of the journal *Educational Theory.*

Pradeep A. Dhillon received her undergraduate degree from Punjab University in philosophy and English literature and a Ph.D. in Education from Stanford University. Her book, *Multiple Identities*, examines the significance of phenomenology in the study of identity formation. She has published in linguistics, philosophy, and philosophy of education. Currently she is Assistant Professor in the Department of Educational Policy Studies at the University of Illinois, Urbana-Champaign, and editor of the *Journal of Aesthetic Education.*

J. M. Fritzman is an Assistant Professor at Lewis and Clark College, and has research interests in social and political philosophy, and in nineteenth and twentieth century Continental philosophy. He has published in the *American Philosophical Quarterly, Clio, Educational Theory, International Philosophical Quarterly*, and *Rhetorica.*

Jan Masschelein is Professor of Philosophy of Education in the Department for Educational Sciences at the Katholieke Universiteit Leuven, Belgium. His primary areas of scholarship are educational theory, critical theory, critical pedagogy, and philosophy of dialogue. He is the author of many articles and contributions in this field and of two books: *Pädagogisches Handeln und Kommunikatives Handeln* (Deutscher Studienverlag, 1991) and *Alterität, Pluralität, Gerechtigkeit. Randgänge der Pädagogik* (Leuven University Press, 1996), the latter co-authored with M. Wimmer.

A. T. Nuyen obtained his Ph.D. from the University of Queensland, Australia, where he is now Reader in Philosophy. His works on Hume and Kant, virtue ethics, and Continental philosophy have appeared in many international journals including *Hume Studies, Kant-Studien, History of Philosophy Quarterly*, and *American Philosophical Quarterly*. He has also published widely in philosophy of education in journals such as *Educational Theory* and *The Journal of Thought.*

David Palumbo-Liu is Associate Professor of Comparative Literature and Director of the Program in Modern Thought and Literature at Stanford University, and a contributing editor to the *Review of Education, Pedagogy, and Cultural Studies*. His latest book is *Asian/American: Historical Crossings of a Racial Frontier* (Stanford, 1999).

Michael Peters is Professor in the School of Education, University of Auckland. His research interests are in the areas of philosophy, education and policy studies. He is the author of a number of books, including *After the Disciplines: The Emergence of Cultural Studies* (ed.) (1999), *Wittgenstein: Philosophy, Postmodernism, Pedagogy* (1999), with James Marshall, and *Education and the Postmodern Condition*, with a foreword by Jean-François Lyotard (ed.) (1995/97), all published by Bergin and Garvey. He is currently Executive Editor of the journal *Educational Philosophy and Theory* and co-editor of the on-line *Encyclopedia of Philosophy of Education* (http://www.educacao.pro.br/).

Paul Smeyers is Professor of Education at the Katholieke Universiteit Leuven, Belgium, where he teaches philosophy of education and methodology of the *Geisteswissenschaften*. His many published articles address issues such as the justification of the content of education, philosophical issues of child-rearing, the importance of commitment, and the ethics of care, with particular reference to the work of Wittgenstein. With James Marshall he co-edited *Philosophy and Education: Accepting Wittgenstein's Challenge* (Kluwer, 1995) and he is co-author of *Thinking Again: Education after Postmodernism* (Bergin and Garvey, 1998). He is the editor of the Journal *Pedagogisch Tijdschrift*. Work in progress includes *Education in an Age of Nihilism* and *The Blackwell Guide to Philosophy of Education* (co-edited with Blake, Smith, and Standish).

Richard Smith is Reader in Education at the University of Durham, where he is currently Director of Combined Social Science, and editor of the *Journal of Philosophy of Education*. He teaches environmental ethics and theory of social science as well as various aspects of education. His books include *Teaching Right and Wrong: Moral Education in the Balance* (Trentham, 1997), co-edited with Paul Standish, and *Thinking Again: Education after Postmodernism* (Bergin and Garvey, 1998) co-authored with Blake, Smeyers, and Standish.

Paul Standish is Senior Lecturer in Education at the University of Dundee. His main research interest is in the relationship between analytical and Continental philosophy and its significance for education. His recent books include *The Universities We Need: Higher Education after Dearing* (co-authored with Blake and Smith) (Kogan Page, 1998), *Education at the Interface: Philosophical Questions Concerning Education Online* (Blackwell, 2000), edited with Nigel Blake, and *Universities Remembering Europe* (Berghahn, 2000), edited with Francis Crawley and Paul Smeyers. He is assistant editor of the *Journal of Philosophy of Education*.

Lynda Stone is Associate Professor, Philosophy of Education, at the University of North Carolina at Chapel Hill, USA. Her interests include philosophy of education, social theory, and feminist theory. She has published widely both in her home country and internationally in such journals as *Teachers College Record, Studies in Philosophy and Education, Journal of Curriculum Studies, Journal of Curriculum Theorizing*, and *Theory and Research in Social Education*. She is editor of *The Education Feminism Reader* (Routledge, 1994).

James Williams teaches philosophy at the University of Dundee. He is the author of *Lyotard: Towards a Postmodern Philosophy* (Polity, 1998) and *Lyotard: Thinking the Political* (Routledge, 1999) as well as articles on Lyotard, Deleuze, Ricoeur, and contemporary French philosophy.

Acknowledgements

We would like to thank Nicholas Burbules whose suggestion it was that we should collaborate on this project. James Williams and Richard Smith are thanked for helpful editorial advice, and Cassie Higgins for her assistance in the preparation of the final manuscript.

Introduction

Jean-François Lyotard: just education in passing

Pradeep A. Dhillon and Paul Standish

In April 1998 Jean-François Lyotard died. There is no doubt that the body of work that he leaves is remarkable: for its range, for its sustained concern with the relation of questions of language and justice, and for its perception of the affinity between questions of education and philosophy itself. His work throws light on numerous matters of critical importance for education: on its aims, legitimation, and accountability; on democracy, citizenship, and globalization; on colonialism and multiculturalism, pluralism and relativism; on capitalism, Marxism, and feminism; on rights and duties, privileges and obligations; on imagination, aesthetics, and moral judgment; on childhood and play. Lyotard's continuing concern with ways of resisting or overcoming the encroachments of nihilism exposes ways in which our contemporary practices have become devalued. There is, it should be clear, no unitary "philosophy of education" here; rather the inducement to think differently about these matters. His insights point repeatedly to the possibility of an education that is more just.

In this introduction we preview thirteen chapters that, in their different and not uncritical ways, each pay tribute to that unresolved body of work. What is the background of this writing? What is the context in which Lyotard is read (or not read)? What themes and influences recur in the work? We begin with general remarks about Lyotard's reception, about the special place of *The Postmodern Condition* (Lyotard 1984a), about the special importance of Kant and Wittgenstein, and about the kind of hope that his philosophy offers.

Philosophy and education: the reception of Lyotard

Lyotard has sometimes been thought the postmodern philosopher *par excellence*. Whether or not this is apt, Lyotard is, it should be clear, a central figure in any debate on the potential, pitfalls, and possibility of a postmodern approach to education. Whether or not postmodernism's influence is now in decline, whether the very term has become yet another name to line up behind in order to denounce the world, and so should be dropped, the questions and issues Lyotard raises will continue to challenge anyone who wants to think seriously about education. "No longer and not yet" is where we find ourselves as educators. Postmodern lessons enjoin us to proceed with a new humility.

Yet the reception of Lyotard's work among educators and philosophers has been mixed, and interpretations uneven. On the one hand, these readings have often been mobilized by assumptions that link the work to ideas of education as liberatory discourse. On the other, analytical philosophers in general, and analytical philosophers of education in particular, have scarcely engaged with Lyotard's thought. This is significant because much of Lyotard's philosophy presents a sustained critique of the analytical tradition, using analytical methods. Style no doubt has been a problem here: some have found Lyotard's work to be elusive and to lack clarity; sometimes, to an Anglophone ear especially, his vocabulary has seemed sensational; sometimes, where ideas have been set spinning, the reader's presumption in favor of cool analysis has been frustrated. It would be unrealistic for us to suppose that the kinds of theoretical and stylistic resistances that operate here will be overcome by a collection such as this, and we think it unlikely that those who have adopted Lyotard in the name of liberatory pedagogy will be much restrained by what follows. But the kinds of issue that these essays enjoin the reader to address point away from the sloganizing tendencies to which Lyotard's work has sometimes been put.

The essays in this collection do indeed presume the postmodern condition, both textually and as the social-historical context within which these questions are raised. If Max Weber told us a story of how we moved from traditional societies to ones that are rule-governed, systematic, and indeed modern, Lyotard strives to show us the ways in which the modern social systems we inhabit have mutated, and their demands for prescriptive performance intensified. The postmodern condition does not reflect a freedom from structuralism: rather it signals an intensification and complication of structural relations. These relations, it is true, are no longer under the regulation of a given set of principles. They lie rather within fractured contexts and demand a focus on the fault-lines along which such fracturing has taken place. For both Weber and Lyotard these changes have come at considerable human cost. The intensification of performativity has ushered in a return of earlier, traditional, even pagan ways of being, in a desire to make sense of a world that is not understandable through established regimes of reason and that does not permit judgement through a consensus on criteria: a desire writ large under conditions of globalization. It is for this reason that the question of the kinds of freedom that are still possible dominates and defeats contemporary thinking.

The Postmodern Condition

Anyone interested in Lyotard and education is likely to take *The Postmodern Condition* (Lyotard 1984a) as a starting point. Commissioned by the

Conseil des Universités of the government of Quebec, this is a study of knowledge in the most highly developed societies. While *modern* ways of knowing are legitimated with reference to a grand narrative of some kind – of the dialectics of Spirit, of the emancipation of the working subject, of humanity as the hero of liberty, of the creation of wealth – the *postmodern* is defined as an incredulity toward metanarratives. The incommensurability that he identifies in our ways of knowing leads to the suggestion that what is needed is a pragmatics of language particles, a diligent attention to the heterogeneity of our language: we should "gaze in wonderment at the diversity of discursive species" (Lyotard 1984a: 26). This heterogeneity he explains by way of Wittgenstein's notion of the language game.

It is clear that Lyotard's concerns here are not abstruse: not only does he respond fully and with remarkable prescience to the profound implications of new technology for education; he also foregrounds the extent to which the social bond is composed of language "moves" (ibid.: 11). It is in this context that he claims: "The true goal of the system, the reason it programs itself like a computer is the optimization of the global relationship between input and output: performativity" (ibid.). And this term aptly connotes the jargon of efficiency and effectiveness, quality assurance and control, inspection and accountability that has become so prominent a feature of contemporary educational regimes. Whatever is undertaken must be justified in terms of an increase in productivity, measured in terms of a gain in time.

Traditional theory is always vulnerable to incorporation into this system: its desire for a unitary and totalizing truth lends itself to the unitary and totalizing practices of the system's managers. So also, it can be added, is radical theory, as we see, for example, where unorthodox ideas can be presented in such a way as to enhance a university's research rating, or where new departures in design or practice can be marketed to relaunch a company and revitalize its portfolio. Criticism can be tolerated and incorporated, and so strengthen the system; ultimately it loses its theoretical force, reduced to token protest or utopian hope.

Contrary to the popular perception, though, science does not expand, Lyotard points out, by means of the positivism of efficiency. It proceeds rather by inventing counter-examples, by looking for "paradox" and legitimating it with new rules in the game of reasoning (Lyotard 1984a: 54). This is not, it should be emphasized, just a matter of innovation. Innovation can take place within the system and consequently can strengthen it. In contrast the break that occurs in response to paradox, with the invention of new rules in the game, is of the order of *paralogy*. This is a move in the pragmatics of knowledge, a move whose importance may not be recognized until after the event (ibid.: 61). Lyotard wants to identify and draw some hope from a postmodern science that concerns itself with undecidables, the limits of precise control, conflicts characterized by incomplete information, "fractals," catastrophes, and pragmatic paradoxes, examples to upset complacent positivist assumptions. Of the views of the several scientists he refers to, Peter Medawar's comments can be taken as indicative: having ideas is the scientist's highest achievement; there is no "scientific method"; a scientist is before anything else a person who tells stories, albeit stories that there is a duty to verify (ibid.: 60). One of the major obstacles to the imaginative advancement of knowledge is precisely the division between the practitioners of science and the decision-makers, those especially who provide the funds. This is a product not of science itself but of the socio-economic system, and it is one in which misunderstanding of science is an important factor. Science itself is open: a statement is relevant if it generates ideas, new possibilities of thinking, new game rules.

Ultimately Lyotard wants to shake the mistaken faith that is placed in consensus as if this were the paradigm of scientific thought. Consensus is a stage of discussion but its end must be paralogy, and this is of profound importance not only for science but for the social bond. The heterogeneity of language games and the search for dissent together undermine the idea of a stable human subject seeking emancipation through the regular- ization of language moves in consensus. Crucially for Lyotard, we must arrive at an idea of justice that is not linked to that of consensus. The prospects for justice are not to be sought in any "alternative" to the present system, for no matter what the particular name under which we might then sign up, it would be vulnerable to the same fate: it would end up resem- bling the system it was meant to replace. In contrast we must recognize our responsibility for the rules of our language and their effects, above all for what validates the adoption of rules: the quest for paralogy (ibid.: 66).

Lyotard recognizes that computerization could become the "dream" instrument for extending the application of the performativity principle. But he also envisages a brighter prospect, at least, a way of dealing with this technological change. The public must be given free access to the memory and data banks, free access, let us say, to the Internet. Then, he claims, the inexhaustible reserve of possible utterances would prevent fixation in an equilibrium. Such a politics would respect both the desire for justice and the desire for the unknown (ibid.: 67).

If the suggestion of totalitarianism here, the emphasis on the way that the system extends across the total field, seems sensational, it is worth remembering that Lyotard sees this as deriving from the cultural imperi- alism, no less, of western civilization: it is governed by the demand for legitimation (ibid.: 27). And indeed the provocation of this vocabulary becomes more acute. Acknowledging the risk of scandalizing the reader, Lyotard speaks of the severity of the system, of the terroristic tendencies of a "scientific" establishment that is governed by homeostasis. "Adapt your aspirations to our ends – or else" is perhaps not a very great exaggeration of the threat that educators find themselves under in some western liberal societies today (ibid.: 62–4).

The force of the case that Lyotard presents here shows that attention must be given to *The Postmodern Condition*, but it is regrettable if exploration ends with this book. Powerful indictment of the problems facing contemporary higher education, and telling evocation of the nature of performativity as it undoubtedly is, there are, we believe, more rewarding texts to address. (Lyotard himself, it should be noted, did not see this text as primarily a work of philosophy.) The contributors to the present volume respond to Lyotard's thought across the range of his writings, and *The Postmodern Condition* is not central. Its prominence is indicative, however, of a more general point about his significance for education: Lyotard's work spans a range of questions that have relevance for education in diverse ways, but there is a sense in which it is especially important for higher education, and this notwithstanding his interest in childhood. This is to be seen most clearly in his concern with the limits of language, with the ways in which different ways of speaking and understanding can be extended, and with ways in which they conflict. Difference and the possibility of paralogy emerge in advanced study in a way that is more problematic, and in certain respects more poignant, than is the case in a person's earlier upbringing. It is then not surprising that several of the chapters that follow take the context of higher education as their main concern.

Wittgenstein and Kant

Lyotard's adaptation of Wittgenstein's notion of the language game has, of course, been much criticized. Valid though much of this criticism seems to us to be, there is a danger that this issue diverts attention from the broader and deeper influence that Wittgenstein undoubtedly has on Lyotard's thought.

Lyotard's philosophy is explicitly based on a normative theory of communication which he develops through a non-anthropomorphic, anti-Hegelian, turn toward Wittgenstein and Kant: particularly the Kant of *The Critique of Judgment* (Kant 1964). Broadly, in his view, language is a social phenomenon, one that precedes and circumscribes individual lives, and is limited in its referential ability. Hence Lyotard's interest in the ethics, politics, and aesthetics of communication, in the fair and just representation of justice, manifested in education within formal institutions and in the practices of daily life; hence his interest in the difference such concerns present for the learning and enactment of citizenship. In his view, judgment, the adjudication between various and multiple ways of looking on the world, is necessary and yet cannot be informed by a set of determinate criteria. To judge with a clear and stable set of criteria would be to presume a totality of knowledge that could result in the most terrifyingly unjust practices. It is this necessity of judgment and indeterminacy of knowledge that, for Lyotard, make difficult issues of majority and minority relations in all contexts. These problems cannot adequately be addressed within the discourses of liberalism or traditional Marxist approaches. They are not to be resolved through a perhaps too easy turn to liberatory pedagogy. They require painstaking and patient work toward just education.

What Lyotard offers as an alternative, in his later work especially, is an ethical turn toward aesthetics in judgment with a special emphasis on the significance of the sublime. This is the place of hope that cannot be articulated nor shown by the protocols of reason, of hope that can be felt. It is thus that he avoids an easy optimism – from what has gone before – without succumbing to pessimism or nihilism. It is by way of Wittgenstein and Kant that hope is restored.

Declining "all universalist doctrines," Lyotard develops a social and political orientation drawn from the Wittgensteinian insight that meaning lies in use, in the diverse yet entangled language games within which we live our lives. In the dispersal of our linguistic practice, nevertheless, there is a unifying element. He draws this out by turning to the Kant of the third *Critique* and also the political writings. He evokes the reflective judgment of Kant's aesthetics, the search for a law from particulars that does not come through a conceptual deduction but is derived "tautegorically" from within the domain over which it must apply. The Kantian sublime is unpresentable, dynamic, sensed only through feeling, and this provides a direction for our universalist longings. Unlike Kant, however, it is in art that Lyotard seeks this rather than in nature.

In the *Philosophical Investigations* Wittgenstein writes:

> We also say of some people that they are transparent to us. It is, however, important as regards this observation that one human being can be a complete enigma to another. We learn this when we come into a strange country with entirely strange traditions; and, what is more, even given a mastery of the country's language. . . . We do not *understand* the people . . . we cannot find ourselves in them.
>
> (Wittgenstein 1997: 223)

Lyotard explained his attraction to Wittgenstein's work in terms of its being a philosophy of limits, and he spoke of Kant in these same terms. His later thought weaves together these legacies. The exploration of difference turns away from performativity and paralogy to some extent, and toward a more sustained focus on the sublime and on what Lyotard calls the *differend*. The chapters in this volume offer various readings of these ideas and their importance. Let us trace here their main contours.

The differend and the sublime

Whatever is said is not said in isolation. It depends for its sense on a language game which supplies the rules for its sense. But any particular phrase or event can be followed by different phrases and so, potentially, be located in different language games. Language games, as we have seen, are heterogeneous, and so there can be a conflict between them. Irresolvable conflicts arise between language games when there is a need to determine the right way to follow a particular phrase or event. Yet, although the rules of exchange for discourse have their limits and their incommensurabilities, fluent systems of exchange can function to the neglect of the real needs and demands of interlocutors. The very conception of language as communication imposes a pressure on interlocutors to accede to the dominant discourse regime.

What is at stake in questions of politics, then, is continuous with literature or philosophy or, perhaps, science to the extent that we must bear witness to differends by finding idioms for them. And for this there must be a prior acknowledgment of the differend, an acknowledgment precisely of this conflict. This requires a refusal to assume that there is always a right way of incorporating a phrase and pursuing a dialogue:

> To give the differend its due is to institute new addressees, new addressors, new significations, and new referents in order for the wrong to find an expression and for the plaintiff to cease being a victim. This requires new rules for the formation and linking of phrases. No one doubts that language is capable of admitting these new phrase families or new genres of discourse. Every wrong ought to be able to be put into phrases. A new competence (or "prudence") must be found.
>
> (Lyotard 1988a: 13)

Lyotard shows what is at stake here, in terms of the injustice of requiring people to represent themselves in terms that are alien. There is a constant danger of injustice here. The very fluency of our communication makes us impervious to the existence of differends and turns them into litigations. The plaintiff is then reined in by the terms in which the court operates. It is art especially that can disturb us into realizing this. In the grotesque court scene at the start of *King Lear* Cordelia cannot "heave her heart into her mouth," however aware she may be of the phrases her father wants to hear, as to do this must be a violation of the feelings she truly has. There is a differend between the truth of her feeling, which as no-thing is inexpressible, and the extravagant boasts of affection made by her evil sisters.

The play makes it possible to bear witness to this differend. We are brought up against an aporia in such a way as to disarm us, to shake confidence in a rational solution. Yet the disabling experience of the differend provides the impetus to the possibility of new thought, to thought that might lead beyond the impasse of these irreconcilable ways of being. Testifying to this incompatibility, it calls upon, and calls for, what is not yet thought. Of the pain and pleasure of this, Lyotard writes:

In the differend, something "asks" to be put into phrases, and suffers from the wrong of not being able to be put into phrases right away. This is when the human beings who thought they could use language as an instrument of communication learn through the feeling of pain which accompanies silence (and of pleasure which accompanies the invention of a new idiom), that they are summoned by language, not to augment to their profit the quantity of information communicable through existing idioms, but to recognize that what remains to be phrased exceeds what they can presently phrase, and that they must be allowed to institute idioms which do not yet exist.

(Lyotard 1988a: 13)

We gain a sense of the limits of our own measure. This *negative presentation*, achieved especially through the aesthetics of the work of art, is liberating for our imagination in that it enables us to see beyond the limits of our thinking and being.

Lyotard's interest in aesthetics is important throughout his writings, but the full influence of Kant now becomes most evident. It is above all in the avant-garde that he sees the most telling evocation of the sublime: there is something there of great value, but its value lies in part in its unapproachability. That the significance of this extends beyond art and through education more generally becomes clear in the essay "The sublime and the avant-garde":

That which we call thought must be disarmed. There is a tradition and an institution of philosophy, of painting, of politics, of literature. These "disciplines" also have a future in the form of Schools, of programmes, projects and "trends". Thought works over what is received, it seeks to reflect on it and overcome it. It seeks to determine what has already been thought, written, painted or socialized in order to determine what hasn't been. . . . But this agitation, in the most noble sense of the word (agitation is the word Kant gives to the activity of the mind that has judgment and exercises it), this agitation is only possible if something remains to be determined. One can strive to determine this something by setting up a system, a theory, a programme or a project – and indeed one has to, all the while anticipating that something. One can also enquire about the remainder, and allow the indeterminate to appear as a question-mark.

What all intellectual disciplines and institutions presuppose is that not everything has been said, written down or recorded, that words already heard or pronounced are not the last words.

(Lyotard 1991d: 90–1)

It may be that such institutions are unthinkable without this ordering: without their systems, theories, programmes, and projects. The something that remains to be determined, however, is not to be understood as something not as yet known but waiting to be incorporated by the *episteme*, some new bit of information, say. Rather it is something that is in principle not assimilable or graspable, not even representable at all. It is a necessary remainder and indeterminacy. And this is the very source of the agitation that is critical to the study of a subject (with all the excitement and intensity that this can mean). An occasion for judgment is provided through an irreconcilability that can receive an appropriate response only through the experience of the sublime. We are at a loss, and we must first bear witness. This might be an avant-garde education. Just education requires us to recognize this.

Loss and hope

What have we lost? What can we hope for? Lyotard's death is an ending, but with regard to endings and beginnings there is a sense in which he challenges our accustomed (philosophical) responses, and this through an ethics of time influenced by his teacher, Maurice Merleau-Ponty. Loss, the sense of an ending, so readily becomes melancholic longing or nostalgia, with all the burdens this has placed on philosophy and politics. The hope that a beginning often brings becomes represented as an enlightenment, the dawn of a new age, a morning. Lyotard enjoins us not to expect any new dawn. There should then be no expectation of a morning, of the authoritative enlightenment that any *system* of thought might seem to provide: no totality of Marx; no Husserlian eidetic reduction, receding into Cartesian modernity; no Leibnizian or Russellian metaphysics. Lyotard wants to give up these totalities, though not the critical impulse that he finds in them (however much he may sometimes laugh at "critique"). And neither should we commit ourselves to mourning. We should resist the human nostalgia for presence, Romantic wistfulness for felt absence; and that work of mourning that seeks representation and resolution of the past.

During the last few years of his life Lyotard taught at the Comparative Literature Department of Emory University, and in 1999 a symposium was held there in his honour. Speaking on that occasion, Jacques Derrida captured in the ambivalent anachrony of an aphorism something of Lyotard's philosophy and pedagogy: "There will be no mo(u)rning." Words already heard or said are not the last words. Something always remains to be determined.

The chapters that follow

The contributors to this volume come from philosophy, education, and literature departments from around the world. None is uncritical of Lyotard but all share the belief that his work is of importance for anyone interested in asking philosophical questions about education today.

The essays are arranged to offer a possible sequence of reading along the following lines. The introductory and partly expository Chapter 1 is followed by three more or less critical essays that address familiar problems regarding Lyotard's work: his appropriation of Wittgenstein's ideas, his opposition to Jürgen Habermas, his relation to capitalism. This leads, in Chapter 5, into a discussion of moral education and the development of the imagination. This theme is expanded in various directions in the essays in the middle of the book that explore the educational resonance of Lyotard's ideas in his early and especially his late work, ideas associated particularly with the differend and the sublime. This section of the book reflects perhaps the most dominant reading of Lyotard at the time of writing, and the one that this Introduction has thus far foregrounded. It is then with a view to unsettling this that we turn in the final chapters toward the different lines of thought that are to be found in Lyotard's middle period. The last two essays echo Lyotard's concern at that stage in his work to identify and move beyond the different forms that nihilism takes, beyond then also the negativity that returns in the acknowledgement of lack in the later work, in Lyotard's conceptions of the differend and the sublime.

The chapter by Michael Peters begins biographically, detailing Lyotard's opposition to French colonialism in Algeria. Lyotard spent twelve years as leader of the Algerian section for *Socialisme ou Barbarie*, thus demonstrating a political commitment against imperialism and colonialism. It was his experience there that shaped his political trajectory thereafter, his break with Marxism, and his subsequent turn to "postmodern" philosophy. The real strength of Lyotard's analysis, Peters argues, is to be found in his understanding of world history in terms of the genre of narrative.

Algeria gave Lyotard a clear example of the injustice of the universal. Subsequently, during the political unrest in France in the late 1960s, Lyotard confronted related injustices in the context of university reform. As a lecturer at Nanterre, Lyotard actively opposed Fouchet's modernizing reforms in the name of freedom of expression and political assembly, and democratic participation by students and staff in university affairs. Peters shows how themes that were to surface later in *The Postmodern Condition* find their source here: the critique of a class monopolization of knowledge and the mercantilization of knowledge and education; an attack on the "hierarchic magisterial relation" of pedagogy; the refusal of a kind of education under capitalism that merely reproduces students to meet the technical demands of the system; and the expression of a moral ideal embodied in non-dialectical forms of dialogue as the ethical precondition for pedagogy.

The much cited suspicion toward metanarratives – especially the Grand Narratives of emancipation emanating from 1789, in some sense from the Greek *polis*, with their promise of a gradual and progressive enfranchisement – is indicative of a more general resistance on Lyotard's part to modern universalism with its politics of redemption. Lyotard's development needs to be understood in part in terms of his changing relation to Marxism. He is at pains to address the new realities confronting Marxism, especially the effects of new techniques on work conditions and on the mentality of workers and employees, the effects of economic growth on daily life and culture, and the appearance of new demands by workers. Capital, which removes, subordinates, or colonizes the language of criticism, imposes its rules on others and attempts to make all discourse commensurable. In Lyotard's view, Peters suggests, the building and mastery of a world economy do not contribute to the reduction of inequalities. It is, of course, possible to draw distinctions between the author, his work, and his historical context, but the "biosophical" approach that Peters adopts in considering Lyotard's experience in Algeria and at Nanterre is of a clear importance to an understanding of his subsequent thought and its development.

Nicholas C. Burbules' essay, "Lyotard on Wittgenstein: the differend, language games, and education," explores a major theme in educational thought influenced by poststructuralism, a theme that he refers to as hostility toward the ideals of consensus and understanding. What are normally taken to be aims of education have been criticized on the grounds that these norms try to bridge gulfs of culture and experience that, under most educational circumstances, cannot be bridged. Thus, argues Elizabeth Ellsworth, the very attempt to do so disrespects these differences, putting those groups that are different from dominant cultures and values at an asymmetrical risk in such contexts. Multiculturalism and feminism similarly have emphasized the insurmountable barriers of difference. Arguments of this kind are often supported by reference to Lyotard's concept of the differend. Burbules is particularly interested in the use that Lyotard makes of Wittgenstein's idea of the language game, and the bearing his interpretation of this has on the broader question of hostility to consensus and understanding. Burbules' own view is that Lyotard's use of Wittgenstein opens a way to this hostility to consensus and understanding, but that this is deeply at odds with Wittgenstein's own position.

Burbules wants to acknowledge that education today is indeed colonized by hegemonic modes of discourse but, he suggests, there is a danger also in the fetishization of difference. It is precisely because people are speaking the same language that misunderstanding between language games is possible. Lyotard's notion of the "phrase regime" does not equate with Wittgenstein's language game, and the slippage between these two has the ironic effect of running together a vast variety of language games. The problems that can arise from Lyotard's account can be revealed and avoided by attention to the relationship in Wittgenstein's thought between the concepts of language game and form of life.

Questions concerning the heterogeneity of language games and the possibility of communication figure also in Nigel Blake's "Paralogy, validity claims, and the politics of knowledge: Habermas, Lyotard, and higher education." Here again there is a concern that Lyotard is in danger of advocating dissent to no purpose, an aestheticization of dissent. The broad educational question that he addresses has to do with the ways in which the pursuit of knowledge relates to the other activities and ways of life of a society, especially in a prevailing climate of performativity. Such matters need to be addressed if we are to become clear about the rights, duties, privileges, and obligations of education, about the relation between research and teaching in universities and their appropriate conduct and organization. Much of the importance of *The Postmodern Condition*, Blake argues, derives from its recognition of the ways in which these problems turn on the nature and legitimacy of the social bond. The chapter explores the feasibility and cogency of the legitimation of higher education by recourse to small narratives, a legitimation in the absence of any larger story of how universities fit in to the rest of our social life. Performativity might then be resisted through the development, subversion, and reinvention of language games. In paralogy, social bonds are rewoven with new threads and in new patterns.

Such, it would appear, is Lyotard's view. But there are other accounts of the social bond, and Blake is particularly concerned to show the ways in which Jürgen Habermas demonstrates the socially bonding nature (*Bildungseffekt*) of linguistic interaction. The resistant potential of communicative interaction, which appeals directly to the conscious assent of the individual, resides in the co-presence in any utterance of tacit assumptions of normative, affective, and cognitive kinds. This cannot easily be theorized if the difference between such claims is reconceptualized as a radical incommensurability, for this suggests that they cannot be co-present in any one utterance. It is perhaps Lyotard's conception of utterances as incommensurable but therefore univocal that prevents him from seeing this. What is most potent in the politics of knowledge, and demonstrated here in part through reference to art history, is perhaps not paralogy but the problematization of dimensions of discourse that are normally non-problematic. Attention to such matters can enable us to question not only the current operation of elements of the system but the normal functioning of their interrelations. This is not to deny any value in paralogy, but it is to doubt its comparative potency in the face of the system.

The only kind of consensus compatible with communicative action is rational consensus, and this is achieved where we aim not at consensus but rather at rational debate. The social bond is strengthened the less rational debate is interfered with. The Lyotardian evasion of calls to consensus is, by the same token, Blake suggests, an evasion of rational discussion. By contrast, nothing is more protective of the possibility and the rights of dissent than commitment to ideals of undistorted communicative action.

The relation between consensus and dissensus is pursued in J. M.

Fritzman's "Overcoming capitalism: Lyotard's pessimism and Rorty's prophecy." Science and education are legitimated, Lyotard urges, neither by Niklas Luhmann's criterion of efficiency of performance nor by Habermas's search for universal consensus. Instead, they are legitimated through paralogy, by the injection of dissensus into consensus. The chapter pursues Lyotard's hopes that paralogy might serve to displace and minimize performativity, and so resist capitalism. This legitimation is not so much a justification of those institutions as an explication of how they perpetuate themselves: by continually evolving, and by changing their theories, research methods, and objects of study.

Fritzman wants particularly to draw attention to the functioning of rules in this evolution. New moves are made in games with their present rules; and rules themselves may emerge in the making of a move, or be constituted in the moment of action. One of the dangers of performativity, however, is that any new moves that are made, anything that looks like becoming critical, can be encompassed and assimilated: individuals are allowed to criticize political and economic systems, but only if their criticisms quickly turn a profit. Hence in the new university the radical is tamed or contained. Lyotard's pessimism arises from the belief that new legislation, the establishment of an opposing regime, inevitably sets up new differends, and so new sources of injustice, and this results in a certain accommodation with capitalism. Any politics then must be a politics of the lesser evil, incorporating the ethical responsibility to bear witness to the wrongs caused by capitalism.

In this context Fritzman examines the current relation between education and business, characterized as this is by the telling expression "learn to earn." That students would generally be poorly served if education did not provide them with the ability to gain a living is to be conceded, but a greater neglect arises where economic success is taken to be the *raison d'être* of education. People's lives will be empty where they have the ability neither to comprehend the world in which they live, nor to make informed decisions about how it might be changed. Hence, students must understand the historically contingent nature of capitalism and the fact that much that seems permanent in human affairs is historically recent and perhaps transitory.

The force of the argument here leads to an emphasis on the imagination in education, and in this the development of the literary imagination is seen as crucial. Fritzman follows Martha Nussbaum in suggesting that failure to cultivate the imagination in this way threatens one of the means that might lead toward the achieving of social justice. The ability to think differently is developed through literature, writing, and discussion. Cultivating the literary imagination, then, is a moral imperative, enabling us to imagine the lives of people very different from ourselves. And an education of this kind might enable us to envisage, and then perhaps to realize, a world in which capitalism is absent.

The importance of cultivating the imagination in education is a theme that is developed more directly in the ensuing chapter, A. T. Nuyen's "Lyotard as moral educator." Lyotard has sometimes been read as the advocate of an extreme relativism and the celebrator of nihilism, a stance that would indeed undermine any project of moral education. In this chapter Nuyen sets out to justify the idea of Lyotard as moral educator by demonstrating the way in which he teaches us to identify the moral problems raised by the postmodern condition, gives us lessons in moral pragmatics, and shows us how to answer the normative question, "Why should I be moral?"

Lyotard provides numerous examples of injustice in his writings, and his purpose is clear: he wants to stress the prevalence of wrongs in the post-modern world *and* to make the normative claim that we have to do something about these wrongs, that we cannot let them go unnoticed. A wrong of this kind arises in the first place by virtue of the fact that the victim's rules of discourse are not valid, or not recognized, within the total-izing discourse: the victim's case is unpresentable within the dominating discourse. Thus, the ethical problem for postmodernity is how to present the unpresentable, how to bear witness to differends.

Like Fritzman, Nuyen is keen to explore the nature of the invention of rules in relation to existing rules, and the particular significance this has for our moral education. We can learn from Lyotard, he suggests, that such rules and regulations do not necessarily undermine individuality and subjectivity because they are regulative rather than determinant. With regulative rules aimed at the ensuring of maximum game playing, inventive individuals would be free to vary rules and regulations, thus inventing new games. Indeed, to take Lyotard seriously is to make it part of the aim of education to encourage inventiveness. The virtuous player would be committed not only to maximizing the possibilities of playing justly, but also to preventing the totalizing of the field by any one game. Such a player would welcome a proliferation of games and, with a deep-ening sensitivity to the unpresentable, would welcome the invention of new ones. Lyotard's postmodern ethics, Nuyen argues, provides important moral and practical lessons for educators in terms of the ethics of invention and the play of the imagination.

The theme of the development of the imagination in relation to justice is further extended in Pradeep A. Dhillon's "The sublime face of just education." Here again the imagination's crucial relationship with aesthetic education is emphasized, and this is achieved by way of an explo-ration of the progressive influence of Kant in Lyotard's later work. Lyotard's discussions of justice reveal ways in which the apparently benign assumptions underlying liberal practices of fairness and commitments to contractual justice have their darker side. An appreciation of this requires once again a consideration of the rule-governed activities that structure our institutions and practices, not least our practices in education.

Lyotard's approach to the problem is initially laid alongside that of John Rawls in order to consider the tension between the honoring of rules and respect for the particular case, especially as this manifests itself in a world that seems not only uncertain but groundless. The central concern of the chapter is with the way in which Lyotard's emphasis on narrativity persuades us to look again at justice in relation to liberal education.

The question of justice and difference is pursued in this chapter through a consideration of the treatment of Shylock in *The Merchant of Venice*. On the strength of a Lyotardian reading of this, the argument moves toward the consideration of the importance for Lyotard of *The Critique of Judgment*. The picture Kant gives us here moves away from that of the autonomous rational self, where concepts are placed under the regimes of reason, in favor of one that is relational. Feeling is tied to the cognitive, and the play of the imagination becomes crucial to the accounts of the freedom of the will and the freedom of aesthetics. This linking of reason and the aesthetic, especially in relation to the sublime, evokes for Lyotard a mode of presentation in which no determined concept could be sufficient to the presentation, and no intelligible language render it adequately (Lyotard 1994: 212). Aesthetic judgment gives us freedom of the imagination. The reflective judgment of aesthetics, the feeling of pleasure that demands it be shared universally, provides what Lyotard calls the "passageway" to intersubjectivity, in a kind of universal empathy. In a line of argument that parallels those adopted by Fritzman and Nuyen, this chapter shows how any education properly sensitive to conditions of heterogeneity must recognize the development of imagination and creativity as critical factors in the development of a politics that is just.

Richard Smith's chapter, "Another space," also explores ways in which attention to literature can unsettle the prevailing discourse and extend perceptions. Here the concern for justice is related to proper sensitivity to the demands of the particular case, and this is pursued through a reading of *Great Expectations*. The careful attention to the particular in Dickens' text is juxtaposed against the anodyne language of performativity and the rhetoric of government education advisers. In the contemporary received idiom of educational policy and curriculum planning, with its anxious detailing of competence statements and learning outcomes, it is difficult, Smith contends, still to think of education as the embodied encounter between teacher and taught, let alone to open the experience to the kind of uncertainty that would allow spontaneity, invention, and an element of risk. All come under the surveillance of quality control, with its uncompromising requirement that all should be transparent. Where a dominating metanarrative asserts its "truths" from the perspective of an authorized discourse, other truths are excluded. All is geared toward maximizing the efficiency of the economic system and of the education system as a subset of that. In this context the embodied encounter between teacher and taught is a matter that is scarcely acknowledged: as if something there, embarrassingly, refused to be represented. That there might be something mysterious to this encounter is a thought that must be expunged in this regime of openness and accountability.

Lyotard's account of the figural is of another space that must be thought of as buried but showing itself obliquely, as what disturbs our discourses and perceptions, in the struggle against the return of the ego and the textual. In contrast to the efficiency and effectiveness, the presentation for inspection and accounting, the frenetic activity eulogized by contemporary educational regimes, the picture of work to be found in *Great Expectations* is in many respects of a significant absence. The rhythms of the black-smith's forge suggest a kind of work and friendship whose life-force comes from elsewhere than from the utilitarian, being lyrical rather than economic or cognitive. Freed from the connotations and criteria of productivity, it is seen to realize a kind of *jouissance*.

Something of this significant absence is found also in the following chapter, co-authored by Paul Smeyers and Jan Masschelein. Under the title "*L'enfance*, education, and the politics of meaning," this takes up again the exploration of the relation between ethical experience and rules, and shows the way that a different perspective on education can be gained by examining Lyotard's writings on childhood. Such a perspective draws attention to the way in which the affective nature of ethical experience can be masked in a certain preoccupation with rules. The affects in question are of an order that is not to be grasped in language, yet they are inescapable.

Smeyers and Masschelein show how Lyotard offers us the means to crit-icize the mainstream of educational theory, a mainstream aimed at the more or less programmatic realization of certain aims, or accomplishment of particular ideas. Action is understood in terms of predetermined goals, all activity is subordinated to this, and this takes place against the back-ground of a bland naturalism: educational theory cannot forget the reality of its "facts", about child development or intelligence or reading ages, perhaps. In contrast, the Lyotardian account emphasizes the irrevocable heteronomy to which the child is subjected: to being touched as a body before it is aware, to being interrupted in its being by the temporality of passing judgment. This is the radical irruption through which meaning comes into sight.

Childhood cannot be captured in the terminology of educational theory, but its truth can manifest itself. A proper sensitivity to this does not so much enlighten, does not provide additional evidence, but rather changes the educator. Lyotard shows us the way to a philosophy of education that starts from what may be called the reality of the child, a reality that is strange insofar as it cannot be represented or laid down; it cannot be understood in terms of facts or data. It may be that coming to understand childhood in terms of *event* is something to which philosophy of education should address itself, hence counteracting among other things that compulsion to classify and measure, to categorize and pigeonhole childhood. The kind of story that could then be told would perhaps open up possibilities for teachers to share something, both of their perplexity at the bogus analysis and prescription that educational theory and policy often provide, and of their frustration at the ineffable and intractable aspects of their responsibility. While many commentators have taken the theme of injustice to be the most important dimension of Lyotard's work for education, Smeyers and Masschelein suggest that more far-reaching implications may lie in the reminder his work provides of the dangers of seeking to contain what must be kept open, of the possibilities of the new that openness can enable.

The Postmodern Condition is rightly celebrated for its anticipation and exposure of the performativity that has increasingly characterized our education systems. What has been less widely understood, especially in educational theory, is the way in which Lyotard's work reveals the limitations and problems of ideals of autonomy and authenticity, and the bearing this has on education. In many respects these ideals have seemed to offer the best hope of resistance against the encroachments of performativity, yet they are partly complicit with its harms. To show why this is the case it is necessary to explore some of the contemporary ills that Lyotard identifies. The chapter by Paul Standish, "In freedom's grip," attempts this by taking up the theme of childhood and relating this to Lyotard's writings on "the jews." What childhood and "the jews" share is the impossibility of their being presented and represented, hence their distortion and disappearance in the face of performativity. The extent of the contemporary demand for presentation and representation is evoked here through Lyotard's dystopian vision of globalization in the megalopolis. The totalitarian threat that this poses is not generally the result of any conspiracy or malevolent wielding of power; on the contrary it is realized in the name of an emancipation that seeks fully to acknowledge rights. Its corresponding denial of silence and secrecy, of a kind of privacy of the self, is then all the more surreptitious. It is by a new acknowledgement of childhood and "the jews" that the possibility of release from these forms of emancipation is suggested. Educators must renounce that intention to grasp and take control, and this must be so at the level both of domination in the classroom, and of constantly holding fast to tidy objectives or lofty aims. There are, it is true, dangers in the kind of education that such a renunciation might underwrite, not so much in the predictable terms of a loss of order, but rather as a result of a certain nostalgia, or of dependence on a sense of lack. Resisting the poignant melancholy that a sublime education might have, Standish turns toward the more affirmative orientation that this renunciation might be given, toward increase of being and jubilation.

Lynda Stone's essay, an exploration of "Lyotard's women," is an attempt to assess the possibility of feminism in Lyotard's writings. The notion of the unpresentable, accompanied by ambivalence and ambiguity and related to

Lyotard's pervasive concern with justice as it is, would seem to be of great potential interest to feminists. Stone's broad judgment, however, is that this has received less attention from feminists than it deserves. Moreover, English-speaking feminists have tended not to read Lyotard's work appropriately: they have missed early writings that are significant to his position on women and on a possible feminist theory. Given this ambivalence it is appropriate to ask the questions: Are women unpresentable? Is a feminist "philosophy" possible? Stone also pursues a further question in the chapter, however. Lyotard's own admission to have made little use of feminist writings perhaps suggests an ambivalence on his part of a deeper kind, especially given the obviously common ground. Is this, she asks, something that Lyotard cannot fully acknowledge?

What cannot be known is basic to Lyotard's writings, as it is to other contemporary French thinkers such as Julia Kristeva, Michel Foucault, Jacques Derrida, and Hélène Cixous. Stone acknowledges the background to this in Marx and Freud, and also more broadly in a strong literary tradition. Most obviously, however, it is the connection between ideas of the unpresentable – variously designated as absent presence, aporia and lacunae, lack or gap, negation, the in-between, radical alterity – and Saussurean structuralist linguistics that must be recognized. Here difference is most centrally in the relationship between the signifier and the signified. This openness of language then helps explain what is always an openness: in the unpresentable, in a "non-pinning down" of relations of center to margin. The move is away from epistemology and toward ethics, involving most characteristically a turn toward justice for the other.

Stone's conclusion is that Lyotard perhaps failed to capitalize on the possibilities within his notion of the unpresentable, and so to recognize and respond to the complexities of transforming the sexual basis of western thought for a new politics. Unlike their English-speaking counterparts, she suggests, French feminists have worked from this radical alterity. The essay points the way to a feminist project of interpreting Lyotard relative to these French thinkers, one that further explores this basic ambivalence toward feminism in his writings.

David Palumbo-Liu's "Fables and apedagogy: Lyotard's relevance for a pedagogy of the other" explores ways in which Lyotard's work has been enlisted in the effort radically to rethink pedagogical practices and values. He begins by considering Peter McLaren's remarks on the relation between the goals of critical pedagogy and the attack from postmodernism on the tenets of modernity. McLaren sees a harmony between on the one hand postmodernism, and on the other critical pedagogy's attempts to analyze and unsettle existing configurations of power, to defamiliarize what is often passed off as the ordinary, and to challenge modernity's conception of knowledge as ahistorical, neutral, and separated from value and power. While McLaren acknowledges Lyotard's usefulness to critical pedagogy, however, he also regrets his reluctance to offer a prescription for educational practice directed toward social justice.

It is true that Lyotard's particular views regarding subjectivity, agency, and voice all militate against prescription, predetermined value, and the logic of representation. Seeking social justice by evoking "names" becomes a suspect activity and, given the social and political practices that Lyotard believes such evocations may come to underwrite, one should be on one's guard against the totalitarian character of an idea of justice, even a pluralistic one. Palumbo-Liu's essay theoretically and historically examines the nature of Lyotard's pessimism in this, and then asks whether and how anything might be recovered for critical pedagogy. In particular the chapter addresses the issue of multicultural pedagogy in the United States, exploring the question of how far Lyotard's work can be "used" in its name without abusing his basic tenets.

It is particularly by focusing on the problematic of narration, Palumbo-Liu argues, that the contours of possibility and negation come into view. A central concern in this is with the way in which ideas of difference and of the singularity of the event are distorted or destroyed by the demands of knowledge production, and by their incorporation into the prevailing modern humanist narrative. Indeed this kind of assimilation is not merely a danger: in the modern university it is actively sought. Contemporary practices of engendering and delivering knowledge reflect its commodification; they point to ways in which knowledge is linked to an institutional morality involving the repression of difference. Lyotard maps out an alternative institutional space for "apedagogy," however, and, in contrast to this modern humanist narrative, a different mode of narration: the "fable." Lyotard's fable is a small narrative that is unhistorical, nonteleological, and nonprescriptive, and it is this that forms the crucial component of apedagogy. Yet this double rejection of narrative and history not only leaves us with no ground to stand on for better or worse (as is commonly remarked); it also prevents Lyotard from seeing his own historical specificity and therefore the limits of his critique.

The hope he leaves us is tinged with melancholic memories of Paris 1968 and the repression that immediately followed. This melancholy not only impinges inappropriately upon an understanding of multiculturalism in the United States in the late twentieth and early twenty-first centuries; it also forecloses the possibilities that were indeed opened up by that moment in the US. Unlike that of France, the ideology of the United States and its history of civil rights activism call for a certain accommodation of pluralism. It is true that this presents opportunities for manipulation, denigration, and commodification, but it also opens the way to contestation and dissensus. Palumbo-Liu argues for the possibility of a critical multiculturalism that, rather than (only) celebrating plurality, explores the fissures, tensions, and sometimes contradictory demands of a society of multiple cultures. Lyotard's portrait of the postmodern condition derives much of its power from its broad rhetorical sweep, and this, Palumbo-Liu suggests, runs the risk of covering over key distinctions: this particular historical juncture takes on a very different tonality and texture in the United States than in France. Such distinctions in no way guarantee the success of critical pedagogy in the United States, but rather suggest that a critical pedagogy that builds a strategy around the contradictions of American pluralistic ideology may have a certain leverage that is unobtainable in the national context that orientates Lyotard's work.

James Williams' "For a libidinal education" turns again to Lyotard's involvement in Socialism or Barbarism and to the views recounted in "Nanterre, here, now." This is taken as a starting point for an exploration of Lyotard's response to the threat of nihilism, especially as he sees this encroaching on education. While it is clear that nihilism manifests itself most dangerously in performativity, Williams shows how it is also present in some of the responses to performativity that Lyotard's work supports. In particular his concern is with the kind of solution that is suggested by his later writings on the differend and by Lyotard's turn to the sublime. A pedagogy based on this later philosophy would have a somewhat marginal or regulative function. The role of some, perhaps all, teachers would be to trigger the feeling of the sublime against Kantian ideas of reason such as humanity. The Lyotardian teacher could then be, on a soft view, the element within a curriculum that reminded us of the limits of our under-standing, morality, and systems of calculation. On a hard view, this teacher would be a last and essentially uncooperative line of resistance to the hegemony of capital and of universalist ideas. Thus, Williams argues, once a goal has been set to testify to the differend or bear witness to the sublime, the role of the philosopher and teacher becomes an essentially reactive one, policing the borders of law, morality, science, and political economy in order to defeat illegitimate passages into the unknowable. The reactive element is unavoidable since what has to be spoken for cannot be approached except through the feeling of the sublime. The other cannot be affirmed as such, and only a negative struggle on its behalf is possible. By adopting an essentially negative stance at the heart of philosophy and pedagogy, we risk a descent into valuelessness and loss of will owing to the absence of positive values or movements to affirm.

Williams contrasts the nihilism that inheres in this way of thinking with the possibilities of an apedagogy that are adumbrated in Lyotard's earlier writings, specifically during the four or five years up to and including *Libidinal Economy* (Lyotard 1974b). Apedagogy, on this view, is neither a straightforward gesture of reversal, where a failed or wrong position is simply negated, nor a promise of a pure land that escapes the mistakes and evil of past ones. In contrast to any politics associated with a set of pure goals, the active passivity of Lyotard's apedagogy, as Williams puts it, is an effort to write and to teach with an objective, neutral eye for the structures in place. It is also, however, an attempt to introduce fissures and cracks into those structures by multiplying them in a destabilizing manner, not allowing one to take precedence. It is an aesthetic effort in its commitment to the material and ideal points likely to give rise to desires and feelings, to the occurrence of intensities. This strategy, which cannot be conceived in terms of a unified method, finds its high point in the style of *Libidinal Economy*, where passionate descriptions and careful attention to particular cases and examples stand in marked contrast to abstract academic theorizing.

Libidinal economics, it should be clear, will provide no pedagogical *program*. The texts that express these views must be taken instead as both models and provocations. Hence the very concept of *a* philosophy of education runs counter to this work, which is rather a style of thinking that seeps into others and opens them up to new possibilities. This requires a refusal to be guided by reference to any transcendent idea – of the human subject or of inter-subjectivity, for example – or to be led by any teleology, in favor of a practice that seeks to multiply discourses and open them up to libidinal events, that is, to intense feelings and desires. It calls for the Stoic love of the event. Such an apedagogy does not lead to an iconoclastic reflection of common values and knowledge. It does, however, imply a less reverential and more questioning attitude, one that allows us to live in an affirmative and libidinally rich manner. This, Williams claims, is a wise and careful way of living with the nihilistic tendencies of the dominant structures of our societies.

The final chapter, "Pointlessness and the university of beauty" by Gordon C. F. Bearn, returns with full force to the problem of performativity and, like Williams' account, seeks something beyond the kinds of response that might be offered in terms of Lyotard's writings on the sublime. Lyotard writes of universities in a melancholic grey, Bearn claims, because they, like the system itself, are guided by a unique technical genre of discourse whose end is performativity. In a climate where everything that comes into the university is assimilated to this genre of discourse, the openness of universities is a sham.

When he wrote *The Postmodern Condition*, Lyotard retained some hope that performativity might be overcome by way of those little narratives that would reveal the paralogical effects of the system. But later he came to think that the system has the consequence of causing us to forget whatever escapes it. His move out of this impasse led him toward a version of the sublime, one later celebrated by Bill Readings in *The University in Ruins* (1996): in the University of the Sublime, then, study is directed toward bearing witness. But this, Bearn argues, was Lyotard's mistake: it is not the sublime that he should have turned to but the beautiful; to the ideal of a University of Beauty. While the University of the Sublime relies on a principle of double negation, the University of Beauty is driven by affirmation.

Bearn's elaboration of what the University of Beauty might be like involves an attempt to recover the intense joys of pointless play, to show

how there can be a good kind of pointlessness. This is not emptiness but intensity, the intensity of being lost in a swarm of different thoughts, ideas, and feelings, involved in myriad points. The central focus of a University of Beauty would be the production of intellectual and emotional intensity, and this would involve breaking through the limitations of our represen-tational ways of thinking. It would be dedicated to releasing these swarming intensities, to breaking through representation, not by negation to emptiness, but by proceeding pointlessly toward maximal intensity. A good textbook, like a good university, keeps those it addresses off-balance, it sets thoughts running: not to bear witness to the differend, but to bring more and more different aspects of a site of investigation into play. A university might – and the best that we see sometimes do – make its goal the production of minds energized in this way. And in this again something of the child's intense joy in pointless play is recovered.

We are wary of an aestheticization of *dissensus* here. But the relation of these last essays to the rest perhaps brings out most clearly what might stand as an aspiration of the volume as a whole, what most of the essays in their different ways try to achieve: invention and intensity, lack of harmony, releasing of affects. It is in this way that we hope to pay tribute to a philosopher whose sustained commentary and critique has made present those aspects of our world that otherwise seemed unpresentable. He taught us to see ourselves, and to see what we were becoming, and tried to give us a sense of how we might be honorable in such dishonorable times. His hopes for his writing were merely that his "pile of phrases" prove useful in helping us think in these times where we no longer have the time to read. This perhaps is just education.

1 Emancipation and philosophies of history

Jean-François Lyotard and cultural difference

Michael Peters

> Within the tradition of modernity, the movement towards emancipation is a movement whereby a third party, who is initially outside the we of the emancipating avant-garde, eventually becomes part of the community of real (first person) or potential (second person) speakers.
>
> (Lyotard, *Universal History and Cultural Differences*, in Benjamin 1989: 315)

Philography/biosophy: Algeria and Lyotard's political writings

> I owe Constantine [an Algerian city] a picture of what it was for me then, when I arrived from the Sorbonne to teach in its high school. But with what colors should I paint what astonished me, that is, the immensity of the injustice? An entire people, from a great civilization, wronged, humiliated, denied their identity.
>
> (Lyotard, *In the Name of Algeria*, 1993a: 170)

Jean-François Lyotard was born in 1924 in Versailles and he died on 21 April 1998 at the age of 73.[1] It is not well known that Lyotard had taught philosophy in secondary schools from 1949 to 1959, teaching in an Algerian *lycée* at Constantine (a city in the northeast), in the period just before the outbreak of the Algerian war. Lyotard became radicalized as a result of his experiences in Algeria during this time and became an active supporter of the Algerian National Liberation Front (FLN) against French colonialist rule.[2]

After the Second World War and the defeat of the Axis powers, many Algerians believed that they also would experience the fruits of French liberty, humanism, and democracy. Traditionally, Algerian migrant labor gravitated to markets in France. In the 1950s this labor market became barred to *fellaghi* who, now jobless, began to direct their anger and desperation against French rule. France responded by sending in French paratroopers under General Massu, and a brutal and bloody war of military occupation ensued.[3] The issue divided the French intelligentsia, compromising the older guard like Albert Camus and rallying the younger, like Lyotard and Pierre Bourdieu, who were both teaching in Algeria at the time.[4]

On returning to France in 1956 Lyotard joined the editorial board of *Socialisme ou Barbarie,* an influential Marxist periodical founded by Cornelius Castoriadis and Claude Lefort in 1948.[5] Under the influence of Castoriadis and Jean Laplanche the journal adopted a distinctive psycho-analytic orientation which was to have an enduring impact upon Lyotard's thinking. The journal itself was characterized by its radical critique of Soviet communism based upon the ideas of workers' management: the Soviet bureaucracy was seen to be caught in the contradiction of using Marxism to suppress the political rights of the very group it claimed to represent.[6] *Socialisme ou Barbarie* was also important in exerting consid-erable influence upon a group of young student activists who were prominent in the student-worker rebellion in Paris in May 1968.[7]

Lyotard resigned from *Socialisme ou Barbarie* in 1963 to join Pouvoir Ouvrier, a revolutionary workers' organization; he was to remain a member for two years. Around this time while a lecturer at Nanterre, Lyotard initiated Le Mouvement du 22 mars, a movement explicitly opposing Fouchet's reforms of 1967 and committed to the freedom of expression and political assembly, and to democratic participation by students and staff in university affairs.[8]

Lyotard was at the University of Nanterre during the events of May 1968, and his political activism centered on the struggle against the modernizing tendency – new selection methods and changed conditions to the baccalau-reate examination – of Fouchet's reforms, which compromised the demand for democratization and, in doing so, severely underestimated the students' desire for genuine participation. Themes that were to surface later in Lyotard's *The Postmodern Condition* (1984a) find their source here: the critique of a class monopolization of knowledge and the mercantilization of knowledge and education; an attack on the "hierarchic magisterial relation" of pedagogy; the refusal of a kind of education under capitalism which merely socially reproduces students to fulfil the technical demands of the system; and the expression of a moral ideal embodied in non-dialectical forms of dialogue as the ethical precondition for pedagogy.[9]

These brief biographical details are not meant to provide anything like a narrative or history of Lyotard's early political life, or even the bones of an obituary: indeed, given his work on narratology, his resistance to the liberal humanist subject, and his rejection of the notion of the "organic" intellectual, it would be inconsistent for me to attempt anything more systematic or chronological. Also it would be a mistake to want to construct yet another hagiography: heroic narratives of its intellectuals are ritually and solemnly demanded by the left.[10] Yet Lyotard's early political engagement and writings, especially his Algerian experiences, are an important preliminary to understanding his "turn" to philosophy, his "depoliticization," his differend with Marxism, and his position regarding emancipation and cultural difference.

The twelve years from 1954 to 1964 represent the years of Lyotard's active political involvement. From 1955 onwards, while a member of *Socialisme ou Barbarie*, Lyotard was assigned responsibility for the Algerian section. His accounts of the anti-imperialist struggle in Algeria – "the Algerians' War" as he called it – Bill Readings argues, "provide a useful empirical corrective to charges that poststructuralism is an evasion of politics, or that Lyotard's account of the postmodern condition is a blissful ignorance of the postcolonial question" (Readings 1993b: xiii).

In "The Name of Algeria" (1993a) Lyotard remembers his debt both to *Socialisme ou Barbarie* and to Algeria. He likens the political orientation of the group *Socialisme ou Barbarie* to the act of repetition when Trotsky established the Fourth International in 1937 to fight against Stalinist bureaucracy: ten years later, he writes, a group of workers and militants "left" the Fourth International. Trotsky, Lyotard alleges, "blinkered" by classism, was unable to see that the bureaucratization of Soviet Russia had created a new exploitative class. Further, Trotskyism, attached to "democratic centralism" and "economism," was unable rethink the nature of workers' struggles in developed capitalist societies or to learn from the democratic modes of their organization and resistance. Finally, Trotskyism does not perform an analysis of the changes that capitalism itself undergoes (by virtue of its own development), even after capitalism has reached the "highest stage" identified by Lenin half a century ago (Lyotard 1993c: 165).

Socialisme ou Barbarie was conceived in terms of the commitment to help rebuild the idea governing the emancipation of workers worldwide, while remaining faithful to the original elements motivating the struggles.[11] It had identified, Lyotard says in retrospect, the secret of all resistance – the *intractable* in the system – which still remains true today even "when the principle of a radical alternative to capitalist domination (worker's power) must be abandoned" (ibid.: 166): that by showing the motive of their resistance (actually inexpressible) to those who resist, the group would help them to remain faithful to this motive, help them not let themselves be robbed of it under the pretext that it is necessary to organize oneself in order to resist (ibid.: 167).

His political writings on Algeria, Lyotard says, are indebted to *Socialisme ou Barbarie*; he says that he could not have written them without the education he received from the group. At the same time he recounts the splitting up of the group, a "depoliticization," and a disappearance of the intractable from the political as the privileged site. Out of the political crises of the 1960s the only belief that Lyotard preserves is that it is "intellectually dishonest to impose the hope that, as Marxists, we should invest in the revolutionary activity of the industrial proletariat" (ibid.: 169). Indeed, this idea, he argues, "must yield to the evidence that the grand narratives of emancipation, beginning (or ending) with 'ours,' that of radical Marxism, have lost their intelligibility and their substance" (ibid.: 169). The dominant presumption of the moderns has been that the true voice has been silenced and that it is a question of realizing this true voice and consolidating its position as heroic subject: the true believer of Christianity, the reasonable citizen of the Enlightenment, the enfranchised proletarian of Marxism. The term "depoliticization," first used twenty-five years ago, announced both "the erasure of the great figure of the alternative, and at the same time, that of the great founding legitimacies" (ibid.: 169). But to give up on the heroic figures of the grand narratives as a basis for achieving emancipation is not to give up on the goal of emancipation:

> The task that remains is to work out a conception and a practice completely different from the ones that inspired "classical" modernity. To readjust the latter, even subtly, to the present state of things would only be to mint and distribute counterfeit coin. Certainly, something of the intractable persists in the present system, but it is not possible to locate and support its expressions or signs in the same areas of the community and with the same means as those of half a century ago.
>
> (Lyotard 1993c: 169)

When Lyotard writes of the Algerians' war he writes as an intellectual and "internationalist;" as one who lent practical support to the FLN. But as Readings (1993b: xviii) argues, the war of the Algerians is not important to Lyotard principally as an example of nationalist struggle for self-determination. The Algerians, he repeatedly insists, are not simply fighting for the right to do to themselves what the French have done to them. Rather, the bloody process of decolonization marks a limit to a modernist and imperialist philosophy of historical progress that is common, under diverse forms, to both left and right. As an affirmation of the local or the particular, the Algerian war throws the universalistic pretensions of the nation-state into crisis: the struggle is not merely over whether French colonists or native Algerians should direct the development of the state and society in Algeria. What counts in these writings is the presentation of the war against the presumed neutrality of "progress" and "development," a struggle not to become the representatives of a process of "universal" human development (capitalist or communist) that has been defined in Europe.

Lyotard's philosophical "turn" and the differend with Marxism

> Inasmuch as there was in Marxism a discourse which claimed to be able to express without residue all opposing positions, which forgot that differends are embodied in incommensurable figures between

which there is no logical solution, it became necessary to stop speaking this idiom at all.

(Lyotard 1988e: 61)

After 1966 Lyotard discontinued his active political affiliation with any radical Marxist group, and indeed this break in his life represents an intellectual separation from Marxism and turn to philosophy. Lyotard's differend with Marxism and his turn to philosophy have to be seen against the background of French intellectual life. In particular, this background comprises the struggle in the late 1950s and early 1960s against humanism in all its forms, and above all Lyotard's turn was a reaction against the phenomenological (existential or humanist) subject which had dominated French philosophy in the postwar period.[12]

The place of Lyotard's political writings in the corpus of his work is a complex question which defies any simple recounting of publication dates. For instance, Lyotard has remarked that *The Postmodern Condition* (1984a), in the eyes of his critics, has occluded his other works; that it was marked by a certain sociology and epistemology rather than philosophy; and that the philosophical basis of *The Postmodern Condition* is to be found in *The Differend* (Lyotard 1988a). While one can name the specific genres that constitute Lyotard's writings – the philosophical, the epistemological, genres of criticism, linguistics, narrative, intellectual autobiography, and aesthetics – politics, as he says, is more complex than a genre, combining "discursive genres (but also phrase-regimes) which are totally heterogeneous" (Lyotard 1988d: 299).

Already in his early works, *Discours, figure* (1971) and *Economie libidinale* (1993, orig. 1974b), Lyotard signaled a conscious shift away from the doctrinaire praxis philosophy which characterized the non-PCF Marxism tradition of *Socialisme ou Barbarie*.[13] The former work attempts to develop a metaphysics of truth without negation; the latter attempts to substitute Freud's economy of libidinal energy (and the notion of primary process) for Marxist political economy. In this situation there is no truth arrived at through dialectics: the supposed ethical and social truths of Marxism, based upon an appeal to an historical ideal, are no better than the falsehoods it wants to overcome. Lyotard (1974b) criticizes the underlying notion of the dialectic. He simply does not believe that a political, philosophical, or artistic position is to be abandoned because it is "sublated." It is not true, according to Lyotard, that the experience of a position means its inevitable exhaustion and necessary development into another position where it is both conserved and suppressed.

Lyotard (1988d), in an interview with Willem van Reijen and Dick Veerman, suggests that "the essential philosophical task will be to refuse . . . the complete aestheticization of the political" which he maintains is characteristic of modern politics. By "aestheticization" Lyotard means an active fashioning or shaping of the community or polity according to the idea of reason. Lyotard in his *Political Writings*, then, addresses the crisis of "the end of the political," that is, "of all attempts to moralize politics which were incarnated in Marxism" (Lyotard 1988d: 300). This means, as Readings (1993b: xviii) suggests, that Lyotard's political writings are characterized by a "resistance to modern universalism," by an argument against what may be called the "politics of redemption." What we are presented with in Lyotard's work, as an alternative, is a politics of resistance, a form of writing which offers resistance to established modes of thought and accepted opinion. The same form of writing also registers an ongoing internal struggle or resistance, characterized by the differend between early and later modes of thinking and, crucially, by Lyotard's differend with Marxism itself.

Lyotard's differend with Marxism and specifically with *Socialisme ou Barbarie* and Pierre Souyri, in particular, is recounted in "A memorial of Marxism: for Pierre Souyri," a rare autobiographical piece.[14] He describes how, in the language of radical Marxism, dialectical logic had become a simple idiom and how "the machinery for overcoming alterity by negating and conserving it" for him had broken down, precipitating a "relapse" into the logic of identity. He writes of his own intellectual biography of the time:

> And what if, after all, the philosopher asked himself, there wasn't any Self at all in experience to synthesize contradictorily the moments and thus to achieve knowledge and realization of itself? What if history and thought did not need this synthesis; what if the paradoxes had to remain paradoxes, and if the equivocacy of these universals which are also particulars, must not be sublated? What if Marxism itself were in its turn one of those particular universals which it was not even a question of going beyond – an assumption that is still too dialectical – but which it was at the very least a question of refuting in its claim to absolute universality, all the while according it a value in its own order? But what then, in what order, and what is an order? These questions frightened me in themselves because of the formidable theoretical tasks they promised, and also because they seemed to condemn anyone who gave himself over to them to the abandonment of any militant practice for an indeterminate time.
>
> (Lyotard 1988e: 50)

What was at stake for Lyotard after twelve years of a commitment to radical Marxism was whether Marxism could "still understand and transform the new direction taken by the world after the end of the Second World War" (ibid.: 49). Capitalism had succeeded in surviving the crisis of the 1930s. The proletariat had not seized the opportunity to overturn the old order. On the contrary, modern capitalism, once its market and production capacities had been restored, had set up new relations of exploitation and taken on new forms. Lyotard lists the following new realities confronting Marxism:

the reorganization of capitalism into bureaucratic or State monopo-
listic capitalism; the role of the modern State in the so-called mixed
economy; the dynamics of the new ruling strata (bureaucratic or tech-
nocratic) within the bourgeoisie; the impact of the new techniques on
work conditions and on the mentality of workers and employees; the
effects of economic growth on daily life and culture; the appearance
of new demands by workers and the possibility of conflicts between the
base and the apparatus in worker organizations.

(Lyotard 1988e: 66)

Of course, today, one can add enormously to this list: the rapid and
unplanned introduction of the "free market" after the collapse of the
eastern communist bloc in the late 1980s; the growth of local mafia, the
black market and the decline of central control in the same territories; the
strong growth of global finance capitalism; the formulation of the so-called
"Washington consensus" and the imposition of "structural adjustment"
policies on the Third World; the US domination of the neoliberal world
policy and lending institutions such as the World Bank and the IMF; the
heralding of the growth of the Asian "tiger economies" and their financial
collapse in the late 1990s; the reintroduction of capital controls and the
studied emulation of China's model. Many of these developments, one
could argue, speak as much to the present world financial crisis and the
policy backlash to the neoliberal free market orthodoxy, as to the internal
transformations of world capitalism (see, for instance, Wade and Venerosa
1998; Cumings 1998; Levinson 1998).

While Lyotard recognizes that there are several incommensurable
genres of discourse in play in society, none can transcribe all others; and
yet, nevertheless, one of them – that of capital – imposes its rules on others
and attempts to make all discourse commensurable. As he says: "This
oppression is the only radical one, the one that forbids its victims to bear
witness against it. It is not enough to understand it and be its philosopher;
one must also destroy it" (Lyotard 1988e: 72).

Emancipation and the politics of cultural difference

In the essay "Universal history and cultural differences" (1989) Lyotard
applies some of the results of his reworking of the "postmodern condition"
and treatment of narrative to the question of cultural difference. He
begins by correcting his bias in his earlier work – in *Instructions païennes*
(1977) and even in *The Postmodern Condition* – where he says, succumbing
to the urge to transcendentize, he granted the genre of narrative an
absolute privilege. Nevertheless, he argues, insofar as we can talk of world
history we must assume that it can be treated in narrative terms. One of the
great questions that face us at the *fin de siècle* is whether we "can continue
to organize the multitude of events that comes to us from the world . . . by

subsuming them beneath the idea of a universal history of humanity?" (Lyotard 1989: 314). Lyotard begins by analyzing the narrative mode of thought by which the moderns organized events and thereby created world history. Modernity, for Lyotard, as the narrative organization of events, begins with Augustine's *Confessions* and Descartes' *Discours* (and is exemplified in Rabelais and Montaigne); it begins with the shift from the "syntactic architecture of classical discourse" to the "paratactic arrangement of short sentences" linked by the conjunction "and." The narrative becomes the way of mastering contingency, of developing series, and of linking sequences that is characteristic of the modern mode of organizing time, especially as it is developed by the *Aufklärung* of the eighteenth century. Lyotard writes in a lengthy passage I will quote in full because it provides a useful summary and contains resonances with his analysis of narrative elsewhere (especially in *The Postmodern Condition*):

> The thought and action of the nineteenth and twentieth centuries are governed by an Idea (I am using Idea in its Kantian sense). That idea is the idea of emancipation. What we call philosophies of history, the great narratives by means of which we attempt to order the multitude of events, certainly argue this idea in very different ways: a Christian narrative in which Adam's sin is redeemed through love; the *Aufklärer* narrative of emancipation from ignorance and servitude thanks to knowledge and egalitarianism; the speculative narrative of the realization of the universal idea through the dialectic of the concrete; the Marxist narrative of emancipation from exploitation and alienation through the socialization of labor; the capitalist narrative of emancipation from poverty through technical and industrial development. These various narratives provide grounds for contention, and even for disagreement. But they all situate the data supplied by events within the course of history whose end, even if it is out of reach, is called freedom.
>
> (Lyotard 1989: 315)

What is useful to emphasize in Lyotard's analysis is that modern (read Enlightenment) philosophies of history constitute a competing series of narratives of emancipation; they all organize the events of world history according to the *telos* of freedom, though each philosophy comprises different events, and the stories are told by different narrators to different audiences for different political purposes. Lyotard does not see himself as "doing" philosophy; rather he is engaging in a form of ideology-critique insofar as the analysis of the phenomenon of language is itself ideological; and he is offering no more than a series of clarifications.

In the first clarification he offers, Lyotard focuses upon the term *continue*; in the second, he turns his attention to the status of the *we* in his original formulation "can *we* continue today to organize the multitude of events that come to us from the world . . . by subsuming them beneath the universal history of humanity?" In asking the question there is the implicit assumption that a *we* still exists, and that this *we* is capable of experiencing the continuity referred to. In what does this "we" consist? Lyotard answers:

> As the first person plural pronoun indicates, it refers to a community of subjects: you and I or they and I, depending on whether the speaker is addressing other members of the community (you/I) or a third party (you/they and I) for whom the other members it represents are designated by the third person (they). The question then arises as to whether or not this we is independent of the Idea of a history of humanity.
>
> (Lyotard 1989: 315)

This brings me to the point of where I opened this paper: the quotation from Lyotard that explains that within the tradition of modernity (in part defined in terms of the grand narratives of freedom) it is precisely the movement "whereby a third party, who is initially outside the *we* of the emancipating avant-garde, eventually becomes part of the community of real (first person) or potential (second person) speakers" (ibid.). Eventually, he says, modernity promises that "there will be only a *we* made up of *you* and *I*" (ibid.). By this he means that the story that rich Atlantic liberal-capitalist democracies like to tell themselves, and project back to 1789 (perhaps, further back to the Greek *polis*), is a story concerning the gradual and progressive enfranchisement of peoples, groups, animals and, ultimately, the biota: the struggle for and the ascription of rights to women, social rights, cultural rights of self-determination, minority rights to cultural maintenance, linguistic or language rights, children's rights, animal rights, the rights of the unborn and of future generations, ecological rights. This is the kind of story, for instance, told by the Hegelian and Italian professor of jurisprudence Norberto Bobbio in his *The Age of Rights* (1995).

I think this constitutes the real strength of Lyotard's analysis: the application of narratology to world history – the capture of philosophies of world history in the net of the narrative genre. It allows him to perform certain operations on the universal by catching it within the narrative structure: if narrative is – to quote one definition – "the semiotic representation of a series of events meaningfully connected in a temporal and causal way" (Onega and Landa 1996: 3), then we are entitled, or compelled, to ask, "whose representation?", "what series?", "why these events?", "why are they connected in this way?" and so on. In other words, the application of narratology to philosophies of history introduces a new awareness of the rules of the genre, and, in a Wittgensteinian sense, a new knowledge of how to play the game, perhaps even how to change the rules. As Susana Onega and her colleagues argue: "Any representation involves a point of view, a selection, a perspective on the represented object, criteria of relevance, and, arguably, an implicit theory of reality" (ibid.). In an age where there is not only a growing sophistication of modes of narrative analysis but also a general public awareness of the stakes of representation, is it at all surprising that incredulity towards grand narratives might be taken as the hallmark of a changing consciousness?[15]

The status of the *we* in the formulation is also a question of its own identity – the identity of the west? – that has been established by the tradition of modernity. If it is the case that the *we* is destined to remain particular – particular in the sense of preserving the linguistic structure *you and I* and, therefore, exclusive of many third parties – then, given that it has not yet forgotten that these third parties were potentially first persons, it is time for mourning: "it must either mourn for unanimity and find another mode of thinking or acting, or be plunged into incurable melancholia by the loss of an 'object' (or the impossibility of a subject): free humanity" (Lyotard 1989: 316).

One way to mourn the universal emancipation promised by modernity may be through what Freud calls secondary narcissism – the alleged condition of the most highly developed societies which results in a kind of terror exemplified at its worst in Nazism and in the idea that we decree the law which is only then applied to *them*. Another way to mourn is to "work through" the loss of the subject who was promised this future, but this does not involve "the unthinking dismissal of the modern subject." Rather, to "work through" the loss of the subject would lead, Lyotard maintains, "to the abandoning of the linguistic-communication structure (I/you/he/she) which . . . the moderns endorsed as an ontological and political model" (ibid.: 317).

Lyotard enters a third clarification based upon an Aristotelian analysis of the modality *can* which I shall not pursue, except to say that it too leads to "an inquiry into the defaillancy (*defaillance*) of the modern subject" (ibid.: 317), a defaillancy which, he speculates, is related to "resistance on the part of what I will term the multiplicity of worlds of names, on the part of the insurmountable diversity of cultures" (ibid.: 319). It is at this point that Lyotard, making use of Kripke's "rigid designators," suggests that names are learned in little stories and pursues his famous example of the Cashinahua, who begin and end each recitation in formulaic ways: "This is the story of . . . as I have always heard it told. Etc." and "Here ends the story of . . . he who told it was . . . (Cashinahua name). Etc." In this situation, to be named is to be recounted in the sense both of reactivating names and nominal relations and of reassuring the community of its permanence and legitimacy. These local narratives differ from the great narratives of legitimation that characterize modernity, which are cosmopolitical in the Kantian sense, transcending particular cultures in favor of a universal civic identity. Lyotard wants to problematize how this transcendence takes place. Does it take place through the structure of narrative as it was shaped syntactically in modernity? Lyotard writes the humanist presupposes the Idea of a universal history and inscribes particular communities within it as moments within the universal development of human communities. This is also, grosso modo, the axiom of the great speculative narrative as applied to human history. But the real question is whether or not there is a human history.

(Lyotard 1989: 321)

Lyotard recalls the epistemological (anthropological) version which "describes savage narrations and their rules without pretending to establish any continuity between them and the rules of its own mode of discourse" (ibid.: 322). He tracks out us for the way in which many universalist movements, including that of labor, derived their legitimacy from an Idea yet to be realized rather than local or popular traditions, and he sees the new independence movements and nationalist struggles to be a retreat into local legitimacy as a reaction against the effects of imperialism. Lyotard suggests, I think without nostalgia, that the rebuilding of the world economy, even if it could boast the achievement of the goals of Keynesianism or economic liberalism, deserves no credit, for to master the game of the global market has little to do with cosmopolitical ends, nor does it concern itself with reducing international inequalities. In other words, "The world market is not creating a universal history in modernity's sense of that term. Cultural differences are . . . being promoted as touristic and cultural commodities . . . " (ibid.: 323).

Finally, what can be said of this *we*, as Lyotard says, "the avant-garde which prefigures today the free humanity of tomorrow?" (ibid.). The figure of the intellectual was once supported by the Idea of emancipation which was part of the history of modernity but that has changed with the "degradation" of educational institutions and, accordingly, the grand figure of the intellectual (Voltaire, Zola, Sartre) has also disappeared. Lyotard suggests:

Now that the age of the intellectuals, and that of the parties, is over, it might, without wishing to be presumptuous, be useful, on both sides of the Atlantic, to begin to trace a line of resistance against our modern defaillancy.

(Lyotard 1989: 323)

Lyotard's work on the narrative analysis of world history has not been without criticism, nor without further development and reflection. He extends his analysis principally in *The Differend* (1988a) and in discussions with Richard Rorty over the virtues of cosmopolitanism.[16] I present his work here in what I called a "biosophical" sense, a sense where, while it may be possible to draw distinctions between the author and his or her work or between authors, their work and their historical context, it is also clear that the category of the subject-author itself is implicated in philosophical questions premised upon it. Algeria was a clear context where Lyotard learned of the injustice of the universal expressed in the statement "We, the French people" and, accordingly, "took arms against a sea of troubles." This context of difference of which Lyotard was painfully aware did not constitute the awareness of a *we* or even of a substitute-we (the *we* of empathetic understanding). It took a precise form of political support given by one who regarded himself as an internationalist. It also shaped his political trajectory thereafter, his differend with Marxism, and his subsequent turn to "postmodern" philosophy.

Notes

1 He had been the Robert W. Woodruff Professor of French and Philosophy at Emory University, Atlanta, since 1995. Lyotard also taught at the University of Nanterre and the University of Paris VIII-Vincennes which he helped to found. Later, he secured a post as professor of philosophy at the University of Paris VIII -Saint-Denis which he held until his retirement in 1989. He was also professor of philosophy at the Collège International de Philosophie in Paris, and a visiting professor of French and Italian at the universities of California at Irvine and Emory from 1991.

2 The Front de libération nationale (FLN) was formed in 1954 and came to power under Ben Bella's one-party state in 1962. After independence most of the French civil service, administrators and technicians abandoned the country. The exception was some 1,000 French school teachers who remained in Algeria.

  French rule had been established in Algeria during the 1830s, and settler domination of Algeria took place from the 1870s. From the late nineteenth century onwards settlers comprised about 10 percent of the population. French colonization was marked by great violence and a mutual incomprehension between the colonizers and the colonized.

3 The French administration sent over 500,000 men to counter the "rebels." After 1956 the French forces concentrated on cutting off Algeria from the newly independent states of Tunisia and Morocco.

4 Frantz Fanon, who had served in the French Army in the Second World War, was working as a psychiatrist in Algeria at the time. He embraced the cause of the FLN and became its chief propagandist. Fanon questioned who was really mad, his Algerian patients or the French oppressors. It is interesting to note that Fanon rejected the "abstract assumption of universality," believing that the logic of reciprocal exclusivity prevented conciliation between the colonizer and the colonized, and, accordingly announced the end of the Rights of Man.

5 Castoriadis died on 26 December, 1997 at age 75. He joined the Greek Trotskyist faction and, escaping the Greek Civil War for Paris in 1945, joined the Paris Trotskyists and began to develop his radical libertarian anti-Stalinist politics based upon workers' management (rather than the party's) of production and society. For an informative obituary see
  http://aleph.lib.ohio-state.edu/~bcase/castoriadis/welcome.html

6 See Castoriadis' "General Introduction" to his *Political and Social Writings* (1988) for an account of the journal.

7 Dany Cohn-Bendit (Dany the Red) in his *Obsolete Communism: the Left-Wing Alternative*, trans. Arnold Pomerans, London, Deutsch (1968) acknowledged that many of his ideas were deeply indebted to *Socialisme ou Barbarie*.

8 See Lyotard's "Preamble to a Charter," "Nanterre, Here, Now," and "March 23"

(an unpublished introduction to an unfinished book on the movement of March 22), in his *Political Writings* (1993b).

9 For an excellent essay which explores Lyotard's suggestion of nondialectical forms of pedagogy see Readings (1995a). For a collection of essays which explore the significance of Lyotard's work for educational theory see Peters (1995).

10 Bill Readings notes: "For all its insistence on historical analysis, the political left has always relished hagiography, since the individual as moral exemplum performs the problematic theoretical reconciliation between historical or economic determinism and individual action, sketches a politics of the present conjuncture" (Readings 1993b: xiii).

11 Lyotard (1993: 166) remarks: "the role of the revolutionary organization is not to direct workers' struggles, but to provide them with the means to deploy the creativity that is at work in them and the means to become aware of that creativity so that they can direct themselves." This formulation is very close to the ethos of critical pedagogy and also to that referred to by Freire in *Pedagogy of the Oppressed* when he quotes Mao: "We give back to the workers clearly what we receive from them confusedly" (Freire 1972: 66, fn6).

12 Lyotard completed his dissertation on phenomenology in 1954. It was recently translated and published in English as *Phenomenology* (1991b).

13 Relevant in this respect also are Lyotard 1973a, 1973b.

14 This essay appears as an afterword in *Peregrinations* (Lyotard 1988e: 45–75). Pierre Souyri was both a friend and a founding member of *Socialisme ou Barbarie*.

15 On narrative see also Martin 1987 and, most interestingly, for an account of narrative ethics see Newton 1997.

16 See particularly the criticisms by the "Hegelians" Klein (1995) and Dallmayr (1997). Klein argues that the terms "master narrative" and "local narrative" perpetuate the Hegelian project of formally differentiating European culture from other cultures, and he suggests that we should regard all narratives as varieties of historical discourse within universal history, but it is not clear to me from his account in what such "universal history" would consist. More importantly, he traces in the work of Lyotard a shift from pragmatic descriptions of narrative mastery in his early work to descriptions of narrative as functions of form. For further sources on the debate with Lyotard see his note 11. Dallmayr phrases the debate in the following terms (taken from his abstract): "Postmodernists believe that a detraction from the egocentrism of Western thought towards the nonidentity of a global and multicultural environment is necessary. . . . Lyotard assert[s] that nonidentity is marked by the absence of all differences, and is symbolic of counteridentity and no-identity." He suggests in an interesting paper, if I can crudely summarize the options, that the shift from identity to nonidentity implies: (i) an axiom of incommensurability, especially in the inability of the west to understand; (ii) a valorization of concrete particularities, approximating a global politics; (iii) a vacuous sphere of nondistinction, i.e., free-floating nomadic intellectuals; (iv) an absence or negation in the very heart of every identity. In relation to these questions but not Dallmayr's specific formulation, see also Melas 1995, Chen 1997 and Cheah 1997. See Rorty 1991 for his response to Lyotard, and Lyotard and Larochelle 1992 for Lyotard's further reflections.

2 Lyotard on Wittgenstein

The differend, language games, and education

Nicholas C. Burbules

This essay is concerned with a major theme of work in education influenced by poststructuralism, namely, a hostility toward the ideals of consensus and understanding. Perhaps the foremost critic in education of these aims of communication is Elizabeth Ellsworth (1989, 1997), who argues that these norms express a rational desire to bridge gulfs of culture and experience which, under most educational circumstances, cannot be bridged. The very attempt to do so, Ellsworth argues, disrespects these differences and puts those different from dominant cultures and values at an asymmetrical risk in these situations. She is far from alone in expressing such views; many writers on multiculturalism and feminism have similarly emphasized the insurmountable barriers of difference.

One of the primary sources drawn upon in buttressing these points is Jean-François Lyotard's concept of the differend, and this idea is explained, by Lyotard, partly in reference to Wittgenstein's idea of the language game. Here I want to explore this lineage, from Wittgenstein through Lyotard to the hostility toward the ideals of agreement and understanding, not primarily to judge whether Lyotard is using Wittgenstein properly here (I think he is not) but to plumb the roots of this hostility, to ask where it comes from, and to assess whether it can sustain any meaningful sense of communication and education.

Lyotard defines the differend as "a case of conflict, between (at least) two parties, that cannot be equitably resolved for lack of a rule of judgment applicable to both arguments" (1988a: xi, 9). This case is contrasted with what Lyotard calls a "litigation," in which the claims of the opposing parties can engage one another because they are defined within a common rule of judgment. A. T. Nuyen's gloss on this quote reflects the import it is typically taken to hold:

> Conflicts can arise when people are engaged in discourses that are incommensurable. Because there are no rules that apply across the discourses, the conflicts become differends. To enforce a rule in a differend is to enforce the rule of one discourse or the other, resulting in a wrong suffered by the party whose rule of discourse is ignored.

> Furthermore the wronged party cannot appeal against the wrong
> because the rules of its own discourse are not recognized and because
> to appeal in terms of the rules of the other discourse is already to have
> given up.
>
> (Nuyen 1998b: 175)

At the very start, one needs to question the model of litigation as a general analogue to the process of communication. "Conflict," after all, can mean many things, ranging from different opinions on a matter of taste, to different judgments about another person's character, to different political views, to disagreements over religion, to competing interests that cannot be mutually satisfied, to opposing rights claims, and so on. Only some of these seem the sorts of matters that could be thought of on the model of a court case, in which there is a direct challenge to the legitimacy of the other's claim, or in which there is the outcome of a clear winner and loser. Such an analogy introduces from the very start an assumption of what Michael Peters (1995a: 391), following Lyotard, calls an "agonistics of language," as if every conversation was a contest, as if every disagreement was a struggle, as if every encounter across sharp cultural difference was characterized by the threat of one party's rules of discourse overwhelming the other's. Indeed, Lyotard often uses analogies like playing a card to "trump" another's as the prototypical move in a verbal contest; yet clearly only some kinds of moves in communication are like this.

There are certainly cases where a wronged party cannot articulate or justify their position within the framework of another vocabulary and value system. The injunction to others to make their case in someone else's terms or to remain silent is the sort of false choice that allows only for the alternatives of conformity or defeat. Lyotard is right to make this point, and it is one of the subtle ways in which systems of justice, without any overt forms of corruption or bias, nevertheless rule out of court any fundamental challenges to their authority. Lyotard is also correct that encounters across different cultural communities do sometimes give rise to differends, incommensurabilities in which one party *cannot* make themselves understood in the terms familiar to the other. (For that matter, the same thing can happen to parties even within the same cultural community.) But what is unsatisfying about these two claims is that they are linked together in Lyotard's argument: as if communicative encounters across cultural difference were typically adversarial, in which misunderstandings or disagreements necessarily give rise to the threat that one party's cultural integrity and credibility are immediately at risk.

Lyotard, in elaborating his view of the differend, repeatedly invokes Wittgenstein's idea of the language game. Here I think Lyotard not only misreads what Wittgenstein meant by that notion, but also fails to see that in fact Wittgenstein's view poses a direct challenge to the agonistic model of language Lyotard is taking for granted. Lyotard's "Nietzscheanized

Wittgenstein" (Bohman 1987: 68) is a stranger to anyone who has studied Wittgenstein closely.

In his most-often quoted passage on language games, Lyotard writes,

> The examination of language games . . . identifies and reinforces the separation of language from itself. There is no unity to language; there are islands of language, each of them ruled by a different regime, untranslatable into the others. This dispersion is good in itself, and ought to be respected. It is deadly when one *phrase regime* prevails over the others.
>
> (Lyotard 1993b: 20, emphasis added)

Steven Best and Douglas Kellner (1991: 175) call this mode of analysis "Lyotard's one-sided celebration of differences, fragmentation, and dissensus."

Now, Wittgenstein's idea of a language game in the *Philosophical Investigations* (1997) plays a very particular purpose in his philosophy. He is trying to make clear, in distinction to his own previous views in the *Tractatus Logico-Philosophicus*, that language does not only serve the purpose of describing the world, that is, asserting propositions that can be tested for truth and falsity; language is used to play many other "games" – joking, praying, promising, and so forth – or what later philosophers called "speech acts," which serve a variety of purposes. These different language games have different purposes and they are characterized by different rules; but they co-exist within the *same* "language," even when people might some-times be confused about which game is being played ("Was that a joke or a threat?"). Misunderstandings between different language games are possible, but these misunderstandings are possible precisely because people *are* speaking the same basic language. Language games, for Wittgenstein, are not different cultural or national languages (French versus Chinese); nor are they alternative "paradigms" or world views; and only in particular instances could they be characterized as "phrase regimes": for example, within forms of life in which language games or speech acts are invested with significant political or institutional weight. But not all language games are like this. The slippage from "language games" to "phrase regimes" conflates, ironically, a vast variety of different language games under a single characterization – a very un-Wittgensteinian thing to do, I would say.

It is also un-Wittgensteinian to invoke the idea of language games to establish the idea of "islands of language," given the way that Lyotard wants to use that image. Here Lyotard's argument is more subtle, but still in the end not very convincing. He says,

> Languages are translatable, otherwise they are not languages; but language games are not translatable, because if they were, they would not be language games. It is as if we wanted to translate the rules and

strategies of chess into those of checkers. . . . A move in bridge cannot be "translated" into a move made in tennis. The same goes for phrases, which are moves in language games; one does not "translate" a mathematical proof into a narration. Translation is itself a language game.

(Lyotard 1985: 53; 1993b: 21)

There are many ideas at work here, not all of them parts of the same argument. It is certainly true that "moves" within different language games are by definition characteristic of those games (just as are moves in games like tennis or chess). But it is not true, first of all, that they are never translatable into other games: there are certain moves and strategies within chess (for example, moving pieces to control the center of the board) that are quite translatable into checkers. A move in bridge *can* be translated into a move in tennis; for example, a method of communicating with your partner (if playing doubles) that you do not want your opponents to understand. To take the linguistic case, phrases in different language games are in fact often translatable into others: as when teachers appropriate the language of contracts and use it as a way of negotiating grades with students; or when a philosopher uses a joke (say, Groucho Marx's quip that "I wouldn't want to belong to any club that would have me as a member") to make a serious point about political philosophy. Of course, *sometimes* such an attempt at translation will seem malapropic, even absurd: it might show that a person does not understand the nature of the language games he or she is playing (using a vulgar joke at a eulogy; or trying to negotiate a peace treaty by giving the recipe for how to make a soufflé). But there is no reason to generalize from these sorts of cases to *all* encounters between language games.

Moreover, even if one takes Lyotard at his word, it seems that he is caught in a contradiction, for he is saying that "there is no unity," no common measure, across these islands; but then one wonders what vantage point Lyotard is occupying that allows him to recognize this fact *and to comment upon it.* Here is what he says:

When I say: There is no common measure, it means that we know of nothing in common with these different language games. We merely know that there are several of them. . . . The fact that I myself speak of this plurality does not imply that I am presenting myself as the occupant of a unitary vantage point upon the whole set of these games.

(Lyotard 1985: 51)

There are three deep problems with this response. The first is that it is a vast overstatement, even on Lyotard's own account, to say that "we know of nothing in common" between different language games. Even if one accepts the untranslatability thesis, which I have just challenged, saying that particular phrases might not be translatable across different language games is not the same thing as saying that they have *nothing* in common. I do not think that point even requires further argument. Second, for Wittgenstein, as I noted earlier, language games exist within "the same" language; they are speech acts that might even use the same words, albeit with different meanings and significance. Now, one might try to extend Wittgenstein's argument to refer to entirely different linguistic traditions, in order to show that they speak right past one another and have nothing in common; but Lyotard does not give us that argument. Finally, it is a significant point to note that agents play multiple language games, and are sometimes even playing multiple games at the same moment; there is no one-to-one mapping between different games, different agents, or different groups of people. Lyotard's "island" imagery assumes that when you are "within" one language game you are cut off from all the others; that when two people speak from within respective language games they speak across a gulf of difference. Given his concerns with disenfranchised groups whose "language games" are not being respected by others, this imagery is understandable. But it conflates the supposed "island" of a language game with the "islands" of social position or cultural otherness, which are not the same thing. And Wittgenstein's idea is especially unsuited to this argument because of his assertion that we can and do play multiple language games, not only the one representing "our" island (as if there were only one).

Finally, there is Lyotard's celebration of "dispersion" (it "is good in itself, and ought to be respected"). By this I take Lyotard to mean that the multiplicity and incommensurability of language games is not only a fact, but a desirable condition; that they should be kept separate and autonomous, and even multiply. Given his assumption, that in cases of a differend the only resolution of conflict must come at the expense of the cultural integrity and credibility of at least one of the parties, one can see why he believes that the less these islands have to do with one another the better. But this position does not sustain a positive conception of social and political philosophy (nor of education). It is not practicable on a wide scale, nor does it present a general conception of communicative relations that can undergird even a state of peaceful and tolerant coexistence, let alone one of possible cooperation and reconciliation. Not all differends may be reducible to litigations; but then litigation is not the only basis for reconciling conflicts.

Lyotard's politicization of discourse, of course, is part and parcel of a broader theoretical emphasis within poststructural theory: "Political struggle for Lyotard is a matter of discursive intervention within language, contesting rules, forms, principles, and positions"(Best and Kellner 1991: 163). There may be no writer who emphasizes so strongly that language is variously the terrain, the weapon, and the stakes in this struggle:

> To speak is to fight in the sense of playing, and speech acts fall within the domain of general agonistics. . . . You don't play around with

language. And in this sense, there are no language games. There are
stakes tied to genres of discourse. When these stakes are attained, we
talk about success. There is conflict, therefore. The conflict, though, is
not between humans or between any other entities; rather, these result
from phrases. . . . No matter what its regime, every phrase is in principle what is at stake in a difference between genres of discourse.

(Lyotard 1984a: 10; 1988a: 137–8)

I am not the first to find Lyotard's enlistment of Wittgenstein as an ally
in this process a strange and even inappropriate misinterpretation:
Richard Rorty (1992: 64), and the co-authors Nigel Blake, Paul Smeyers,
Richard Smith, and Paul Standish (1998: 33) make similar points. But
neither of these analyses develops the view I am stressing here, that in fact
Wittgenstein's view offers an alternative to, and a critique of, Lyotard's
"islands of language" and the fundamentally agonistic view of language
this assumes. Michael Peters, on the other hand, defends Lyotard's interpretation of Wittgenstein. He calls it a "playful and innovative" reading
(Peters 1995a: 391; see also 1989: 100–1); although in a more recent correspondence with me he suggested that a better term would be "creative
misappropriation." I suspect that he would stress the first term in that
phrase; I would stress the second.

Lyotard's version of a language game is, first, internally structured by a
system of rules that are constitutive of, and unique to, that game (as are
the rules of chess or of baseball). Second, a language game is dependent
for its legitimacy on these rules (that is, it cannot be justified to those who
do not share those rules). Third, any language game inherently contains
a paradox, because no system of rules can entirely support itself (there
must always be elements within a language game that cannot be justified
on its own terms; as, for example, when science needs to appeal ultimately
to narratives or allegories – the Book of Nature – to explain and justify
itself). Therefore, fourth, these legitimating narratives can never provide
an overarching set of rules, a "common measure," by which competing
language games can be judged or compared (that is, they are incommensurable). Finally, fifth, this condition makes language games
untranslatable with each other, where the limit case is the differend,
where competing language games cannot engage one another at all
(Lyotard 1984a: 10).

However, on each of these points Lyotard misunderstands what
Wittgenstein means by a language game. A language game is not a world
view, an argument, a paradigm, or a culture: it is a specific set of discursive
practices tied to specific purposes. Hence, first of all, while language games
certainly comprise rules, these rules do not circumscribe the practice; the
practice comes first (hence, Wittgenstein says, we can learn to play a game
without ever being able to identify or articulate all of the rules). Second,
language games do not depend for their legitimacy on these rules; they

depend for their legitimacy, Wittgenstein says, on the *forms of life* that sustain them – and a language game makes no sense outside of that form of life. Third, it is not a paradox to say that no such system of rules can support itself; we should never expect a language game to "justify" itself. It is more accurate to characterize Wittgenstein's view as "one does not have to play any particular language game; but if one does, there is a right and a wrong way to play it." Argument is entirely external to this process or, more precisely, argument is one type of language game, not a character-istic of language games ("phrase regimes") generally. Fourth, a point so crucial that I will return to it at length in a moment, Wittgenstein rejects the entire notion that there can be, or needs to be, a "common measure" operating across language games that allows them all to be understood as language games: this is his idea of a family resemblance across language games, which relates them all as games without identifying an essential core characteristic or characteristics that they all must share. Finally, fifth, as Lyotard himself notes, translation is itself a language game (not a meta-language game), and so it is very strange for him to suggest that translation between language games is a general issue or problem. Perhaps in the case of a litigation or a differend, where there is an actual conflict of interests or desires that needs to be reconciled, it makes sense to ask whether a common ground on which to negotiate or adjudicate that conflict exists; but this is not a *general* problem between language games. We do not typi-cally worry about achieving a "translation" between, say, a joke and a prayer, or between an apology and a mathematical proof, or between a scientific journal article and a poem.

One must ask, therefore, why Lyotard has chosen to emphasize the agonistics of language and, within it, the cases of untranslatability between "islands of language." He is certainly not the first to use Wittgenstein in this manner: Thomas Kuhn, in *The Structure of Scientific Revolutions*, makes a similar kind of argument – indeed, it is Kuhn above all who established the idea of "incommensurability" between "paradigms" as a virtual truism for many today (although he later backed off that interpretation of his work). But Lyotard goes beyond these views to consider incommensurability, not only as a failure of translation, but as a positive good; and to consider consensus as a threat (Blake *et al.* 1998: 11). "Consensus," he says, "does violence to the heterogeneity of language games" (Lyotard 1984a: xxv). If one believes this, then highlighting the incommensurability of the differend, and protecting it from compromise through litigation, or through being homogenized through translation, becomes the only way to avoid doing violence to radical difference. One cannot (consistently) claim to understand or appreciate all of those differends; nor can one presume to speak for them. But one can argue for their preservation (the "dispersion" of language) as a good in itself.

But why would one believe that consensus necessarily does *violence* to heterogeneity? Why would one call it "deadly," as Lyotard does? One thing that this claim could be taken to mean is that consensus *reduces* hetero-geneity: that where there were two or more contending views, there is now only the one shared view. But the idea that consensus in this sense elimi-nates heterogeneity assumes that reconciliation inevitably happens on one party's terms (in which case the other party "loses"), as opposed to circum-stances in which a consensus or rapprochement gives rise to a new position, in which case there is an *increase* in the options available, not a diminishment of them. But, like many "Nietzscheanized" theorists, Lyotard seems to assume that for one point of view to win the other must always lose; there is no third way:

> Grant me, in fact, that within the hypothesis of a discussion in which the stakes are not the same for each of the two interlocutors, consensus appears impossible to obtain. . . . This corresponds precisely to Wittgenstein's conception of a language game. The procedures for discussion and argumentation are dependent on these stakes.
>
> (Lyotard 1997: 129–30)

Another thing that Lyotard's "violence" might be taken to mean is that people who yield to consensus do so within an asymmetrical relation in which they do not appreciate what they are giving up by doing so. They suffer violence by losing their uniqueness and integrity, without realizing it; and once gone, they cannot be recaptured. To use a Foucauldian term, they have become "normalized." I think that there are cases in which this is a disturbing prospect and cases in which it is not. To judge whether this is a violence or wrong to them, one needs to consider a range of specific features of the situation: the conditions under which this agreement is obtained and the extent to which it is voluntary or coerced (this is rarely likely to be a clear-cut and unproblematic judgment); the nature of the differences that are lost or compromised (are all differends worth preserving?); or whether there were alternatives to this change (it is important to recognize that in particular circumstances the actual choice is not simply between preserving the differend or eliminating it).

Another thing that Lyotard's "violence" might be taken to mean is that consensus among some parties inevitably excludes or silences others, those not party to the agreement. I think that this concern is more salient than some of the others, because it asks us to interrogate the circumstances under which consensus is "voluntarily" obtained, to weigh its effects not only on those party to it, but on others whose views are not even taken into consideration. Indeed, it is sometimes only by excluding or silencing some voices and points of view that an agreement can be secured among the voices and points of view remaining. Here again, however, in order to make this judgment we need to consider a number of particulars about the case, the parties to it, their motivations, and so on.

Lyotard gives one other argument about the "violence" that is done through consensus. This argument derives from his view of *performativity*, the "technical language of efficiency and inefficiency" that increasingly comes to dominate public language in contemporary society. As Robin Usher and Richard Edwards define it,

> Performativity does not legitimize knowledge but rather embodies what science has become in the postmodern condition, which in itself has been made possible by the development of technology. In this situation, knowledge becomes a commodity to be exchanged, to be produced, sold, and consumed.
>
> (Usher and Edwards 1994: 165–6)

This logic of performativity tends to "colonize" other ways of speaking and acting about social concerns; in particular, it tends to crowd out prescriptive discourses about justice and respect for difference. As a result, one might argue, the impulse to regard all language games as commensurable serves the performative orientation, in which all differences are simply problems to be solved or overcome in the pursuit of one large market of ideas, products, and ends. While Lyotard does not make this connection directly, I think that another way in which consensus could be said to do "violence" to the differend is by facilitating the approximation of all points of view and value orientations to this one dominant regime. Here, too, I think that the picture is more complex than one of simple domination; but to a significant extent Lyotard would be right that discordant or oppositional views only gain a hearing within this framework when they express themselves within a technical discourse that may be incompatible with the presentation of fundamental criticisms or radical alternatives.

What is the alternative, if any, to this "violence"? J. M. Fritzman suggests that the choice is a "politics of the lesser evil" which

> would attempt to phrase wrongs so that they may be recognized as such. . . . A politics of the lesser evil will not forget that there are differends which cannot be transformed into litigations, and so will seek to make decisions that will minimize the wrongs that necessarily occur.
>
> (Fritzman 1990: 477–8)

Elsewhere, however, Lyotard seems to go beyond this politics of the lesser evil. A. T. Nuyen expresses this positive view as an "ethical injunction to bear witness to differends" (Nuyen 1998b: 175). Nigel Blake, Paul Smeyers, Richard Smith, and Paul Standish suggest, similarly, that we ought to "explore the manifold language games, many of which modernism has marginalized, and find out how and where they are useful, how and where they can help us with what we want to understand" (Blake *et al.* 1998: 142). Lyotard goes even further, however, not only to recognize and to preserve differends but to try to create new ones: "the task is one of multiplying and refining language games . . . an enterprise of experimentation on language games" (Lyotard 1985: 49).

But, then, more recently, Lyotard confronts us with a new dilemma: one does violence by rejecting differends or by forcing them into conformity, but one also does violence by trying to learn new ones:

> Your partner is playing a game you don't know. . . . You ask what it is that he/she is playing, *he/she doesn't answer you.* What is it reasonable to do? . . . I think what is reasonable is to try to learn the other's game. . . . Violence stems from this dilemma: either you reject the unknown game of your partner, you even reject the fact that it is a game, you exclude it . . . and this is a violence done to the event and to the unknown of such a kind that you stop writing and thinking; or else, you do violence to yourself in trying to learn the moves that you don't know and that your silent partner imposes . . . upon the words and sentences. This is called the violence of learning to think or write, which is implied in every education. I believe this violence is inevitable, because I believe the encounter with this bizarre partner is inevitable.
>
> (Lyotard 1997: 145, emphasis in original)

So, perhaps we return to the politics of the lesser evil after all.

In the end, I believe, Lyotard's positive position is very confusing. On the one hand, invoking the concept of "deadly" violence, a strange usage in the context of consensus and of playing a game, certainly seems to suggest that the exercise of violence should be avoided or at least minimized. We do this not only by endeavoring to recognize and preserve differends but also by trying to create new ones: his process for doing so he terms *paralogy*, defined by Fritzman as "imaginative moves which directly contest the procedural rules that claim to regulate and adjudicate conflict" (Fritzman 1990: 380). James Bohman elaborates paralogy as:

> the undermining of established language games through the activation of differences, through constant innovation and experimentation. Its principles are not the universality of reason and the need for consensus but the irreducibly local character of all discourse, argumentation, and legitimation and the need to undermine established agreements . . . its underlying notion of justice appeals not to consensus but to "the recognition of the specificity and the autonomy of the multiplicity of entangled language games, the refusal to reduce them; with a rule that nevertheless would be a general rule: let us play . . . and let us play in peace."
>
> (Bohman 1987: 70; the passage in quotes is from Lyotard)

On the other hand, Lyotard says in the preceding quote that "violence is inevitable." What is he trying to claim here? Can violence and peace co-exist? In order to understand where this argument has gone wrong, we need to approach the problem from an entirely different perspective, I believe.

Language contains both centripetal and centrifugal impulses. At any moment a word, an idiom, a slogan, a metaphor is undergoing a process in tension between the novelty of its initial expression and its capacity for yielding up new interpretations, on the one hand, and the tendency to become static, reified through repetition, and clichéd, on the other hand. If language becomes too static, it becomes meaningless through habituation, as in the slogans of the novel *1984*; if there is too much invention and local differentiation, then it loses its capacity to support communication directed toward the possibility of shared understanding and, sometimes, agreement. Lyotard writes at times as if the only alternatives for language were either metanarratives, which overwhelm difference and creativity, or a multiplicity of incommensurable language games. From this vantage point, the only choice, then, is between the violence of "consensus," which destroys the differend, and violence to one's self in encountering and trying to reconcile one's self to the "bizarre." Yet in other places Lyotard writes as if the choices were between playing different language games, learning other games, and creating new games, "in peace." And so he seems torn between agonism in the sense of a contest, a game, and agonism in the sense of a war: "conflict," the term he uses repeatedly, is not sufficiently fine-grained to help us distinguish the two.

Like some other poststructuralist writers, Lyotard has a tendency to fetishize difference – one might even say he constructs a metanarrative of difference – as if this were the overarching principle of language. Yet sameness and difference, consensus and conflict, understanding and misunderstanding, are all twin principles of language; neither makes sense without the other (Burbules 1997). General pronouncements about incommensurability or the untranslatability of the differend do not help us recognize or understand the nature of differences we encounter between language games and *when* rules or concepts may be applicable between them, and when not. Sometimes translations fail; but this is not the same thing as untranslatability.

A general hostility to consensus or metanarratives does not help us understand when provisional grounds of agreement might yield relatively stable principles or generalizations that are useful in organizing our lives. And if we need to be reminded, rightly, of how these provisional grounds of agreement only include some actors and not others, that should make us question the boundaries of inclusion and exclusion entailed by those agreements, and perhaps choose others. But any other choice would entail its own inclusions and exclusions, only different ones, and that is the level at which an honest choice needs to be made. A perpetual openness to difference, whatever that would look like, might avoid creating any exclusions, but it would also never create any inclusions either; and no social existence could exist under such a principle.

Finally, there is the level at which this issue affects the person. As Wittgenstein himself pointed out, we cannot doubt everything. We cannot destabilize everything, especially not all at the same time. We must keep some points fixed still *in order to question others.* And if we want to question *those* fixed points, it can only be by (at least provisionally) affirming others. This general way of looking at language and understanding, it seems to me, yields a fundamentally different analysis of these problems than that offered by Lyotard. And the starting point to unraveling the antinomies with which Lyotard has left us is one of the core Wittgensteinian ideas, intimately linked with his idea of language games, and yet as far as I can see discussed nowhere by Lyotard, for all the times that he invokes the language game notion.

In defining language games Wittgenstein asked, first, What is a game? And he found out that he could not give a strict set of criteria or a definition that demarcated games; as he put it, one can only say "This *and similar things* are called 'games'" (Wittgenstein 1997: sect. 69). Games share a set of criss-crossing, overlapping features, none held by all instances, and some instances, perhaps, having a set of features that share little or nothing in common with other particular instances. So what comprises all of these instances as instances of the category "game"? *Family resemblances,* Wittgenstein said, just as family members have a set of similar characteristics, but perhaps no single set of common characteristics. What I want to argue in the last part of this essay is how the family resemblance notion erases the dichotomy between metanarratives and a multiplicity of incommensurable language games as the only alternatives. It directly challenges the key point in Lyotard's argument about "islands of language," quoted at the beginning of this essay: "When I say: There is no common measure, it means that we know of nothing in common with these different language games." Family resemblance explains how, even when there is no single "common measure," it does not mean that there is necessarily "nothing in common." By erasing this either/or dichotomy, the family resemblance idea opens up a whole new approach to the issues of understanding and misunderstanding, of consensus and conflict, among language games.

Dorothy Lee writes, "I want to criticize understanding, because I myself do not want to be understood" (1976: 86). Now, I suppose that the only consistent response to such a statement is, "huh?" But venturing to understand what Lee means here (I hope she doesn't mind), I think that she seems to be rejecting the condescending, and sometimes domineering, attitude of others who say, patronizingly, "I understand you completely." No one can be understood completely, and the claim that one does fully understand another seems to lock the complexity and ambiguity of a living person into a set of assumptions, theoretical categories, and stereotypes. Lee's complaint is typical of the contemporary hostility to understanding discussed at the opening of this essay; and in many educational settings and others, multicultural studies are taken as a series of object lessons in how the Other must remain utterly inscrutable. To suggest otherwise is to be aligned with "humanists" who believe that "we are all basically alike" or naïve communication theorists who believe that all linguistic barriers can, with persistence and good will, eventually be broken down. It seems that the only possible choices are that differences must be either utterly transparent or utterly opaque.

We must reject that dichotomy. Both options, in my view, have done serious damage; though if they were the only two choices, I would probably agree that the one less likely to harm would be deferring to the uniqueness and integrity of others. But they are not the only two choices. Understanding and misunderstanding are not opposing alternatives; they are aspects of the same process by which meaning is shared between persons.

To understand is never to understand "completely." Because of the unique qualities of each person's knowledge and experience, what is understood from others (however similar they might be to us) is always understood *differently*. Whether one has understood sufficiently for communication to proceed further, for coordinating practical efforts, for achieving a level of empathy and intersubjective connection, is a matter to be discovered. At the same time, however, there will always be something in what was meant that was not understood, and something in what was understood that brings in elements from the listener's knowledge and experience, not the speaker's. Sometimes in being understood differently, a mistake is made, a mistake that interferes with further communication, coordinating practical efforts, or intersubjective connection; and then one must try to understand again. Other times, however, this difference in understanding is productive; as when others see more in what we say than we realize we meant. Sometimes it might even seem that a mistake has been made, but on further discussion it turns out that what was understood is a truer representation of what the speaker meant than what they actually thought they said. In all of this, understanding and misunderstanding are ever-present conditions; because one is always understanding differently, the judgment about whether it constitutes understanding or misunderstanding comes *after*; it is not immediately apparent and, to an extent, both features are always commingled (perhaps Lyotard's reading/misreading of Wittgenstein can be seen as a nice case study of this intermingling).[1] In most cases what we need to decide is whether we have understood *enough*. When one judges that it is not sufficient one says, "You have misunderstood." But this is a judgment *following* the effort.

Following from this analysis, we can see how most claims of incommensurability are exaggerated and even self-fulfilling. It is almost inconceivable to imagine a case in which anything was understood perfectly, or a case in which something was understood *not at all* (although we frequently speak this way). Just as misunderstanding is a condition of understanding, to the extent that we do understand, so also is understanding a condition of misunderstanding. If no engagement of understandings occurs at all, then it is impossible even to say "you have misunderstood me": for one thing, the speaker must understand the listener sufficiently to recognize that what was understood was different from what was meant; but this also means that what the listener says is related enough to what was said for the contrasts to be apparent. So incommensurability, in the sense of two spheres of meaning that do not engage one another at all, could occur only when the two parties were speaking entirely different languages; and even then I would argue that some level of understanding (through gestures, expressions, and so on) can often still be achieved, if inadvertently.

Lyotard's claims about the incommensurability of language games, then, must be seen as an overstatement. They are not "islands of language" and could not be so (for one thing, as Wittgenstein would point out, we recognize them all as language games). Sometimes, as I have argued, points of similarity or connection can be established between them, and sometimes, perhaps more often, they cannot. But this is not a conclusion to assert a priori or in general. There are differends – "the unstable state and instant of language wherein something which must be put into phrases cannot yet be" (Lyotard 1988a: 13) – but the existence of them does not render different language games utterly incommensurable. When Lyotard says that languages are translatable, but language games cannot be, he neglects the family resemblance characteristic that, for Wittgenstein, is partly constitutive of what language games are; where there are family resemblances, translation is always a possibility, even if only an imperfect and incomplete translation (as all translations necessarily are, to some extent).

Incommensurability is actually a problem of a very different sort. While it literally means matters that cannot be compared or judged by a common standard, in ordinary usage it is taken to mean many different things: (a) heterogeneity; (b) no overlap (islands); (c) mutual incomprehensibility; (d) incompatibibility; (e) untranslatability; (f) non-combinability; or (g) non-reducibility, one to the other. Elements of each of these meanings can be found in the various ways in which Lyotard speaks of language games. But to ascertain whether two language games actually can be compared or judged by a common standard (as with translation generally), one can only try to do so and see whether it works out. Sometimes it will work in certain respects, or for certain purposes, and not for others. Sometimes it will work only at the expense of a severe effort or sacrifice being made by one or more of the parties to the relation, and sometimes this price will be judged too steep. And with this last point, I think, we begin to understand what is really at work in this problem area.

One cannot infer incommensurability from the mere fact of disagreement, even serious disagreement. It cannot be inferred from the mere fact of misunderstanding, even egregious and persistent misunderstanding. It cannot be inferred from an inability, in practice, of achieving a workable translation. Incommensurability is an assertion at the level of meaning, the metaphysics of language, if you will; it is sweeping, conclusive, and often self-perpetuating, because once one assumes incommensurability, serious efforts at communication might as well cease (why persist in the face of inevitable futility?). But at the level of communication, what we are experiencing are disagreement, misunderstanding, and the inability of achieving a workable translation (not incommensurability). These are difficult enough problems, and they represent real failures at making a meaningful connection. But overlaying them with the conclusion "and therefore these views are incommensurable" is to prejudge the possibilities of future efforts, or efforts made by others, or efforts made under other circumstances – for sometimes the failure is attributable to these sorts of factors, not to the intrinsic character of the views being discussed.

Wittgenstein, once again, made clear that language games are intimately related to a context, or form of life, that sustains them and gives them relevance. Language games are not phenomena that can be understood or appreciated apart from that: for example, no one can understand chess, no matter how long one tries to explain the rules to them, if they do not understand the idea of a game, specifically a board game – some cultures may find the entire idea of staring at and moving pieces of wood on a board very mysterious, even bizarre. What is causing the confusion here is *not* the language game, or the incommensurability of its rules; it is the foreignness of a form of life. And here, finally, I think that we arrive at the deeper problem that we need to think through.

Just as Lyotard says, rightly, that translation is a language game, so also I would say that consensus is a kind of language game: or, more precisely, an element within many different possible language games (and, significantly, there are other language games in which reaching consensus is *not* the point). Consensus can mean answering a question, solving a problem, arriving at a compromise, resolving a disagreement, negotiating a deal, and so on. Each of these is a different sort of language game, relating to a different sort of conflict or problem, and while there are similarities between, for example, scientists debating the significance of an experimental result in a laboratory, and a purchaser and seller trying to settle on the acceptable price for an automobile, it is a dangerous oversimplification to say that just the same sorts of processes are at work in all of these instances. There may be a family resemblance that allows us to cluster them all as instances of "consensus," but there are significant differences as well. Specifically, these activities inhabit different forms of life, and it is often at that level that significant differences reside: for instance, with what might be considered "cheating" or inappropriate behavior within each game. Saying that consensus does violence to language games obscures the very different things that consensus can mean; at the same time, saying that the failure of consensus is a sign of incommensurability between language games attributes the breakdown to the wrong factors. Incommensurabilities, or deep conflicts, are more often attributable to the differences among the forms of life that sustain language games and give them relevance than to the essential features (rules, phrases, and so on) of the language games themselves.

Here, we are less concerned with the "metaphysics of language," and more concerned with the social orders in which, and between which, communication happens. I think that the sorts of deep conflicts that trouble Lyotard are rarely the result of clashes between language games themselves. They are over other sorts of disputes: What *is* the language game we are playing? *Whose* game are we playing? Who decides which language game we are playing? What constitutes cheating or inappropriate behavior in this language game? If we are playing multiple language games (I would argue that each of us is rarely playing only one), which one is most salient at this moment? Does X count as a language game? Who gets to participate in this language game (or these language games)? Who decides when the language game is "finished" and who has "won" or "lost," or even if this is a language game *about* winning and losing? Here, with these sorts of questions, is where the conflicts typically reside. And these are not conflicts *between* language games *per se*, not in the sense that Lyotard means it; they are conflicts *over* those games (whose game, what sort of game, and so on). These disputes take on the significance they do because they arise within and between the forms of life that sustain and give relevance to these different games. (Imagine a scientist who approached a dispute over evidence in the laboratory the way he would approach wrangling over the price of a car. Both can be considered to be playing the game of reaching consensus, but the scientist's actions might very well be judged disruptive and inappropriate, if not incompatible with the spirit of "ascertaining scientific truth"; he or she would be accused of playing the *wrong* game for these circumstances).

Wittgenstein: "It is what human beings *say* that is true and false; and they agree in the *language* they use. That is not agreement in opinions but in form of life" (1997: sect. 241, emphasis in the original).

If my argument has succeeded, I have translated the problem of incommensurability (as Lyotard characterizes it) from a problem of conflict between languages, or between phrases, or between rules, or between language games, to a problem of conflict between forms of life. Lyotard is entirely correct that differends exist; that they often exist against the background of power differences that delegitimate and suppress the views of non-dominant groups (who are unable to make their case in the language game of litigation); and that as a result a certain openness to heterogeneity in language games is part of a just social order. But he is wrong that the existence of differends proves something about the general incommensurability of language games; that misunderstanding will be inevitable, and total, when people try to translate between different language games; and that as a result any pursuit of consensus "does violence" to the language games of others. Conflicts between languages, phrases, rules, or language games are always the potential conditions of an experiment in translatability; a translation that, to be sure, may fail. But the failures of understanding, translation, and agreement are human failures, not generally problems of language (or of language games). It is *our* values, *our* forms of life, and *our* refusal or inability to respect or consider the forms of life of others that give rise to the breakdowns in understanding that Lyotard decries. And it is in encounters with strange, disturbing, or challenging language games that we stand to learn by reflecting upon ourselves. We can, as Lyotard says, try to learn to play the other's game; but unlike him, I would not say that this means "doing violence" to what we think. It may mean coming to recognize and rethink the form of life that we take for granted, which makes this other language game seem so "bizarre" to us.

In closing, I hope that this essay provides an answer to those, influenced perhaps by Lyotard, who are prepared to jettison the values of understanding or consensus, to see in them only the vampire-like threat of sapping Others of their otherness, normalizing them to dominant language games. Some authors, such as Hans-Georg Gadamer or Jürgen Habermas, are much more optimistic about the possibilities of understanding or agreement. But both the pessimists and the optimists here miss the point, I would suggest. The issue is not with the nature of language, but with the practice of communication. The available language both facilitates and constrains the possibilities of communication (it is not a remarkable observation to say this); but whether communication can generate shared understandings or agreements is not determined by the available language so much as by the ways in which persons enact the communicative relation. This is a social problem, and a moral problem, more than a linguistic or epistemological one.

Certain forms of life invest language games with an import that can be deadly serious: for example, whether one utters a confession when interrogated. Such contexts (forms of life) make issues of difference in language or in language games not mere matters of understanding or making one's self understood, but interactions that have asymmetrical consequences for the different participants. And when a hegemonic mode of speaking and thinking, like performativity, threatens to "colonize" other types of speaking and thinking about social concerns, then the push to treat all language games as commensurable (comparable by a single set of standards) can be seen as an aspect of this colonization. Similar points could be made about the language of science, or litigation, or bureaucracy, all ascendant in educational discourse today. But the fetishization of difference as a corrective has its own excesses as well; and here too this orientation only makes sense within a particular form of life – one that could be as constraining in its implications for learning and social development as any other. Addressing these various forms of life and the language games that they do and do not make possible poses a new set of questions, not about the desirability of understanding and agreement *in general* (as if one could make a judgment of such things in general), but about the conditions that make understanding and agreement possible, and for whom, and for what purposes.[2]

Notes

1 Or my reading/misreading of Lyotard.
2 I appreciate the suggestions and support of Paul Standish, Pradeep Dhillon, and Michael Peters.

3 Paralogy, validity claims, and the politics of knowledge

Habermas, Lyotard and higher education

Nigel Blake

How does the pursuit of knowledge fit in with the other activities and ways of life of a society? Is it important or fundamental to them? In particular, has it any importance which is not subsidiary to other activities, most specifically those of economic survival and growth, or of political and social control? Such questions are obviously fundamental to any attempt to judge the rights and duties, the privileges and obligations of education, and in particular higher education. They are fundamental to any inquiry into the relation between research and teaching in universities and their appropriate conduct and organization.

The importance of *The Postmodern Condition* (Lyotard 1984a) as philosophy of higher education is to conceive this constellation of problems as turning on the nature and legitimacy of the social bond. For there was a time when such questions were "merely academic" in the pejorative sense of practical irrelevance: fundamentally, any concerned person could piece together the answer because all of them knew and understood, and what's more, all (more or less) *subscribed* to, one or other Grand Narrative which would tell a plausible story of how universities fit in to the rest of our social life. These matters hardly needed rehearsing. But if Grand Narratives are just no longer credible, as Lyotard claims, then the question ceases to be merely academic. Nonetheless, if we abandon the Grand Narratives, we do not abjure recourse to narrative in any form at all. We cannot, for it is in our acceding to narrative of some sort that we accept in practice (if not in theory) the legitimacy of social institutions: a legitimacy which cannot finally be demonstrated by recourse to rules, since rules themselves need legitimation. And in recourse to *small* narratives lies our remaining chance to legitimate higher education. For although, "Once the unifying thread of Grand Narrative is snapped, the narrative is dispersed in clouds of narrative language elements" (Lyotard 1984a: xxiv), nonetheless the potential for legitimate social bonds and the possibility of legitimation of institutions is not lost but relocated: "Conveyed within each cloud are pragmatic valencies [potentials for creating social bonds] specific to its kind. . . . There are many different language games – a heterogeneity of elements. They only give rise to institutions in patches" (ibid.: xxiv). For, "The social bond is linguistic, but is not woven with a single thread" (ibid.: 40).

Here is a picture which seems still to contain a space for the university. If universities can find a role at least in some small narrative, then they can legitimate at least some kind of presence in society, no less valid than anything else legitimated by small narrative. Meanwhile the totalizing power of Grand Narrative is taken over by the performativity of a socio-economic system which recognizes no other goals than instrumental effectiveness and efficiency. But nonetheless, performativity itself lacks any normative authority. So by that same token, there can be no normative objection to the university, however annoyingly resistant it might be to performativity and however ferocious the assaults of managerial efficiency upon it. And how might the university attempt to resist performativity? As a school for paralogy: for the development, subversion and reinvention of language games, including small narratives. In paralogy, social bonds are rewoven with new threads and in new patterns, and not those most performatively assimilable.

In effect, Lyotard implies that in their current historical predicament, only a defense in terms of social bonds and their legitimation in small narratives can support the universities. But in positing the issue of the social bond and its linguistic constitution as central, Lyotard sidesteps theories of higher education which start from abstract epistemological considerations or from value-theoretic premises. And in explaining the social bond as a linguistic construct, he seems to release these questions from dependency on tendentious philosophical argument in epistemology and ethics and to reconceive them as much as socio-linguistic meta-questions, perhaps more readily capable of resolution. As James Williams (1998b) points out, this is a resolutely materialist project. Not least, it posits the social bond as historically contingent, thus enabling us to consider questions referring specifically to higher education in the context of modernity or postmodernity. Indeed, we begin to see that our opening questions are themselves specifically modern (and postmodern) questions.

However, resolution still does not come that easily. At least one major contemporary of Lyotard offers an alternative account of the social bond, very relevant to our questions here, and also in terms of linguistic construction: an account, moreover, which Lyotard was determined to repudiate. Jürgen Habermas, in his work from the later 1970s onwards, posits linguistic interaction as the form of action which binds social relations between individuals. And if he does not use the phrase "social bond," he does nonetheless refer to the "binding/bonding effect" of linguistic interaction. As I once pointed out, according to Habermas,

> speakers and hearers cannot communicate unless they both implicitly impute certain obligations to whoever speaks. There is a "speech act immanent obligation" incumbent on any speaker, and anticipated by

any hearer, that the speaker will be able to justify whatever validity claims he raises.

(Blake 1995: 358)

And Habermas himself says, "in communicative action one actor seeks rationally to motivate another by relying on the ... binding/bonding effect (*Bildungseffekt*) of the offer [to redeem his implicit validity claims] contained in his speech act" (Habermas 1989: 58).

A validity claim is any presupposition, if only implicit, that some utterance states a true proposition, or is morally justified or affectively appropriate. Habermas believes that all utterances presuppose all three kinds of validity claim, cognitive, normative and affective, even if most of these are uncontroversial and unproblematic.[1] Mutual understanding is impossible if a hearer doubts the sincerity of the speaker's own implied claim that he could redeem or validate these presuppositions if called upon to do so. The necessity of general mutual understanding imposes an obligation to make good such claims if necessary. What constitutes the interpersonal bond is the speaker and hearer's mutual faith in each other, in this respect. The bond is a bond of obligation, and a failure to try to meet the obligation weakens it.

More specifically, Habermas describes theoretical discourse, which is central to the pursuit of knowledge and the discourse of universities, in terms of the importance, in that discourse in particular, of undistorted or communicative interaction. (Moreover – a separate point – theoretical discourse requires speech conditions which aspire to some kind of ideal openness, however problematic (Blake 1995: 357–60)). But since he also argues to the *logical priority* of communicative speech over other forms of speech interaction, he implies a view of higher education as dealing with quite fundamental kinds of discourse for any society.[2] For it is moreover the logical priority of communicative interaction over the varieties of what he calls strategic interaction that secures, for Habermas, the legitimacy of the interpersonal bond. Since strategic interaction is, as I presently explain, a distortion of the communicative and thus parasitic on it, communicative interaction is the *sine qua non* of social solidarity. In this inheres its own legitimacy. And without the social bonds which are formed in communicative interaction, the question of their legitimacy in turn cannot even arise. For Habermas, legitimate social bonds are constructed in communicative interaction if anywhere, or not at all. All other legitimate social bonds must be at least compatible with those formed in communicative interaction.

Further, and by contrast, Habermas specifies *strategic* interaction as a form of manipulation, characteristic of debased but endemic modes of interaction in the political and economic spheres, where the dominant media are power and money (White 1988: 104–15). Thus he implicitly indicates some detailed answers to the kinds of question about higher education and other spheres of society that interest us here. In particular, his substantive answers are not dissimilar, where they may be compared, to those of Lyotard. Both see the regimes of manipulation characteristic of business, mass media and modern politics as inimical to the pursuit of knowledge under ideal or even simply undistorted conditions, and to its role in our social and moral life: a role which many would take to be the special concern of universities.[3]

Importantly, in Habermas the interpersonal bond is formed in and with the formation of consensus between participants in conversation. In contrast, strategic interaction forms, by definition, a delusory and specious sense of consensus for the hearer. That specious "consensus" is understood as bogus by the speaker, since it is created as bogus by him in the first place, for his covert and manipulative purposes. The hearer trusts the speaker, but is badly mistaken in doing so; the bond of trust is delusory (as so often in the speech of management, politics, mass media and so on). So Habermas associates an intentional corruption of consensus with a breaking of interpersonal bonds. But conversely, for Habermas, the securing of a more general social bond has seemingly to follow from a maximization of consensus; and so the optimization and maximization of communicative interaction within society is central to that project. So we may infer from Habermas that maximizing and deepening consensus is an important role for higher education.

Yet to Lyotard, for reasons never made explicit in *The Postmodern Condition*, the maximization of consensus is apparently a horror to avoid. And so he seeks an alternative account of the legitimation of the social bond. Lyotard posits small narratives and restrictedly local consensus as alternative candidates for this job. (I refer later to the role consensus plays in his own account.) So if Grand Narrative is dead, then, as we have seen, there is no consensual source of legitimation for the whole of society at large. This is the crux of the dispute between Lyotard and Habermas. Accordingly, one way of reading *The Postmodern Condition* is as an indirect repudiation of Habermas's analyses and program. Lyotard's Introduction goes directly to Habermas's views in the second paragraph, and a page or so later a brief dismissal of them completes the background for positing the key question of the book; how can the social bond be legitimated, if not by appeal to general consensus (or to metanarrative)? This is the question to which Lyotard returns in the final section of the book, elaborating there a little on his reading of Habermas, which in this particular text otherwise remains exceedingly vague.

However, Lyotard's sketchy comments on Habermas are not just inadequate but misleading, and embarrassingly so. It is a scholarly question of some interest in its own right as to why a thinker who has much the same political and moral motives should nonetheless treat a distinguished colleague so unsympathetically. But the question has more urgent practical importance too, for it is also hard to deny that Lyotard illuminates quite vividly "the condition of knowledge in the most highly developed societies" (Lyotard 1984a: xxiii), in particular the threats to the growth of knowledge from the "terroristic" demands of performativity. Lyotard's emphases on heterogeneity, contestation, undecidability, and uncertainty (but not, I shall argue, incommensurability), at levels from macro to micro, are surely healthy and important. And it is hard to deny that Lyotard turns light onto significant aspects of the pursuit of knowledge which are not emphasized in Habermas. All of this must be of urgent concern to any critical theorist of education, and higher education in particular.

Yet any reader sympathetic to Habermas can only find the contrast between these thinkers drawn much too sharply by Lyotard (and his sympathetic commentators), and even carelessly drawn. If both writers contribute something important to our understanding of epistemics, then it is important to locate and interrelate their contributions more carefully than does Lyotard. I believe that if the former illuminates better the politics of knowledge, the latter has important things to add about economies of meaning.

But I will also argue that Lyotard's own contribution is more fragile than he allows, and that Lyotardians need Habermas as an ally rather than a rival. Lyotard recognizes the power of performativity to block and divert science, *sciences*, *Wissenschaft*, the growth of knowledge. His picture of the operation and counter-resistant potential of paralogy is, as we know, modeled on the cultural success of aesthetic modernism. But he overlooks the ways in which the institutionalization of modernism in the art world has arguably robbed it of the critical potency to which it could originally lay claim. As a picture informing intellectual discourse, the theory of paralogy offers itself as a guide to academic endeavor in a parallel way to the guidance modernist theory offers to art practice. But the fear must be that any academic institutionalization would rob paralogies of their critical potency, just as surely as the art world has castrated aesthetic modernism. If this fate is to be resisted, then we require the more sophisticated grasp of the politics of knowledge that Habermas has to offer.

Let us get an outline of the points at issue between the two thinkers, first by juxtaposing Lyotard's brief comments on Habermas in his Introduction with some extracts from an essay of Habermas that should have been available to Lyotard at the time of his writing. Habermas's essay "What is universal pragmatics?" was published in 1976 in Karl-Otto Apel's collection *Sprachpragmatik und Philosophie* (Apel 1976). I do not know if Lyotard knew of this, but he does refer to the essay "Legitimationsprobleme" (Lyotard 1984a: n.227) which was also published in 1976 in Habermas's *Zur Rekonstruktion des Historischen Materialismus*. The English translation anthology *Communication and the Evolution of Society* (Habermas 1979) collects the latter book and the former essay between the same covers. It will be apparent that, whether or not Lyotard read the essay, his claims against Habermas had already received at least an implicit preliminary answer before the original French publication of Lyotard's text in 1979. The 1970s were, for Habermas, a period of transition between the philosophical anthropology of *Knowledge and Human Interests* (Habermas 1971), and the linguistic turn resolved in *The Theory of Communicative Action* of 1981 (German publication). But even by 1976, his work need no longer have been read as a simple recasting of the earlier views, particularly focused on the task of relocating Marx and Freud within the Enlightenment project of emancipation.

To begin with Lyotard's misgivings about consensus and his famous association of consensus, as an ideal, with an increasingly discredited Enlightenment narrative, consider these words from his second paragraph:

> to the extent that science does not restrict itself to stating useful regularities and seeks the truth, it is obliged to legitimate the rules of its own game. It then produces a discourse of legitimation with respect to its own status, a discourse called philosophy. . . . For example, the rule of consensus between the sender and addressee of a statement with truth-value is deemed acceptable if it is cast in terms of a possible unanimity between rational minds: this is the Enlightenment narrative, in which the hero of knowledge works toward a good ethico-political end – universal peace. . . . Thus justice is consigned to the grand narrative in the same way as truth.
>
> (Lyotard 1984a: xxiii–xxiv)

At a simple level of paraphrase, what does this grammatically tortuous passage mean?

I take it to be saying that if unanimity between rational minds (in other words, consensus) is a real possibility, then science can be legitimated in terms of a "rule of consensus." (And Lyotard does not doubt this possibility.) Science is a legitimate pursuit, one complicit with a legitimate social bond, because it produces unanimity between rational people (much as Habermas argues). Moreover, unanimity between rational minds is a good ethico-political end. It fosters justice and therefore peace within the social order. The narrative of Enlightenment is the very story of how the pursuit of knowledge can promote justice and peace. (And any such story obviously offers strong justification for the autonomy of higher education.)

What worries me about this passage, implicitly but clearly referring to Habermas, is the phrase "the rule of consensus." Consensus seems here to be presented as an ethical or political good or value, which one might or might not adopt as a precept for practice: a regulative ideal. If one does so, then Lyotard seems to suggest that the most obvious reason for doing so is an ethical commitment to the ideals of the Enlightenment, such as Habermas's.

But to say this is to misconstrue badly the analytic role that the idea of consensus plays in Habermas's own account of the social bond. For him, as we have seen above, consensus is not a regulative ideal governing the proper maintenance of that bond, but constitutive of the very possibility of any interpersonal bond in any language community, not just a society governed by Enlightenment ideals.[4] It is this constitutive social role of consensus rather than any social commitment to the Enlightenment Project which legitimates the social bond for Habermas. So impugning the Enlightenment narrative, as Lyotard here signals he will do, is irrelevant to any evaluation of Habermas's account of legitimation. There is a logical hiatus between the legitimation of science in terms of its potential for producing consensus, and the adoption of consensus as an ideal for the promotion of justice, harmony, and peace. Legitimation is one thing; ideals are another.

Nonetheless, the illuminations provided by Lyotard's reflections on the Enlightenment narrative are sufficiently vivid to motivate my desire to reconcile the two thinkers where possible. So what reasons does Lyotard think he has for repudiating some supposed "rule of consensus" as a regulative ideal rather than constitutive necessity? "Is legitimacy to be found in consensus obtained through discussion, as Jürgen Habermas thinks? Such consensus does violence to the heterogeneity of language games. And invention is always born of dissension" (ibid.: xxv).

The first claim here, that the aim of consensus "does violence to the heterogeneity of language games" badly lacks plausibility as a response to Habermas. The concept of a progressive decentering of consciousness, over the historical *longue durée*, into three different forms (the technical, hermeneutic, and critical) in the process of cultural modernization (from prehistoric times) is already fundamental to *Knowledge and Human Interests* (Habermas 1971). By the time of the essay here in question, this thesis was already being recast in terms of the mutual autonomy of three spheres of implicit validity claims, each with their own characteristic linguistic pragmatics (the cognitive, the normative, and the affective, echoing distantly but loudly the trilogy of the Kantian Critiques). If this is not the supposedly profuse heterogeneity of Lyotard's "clouds of narrative language elements," neither is it a picture of linguistic homogeneity. Lyotard could never reasonably object that Habermas offers a monolithic account of rationality. Habermas explicitly repudiates such an account. And if Lyotard's objection is not that Habermas deals in homogeneity, but lacks sufficient detail and discrimination in his account of the heterogeneity, then this claim needs a lot more argument than it gets.

It needs more than just more detail: it needs more precision. Lyotard's later invocation of Wittgensteinian language games is at home in either of two kinds of analysis: pragmatics or semantics. Habermas has nothing to say about semantics: semantics is simply not pertinent to his project. But by that same token, a Habermasian picture is perfectly compatible with talk of radical heterogenity in the semantic field (heterogeneity of modes of meaning), because Habermas has nothing at stake here. As to pragmatics,

Habermas himself fully recognizes diversity, and discusses a variety of pragmatic forms in *The Theory of Comunicative Action* (Habermas 1984a). But he
seeks to classify that diversity in other terms: in terms of the logic of the
differing kinds of validity claims presupposed by speech acts. Like J. L.
Austin (1962, Lecture XII), the other primary source (with Wittgenstein)
for modern philosophical discussion of linguistic pragmatics and on whose
work he draws, Habermas both recognizes diversity in speech acts and
believes they can properly and informatively be classified; that similarities
and connections also obtain, no less than differences and forms of logical
independence.[5] Moreover, none of this heterogeneity implies any incommensurability or incompatibility between different classes of speech act,
pace the claim to the contrary which Lyotard comes to emphasize. In fact,
one of the most powerful and interesting of Habermas's claims, which we
have noted, is precisely that these spheres of validity claim are not merely
compatible but co-present in any possible utterance. And we will ask again
presently what the idea of incommensurability adds to that of simple
difference.

We must also note here the frankly bizarre attribution to Habermas
which Lyotard makes near the end of his essay, "that humanity as a
collective (universal) subject seeks its common emancipation through the
regularization of the 'moves' permitted in all language games" (Lyotard
1984a: 66), an attribution which clearly puts Habermas in a paradoxically
totalitarian light for a radical liberal, proposing an emancipation which
looks like no emancipation at all. This is a travesty of Habermas. A concern
to classify speech acts is not a concern to regularize them (and besides,
concern with pragmatics is not to the front of *Knowledge and Human
Interests*, the obvious target at that time of writing). Habermas's concern
with pragmatics has never been some meaningless (and impossible) rationalization of language games, but the removal of distortions in the way
such "games" are "played." It is the fight against distortion which constitutes emancipation, not rationalization in any sense of standardization or
normalization ("regularization" is Lyotard's word).

In Habermas's later work, the aim is quite certainly not to discipline
what people say (though there are clearly moral objections to manipulation), but on the contrary to liberate them from constraints on their
fullest expression. Indeed, to be against distortion is to be in favor of the
most vivid appreciation and display of differences, where these are real.
And this actually entails openness to innovation in language games, surely,
an important point to which I will return. For there is an important
difference between making an overtly anomalous or innovative move in a
game or a language game, and covertly cheating within the settled rules of
a game. The schoolboy who picked up the ball and ran with it, and
prompted the development of the game of rugby, was hardly cheating or
deceiving anyone. If Lyotard were to approve the agonistics of speech in
terms of psychosocial manipulation of the hearer or political distortions of

conditions of speech, we should surely damn him. Even in agonistics, there is fighting fair and fighting dirty. The distinction makes a difference. Paralogy is not deceit.

Of course, to classify is not to regularize but it may be used to help explain something, and that is part of the role that classification plays for Habermas: to see fundamental aspects of the human condition beneath the surface profusion of human language. It is, I suspect, this to which Lyotard really objects. If so, then this should be distinguished carefully from an allegation of insensitivity to difference or repudiation of innovation by Habermas. Nothing of consequence is demonstrated by Lyotard until it can be shown that there are real instances of linguistic innovation which simply cannot be related to the basic semantic dimensions of the cognitive, normative, and affective (or in an earlier idiom, the technical, hermeneutic, or critical interests in knowledge). And since this is precisely the categorization which Lyotard uses himself (as a good post-Kantian) at many points in *The Postmodern Condition*, we are entitled to considerable skepticism as to his chances.[6] (I suspect his aesthetic modernism may be misleading him here. I will return to this.)

The second objection, that invention is always born of dissension, simply lacks bite as an argument against legitimation in terms of consensus, if we characterize Habermas's position by reference to "What is universal pragmatics?" This essay begins,

> The task of universal pragmatics is to identify and reconstruct universal conditions of possible understanding. . . . I take the type of action aimed at reaching understanding to be fundamental [to all forms of communication]. Thus I start from the assumption (without undertaking to demonstrate it here) that other forms of social action – for example, conflict, competition, strategic action in general [aimed primarily at manipulating the hearer] – are derivatives of action oriented to reaching understanding.
>
> (Habermas 1979: 1)

If Habermas offered no argument at this point, such an argument became clearer in later work. The idea of the primacy of the communicative becomes a fundamental one for Habermas, and its pertinence to Lyotard's second objection is surely already patent here. Dissension, disagreement, contestation, conflict: none of these are real unless the participants themselves do in fact understand that they obtain, even if they have different interpretations (which may be made explicit) of just what is at stake. Thus they presuppose that at least some degree of understanding has been reached between participants even if full agreement may not have been. Witting participants to any epistemic conflict must at least see that there is some difference between their views. So if understanding inherently requires some form of consensus (as Habermas immediately goes on to argue in this article), then even these Lyotardian values of dissent, competition, and the rest, themselves presuppose consensus at some prior level. This is a simple point, not unlike Neurath's famous objection to universal skepticism: his parable of the futility of trying to repair a boat at sea by replacing not just one timber, but every timber all at once. Just as one cannot doubt everything at once, because doubt presupposes a background of the taken-as-true, so too there can be no meaningful dissensus about everything at the same time.

So if invention is indeed born of dissension – even "always," which is surely straining the point – neither dissent nor invention are incompatible with broad swathes of fundamental and general consensus. Nor can they, therefore, constitute much objection to legitimation in terms of consensus. Even if consensus legitimates the social bond, it does not follow that consensus is the uniquely desirable state of every dialogue at all times. And it is worth remembering that Lyotard does not really deny the necessity of some degree of consensus either – too often is he presented as the scourge of consensus in any form. On the contrary, he characterizes both language games and general culture in terms of consensus. Of language games, he writes that "their rules do not carry within them their own legitimation, but are the object of a contract, explicit or not, between players" (Lyotard 1984a: 10): and what is a contract if not some form of consensus? And he defines culture in terms of consensus: "The consensus that permits . . . knowledge to be circumscribed and makes it possible to distinguish one who knows from one who doesn't (the foreigner, the child) is what constitutes the culture of a people" (ibid.: 19). Nonetheless, Lyotard treats the prospect of a *general* consensus implicitly as some kind of nightmare, and it still seems remarkable in the light of these two weak objections (heterogeneity, invention) that he refuses to consensus any more general role in social legitimation, despite recognizing its constitutive role in language and culture. As we know, he seems to fear that a pursuit of consensus would constitute a complete closure on creativity, closure on the growth of knowledge itself and the surrender of social progress to the internal demands of "the system." Is not that the dystopian goal towards which we seem driven by a triumph of performativity?

Lyotard's desire to emphasize the heterogeneity of language games relates to this fear of total consensus. It is part of his strategy for grounding the ever-present possibility of dissensus (and thus to argue to the possibility and validity of the dissenting and resistant academy, as we saw at the beginning of this essay). But in pursuit of this strategy, he wants to argue not just that language games are heterogeneous but that they are incommensurable: not just actually different, but moreover mutually irreducible or non-assimilable in principle.

It is important to appreciate how pointlessly excessive this move might seem, of strengthening the claim from a heterogeneity of language games to their actual incommensurability. For instance, one does not ask whether the rules of chess, rugby and pool are commensurable. It would be a category mistake to do so – neither the answer "Yes" nor "No" would tell us anything. Certainly there is no *Ur*-game of which rugby and chess are different episodes, strategies or styles of play, and some might suppose that this itself is all that Lyotard means by incommensurability, and that he is therefore right about it. But by the same token, there is no potential conflict between them in terms of rules, and so no resistance to resolving such a conflict. Questions about the possibility or impossibility of overarching systems of rules just do not arise in such cases. Here, different rules are simply constitutive of different games and the games are logically independent, neither commensurable nor incommensurable (any more than different people are "incommensurable" with each other).

If games are an appropriate model for language games, then incommensurability is out of place as a question about them too. Certainly, we may elsewhere need to compare and contrast other kinds and bodies of rules where commensurability is indeed a serious question, for instance the relations between the statutes of law and the regulations of institutions such as universities or corporations, which can indeed be found in harmony or in conflict with the law. (This kind of real in/commensurability is obviously pertinent to the problems of justice which exercise Lyotard in *Le Différend* (1983c).) Questions of commensurability do arise where we deal with regulative rather than constitutive rules.[7] Regulative rules govern activities which it is possible (but wrong) to pursue without regard for those rules. But questions about language games are not regulative, but rather questions about constitutive rules, like the rules of chess, some of which do not govern *correct* play so much as make the game (or language game) what it is in the first place. Talk of incommensurability is misleading in connection with constitutive rules.

So why did this apparently pointless move of claiming incommensurability, and thus confusing constitutive and regulative rules, seem worthwhile for Lyotard? The answer with regard to *The Postmodern Condition*, it seems clear, is his desire to repudiate functionalist sociology (compounded with inadequacies in his analysis of pragmatics: inadequacies Habermas avoids). For it is functionalism which raises the nightmare of complete consensus and shows what is frightening about it.

Lyotard very reasonably proposes (Lyotard 1984a: 11) that we cannot discuss the condition of knowledge in society without some prior conception of what society is. Writing in the late 1970s, two kinds of sociology were available to him: a Marxist account, and a variety of functionalisms. Both, he notes, had been compromised. In particular, Marxism had been suborned in the service of Soviet state socialism, a large, heavy nail in the coffin of Grand Narrative. But functionalism seemed yet worse compromised. By functionalism, he means that tradition from Comte to Luhmann, by way of Talcott Parsons, which conceives of society as "a unified totality, a 'unicity'" (ibid.: 12). The guiding metaphor here changes from that of an organism to that of a self-regulating mechanism in Parsons; and by Luhmann, the model is fully cybernetic. The system has no goal but is rigidly self-maintaining. And the normative implications of this are wholly "cynical" (Lyotard's word: ibid.: 11)). Social norms themselves are now conceived as having no reality other than as functors of the system, and no independent validity. We have the morals we have because they keep the system functioning in stable fashion.

Obviously no such view is going to have much to offer to the autonomy of higher education. So if the social bond is indeed to be conceived as normative, and critical answers offered to questions about knowledge in society, functionalism must be repudiated.

> "Traditional" theory [functionalism] is always in danger of being incorporated into the programming of the social whole as a simple tool for the optimization of performance; this is because its desire for a unitary and totalizing truth lends itself to the unitary and totalizing practice of the system's managers. "Critical" theory, based on a principle of dualism and wary of syntheses and reconciliations, should be in a position to avoid this fate.
>
> (Lyotard 1984a: 12)

Thus far, it is surely easy to feel strong sympathy with Lyotard. And a mistrust of any "unicity" will obviously constitute a strong motive for mistrust of consensus. The strategy of emphasizing the heterogeneity of language games, to the excessive degree of theorizing their incommensurability, seems to aim at locating another level of rules within society, a semantic level prior to and resistant to mere social pressure (though not without its own linguistic plasticity), where consensus can be local and strong but never universal. The observation of rules at this level will constitute a nexus of social bonds which owe nothing to any broader consensus presumed and attributed to the putative functional whole. And the presumed incommensurability of rules at this level, their non-subsumability under any set of more general rules, is offered, it seems, as a guarantee against any rationalization of this level by normalizing mechanisms, fostering an oppressive consensus.

Does this strategy for resistance to unicity actually do the job it is supposed to do? Where Lyotard emphasizes a supposed incommensurability between "language games," we need first to be wary of two ambiguities in usage. First, he comes to speak of whole areas of activity such as science or law as "language games," where many readers of Wittgenstein would call them "forms of life."[8] But for Wittgenstein, the notion of a language game is originally invoked to describe either the semantics of particular words or phrases, or the pragmatics of particular speech acts.[9] Whole discourses such as science or law are clearly categorically different from words or speech acts, and are likely to require different kinds of analysis, a difference obscured by referring to these as well as "language games." Second, Lyotard defines "language game" as referring to "rules specifying [the] properties and uses to which [various categories of utterance] can be put." (Lyotard 1984a: 10) But this is ambiguous between semantic and pragmatic interpretations. Does he refer to a categorization in terms of pragmatics or in terms of semantics? For instance, is "promises" a (pragmatic) category of utterance? Or is law a category (semantic)? Is "observation statement" the kind of category of utterance that interests him, or is it rather categories such as "science"?

For of course, neither science nor law, for instance, can be reduced to a single kind of speech act – there is no such thing as "the" legal or scientific speech act. Science, for instance, will include maxims, principles, statements of fact or generalizations, methodological injunctions, prohibitions or prescriptions on inferences, and much else. But ironically, Lyotard's own insistence on irreducible difference between speech acts and the absence of any overarching rules will invalidate any attempt to infer incompatibility between forms of life, such as science and law, at this pragmatic level. Precisely because speech acts just have different rules, there is no overarching set of rules which could disclose a categorical pragmatic difference between any two *collections* of kinds of speech act. So if any field such as law or science (which some of us would call "forms of life") includes a plurality of simply different kinds of speech act, there seems to be no *pragmatic* principle, no overarching set of rules in pragmatics, which will indicate the individual integrity and mutual difference of these fields or forms of life. Any observations of such differences can only be purely contingent and questionable. For instance, it is clear that simple constatives of fact are found in both legal and scientific discourse, and by no means clear whether there is any significant *pragmatic* difference between them (as of course there is, by contrast, between the notion of law in jurisprudence and science).

Nonetheless, it remains wholly implausible to say there is no difference between law and science, and so if pragmatic considerations will not distinguish them, arguably more weight needs to be given to semantic differences between the two. What binds disparate utterances together in the discourses of science or law is not their pragmatics but their semantics. It is wholly implausible to disregard the fact that science and law, for instance, are *inter alia* just about different things. Yet why should such an obvious solution seem uninteresting to Lyotard?

The answer is surely that semantic rules do not constitute the kind of social bond which can ground resistance to normalization. For as Wittgenstein himself made clear, meanings are not mutually independent, not islands (like the atomic propositions and logically proper names of the *Tractatus*, which he came to repudiate) but elaborately and intricately interconnected.[10] To describe the grammar of a concept is to map its interconnections with others. But there is seemingly no limit a priori to the possible interconnectedness of concepts. Of course, Lyotard himself does talk of islands or clouds of meanings, rhetorically supposing that the semantic field is simply cleft through, at a minute level, into mutually independent archipelagoes of language games (to mix metaphors). But this in itself presupposes an interconnectedness between the language games in any particular group. And it consigns questions about the place, nature and number of the clefts to linguistic description, not to a priori demonstration. Thus, in principle, there might not be any such clefts. We have to "look and see" to find out.

So while we cannot rule out the possibility of clefts and faults in the semantic field, it is not obvious what or where they are: where interconnections are simply no longer to be found, however tenuous. Therefore, normalization of the semantic field might be a real possibility. Normalization would not, absurdly, erode differences between meanings; but it might threaten to link everything up in an inescapable web, such that one set of meanings could readily be harmonized with any other and semantic cleavages covered over. This might seem to be the threat that the functionality of society poses in the semantic field. The social bonds created in semantics might too readily be integrated. And if pragmatics fails to individuate irreducible fields either, where then would lie the potential for dissent and invention?

The unhappy upshot seems to be that appeal to the notion of a language game is not going to disclose any level of incommensurability and irreducible resistance to normalization in the social field, either in the pragmatic or the semantic construal of language games. So if there is a gap in the argument here, is it one we should seek to make good?

On the contrary, Lyotard's linguistic program is in fact disastrously complicit with sociological functionalism anyway. For nothing is more congenial to functionalism, particularly in its systems-theoretic form, than precisely an emphasis on the linguistic heterogeneity and conceptual autonomy of different sectors of culture and society. A clarity and moreover stability of differentiation is itself a major precondition of the efficiency and self-correcting stability of any system as a whole. While functionalism theorizes the influence of one sector of society on another, and thus precludes their *social* autonomy, it also presupposes clear boundaries between sub-systems so that flows of power and knowledge can be discerned and regulated. So describing these flows does nonetheless presuppose the conceptual and *cultural* autonomy of sub-systems, their mutual intellectual and epistemological difference. Once boundaries erode or blur, one begins to lose sight of any systematic functioning and to lose any grip on the system. From a political point of view, conservatism values stable sub-systems, and *pace* Lyotard, their cultural autonomy is functional for the status quo.

Consider the very example of modernist art, so important in Lyotard's other writings. Aesthetic modernism is a form of formalism, explaining and valuing modern art in terms not of its cognitive meanings or ethical or political commitments, but of its radical formal innovations and their aesthetic power. This formalism can be "spun" in opposite political directions. For Adorno (1977), preeminently, aesthetic modernism as an instance of high culture discloses a realm of experience which, in its radical difference, constitutes an oppositional political formation. The autonomy of high art (as opposed to "kitsch") is here seen as the ground of its political radicalism.[11]

However, radical theorists in recent years have reminded us that, in marginalizing or even repudiating the cognitive and normative aspects of art, one certainly robs it of other forms of critical address. And it is arguably historical fact that the prioritization of aesthetic autonomy has accompanied the commodification, and thus the political normalization, of works of art. Great paintings make great investments, while much work of importance is rarely seen outside the élite circuits of expensive galleries or private collections. Public exhibitions become major marketing exercises (don't leave without your Monet carrier bag or your Cézanne mug).[12] Political, religious and social meanings and exhortations get in the way of all this.

The classic instance of the autonomy of art sustaining its assimilation by the system is the story of abstract expressionism (dear to Lyotard) in the 1950s. A major American exhibition was sent to tour the "free" world (with great success), to present abstract expressionism as the ultimate instance of American liberal individualism, innovation and of course, the genius cultivated therein. Never mind that most of the leading artists of the movement were adherents of the far left, and discussed their work at least sometimes in political terms: Jackson Pollock claimed that his was the way to paint in the era of the hydrogen bomb, while Mark Rothko claimed some of his work responded to the Holocaust. Nonetheless, formal innovation was the organizing category of the exhibition. The exhibition was an elaborate propaganda exercise in Cold War politics. This is not inference: the exhibition is known to have been funded by the CIA.[13] (An entertaining detail: the wife of John D. Rockefeller was at the time a trustee of the Museum of Modern Art (New York), which sponsored the show, a "coincidence" to strain credibility.) Less melodramatically, the Museum of Modern Art itself has always organized its collection in terms of formal innovation, drawing formal (and often superficial) connections between works which were actually made with strong but divergent ethical and political ambitions.[14]

It has often been remarked that the formal experiments of modern art seem to be the models for Lyotard's concept of paralogy – of moves within language games which are eccentric or subversive in terms of the game and which, if successful, alter the nature of the game itself. So, for instance, cubism articulated a rich variety of, in Lyotard's word, "agonistic" ways of depicting pictorial space and the objects disposed within it, radically disruptive of settled expectations; ways which nonetheless proved open to rich elaboration and complex development. The possibilities for pictorial art after cubism were quite different from before; and earlier possibilities were, if not lost, then nonetheless robbed of their previous self-evidence. Another model for paralogy is that of the Kuhnian paradigm, of course; but intriguingly, this too has been taken to be modeled on the history of innovation in modern art.[15]

Herein lies precisely the impotence of paralogy with respect to functionalism. Paralogy functions only *within* language games (or forms of life), not across or between them. Formal experiment and innovation in art does not disrupt the mutual autonomy and categorical primacy of cognitive, normative and affective spheres of human experience. For the same reason, nor can any other kind of formal experiment or paralogy in any other sphere, to answer an earlier question. And theorizing language games or forms of life as mutually incommensurable actually *guarantees* this debilitating autonomy. It is precisely insofar as the formal experiments of modern art are theorized as of relevance to *nothing but* modern art that it is robbed, in such ways as I have sketched, of its broader normative critical potential. For instance, in disrupting canonic forms of representation, cubism also put in question the canonic ethical values and meanings of supposedly realist genres: the authority of the portrait, the idyll of the landscape, the classicizing eroticism of the nude. Cubism enacted normative, no less than formal critique in art. Yet formalism such as Lyotard's occludes such aspects, for all its Adorno-like validation of the aesthetic as "alternative."

One must fear that the notion of paralogy in the sciences, natural and social, or in philosophy or literary theory for instance, must be equally congenial to the functioning of a heavily managed system. It may indeed explain why "performativity" has to recognize its boundaries, to stop, for instance, at the door of the laboratory (as increasingly it sees no need to do, we must concede). But it does not provide any hope of academic or cultural paralogy upsetting the system in general.

Of course, paralogy is not intended by Lyotard to be seen as a function of intellectual life alone, but as a more general model for political or ethical activism. Is this credible? Only, I suggest, if we abandon the notion of the incommensurability of language games. For otherwise, what is the value of a program for political radicalism which must see itself in turn corralled within its own autonomous sphere? What is political activism if its effects are not potentially far-reaching, through unexpected areas of society? It is political reform, and reform within the limits and premises of the system.

It is again worth comparing Habermas here. Arguably, Habermas the consensualist has a sharper conception of the nature of pressures on intimate social bonds, on the linguistic fabric of society and the implications for legitimation. In his theorization of the "colonization of the lifeworld" by the media of money and power and by "expert cultures" which come to dominate areas of ethico-political thinking (for instance personal counseling, financial consultancy, public relations "experts," policy study institutes), it is arguably Habermas who is the more alert to the functioning of the system as a system. And in his conception of communicative interaction and the nature of the utterance, he defines radical potentials for resisting and even reconfiguring or removing the internal boundaries of the system, just as non-formalist aesthetics finds a radical potential for art by blurring its boundaries with politics and ethics, and confusing the flows of power and influence while rendering them harder to discern.

Habermas recognizes the brute necessity of what he calls "systemic sociation" in a modern society. In so complex a system, not every form of relationship or role can consciously be recognized, understood, negotiated and agreed upon. Necessarily, there is much that "works" in our society precisely in bypassing appeal to the conscious agreement of individuals. Think of the adjustment of consumer demand by manipulating interest rates, the salvation of the modern city by one-way traffic systems and parking regulations, the protection of individual health by environmental controls. However, the mode of interaction in which systemic sociation captures the individual is strategic interaction. What matters is not that the individual and the system "understand" each other but that the individual believes what he or she is told and accepts what he or she is told to do. Yet in this resides the constant danger of manipulation through which the "system" so easily oversteps its moral limits and invades the sphere of legitimate individual and institutional autonomy. Thus today, for instance, the economic pay-off of the more debased forms of distance education virtually preempts principled consideration within the universities of its problems and potentials in primarily educational terms.

The resistant potential of communicative interaction, that non-manipulative form which appeals directly to the conscious assent of the individual, resides in the co-presence in any utterance of the three different kinds of validity claim, even where much seems too unproblematic to matter. Examples of actual but non-problematic presuppositions might include the normative claims involved in descriptive speech (for instance, the norms informing the conduct of science), or the affective assumptions which accompany moral claims (that moral imperatives are emotionally bearable, for instance), or the silent cognitive assumptions which accompany a moral or aesthetic program (that human life and experience is such as to make such a program viable). This co-presence cannot easily be theorized if the difference between such claims is reconceptualized as a radical incommensurability, for this suggests that they cannot be co-present in any one utterance.[16]

Yet it is precisely the problematization of these co-present tacit assumptions which has the power to blur and question the boundaries between elements of the system, disrupting flows of control and re-empowering individuals and groups in the teeth of systemic sociation. What is most potent in the politics of knowledge is not so much our ability to make innovative and eccentric meanings and disrupt settled logics, but rather to activate dimensions of consciousness which are normally quiescent. This can put in question not just the current operation of elements of the system, but the normal functioning of their interrelations. What is most powerful in discourse is perhaps not paralogy but the problematization of dimensions of discourse which are normally non-problematic. Thus, in modern art, the potency of cubism lay not only in disrupting canonic *formal* expectations, but by activating thereby an otherwise unconscious set of cognitive and normative assumptions and habits of emotional response. This is not to deny any value in paralogy, but it is to doubt its comparative potency in the face of the system.

Where, then, does this leave the search for consensus? For does not the very pursuit of maximal consensus preclude this process of problematization? On the contrary, it depends upon it; and moreover it remains an ever-present possibility and occasional necessity, even when consensus seems settled. For the only kind of consensus compatible with communicative, rather than strategic, interaction is a rational consensus: not one which depends on pre-rational manipulation of others or moral pressure or emotional blackmail, but precisely one achieved through rational debate. And rational debate is by definition that which is concerned solely with the rights and wrongs of an argument. It is absolutely not a debate whose primary aim is to maximize consensus. Critics of Habermas seem often to miss this point. Even though the optimization of the social bond is constituted by the maximization of consensus, that does not entail that this goal is the proper or primary aim of discussion and debate. At best, it is its byproduct. But the social bond is strengthened the less rational debate is interfered with. The legitimacy of consensus dictates the optimization of open and probing discussion between dissenting speakers, not the suppression of either.

We see here that the pursuit of rational consensus cannot possibly be conceived as inimical to dissent, for it is only by giving dissent its due, only by responding openly to the power of dissenting and innovative argument, that we may reach a consensus with any claim to rationality. The Lyotardian evasion of calls to consensus is, by the same token, an evasion of rational discussion. And by that token, it puts in question the very value of dissent. What Lyotard is in danger of giving us is "dissent to no purpose": an aestheticization of dissent. By contrast, nothing is more protective of the possibility and the rights of dissent than commitment to ideals of undistorted communicative action.

Notes

1 That all three kinds are presupposed is widely misunderstood. Many assume that Habermas aligns all utterances with just one type of validity claim each; but not so. All he says in that respect is that typically (but only typically, and thus contingently) utterances tend to "thematize" particular claims, i.e. that the non-thematized claims are unproblematic and may be disregarded in

normal circumstances. But that does not mean they are not implied. As he writes of his own initial discussion of validity claims,

> In our previous examples we have assumed that the speaker raises precisely one validity claim with his utterance. . . . This picture is incomplete inasmuch as every speech act in a natural context can be contested (that is, rejected as invalid) under more than one aspect . . . speech acts can always be rejected under each of the three aspects.
>
> (Habermas 1984a: 306–7)

It is surely this kind of view that informs, for instance, his argument against positivism in the social sciences.

2 Habermas furthermore characterizes theoretical discourse as that subset of communicative action in which argumentation is radicalized by its pervasive reflexivity. And this further characteristic implies that the university deals specifically with fundamental discourses of a *modern* or modernizing society. See Blake 1995: 363.

3 See White 1988: 107–22 for erosion of the cultural sphere and expert cultures.

4 For the distinction between regulative and constitutive rules, see J. R. Searle (1969: 33 ff.).

5 Kant is the earliest source for modern philosophical discussion of linguistic pragmatics.

6 For instance, at Lyotard 1984a: 40, he actually relies on the theoretical/practical, cognitive/[normative] distinctions to further his argument and explicitly refers the distinction back to Kant. Similarly, at Lyotard 1984a: 9–10, he relies on the parallel cognitive/prescriptive distinction. These terms crop up at many other places too.

7 See again Searle, 1969.

8 There are others, including contributors to this volume, who believe "form of life" is primarily to be construed in the singular in Wittgenstein, referring to the contingent but utterly general relation between language, belief and practice in human existence. I recognize this usage, but am not alone in insisting that the plural usage is also present and important in *Philosophical Investigations* and bears pertinently on Lyotard's construction of Wittgenstein.

9 I have dealt in some depth with some consequences of this elision in *Thinking Again: Education after Postmodernism* (Blake *et al.* 1998: ch. 7).

10 On this point, I would strongly take issue with Michael Peters (1995c: 391), who seems to me too ready to accept Lyotard's reading of Wittgenstein.

11 On kitsch see Clement Greenberg, "Avant-garde and kitsch," (1939: 39).

12 Both items are real and have been sold in London in recent years. The author is pleased to possess neither of them.

13 For a number of papers dealing with this remarkable episode, see Frascina 1985.

14 Paradigmatically, the catalogue for the opening exhibition of the Museum (see Barr 1936).

15 It is irresistible to point out that the most dramatic innovations of all, those of the cubism of Picasso and Braque, were cited as exemplars by Roman Jakobson in early formulations of semiotics.

16 It is perhaps Lyotard's conception of utterances as incommensurable but therefore univocal which blinds him to the co-presence of cognitive, normative and affective dimensions of utterances. And perhaps it is this in turn which misleads him into talking as if modern art, and paralogies more generally, can transcend this Kantian trichotomy, which otherwise he himself seems never consciously to abandon.

4 Overcoming capitalism

Lyotard's pessimism and Rorty's prophecy

J. M. Fritzman

No doubt, in pointing out what I regard as a misunderstanding which it is important to uncover, I shall be careful in my refutation, and respectful in my criticism. I shall certainly refrain from joining myself to the detractors of a great man. When chance has it that I find myself apparently in agreement with them on some one particular point, I suspect myself; and to console myself for appearing for a moment in agreement with them on a single partial question, I need to disown and denounce with all my energies these pretended allies. Nevertheless, the interests of truth must prevail over considerations which make the glory of a prodigious talent and the authority of an immense reputation so powerful.

(Constant 1988: 318)

This chapter chronicles Jean-François Lyotard's increasing pessimism regarding the possibility of successfully resisting capitalism.[1] Initially, he hopes that paralogy can resist capitalism. Later, he realizes that paralogy actually enhances capitalism's performativity. He then urges that the ethical task is to bear witness to the differend, and so to the injustices of capitalism, but without hope that capitalism might be abolished. Eventually, he asserts that capitalism is an instance of the universe's increasing complexity. Lyotard's insights should be retained, but his pessimism abandoned. Richard Rorty's concept of prophetic imagination helps overcome Lyotard's pessimism. However, Rorty's own position must be subjected to criticism, for which he himself provides the resources, in order to arrive at an acceptable approach to overcoming capitalism.

I

Lyotard believes that performativity – operational efficiency, determined by cost/benefit or input/output analyses – is a fundamental principle of capitalism. In *The Postmodern Condition* (Lyotard 1984a), he opposes the legitimation of science and education through performativity, advocated by such systems theorists as Niklas Luhmann. Systems theorists conceptualize society as an overarching, totalizing system which is constituted through the interactions of its sub-systems, such as religion, politics, the family, and the economy. They urge that what needs to be taught are only the skills and knowledge required to preserve and enhance society's performativity. The content of what is taught is determined by the system's technological requirements, and educationalists are evaluated by how efficiently this content is conveyed. When education is legitimated through performativity, Lyotard notes, knowledge is not thought to have any intrinsic worth, but instead is valued only as a commodity which can be sold; it no longer possesses "use value," but only "exchange value" (Lyotard 1984a: 4–5).

Jürgen Habermas also seeks to resist legitimation through performativity. Habermas hopes to obtain universal and rational consensus through an argumentation where undistorted communication obtains. Lyotard supports Habermas's goal, but not his strategy: "The cause is good, but the argument is not" (ibid.: 66). Although recognizing the importance of consensus, Lyotard believes "consensus is only a particular state of discussion, not its end. Its end, on the contrary, is paralogy" (ibid.: 65–6). He uses "paralogy" to refer to the introduction of new rules of procedure, as well as ideas and goals, which disrupt and destabilize an existing consensus:

> Consensus is a horizon that is never reached. Research that takes place under the aegis of a paradigm tends to stabilize; it is like the exploitation of a technological, economic, or artistic "idea". It cannot be discounted. But what is striking is that someone always comes along to disturb the order of "reason".
>
> (Lyotard 1984a: 61)

Science and education are legitimated, Lyotard urges, neither by Luhmann's criterion of efficiency of performance nor by Habermas's search for universal consensus. Instead, they are legitimated through paralogy, by the injection of dissensus into consensus. This legitimation is not so much a justification of those institutions as it is an explication of how these institutions perpetuate themselves. They do so by continually evolving, changing their theories, research methods, and objects of study.

Employing Wittgenstein's notion of language games, Lyotard believes that the rules of a game collectively constitute that game, and that the rules determine which moves are permitted. Changing the rules alters the nature of the game (ibid.: 10). Procedural rules determine the moves that are permissible within a game. These rules may be changed, however, thereby constituting a different game which permits different moves:

> We know today that the limits the institution imposes on potential language "moves" are never established once and for all (even if they have been formally defined). Rather, the limits are themselves the

stakes and provisional results of language strategies, within the institution and without. . . . Reciprocally, it can be said that the boundaries
only stabilize when they cease to be stakes in the game. This, I think, is
the appropriate approach to contemporary institutions of knowledge.

(Lyotard 1984a: 17)

The imagination may discern a winning move which violates the
existing rules of the game. Hence, procedural rules can become stakes in
the game. The rules themselves may emerge in the making of the move;
they may be constituted in the moment of action. So moves in a game
might be *described* by appealing to rules, but it would be misleading to say
that they are *governed* by those rules. Here is how Lyotard explains this
aspect of paralogy to Jean-Loup Thébaud in *Just Gaming*:

The point is not that one keeps the games, but that, in each of the
existing games, one effects new moves, one opens up the possibility of
new efficacies in the games with their present rules. And, in addition,
one changes the rules: one can play a given game with other rules, and
when one changes the rules, one has changed the game, because a
game is primarily defined by its rules.

(Lyotard and Thébaud 1985: 62)

Lyotard hopes that paralogy might serve to displace and minimize
performativity, and so resist capitalism.

Even in *The Postmodern Condition*, though, there are intimations that
paralogy might not be able successfully to oppose capitalism. It is true that
Lyotard rejects Habermas's appeal to a universal consensus as a way of
resisting performativity:

Such consensus does violence to the heterogeneity of language games.
And invention is always born of dissension. Postmodern knowledge is
not simply a tool of the authorities; it refines our sensitivity to differences and reinforces our ability to tolerate the incommensurable. Its
principle is not the expert's homology, but the inventor's paralogy.

(Lyotard 1984a: xxv)

Yet, Lyotard also argues that it is paralogy which engenders science's
continuation and technology's progress. Paradoxically, in order to
maximize performativity, paralogy, not homeostasis, must be encouraged.
Lyotard recognizes that the system often is made less efficient, not more,
when it resists paralogy, and that performativity frequently is enhanced by
paralogy. In that case, however, paralogy cannot oppose performativity in
the last instance, even if a change in the game's rules makes obsolete a
particular way of maximizing outputs.

To simplify, Lyotard employed "postmodern" as a synonym for

"paralogy," and "modern" for the existing consensus that is capitalism. "Postmodern," then, does not to refer to a temporal period, but instead to a moment within modernism. He urges that "the postmodern would be that which, in the modern, puts forward the unpresentable in presentation itself" (ibid.: 81). He also writes: "A work can become modern only if it is first postmodern. Postmodernism thus understood is not modernism at its end but in the nascent state, and this state is constant" (ibid.: 79). The postmodern, then, would refer to the eruption of the new – that is, to changes in rules, practices, and institutions – within modernism. The problem, as Lyotard acknowledges, is that modernism is adept at forgetting and eliding the unpresentable. Put otherwise, the postmodern would refer to the emergence of novelty, prior to its being assimilated or absorbed within the modern. Avant-garde art would be an example of this. Works of art which formerly scandalized, shocked, or disgusted the public are viewed now with benign neglect and indifference. Similarly, art that was intended to protest the influence of money on public taste now sells for top dollar at auctions. Insofar as the modern eventually recoups what initially is novel, the postmodern cannot overthrow the modern. Rather, the postmodern is subsumed and so becomes the modern. Hence, paralogy cannot defeat capitalism. This is so because paralogy is the "motor" of capitalism.

This point can be explicated further by turning to Joseph A. Schumpeter's discussion in *Capitalism, Socialism and Democracy* (1950). Although not employing the term "paralogy," Schumpeter articulates Lyotard's insight when he writes that "the essential point to grasp is that in dealing with capitalism we are dealing with an evolutionary process. . . . Capitalism . . . is by nature a form or method of economic change and not only never is but never can be stationary" (Schumpeter 1950: 82). Schumpeter further claims that capitalism "incessantly revolutionizes the economic structure *from within,* incessantly destroying the old one, incessantly creating a new one. This process of Creative Destruction is the essential fact about capitalism" (ibid.: 83). Like a virus, capitalism mutates, thereby outmaneuvering the measures introduced to fight it.

II

As Lyotard uses these terms in *The Differend* (1988a), "litigations" and "damages" are different from "differends" and "wrongs." Litigations are disputes where certain criteria obtain which make possible the adjudication of those disputes. Differends are disputes where such criteria do not exist. Litigations result from damages, while differends result from wrongs. Lyotard states:

> As distinguished from a litigation, a differend would be a case of conflict, between (at least) two parties, that cannot be equitably resolved for lack of a rule of judgment applicable to both arguments.

One side's legitimacy does not imply the other's lack of legitimacy. However, applying a single rule of judgment to both in order to settle their differend as though it were merely a litigation would wrong (at least) one of them (and both of them if neither side admits this rule). Damages result from an injury which is inflicted upon the rules of a genre of discourse but which is reparable according to those rules. A wrong results from the fact that the rules of the genre of discourse by which one judges are not those of the judged genre or genres of discourse.

(Lyotard 1988a: xi)

Lyotard argues that there are conflicts where the differing parties do not share criteria which would allow their dispute to be adjudicated. Such disputes are differends rather than litigations. Further, not every differend can be replaced with a litigation. To attempt to adjudicate a differend as though it were a litigation necessarily wrongs at least one of the parties. Lyotard believes that differends are inevitable. To understand why he sees differends as arising inevitably, it is necessary to describe briefly Lyotard's notions of "phrase," "phrase regimen," and "genre of discourse" developed in *The Differend.*

A phrase is the ultimate unit of analysis. Phrases are indubitable and immediately presupposed: "To doubt that one phrases is still to phrase, one's silence makes a phrase" (ibid.: xi). There neither was a first phrase, nor will there be a last phrase. Each phrase necessarily must link with a previous phrase and then link to the next succeeding phrase. The linkages which occur are not necessary. Which phrases actually are linked together is a contingent matter. It is necessary that phrases link, but how they link is contingent. Phrases linked together constitute phrase regimens, and each phrase belongs to some regimen. Examples of phrase regimens would include defining, describing, knowing, ordering, questioning, reasoning, recounting, showing, and so forth. It is not always possible to determine the regimen to which a phrase belongs, since "a linkage may reveal an equivocalness in the previous phrase" (ibid.: 81). Phrase regimens are heterogeneous, and phrases belonging to one phrase regimen cannot be translated into another regimen. There is no metaregimen that would commensurate phrase regimens.

Further, since definition is itself a phrase regimen, it is impossible to define "phrase." To the objection that, lacking a definition of "phrase," it will not be known whether the same thing is being referred to by all parties, Lyotard replies that "it's not easy to know what one is phrasing about, but it is indubitable that 'one is phrasing,' be it only in order to know this" (ibid.: 69). The phrase functions, then, in a manner analogous to that of a primitive within a logical system. While a logical primitive is defined *operationally*, it does not receive an explicit interpretation.

Although phrases belonging to one phrase regimen cannot be translated into any other, phrases belonging to heterogeneous regimens can link together to constitute a given genre of discourse: "Genres of discourse supply rules for linking together heterogeneous phrases, rules that are proper for attaining certain goals: to know, to teach, to be just, to seduce, to justify, to evaluate, to rouse emotion, to oversee" (ibid.: xii). However, the rules for many genres – for example, philosophy – have not been determined: "There are many genres of discourse whose rules for linking are not stated" (ibid.: 80).

Differends are inevitable. As has been seen, it is necessary that phrases link, but how they do so is contingent. Given an actualized phrase – for example, "a friend may well be reckoned the masterpiece of nature" – there are countless possible phrases that could link on to it. Yet only one of the possible phrases actually will be phrased next, and there are no criteria external to those of phrase regimens and genres of discourse to decide which of the possible phrases actually will be phrased (ibid.: 140). Not only can there be a differend between actualized phrases, there also is a differend between the phrases that "wait" to be phrased.

The differend frequently takes the form of the "double bind." The logical machinery of the double bind goes like this: Either the proposition is the case or it is not the case; now, if it is not the case, then (of course) it is not the case; but if the proposition is the case, then it can be shown that it nevertheless is not the case.

> Either you are the victim of a wrong, or you are not. If you are not, you are deceived (or lying) in testifying that you are. If you are, since you can bear witness to this wrong, it is not a wrong, and you are deceived (or lying) in testifying that you are the victim of a wrong.
>
> (Lyotard 1988a: 5)

An example of such a differend would be the mechanism of the patriarchal definition of "femininity," analyzed by Sarah Lucia Hoagland, according to which wimmin are conceptualized as weak and passive, and so dependent upon men. A woman's attempts to resist the imposition of this definition are not viewed as disconfirming evidence of its correctness. Rather, the resistance is invisible *as* resistance, and is seen only as corroborating the definition's adequacy:

> One of the most pervasive effects of the male naming of wimmin feminine is the obliteration of any conceptual hint of female resistance to male domination, resistance to attempts to limit or control a woman's integrity. One searches in vain for portraits and historical depictions of female autonomy, female resistance, female bonding. Patrihistorians claim that wimmin have remained content with our lot and have accepted male domination throughout time with the

exception of a few suffragists and now a few "aberrant" feminists. Yet upon examination it becomes clear that within the confines of the feminine stereotype, no behavior, no set of actions *count* as resistance. Any behavior that cannot be squeezed into the confines of the feminine, passive stereotype has been discounted as an aberration or it has been buried.

(Hoagland 1982: 89)

To articulate this in the form of a differend, the patriarchs would say to the womon: "Either you are resisting the definition of 'femininity,' or you are not. If you are not resisting, then you would be wrong or lying to claim that you were. If you are resisting, however, then you are not behaving in a feminine manner, and so your putative resistance is not resistance at all but instead evidence of some psychological imbalance or mental disturbance". As Hoagland perceives, "we have been unable to re-cognize resistance to male domination among wimmin because under the male-identified feminine stereotype, resistance is considered abnormal, an indication of insanity, or incredibly, proof of submission" (ibid.). The womon suffers a wrong. What she experiences as an injustice cannot be phrased within the idioms recognized by the patriarchs. Perhaps all she can say is: "Their definition of 'femininity' makes me feel as though I am not important," or "Something about that definition makes me feel uncomfortable." She also suffers a wrong if she lacks an idiom in which to phrase her feelings to herself as an experience of injustice. Remember, silence too is a phrase.

Imagine, then, that what the womon experiences as an injustice cannot be phrased within an idiom recognized by the patriarchs, that she herself lacks an idiom in which to phrase her feelings, and so she remains silent. The patriarchs infer: "Obviously, this womon hasn't any basis for complaint since she doesn't resist, but instead remains silent." The patriarchs believe that her silence demonstrates that their definition of "femininity" is adequate, and that her feelings – "And since she doesn't speak, how could we know of them?" – lack any referent. However, this is an invalid inference. To remain silent is not the absence of phrasing. Silence is itself a phrase positioned by at least one of the phrase instances: addressee, addressor, reference and sense. Lyotard's comments regarding the silence of the survivors of the holocaust also apply, *mutatis mutandis*, to the case above:

Silence does not indicate which instance is denied, it signals the denial of one or more instances. The survivors remain silent, and it can be understood 1) that the situation in question (the case) is not the addressee's business (he or she lacks the competence, or he or she is not worthy of being spoken to about it, etc.); or 2) that it never took place . . .; or 3) that there is nothing to say about it (the situation is senseless, inexpressible); or 4) that it is not the survivors' business to be talking about it (they are not worthy, etc.). Or, several of these negations together.

(Lyotard 1988a: 14)

In asserting that the woman's silence is evidence that their definition of "femininity" is unproblematic, the patriarchs infer that silence entails consent. However, her silence also could indicate that she does not know how to articulate her suffering.

Can this differend between the patriarchs and the wimmin be substituted with a litigation? Yes, if an idiom can be found in which the woman's actions can be recognized by the patriarchs as instances of resistance to their definition of "femininity."

While some differends can be replaced with litigations, this may not be true of all differends. Further, the exchange of a differend for a litigation is not a matter of translation. A differend exists when there are no criteria by which to adjudicate a dispute. Conflicting parties might agree to accept a set of criteria which will allow their dispute to be adjudicated, and so overcome their differend. In such a case, however, the parties have reformulated the terms of their dispute. That is, the parties have agreed to substitute their earlier dispute for a new one, exchanging their differend for a litigation. Since this substitution itself proceeds without criteria, it would be incorrect to speak of translating differends into litigations. Indeed, in cases where a litigation supplants a differend, another differend is created: one between the terms of the earlier and later disputes.

Why would capitalism be unjust on this analysis? Because it makes phrases link according to rules of exchange governed by performativity, and it pretends that there are no alternatives. Or, if capitalism acknowledges other alternatives, it permits them to function only insofar as they are subsumed under and contribute to the performativity of the system. Capitalism, as Lyotard puts it, never needs to have the last word. It always does, however, want to have the next word, and as soon as possible. "Part of the power and flexibility of our profit-oriented economy," Peter Coyote writes in his memoir, "is that it can co-opt nearly everything. Everything but *doing things for free*" (Coyote 1998: 35). Kant's monarch says that subjects are permitted to debate as much as they wish, provided they obey. Capitalism says that individuals are allowed to criticize its political and economic systems, but only if their criticisms quickly turn a profit.

Because Lyotard believes that differends are inevitable, he understands politics as the pursuit, not of the good, but of the lesser evil:

It cannot even be said that (necessarily, civil) war, class struggle, or revolutionary violence are more just than the tribunal because they would expose the differend instead of masking it under litigation.

Vengeance is not an authorization. . . . It shows that another tribunal and other criteria of judgment (should there be any) are possible and seem to be preferable. But, supposing the change took place, it is impossible that the judgments of the new tribunal would not create new wrongs, since they would regulate (or think they were regulating) differends as though they were litigations. This is why politicians cannot have the good at stake, but they ought to have the lesser evil. Or, if you prefer, the lesser evil ought to be the political good. By evil, I understand, and one can only understand, the incessant inter-diction of possible phrases, a defiance of the occurrence, the contempt for Being.

(Lyotard 1988a: 140)

Rather than pretending that differends never exist or that they always can be treated as litigations, thereby acting as though wrongs could be treated as damages, politics should seek to bear witness to differends. A politics of the lesser evil would attempt to phrase wrongs so that they may be recognized as such, instead of being construed as damages. Of course, political decisions must be made, since not to decide is itself a decision which favors one set of options over others. Where there exists a differend between disputing parties, any decision will constitute a wrong done to at least one group.

In light of this, what is to be done? A politics of the good would not acknowledge the existence of differends, but instead would treat all disputes as litigations. In confronting a differend, then, it would privilege a certain set of criteria, and so would wrong at least one party. A politics of the good would not allow that there exist other sets of criteria, and so it would be blind to the wrongs it inflicts. Instead of a politics of the good, Lyotard believes that a politics of the lesser evil must be developed. A politics of the lesser evil will not forget that there are differends which cannot be substituted for liti-gations, and so will seek to make decisions that minimize the wrongs that necessarily occur. A politics of the lesser evil will attempt to leave open as wide a set of political options as possible. This still will result in a wrong being done to at least one party of any dispute which is not a litigation, but the wrong would be the least wrong possible, and it would be recognized and acknowledged as a wrong by those making that judgment.

This results in a certain accommodation with capitalism. Rather than attempting to overcome capitalism – which itself would constitute a wrong, since there are no criteria which would allow the dispute between capitalism and socialism to be adjudicated – Lyotard instead urges that persons have an ethical obligation to bear witness to the wrongs caused by capitalism:

Marxism has not come to an end, but how does it continue? Marx in 1843: "a class with radical chains, a class of bourgeois society which is not a class of bourgeois society, a sphere which has a universal character by its universal suffering and claims no particular right because no particular wrong but wrong generally is perpetrated against it." The wrong is expressed through the silence of feeling, through suffering. The wrong results from the fact that all phrase universes and all their linkages are or can be subordinated to the sole finality of capital (but is capital a genre?) and judged accordingly. Because this finality seizes upon or can seize upon all phrases, it makes a claim to universality. The wrong done to phrases by capital would then be a universal one. Even if the wrong is not universal (but how can you prove it? it's an Idea), the silent feeling that signals a differend remains to be listened to. Responsibility to thought requires it. This is the way in which Marxism has not come to an end, as the feeling of the differend.

(Lyotard 1988a: 171)

Denying Marxism's demise, Lyotard insists on the injustice of capitalism while adopting an incredulity toward Marx's analyses that sought to demonstrate its crimes. Marxism's continued existence, then, no longer would be a matter of revolutionary praxis, but rather a bearing witness to capitalism's evils. This analysis presupposes, though, either that allowing capitalism to continue – instead of seeking its destruction – would be the lesser evil, or that capitalism cannot be overcome.

III

In *The Inhuman* (1991c), Lyotard suggests that capitalism cannot be overcome. Capitalism is not the result of any plan or intention. Indeed, it is not a human creation at all, but rather a manifestation of the universe's movement toward increasing complexity. Thus, while capitalism can be resisted and its course slowed – indeed, there is an ethical obligation to resist, bearing witness to the differends it engenders – it ultimately cannot be overcome or halted. Capitalism cannot be stopped, in the last instance, any more than entropy. This is so because, according to Lyotard, capitalism is an instance of entropy.

If true, this would mean that the project of Marxism, and the moral vision which underlay it, always were delusive. Resistance would be futile. Once it seemed that capitalism could be surmounted. Now it is seen to be a part of the nature of things. All that could be done, realistically, would be to struggle against those injustices and indignities which are not the result of the functioning of capitalism itself: searching for archipelagos of justice – or, as Lyotard would have it, islands of the lesser evil – in an ocean of injustice.

IV

Given the need for brevity, the propositions in this chapter will be didactic and dogmatic, the theses schematic and provisional. What is correct in

Lyotard's analyses? The notion of the differend and of justice as the lesser evil. The insight that capitalism is not the result of any plan. The belief that there is an ethical obligation to bear witness to the differend, and so to testify against capitalism's injustices. Lyotard also is correct in claiming that there is a differend between socialism and capitalism, and so any attempt to institute socialism in capitalism's place would constitute a wrong against capitalism.

What requires correcting? The claim that capitalism is unstoppable because it is an instance of entropy, where entropy is understood as increasing complexity, as well as the claim that capitalism is not a human product. However, although attempting to overcome capitalism constitutes an injustice against capitalism, it is the least bad option. Finally, he correctly perceives that socialism would generate differends too. Hence, the ethical task to bear witness to the differend would remain after socialism's advent.

The notion of complexity must be rethought. When Lyotard asserts that the universe itself is moving toward increased complexity, he confuses the notion of complexity used in communication theory with the concept of entropy employed in physics. Roughly speaking, the communication theorists' complexity is the opposite of physicists' entropy. Complexity refers to a meaningful sequence of bytes, which then is defined as information, while entropy denotes the process toward the increasing randomization of bytes.

Further, what counts as complexity always is the result of an interpretive stance. Talk of increased complexity which purports to be more than a pragmatically useful means of expression must be rejected. Any method for specifying increased complexity can be employed only after it has been decided which features will be considered relevant. That is, any method for specifying increased complexity must presuppose a determination of what is to count *as* complexity. Once it is decided which features are relevant, increased complexity can be measured by means of methods which enumerate these features, which chronologically appear later. Such a procedure is unobjectionable when its adoption is based on pragmatic considerations. However, any claim that it provides a literal explication of complexity must be rejected as circular, for the features enumerated are taken as indications of increased complexity because what is to count as complexity has been presupposed, while the decision to regard certain features as indications of increased complexity is defended by instancing the later presence of those features. The points regarding complexity in biological evolution made in *The Dialectical Biologist* by Richard Levins and Richard Lewontin (1985) apply, *mutatis mutandis*, to Lyotard's notion of complexity too. Levins and Lewontin write:

> The supposed increase in complexity . . . during evolution does not stand on any objective ground. . . . How are we to measure the

complexity of an organism? In what sense is a mammal more complex than a bacterium? Mammals have many types of cells, tissues, and organ systems and in this respect are more complex, but bacteria can carry out many bio-synthetic reactions, such as the synthesis of certain amino acids, that have been lost during the evolution of the verte-brates, so in that sense bacteria are more complex. There is no indication that vertebrates in general enter into more direct interac-tions with other organisms than do bacteria, which have their own parasites, predators, competitors, and symbionts. And even if we are to accept sheer structural variation as an indication of complexity, we do not know how to order it, not to speak of assigning a metric to it. Is a mammal more complex structurally than a fish? Yet 370 million years passed between the origin of the fishes at the end of the Cambrian and the first mammals at the beginning of the Cretaceous. If one starts with the assertion that structural complexity has increased, it is possible to rationalize the assertion a posteriori by enumerating those features, for example, a very large hindbrain, that appear later in evolution and declaring them to be more complex. The evident circularity of this procedure has not prevented its wide-spread practice.

(Levins and Lewontin 1985: 17)

This does not mean that all talk of the complexity must be rejected. The notion of the complexity is acceptable if construed heuristically. Problems of circularity only arise if the pragmatic basis of this concept is forgotten.

Although Lyotard is correct in claiming that capitalism is not the result of any plan or intention, it nevertheless is a human product. One of the great merits of David McNally's *Against the Market* (1993) is its detailed examination of the emergence of capitalism from feudalism. Citing Marx, McNally argues:

Central to the genesis of capitalism . . . are those historical processes which bring about the separation of a large and growing proportion of the labouring population from means of production which could provide them with an adequate subsistence. It follows that the emer-gence of a *labour market* is central to the rise of capitalism. And, emerging, out of an overwhelmingly agricultural society, the origins of the capitalist labour market must be sought in "the expropriation of the agricultural producer, of the peasant, from the soil."

(McNally 1993: 7–8)

Capitalism did not emerge of a sudden, but rather slowly evolved as the result of a series of disparate erodings of the practices and institutions which constituted feudalism.

Can capitalism be overcome? It is clear that much can be done to contain it and to limit its most harmful effects, and that the market can be subject to rational controls. For example, the United States Constitution could be amended to allow for the overturning of the 1886 Supreme Court decision, *Santa Clara County vs. Southern Pacific Railroad*, that a private corporation has the status of a "natural person" and so is protected by the Bill of Rights. This would allow corporations to be regulated in much the same way as are television and radio stations. The shareholders or owners of a corporation might be required to demonstrate, on a regular basis, that the corporation benefits the community, and so on. It addition, federal and local governments could put severe restrictions on the ability of corporations to transfer money in and out of the country, to relocate or close manufacturing plants, and to lay off or fire their employees.

Yes, but can capitalism be abolished? Is there any hope for socialism?

V

Rorty writes that

> the leftist use of the terms "capitalism," "bourgeois ideology," and "working class," depends on the implicit claim that we can do *better* than a market economy, that we know of a viable alternative option for complex technologically oriented societies. But at the moment, at least, we know of no such option.
>
> (Rorty 1998: 234)

He then presents leftist intellectuals with an alternative: "We have either to spin some new metanarrative that does not mention capitalism, yet has the same dramatic power and urgency as the Marxist narrative, or else to give up the idea that we intellectuals are notably better at holding our time in thought than our fellow citizens," adding that "since I have no idea how to do the former, I suggest we do the latter" (ibid.: 235). Nevertheless, despite his intentions, Rorty unwittingly provides the resources both for detecting the implicit and fallacious appeal to ignorance in his claim that leftists must acquiesce to market economies because there presently are no known better options, and for rejecting his alternative as a false dilemma.

Regarding capitalism as an insurmountable horizon is the way to ensure that it will remain so. What is required, then, is a way of conceptualizing a world without capitalism that does not seem a cloud-cuckoo-land. As Rorty recognizes when discussing feminism:

> Assumptions become visible *as* assumptions only if we can make the contradictories of those assumptions sound plausible. So injustices

may not be perceived as injustices, even by those who suffer them,
until somebody invents a previously unplayed role. Only if
somebody has a dream, and a voice to describe that dream, does
what looked like nature begin to look like culture, what looked like
fate begin to look like a moral abomination. For until then only the
language of the oppressor is available, and most oppressors have
had the wit to teach the oppressed a language in which the
oppressed will sound crazy – *even to themselves* – if they describe themselves as oppressed.

(Rorty 1998: 203)

Hence, a first step in resisting oppression must be the invention of a
language in which certain experiences can be described as those of
oppression, a language where such descriptions have a *prima facie* claim to
sanity. Once an oppressed group invents a new language, its terms and
categories may be incommensurable not only with its previous self-
descriptions, but also with the language of its oppressors. As a result, "we
have to give up the comforting belief that competing groups will always be
able to reason together on the basis of plausible and neutral premises"
(ibid.: 206). It is at this point that Rorty's pragmatism touches Lyotard's
notion of the differend, since it allows that disputing parties may not
share a set of criteria which would allow their conflict to be treated as a
litigation.

Rorty refers to the process of revising moral categories, inventing new
self-descriptions, and creating new languages as "prophecy." "Prophecy,"
he maintains,

is all that non-violent political movements can fall back on when
argument fails. Argument for the rights of the oppressed *will* fail just
insofar as the only language in which to state relevant premises is one
in which the relevant emancipatory premises sound crazy.

(Ibid.: 207–8)

As he understands this process of engendering new self-descriptions
and languages, prophecy is not a radical project, but instead a utopian
vision. In contrast to radicals – who believe that "there is a basic mistake
being made, a mistake deep down at the roots," that "deep thinking is
required to get down to this deep level, and that only there, when all the
superstructural appearances have been undercut, can things be seen as
they really are" – utopian prophets "do not think in terms of mistakes or of
depth. They abandon the contrast between superficial appearances and
deep reality in favor of the contrast between a painful present and a
possibly less painful, dimly-seen, future" (ibid.: 214).

The resources for utopian prophecy come from the imagination. Rorty
notes that Marilyn Frye writes that feminists must "dare to rely on ourselves

to make meaning and we have to imagine ourselves capable of . . . weaving the web of meaning which will hold us in some kind of intelligibility" (Frye 1983: 80). Such imagination presupposes the courage to redefine what is rational, moral, allowable – and what is not. Frye also maintains that "there probably is really no distinction, in the end, between imagination and courage" (ibid.: 80). "Such courage is indistinguishable," Rorty adds, "from the imagination it takes to hear oneself as the spokesperson of a merely possible community, rather than as a lonely, and perhaps crazed, outcast from an actual one" (Rorty 1998: 215).

Creating such a language is no easy task, especially since the claim that they are oppressed may appear, initially, as ludicrous to the victims as it does to the perpetrators. As Hoagland recognizes:

> To dominate a people one must first use force, but eventually one finds other means. One effective means of maintaining power is to rob the oppressed of any positive self concept and to prevent us from identifying with each other. Then one can portray us as accepting, indeed desiring our lot, and each individual sees herself as alone and abnormal when she resists.
>
> (Hoagland 1982: 94)

Such considerations lead Rorty to argue that courageous imagination alone may not be enough.

So that the dominated can resist, and not see themselves as alone and abnormal, they require a community – "an invisible club, a very good club" (Rorty 1998: 221) – in which novel self-descriptions and languages can be developed and articulated. As Rorty understands it, this is one of the points of feminist separatism. Concerning "the new being and meaning which are being created now by lesbian-feminists," Frye maintains that "we *do* have semantic authority, and, collectively, can and do define with effect." "It is only by maintaining our boundaries," she continues, "through controlling concrete access to us that we can enforce on those who are not-us our definitions of ourselves, hence force on them *the fact of our existence* and thence open up the *possibility* of our having semantic authority with them" (Frye 1983: 106). Rorty explicates Frye's claims this way:

> Individuals – even individuals of great courage and imagination – cannot achieve semantic authority, *even semantic authority over themselves*, on their own. To get such authority you have to hear your own statements as part of a shared practice. Otherwise you yourself will never know whether they are more than ravings, never know whether you are a heroine or a maniac. People in search of such authority need to band together and form clubs, exclusive clubs. For if you want to work out a story of who you are – to put together a moral identity – which decreases the importance of your relationships to one set of people

and increases the importance of your relationships to another set, the physical absence of the first set of people may be just what you need.
(Rorty 1998: 223)

Suppose that persons do work together to articulate new ways of understanding economic relationships, and that they proceed to form cooperatives, communities, communes, or clubs. Nevertheless, it will be objected, the history of utopian communities demonstrates that they inevitably collapse. Even when the internal structure of such a community is socialist, it still exists within a larger capitalist context, and ultimately it will not be able to compete successfully. The name of the game for capitalism is the maximization of profits, and socialism always will lose whenever it plays that game. Socialism's bottom line is human needs and dignity, but profits often are increased by overlooking such niceties. The project of socialism in one country always will fail, and it always has been suffocated before it could be adopted globally. Further, capitalism has proven sufficiently supple to block the efforts of those who would resist it.

These objections are all too familiar. Capitalism might not be to everyone's liking, it will be said, and it may offend the moral and aesthetic sensibilities of malcontents. Socialism has failed whenever it was tried, it will be added, and that is sufficient reason to conclude that it never will succeed. Further, in spite of the above grandiose appeals to the power of the imagination, it must be admitted that it seems there is no realistic alternative to capitalism. Like the poor, capitalism will always be present – it will see to that! A reasonable individual, Plato's Socrates seemingly advises in a similar context,

> keeps quiet and minds his own business – as a man in a storm, when dust and rain are blown about by the wind, stands aside under a little wall. Seeing others filled full of lawlessness, he is content if somehow he himself can live his life here pure of injustice and unholy deeds.
> (Plato 1991: 176; 496e)

So, the sensible course of action would be to reach an accommodation with capitalism.

What such reasoning overlooks is that success emerges from failure as does truth from misrecognition. Slavoj Žižek perceives that

> if we want to spare ourselves the painful roundabout route through misrecognition, we miss the Truth itself: only the 'working-through' of the misrecognition allows us to accede to the true nature of the other and at the same time to overcome our own deficiency.
> (Žižek 1989: 63)

Put otherwise, failure has a pedagogical function. Through successive setbacks, persons learn which tactics and strategies were not useful or need modification. Thus, failures ultimately remain failures, rather than stepping stones to victory, only if the struggle is abandoned. There can be no guarantee of victory, of course, but failure is insured if defeat is believed inevitable. Those who wager that capitalism can be overcome never will lose their bet, although they may not win. As long as capitalism exists, the bet has not been won. Even then, however, it still can be hoped that capitalism will be surmounted, and so the bet has not been lost. Following the paradoxical logic of Pascal's wager that God exists, the only way to lose the bet that capitalism can be overcome is never to place it.

As his own writings demonstrate, then, Rorty is wrong in believing that the vision of socialism should be abandoned just because that vision seems unrealizable. Even if it were conceded that he is correct in maintaining that there currently is no viable alternative for complex technologically oriented societies other than a market economy – and McNally's *Against the Market* would urge that he is not correct – his discussion of the imagination demonstrates why that would be an insufficient reason for acceding to capitalism. Rather, what is required is a concerted effort to imagine a world without capitalism. One way to begin this task would be to identify the injustices generated by capitalism, analyze the precise mechanisms by which they occur, and then attempt to imagine an alternative world in which such mechanisms either did not exist or else did not cause those injustices. It would be a mistake, however, to concentrate solely on this task. As noted above, it is clear that much can be done to ameliorate the worst effects of capitalism. So leftists must adopt a two-sided approach. They must attempt to imagine and then realize a socialist alternative to capitalism. Simultaneously, though, they must also attempt to reform capitalism, insofar as this is possible, while also bearing witness to its injustices. However, to a large extent these two sides, while they can be distinguished conceptually, will prove indistinguishable in practice. Rorty is almost certainly correct in urging that present conditions will not be improved through some revolution. Rather, it is probable that capitalism will be overcome piecemeal, through a series of reforms and changes which have the cumulative effect of transforming it into socialism.

A critic might charge that this chapter so far has suggested ways in which capitalism can be ameliorated, but not ways in which it might be overthrown. Its conclusions would seem compatible with Rorty's recommendation that

> we start talking about greed and selfishness rather than about bourgeois ideology, about starvation wages and layoffs rather than about the commodification of labor, and about differential per-pupil expenditure on schools and differential access to health care rather than about the division of society into classes.
>
> (Rorty 1998: 229)

Behind that objection – if that is what it is – lies an unexamined distinction between reform (which is suspected of always being complicitous with the status quo) and revolution (which overthrows existing social institutions). As McNally illustrates, however, it is capitalism's effects, not its emergence, that are revolutionary.

VI

It is rational to hope that capitalism eventually can be overcome. In *Capitalism, Socialism and Democracy*, Schumpeter argues that insofar as it succeeds, capitalism undermines the social institutions on which it depends and which allow it to exist. He writes:

> Since capitalist enterprise, by its very achievements, tends to automatize progress, we conclude that it tends to make itself superfluous – to break to pieces under the pressure of its own success. The perfectly bureaucratized giant industrial unit not only ousts the small or medium-sized firm and "expropriates" its owners, but in the end it also ousts the entrepreneur and expropriates the bourgeoisie as a class which in the process stands to lose not only its income but also what is infinitely more important, its function.
>
> (Schumpeter 1950: 134)

Schumpeter does not mean that capitalism inevitably will lead to socialism, but instead that socialism is the probable – although no more than that – outcome of capitalism's collapse. Since *Capitalism, Socialism and Democracy* is fifty years old, it might be objected that Schumpeter's analysis suggesting that capitalism will implode must be incorrect because it has not occurred. However, he never claimed that capitalism's demise would happen overnight. Indeed, recent events on Wall Street provide evidence of the correctness of his analysis.

Goldman, Sachs & Company, founded by Marcus Goldman more than 130 years ago, in 1869, had been Wall Street's remaining large investment-banking partnership. Referring to the company's decision to dissolve its partnership structure and convert itself into a public company by issuing stock on the New York Stock Exchange, John Cassidy writes that "there are signs that the firm's success is generating, as Marxists used to say, internal contradictions" (Cassidy 1999: 28). Cassidy believes that Goldman's decision to become a public company corroborates the correctness of Schumpeter's argument that "free-market capitalism eventually undermines the very institutions that give rise to its success" (ibid.: 29). Goldman's financial success had been secured by its partnership structure. Many of the firm's investment bankers eventually became partners. In this way, their own interests were linked to Goldman's financial success. "At most firms," according to Cassidy, "loyalty is purchased in return for six-figure salaries and seven- or, occasionally, eight-figure bonuses. If the bonuses aren't big enough, star performers pack up and leave. The great strength of Goldman's partnership structure is that it encourages cooperation and loyalty" (ibid.: 32). This resulted in an annual staff turnover of only 3 percent, the lowest of any Wall Street firm. Goldman's partnership structure allowed the firm to articulate its business philosophy as "greedy, but long-termed greedy." Observing, however, that "on Wall Street, the most inexorable force is money" (ibid.: 35), Cassidy argues that the present partners' decision to transform Goldman into a public company was motivated less by considerations of Goldman's long-term institutional interests than by concerns for the partners' short-term financial interests:

> The point is best illustrated with some arithmetic. Given the high prices at which stocks in other investment banks are trading on Wall Street, Goldman's partners will probably receive about two and a half or three times the current value of their equity in a public offering. A Goldman executive who has been a partner for four or five years and built up, say, $20 million in his capital account could expect to get an equity stake worth between $50 million and $60 million. A senior partner who has already squirrelled away, say, $50 million in accumulated earnings could expect to pocket somewhere between $125 million and $150 million.
>
> (Ibid.: 35)

This occurs, as Cassidy notes, in accordance with Schumpeter's observation that "capitalism creates a critical frame of mind which, after having destroyed the moral authority of so many other institutions, in the end turns against its own" (Schumpeter 1950: 143). Referring to Goldman's business philosophy of "greedy, but long-termed greedy," Cassidy concludes:

> The partnership structure, which tied people to Goldman for decades and gave them a strong incentive to act in the long-term interest of the firm, was what made this philosophy viable. Once the partnerships are gone, Goldman people will be like everyone else on Wall Street – greedy, but short-term greedy – and the implications of this change are profound. Goldman will still be immensely powerful, but it will have sold its greatest asset, and it will be answerable to outside shareholders. The history of other ex-partnerships demonstrates that this can be an unhappy experience, and often culminates in the firm's becoming part of a larger conglomerate. All told, it is hard to see Marcus Goldman's creation enduring for another hundred and thirty years.
>
> (Cassidy 1999: 36)

Although Goldman's partnership structure encouraged co-operation and loyalty, those values were trumped by the prospects of fabulous wealth.

What is important, though, is not to denounce the propensity towards avarice, but instead to recognize that the partnership structure created those prospects, and so led to its own unraveling.

Schumpeter would maintain that what is true of Goldman holds generally. The case of Goldman shows, he would claim, that capitalism's very success undermines the institutions on which it depends. This strongly suggests that capitalism is doomed. Once capitalism collapses, some other structure will inevitably succeed it, probably some form of socialism:

> The capitalist process not only destroys its own institutional framework but it also creates the conditions for another. Destruction may not be the right word after all. Perhaps I should have spoken of transformation. The outcome of the process is not simply a void that could be filled by whatever might happen to turn up; things and souls are transformed in such a way as to become increasingly amenable to the socialist form of life. With every peg from under the capitalist structure vanishes the impossibility of the socialist plan.
>
> (Schumpeter 1950: 162)

Schumpeter frequently reminds his readers, however, that this does not mean that capitalism necessarily leads to socialism, but rather that socialism is a likely outcome of capitalism's collapse. It seems that history has shown that socialism cannot compete with capitalism when the former is confined to a community or nation while the latter provides its horizon or context. Things may be otherwise, though, if global capitalism does become the victim of its own success. For in that event, capitalism itself may become inefficient – by its own criterion – and so socialism then might have a chance. In such circumstances, it also is possible that capitalism would no longer be seen by the majority of persons as the road to their own well-being, but instead be revealed as a mechanism that tends to enrich the few but impoverish everyone else. In that case, persons may opt for socialism while acknowledging its inefficiencies in generating wealth.

It is possible that capitalism will implode, and there are reasons for believing that this is probable. What is important, then, is to develop a vision of the world where the absence of capitalism is conceivable, and where socialism is perceived as a sensible and likely alternative. Since capitalism's demise likely will involve considerable want and suffering on the part of many people, it also is important that leftists be able to articulate a vision that can be counterposed to the attempts, which almost certainly will arise, to scapegoat religious, racial, and ethnic minorities.

VII

One of the telling expressions that has arisen from the intersection of education and business is "learn to earn." Under present conditions, of course, surviving generally involves earning a living (another telling expression). Hence, students would be served poorly if educationalists did not impart the knowledge, habits, and disciplines needed to succeed financially. Nevertheless, students would be even more ill-served if economic success were taken to be the goal of education, its *raison d'être*, as "learn to earn" would have it. Persons who only learn to earn may have full stomachs, but their lives will be empty. Further, they will have the ability neither to comprehend the world in which they live, nor to make informed decisions about which aspects of it should be preserved and which changed. So students must understand the historically contingent nature of capitalism in particular, and comprehend that much which seems permanent in human affairs is historically recent and, likely, transitory.

The ability to imagine alternatives, to think otherwise, can be developed and expanded not only by historical studies, but also through literature and writing. Literature, as Rorty points out, not only can help persons to become more autonomous, it also can assist individuals to become less cruel. Literature accomplishes the latter by helping readers to perceive "the effects of social practices and institutions on others" and "the effects of our private idiosyncrasies on others" (Rorty 1989: 141). Martha Craven Nussbaum would agree with this. In *Poetic Justice: The Literary Imagination and Public Life*, she defends the literary imagination, seeing it as "an essential ingredient to an ethical stance that asks us to concern ourselves with the good of other people whose lives are distant from our own" (Nussbaum 1995: xvi).

Merely appealing to an ethics of impartial respect for human dignity is insufficient, Nussbaum urges, because such appeals "will fail to engage real human beings unless they are made capable of entering imaginatively into the lives of distant others and to have emotions related to that participation" (ibid.: xvi). Acknowledging that the literary imagination's appeals to empathy and the emotions have their dangers, and must be complemented by rules and formal decision procedures, Nussbaum nevertheless maintains that such appeals can provide "a powerful, if partial, vision of social justice and provide powerful motives for just conduct" (ibid.: xvi). What is required, then, is a continuous interplay between empathy and the emotions on the one hand, and rules and procedures on the other:

> We are seeking, overall, the best fit between our considered moral and political judgments and the insights offered by our reading. Reading can lead us to alter some of our standing judgments, but it is also the case that these judgments can cause us to reject some experiences of reading as deforming or pernicious.
>
> (Nussbaum 1995: 10)

This is why cultivating the literary imagination is crucial: "Storytelling and literary imagining are not opposed to rational argument, but can provide essential ingredients in a rational argument" (ibid.: xiii). Writing that her "central subject is the ability to imagine what it is like to live the life of another person who might, given changes in circumstances, be oneself or one of one's loved ones" (ibid.: 5), Nussbaum claims that "the novel determinedly introduces its readers to that which is in a way common and close at hand – but which is often, in its significant strangeness, the object of profound ignorance and emotional refusal" (ibid.: 10). Since "thinking about narrative literature does have the potential to make a contribution to the law in particular, to public reasoning generally" (ibid.: xv), she believes that the literary imagination should be a part of public rationality.

Nussbaum is aware that "our society is full of refusals to imagine one another with empathy and compassion, refusals from which none of us is free" (ibid.: xvii), and that these refusals represent failures of the literary imagination. It might be objected that this shows that there is an incorrigible defect in the imagination, and that it therefore should be abandoned in favor of unemotional and indifferent institutional rules and procedures. Referring to the literary imagination's "ability to imagine nonexistent possibilities, to see one thing as another and one thing in another, to endow a perceived form with a complex life" (ibid.: 4) as "fancy," Nussbaum responds:

> The remedy for that defect seems to be, not the repudiation of fancy, but its more consistent and humane cultivation; not the substitution of impersonal institutional structures for the imagination, but the construction of institutions, and institutional actors, who more perfectly embody, and by institutional firmness protect, the insights of the compassionate institution. We need not and should not rely on the fancy of individuals alone. Institutions themselves should also be informed by "fancy's" insight.
>
> (Ibid.: xviii)

It is for these reasons, Nussbaum argues, that "if we do not cultivate the imagination in this way, we lose, I believe, an essential bridge to social justice. If we give up on 'fancy' we give up on ourselves" (ibid.: xviii). Cultivating the literary imagination, then, is a moral imperative. It enables individuals to imagine and empathize with the conditions of other persons, persons whose lives may be quite different from their own.

The literary imagination also is developed through writing and discussion. It frequently is believed that writing is no more than the externalization, on paper, of internal thoughts. Although it is true that individuals can write thoughts already formulated, writing also creates knowledge, and reasons often are found by writing. Not only do persons write about what they already know, but they produce knowledge as they write, and discover what they think as they write. In this connection, educationalists should be concerned that students develop the ability to discuss issues cogently and to write intelligent, reflective pieces in clear, grammatical English. It is important that students learn to think, in a disciplined way, about books and issues they raise. Part of that discipline consists in being able to analyze, evaluate, and formulate arguments. This involves knowing how to identify basic assumptions, develop a line of reasoning, recognize the steps that lead to a conclusion, and determine whether an argument is sensible. In this way, hopefully, students will develop intellectual curiosity and the competencies to reason logically, evaluate critically, communicate effectively, appreciate aesthetic and creative expressions of humanity, as well as imagine creatively.

A major goal of educationalists should be to enable students to cultivate the imagination. In addition to teaching the required subject matter, educationalists should aim to provide the resources which will enable students to question what passes as common knowledge and accepted wisdom, evaluate their own and others' positions, and formulate new ideas. The imagination is developed as students gain the ability to summarize assigned material, and to write papers in which ideas and arguments are articulated, criticized, defended. Equally important is the ability to think critically about their own beliefs and those of others. Critical thinking consists in understanding several sides of a debate, and seeing both the advantages and limitations of an opinion. Learning to call into question opinions is as crucial as arguing for them. If students only learn to give reasons for opinions already held, they merely are giving rationalizations for prejudices. Students need to learn to think for themselves, defending, criticizing, and articulating their beliefs.

Students should be encouraged to share their questions and observations with the rest of the class, and to engage critically with the material, educationalists, and each other. Through discussion, students will encounter directly differing interpretations of the material, become aware of the history of these views, and be encouraged to articulate their own critical perspectives. In interacting with the material and each other, students will acquire a knowledge and appreciation of themselves, their society, other cultures, and the natural world. This is accomplished by having students meditate on books imaginatively, drawing connections between the material studied in the classroom and concerns arising from their involvement with jobs, families, and community. It this way, students will acquire moral and ethical commitments to their neighbors, society, and the natural world.

The ability to think differently is developed, then, through literature, writing, and discussion, Hopefully, persons will be able to imagine a world in which capitalism's absence is thinkable, and so achievable.[2]

Notes

1 Pam R. Sailors and Norah Martin are thanked for numerous suggestions which led to useful revisions. Preliminary versions were presented to the Conference on Value Inquiry at Central Missouri State University on 23 April 1999, to the Midsouth Philosophy Conference at the University of Memphis on 6 March 1999 (Henry Theriault is thanked for the helpful commentary), and to the Department of Philosophy at Lewis and Clark College on 15 February 1999.
2 Further discussions of these issues may be found in the other chapters in this volume, as well as in Michael Peters' anthology on *Education and the Postmodern Condition* (Peters 1995b).

5 Lyotard as moral educator

A. T. Nuyen

Lyotard may not be an educator in the strict sense of the term. However, most commentators agree that the discussion of pedagogical issues in *The Postmodern Condition* (Lyotard 1984a) and elsewhere is sufficient to earn him the credentials of an educator. In any case, he *was* an instructor in philosophy who taught and inspired many generations of students. What is perhaps harder to justify is the label "moral educator." In what follows I shall try to justify it by showing that there are important and instructive moral lessons to be learned from Lyotard. In particular, I try to show that Lyotard, first, teaches us to identify the moral problem, or the ethical question, of the postmodern condition, second, gives us lessons in moral pragmatics, and third, shows us how to answer the normative question, "Why should I be moral?"

The ethical question

While Lyotard nowhere discusses the moral problem in the context of an ethical theory, the views and arguments he presents in various works do constitute a coherent ethics. I have elsewhere referred to it as "Lyotard's postmodern ethics" (Nuyen 1996a). Admittedly, for many of Lyotard's critics, the phrase "Lyotard's postmodern ethics" is a kind of oxymoron, insofar as ethics is about the right and the just, the good and the obligatory, and insofar as Lyotard advocates a pluralism without universal rules, a postmodernism without "metanarratives."[1] Against Lyotard's critics, it can be shown that there is a line of thought in Lyotard's postmodernism that is decidedly ethical, a line of thought consistent and robust enough to be called an ethics. As in any ethics, there is a clear identification of an ethical problem.

In *The Postmodern Condition*, Lyotard defines "postmodern as incredulity toward metanarratives" (Lyotard 1984a: xxiv). A metanarrative in turn is a "metadiscourse" which contains universal rules and principles to which we can appeal to resolve a dispute that may arise between the "small discourses," or "language games" (*petits récits*), in which different people are engaged. The history of philosophy is replete with metadiscourses "such as the dialectics of Spirit, the hermeneutics of meaning, the emancipation of the rational or working subject, or the creation of wealth" (ibid.: xxiii). Thus, for instance, two theorists engaged in different political discourses may attempt to resolve their dispute by appealing to a metadiscourse concerning "the emancipation of the working subject" (such as Marxism). The appeal to a metadiscourse is an attempt to legitimate one's own discourse. Legitimation, according to Lyotard, is characteristic of modernity. Indeed, he uses the term "*modern* to designate any science that legitimates itself with reference to a metadiscourse of this kind." (ibid.: xxiii). Lyotard's main argument in *The Postmodern Condition* is that the modernist practice of legitimation ultimately fails. This is a familiar argument and I shall not rehearse it here (see Nuyen 1992). It is sufficient to note that the argument leads to the claim that in the postmodern condition, metadiscourses have lost their authority, and it is no longer possible to appeal to rules and principles that apply across discourses. In the postmodern condition, there are no universal rules and principles. There are only language games, or small discourses, each defined by its own set of rules.

In the absence of metadiscourses, a conflict between language games cannot be resolved to the satisfaction of all parties to the conflict. Without universal rules and principles, all that we have are rules and principles internal to each game, or each small discourse. To apply the rules internal to one discourse in the case of a conflict is not to resolve it: it is to allow that discourse to dominate others that are in conflict with it, or to allow it, as Lyotard puts it, to "totalize" the field. Thus, either a conflict remains unresolved, or it is dissolved into a totality dominated by one of the discourses in conflict. Lyotard calls this kind of conflict the differend, defining it as "a case of conflict, between (at least) two parties, that cannot be equitably resolved for lack of a rule of judgment applicable to both arguments" (Lyotard 1988a: xi). If the postmodern condition means the death of metanarratives, then the differend is its effect.

Given the varying degrees of discursive powers, a differend invariably results in one discourse dominating others, in a totality. In such a totality, the losing side suffers what Lyotard calls a *wrong*. The nature of the differend is such that the losing side cannot appeal against the *wrong* because it can only do so in terms of the rules of its own discourse which have no validity within the dominating discourse. In *The Differend* (1988a), Lyotard discusses numerous examples. For instance, the victims of the Holocaust may be said to suffer a wrong in the hands of someone like the revisionist historian Robert Faurisson who denies the existence of gas chambers by sticking to a historical discourse the rules of which effectively silence them. Lyotard describes Faurisson's argument as follows:

> in order for a place to be identified as a gas chamber, the only eyewitness I will accept would be a victim of this gas chamber; now,

according to my opponent, there is no victim that is not dead; otherwise this gas chamber would not be what he or she claims it to be. There is, therefore, no gas chamber.

(Lyotard 1988a: 3–4)

As pointed out above, Lyotard discusses numerous examples of the differend in his book. Confronted with the number of examples making the same point, it is easy to gain the impression that Lyotard is laboring the point. However, Lyotard's intention is clear: he wants to stress the prevalence of wrongs in the postmodern world *and* to make the normative claim that we have to do something about these wrongs, that we cannot let them go unnoticed. In giving us one example after another and in returning again and again to the Holocaust, Lyotard wants to strengthen the normative claim. To repeat, the normative claim is that "[e]very wrong ought to be able to be put into phrases," that "in the differend, something 'asks' to be put into phrases, and suffers from the wrong of not being able to be put into phrases right away" (Lyotard 1988a: 13). Given the ethical demand that wrongs be put into phrases, the postmodern condition throws up an ethical problem: how can wrongs be put into phrases? It is a problem because, as we have seen, the wrong arises in the first place by virtue of the fact that the victim's rules of discourse are not valid, or not recognized, within the totalizing discourse. As Lyotard puts it, the victim's case is *unpresentable* within the dominating discourse. Thus, the ethical problem for postmodernity is how to present the unpresentable, how to "bear witness to differends" (ibid.: 13). Furthermore, Lyotard leaves the reader in no doubt that we have to face this ethical problem with the utmost urgency, that what is at stake is the question of life and death itself. For, what happened to the Jews can happen again: "the question 'Auschwitz' is also the question 'after Auschwitz'?" (ibid.: 101). Indeed, we know that it did happen again under Stalin; we know that after the "extermination (Auschwitz) . . . [was] . . . a sacrificial 'beautiful death' (Stalingrad)" (ibid.: 106).

Lyotard has been most consistent about the ethical demand in the postmodern condition in the various writings since the late seventies, even though the contexts of the separate discussions do not always make it clear that he has in mind the same ethical problem. However, the link is clear enough to be seen, and even the language remains more or less the same throughout. Thus, toward the end of the essay "Answering the question: what is postmodernism?" Lyotard warns us that "we can hear the mutterings of the desire for a return of terror," and urges that what must be done is to "wage a war on totality" and to be "witnesses to the unpresentable" (Lyotard 1984a: 82). In a recent book, *The Inhuman*, Lyotard declares that the question of presenting the unpresentable is "the only one worthy of what is at stake in life and thought in the coming century" (Lyotard 1991c: 127). Lyotard has identified an ethical problem, an urgent one "worthy of what is at stake in life and thought." In the first half of *Just Gaming* (Lyotard and Thébaud 1985), we find anticipated the arguments of *The Postmodern Condition* and *The Differend*. In a claim that is to become the theme of *The Postmodern Condition*, Lyotard says that there is "no meta-language, and by metalanguage, I mean the famous theoretical discourse that is supposed to ground political and ethical decisions that will be taken as the basis of its statements" (Lyotard and Thébaud 1985: 28). Then, anticipating the argument in *The Differend*, Lyotard argues that "language games are not translatable, because, if they were, they would not be language games" (ibid.: 53). Since language games, or small discourses, are not translatable, "to import into a language game a question that comes from another one and to impose it" amounts to "oppression" (ibid.). Given the fact that there is a multiplicity of language games, the ethical problem is how to avoid oppression. Failing to do so gives rise to the problem of injustice, a problem that any ethical theory worth its salt must aim to solve, to resolve. Failing to do so will perpetuate wrongs, such as the wrong suffered by the Jewish people under Nazism, or the wrong suffered by oppressed people everywhere.

What is the lesson from Lyotard? If Lyotard is right, at the ethical core of all conflicts, ranging from conflicts in the school yard leading to bullying to conflicts in the Balkans leading to ethnic cleansing, is the problem of "presenting the unpresentable." When we say that people are talking "at cross purposes," that they are not "on the same wavelength," that they cannot "empathise" with each other and so on, we are in fact referring to the same ethical problem identified by Lyotard. The lesson we should learn from Lyotard is that the problem of presenting the unpresentable can have the greatest ethical consequences. This is an important lesson for moral educators in the postmodern condition.

Moral pragmatics

Lyotard's postmodernism has many different kinds of educational implications. Understandably, educationists have focused on the pedagogical issues thrown up by Lyotard's diagnosis of the legitimation crisis (see Peters 1995b). However, other educational implications are also important. Indeed, some would say that it is much more important to come up with an educational strategy for the moral question. We have seen that for Lyotard the moral question is the problem of presenting the unpresentable in the postmodern condition. But Lyotard does not just give us a diagnosis of the ethical problem in the postmodern condition. In various writings, he also suggests a response to the problem. This response consists of a political strategy and what might be called a reflective strategy. If I am right in thinking that Lyotard has offered us both a reflective strategy and a political strategy for dealing with the *wrongs* of differends, then it follows that to educate for such ethical problems is to educate in both of these aspects. To see Lyotard as a moral educator, we need to examine his political and reflective strategies for dealing with the ethical problem and to draw educational implications from them.

The political strategy can be found in *Just Gaming*. Here, Lyotard offers a strategy to avoid one discourse totalizing the others (Lyotard and Thébaud 1985). The aim of the strategy is to "maximize as much as possible the multiplication of small narratives" (ibid.: 59). Toward this aim, we ought to declare as an injustice the preventing of game playing, and to prohibit any activity that effectively restricts game playing. Lyotard writes: "Absolute injustice would occur if the pragmatics of obligation, that is, the possibility of continuing to play the game of the just, were excluded" (ibid.: 66). What is advocated is similar to the libertarian strategy of prohibiting activities which cause harm to others. Indeed, Lyotard himself describes his position as "libertine or libertarian" (ibid.: 62). Lyotard's conception of injustice allows us to declare unjust, for instance, terrorist activities such as hostage taking, kidnapping, blackmailing, and inflicting terror itself. Terrorism is unjust because it prevents others from playing their games: "The people whom [the terrorist] massacres will no longer be able to play the game of the just and the unjust" (ibid.: 67). To demonstrate the practical power of his conception of injustice, Lyotard claims that we can use it to denounce the role of the Americans in Vietnam and that of the French in Algeria. For they "were doing something that prohibited that the whole of reasonable beings could continue to exist. In other words, the Vietnamese or the Algerians saw themselves being placed in a position where the pragmatics of obligation was forbidden them" (ibid.: 70).

A question arises at this point, one that seems to have escaped Lyotard's notice. It is whether the negative rule about what is unjust, or the non-exclusion rule, is itself coherent. For, in applying it against terrorism, are we not excluding the terrorist from playing his or her terroristic game? Does the rule not preclude its own application? While Lyotard does not seem to be aware of this question, he inadvertently renders it inoperative by his answer to another question, namely: is it sufficient just to have a negative rule about what is unjust? Should such a rule not be based on, or grounded in, some positive conception of justice? Lyotard himself puts the question this way: "Can we have a politics without the Idea of justice?" (ibid.: 76). Faced with this question, Lyotard admits that he hesitates between two positions: the "pagan position" of not grounding the negative rule, regarding it as something we have made up as we went along, and the "Kantian position" of regarding it as something grounded in a Kantian regulative Idea such as the Idea of justice as the proliferation of games, or the maximization of games. Taking the "pagan position" means that we regard the maximum "multiplication of small narratives" simply as a conventional rule. The problem with the "pagan position" is that there is nothing that prevents the society from making up different rules, for example, a rule that accepts rather than rules out terrorism: "A rule by convention would require that one accept . . . even Nazism. After all, since there was near unanimity upon it, from where could one judge that it is not just?" (ibid.: 74). Thus, a politics that rules out terrorism is not possible without some Kantian Idea of justice.

With the Kantian position, we have a "regulator, that is a safekeeper of the pragmatics of obligation" (ibid.: 76). However, how can we take the Kantian position without being committed to the Kantian metadiscourse? In the end, Lyotard settles for a modified Kantian position in which the Idea of justice (as the proliferation of games) is posited as merely a *regulative* idea rather than a determinate idea, that is, as an idea not itself grounded in any transcendental reality, any noumenality, or any Kantian finality. In particular, we are not to posit along with it any Kantian totality such as the Kingdom of Ends. Rather, we act *as if* we are dealing with a community of rational beings who have come to accept the rationality of the idea of maximizing game playing. With this as a regulative idea, we have a solution to the question not noticed by Lyotard, namely how to apply the negative rule against terrorism without contradiction. We can say to the terrorist that his or her game is excluded because it minimizes rather than maximizes game playing. It is true that in applying the rule against terrorism, we exclude it, but there is no inconsistency because the rule is not applied for its own sake but rather for the sake of the regulative Idea of maximum game playing. Terrorism is ruled out because it is destructive of all other games; indeed, it is destructive of terrorism itself, as one terrorist group invariably tries to exclude other terrorist groups. By contrast, in excluding terrorism, the only thing we exclude is terrorism.

What we can learn from Lyotard's political strategy is that it must be part of the aim of education to instill in the learner the idea that we must accept certain restrictive rules and regulations as necessary for maximum game playing. What the strategy implies is that there is a need for those elements of education that strengthen the idea of citizenship and the idea of acceptable and unacceptable behavior. One problem frequently encountered here is the resistance to rule-following, which is typically seen as restrictive and undermining individuality and subjectivity. However, what we can also learn from Lyotard is that such rules and regulations do not necessarily undermine individuality and subjectivity, because they are regulative rather than determinant. Being regulative with the aim of ensuring maximum game playing, inventive individuals would be free to vary rules and regulations, thus inventing new games. Indeed, to take Lyotard seriously is to make it part of the aim of education to encourage inventiveness. One effective way to prevent one game totalizing the field is to have a proliferation of games.

In addition to the political strategy I have outlined, we can discern in Lyotard's writings what I call a reflective strategy. To guard against totalization, we need to reflect on what is not there in the games we play, what is not presented in the familiar discourses. Just because something is not there, not presented, does not mean that it does not exist, or has no right to exist. Silence does not mean absence or irrelevance. The failure to reflect in this way amounts to taking one's own discourses, or at best all the existing discourses, as representing the totality of all there is. While this is not yet the terror of one totalizing grand narrative, it is what sets the course toward such terror. Thus, the war against totality is the struggle to raise and maintain the consciousness of what is not presented in the existing discourses; it is to present the unpresentable. The first crucial step is to develop the consciousness of the unpresentable. Since it cannot be put into phrases, we have to develop a *feeling* for it. This feeling can be generated if we *reflect* on our thinking. This feeling is a reflective judgment. "Reflective judgment" is a phrase used by Kant in the Third Critique to refer to an aesthetic judgment which is reflective, because it arises when thinking reflects on itself. It is not surprising that Lyotard turns to Kant for insights for a strategy to develop the consciousness of the unpresentable.

In the judgment of the sublime, thinking reflects on the fact that the imagination is inadequate to the demand of reason, and that reason is able to overcome this inadequacy. The sensuous resources of the imagination are inadequate to present rational ideas (such as the idea of God) in sensuous intuitions. Such ideas are said by Kant to be "indemonstrable." Reason overcomes this inadequacy by encouraging the imagination to come up with metaphors and symbols to represent its ideas. The inadequacy of imagination revealed by thinking gives rise to the feeling of displeasure, and the overcoming of this inadequacy gives rise to the feeling of pleasure. The pleasure mediated by displeasure is what Kant calls the feeling of the sublime. This feeling represents the triumph of reason. However, it does not mean that the imagination is totally subordinated to reason. Indeed, when reason comes to conceptualize the metaphors and symbols invented by the imagination, or what Kant calls "aesthetic ideas," reason discovers that no concepts are adequate to them. As Kant puts it, aesthetic ideas are "inexponible." The inexponible is the other side of the indemonstrable. What reason does then is to encourage the imagination to come up with further aesthetic ideas to represent what it has already invented. What Lyotard finds significant in all this is that indemonstrable concepts are unpresentable in sensuous images, whereas inexponible aesthetic ideas are unpresentable in concepts. Yet the mind finds a way of presenting the unpresentable. If the ethical problem is to find ways of presenting the unpresentable, then the way to respond to the problem is to learn from Kant.

From Lyotard's explorations of Kant's *The Critique of Judgment* (Kant 1964), two lessons can be drawn. As Lyotard explains it in his *Lessons on the Analytic of the Sublime* (Lyotard 1994), Kant's account of the sublime can be taken as an account of the presentation in thought of the unpresentable ideas of reason. Thus, in the feeling of the sublime, we have a solution to the problem of presenting the unpresentable. Learning from Lyotard, we can say that there is a need for inculcating in the learner the feeling for the sublime. Elsewhere I refer to such educational programs as education in sublimation (Nuyen 1996b). But the mind is able not only to present unpresentable (that is, undemonstrable) ideas of reason, but also to present unpresentable (that is, inexponible) aesthetic ideas. This is where the imagination comes to the foreground. I have argued elsewhere that to deal effectively with the ethical problem of the postmodern condition, we need to construct a program of education for imaginative knowledge (Nuyen 1997). The role of the imagination has been widely recognized by educators (see Greene 1995). In moral education in particular, the imagination has long been recognized as a vital ingredient in moral development. For instance, it would be hard to imagine a better way of teaching the Golden Rule, "Do unto others," and its negative form, "Do not do unto others," without asking the learner to use his or her imagination, thus imagining what it would be like to be in the other person's shoes. However, it is Lyotard who has drawn our attention to the fact that a great deal more is at stake, and hence to the urgency of developing the imaginative powers to their fullest possible extent.

The normative question

By "the normative question" I mean the age-old question "Why should I be moral?" To ask this question is to ask for a justification of morality's claims on us, or for a justification of the obligations of morality. The first systematic attempt to answer this question was made nearly 2,500 years ago by Plato when it was put to him by Glaucon. The fact, if it is a fact, that there is still no satisfactory answer to this question after 2,500 years, that moral skepticism, even nihilism, is still a serious threat, is, to paraphrase Kant, a scandal of moral philosophy. As if out of fear of an outbreak of the scandal, or perhaps in an attempt to contain it, many philosophers have recently revisited the normative question and tried to answer it. Notable efforts include Michael Smith's *The Moral Problem* (1995) and Christine Korsgaard's *Sources of Normativity* (1996). I believe that Lyotard's postmodern ethics constitutes just as good an answer, if not a better one, to the normative question.[2] The frequency with which the normative question arises in the educational context is notorious. Teachers (and parents) cannot help but notice the persistence and stubbornness of the question "Why should I do that?" The ability to supply an answer to the question is the mark of a moral educator.

As pointed out in the first section of this paper, Lyotard's view is that in the postmodern condition, we can no longer appeal to a metanarrative to justify universal rules, including moral rules. But it does not follow that there are no rules to follow, no obligations to be had. For instead of metanarratives we have the *petits récits*, the little games, the small discourses, each with its own rules. To play a game entails obeying the rules of the game. Indeed, it may be said that a game player is committed not just to the rules of the game but also to the kind of behavior that is beneficial to the game, or at least to the avoidance of behavior that is destructive of the game. There is a parallel here between Lyotard's *petits récits* and MacIntyre's "practices" (MacIntyre 1981). Drawing from MacIntyre, it may be argued that a game player is committed to practicing the virtues that are good for the game, or at least to avoiding the vices that are destructive of the game. It is likely that any game whatsoever must include some rules that are moral in the traditional sense. For instance, the rule against cheating seems necessary for any game, for the simple reason that no game can meaningfully be played if cheating is rampant. Also, there are certain minimum obligations that a game player must take on, such as the obligation to respect any legitimate move made by another player of the game, or to respect other persons as players of the game. With this in mind, we can justify a whole host of rules traditionally seen as moral rules. For instance, we may say that insofar as one wants to play the marriage game, one ought to be faithful to one's spouse because cheating is destructive of the game. (If the partners cheat openly in a marriage then what we have is not a marriage as we understand it: it may be called an "open marriage" or whatever, but that is a different game. Even so, unfaithfulness is acceptable in an "open marriage" only because it does not amount to cheating in the context of that game.)

The first step in answering the normative question, then, is to say that each game has its own rules and to play it we must obey its rules. Some of these rules are moral in the traditional sense of the word. The rules are binding but the real source of normativity, of the force of obligation, lies in the agent himself or herself who chooses to play a certain game, thus chooses to play by the very rules that define the game. One ought to do certain things because that is how the game is played, just as a member of a club ought to observe club rules. However, the moral skeptic is bound to ask: why can't I choose not to play any game at all, thus choosing to follow no rules and to place myself under no obligations whatsoever? Unfortunately for the skeptic, not playing any game at all is not an intelligible option, indeed not really a choice. For simply to exist, to be, is to play some game or other. Ultimately, the skeptic's choice is the Shakespearean choice between to be or not to be, the choice between to exist or to commit suicide. One is here reminded of the Sartrean paradox that to exist is to be condemned to be free. To press home the point against the skeptic, we can remind him or her that simply to raise the normative question, to ask "Why should I be moral?" is already to be playing a game: the game of communication. As such, the skeptic is already committed to obeying certain rules, to accepting certain obligations. As Habermas has pointed out, there is such a thing as *communicative ethics* (Habermas 1984b, 1987). Of course, one need not accept all the communicative rules stipulated by Habermas – Lyotard certainly would not – but there is no escape from the fact that there are rules and obligations. For instance, the skeptic must, among other things, be sincere in asking the normative question (or else we have no reason to take it seriously), and be committed to respect the answer that is given whether or not it is an acceptable answer, that is, not to treat what the respondent has to say as, for example, meaningless noises or the babbling of a deranged person.

What I said earlier constitutes only a partial answer to the normative question. Before completing the answer, it is useful to note that so far the postmodern position is not all that different from, say, Korsgaard's (1996). For Korsgaard, the source of normativity lies in the agent's own laws formulated as part of his or her choice of a practical identity. Again, it is not open to the skeptic to choose not to have any identity at all, for to exist is to assume some identity or other. The idea of assuming a practical identity is close enough to Lyotard's idea of playing games. However, Korsgaard's position is vulnerable to the objection that there is really no normative force at all in the laws of one's own making, because what one makes one can unmake. As one of Korsgaard's critics has pointed out, one "might think that, if you are the author of the law, then it *cannot* bind you. For how can it have authority over you when you have authority over it?" (Cohen 1996: 167). Lyotard's postmodern view I outlined earlier is not vulnerable to this objection. The reason is that one does not have authority over the rules and laws of a game. This does not mean that such rules and laws are sacrosanct, or written in stone. They can be changed, but never by any one game player, and bearing in mind that a large enough change will redefine the game. For any one game player, the rules of the game, its ethics, are binding until such time as he or she *together with all other game players* decides to change them.

Another similarity with Korsgaard's view is also worth noting. For Korsgaard, to exist as a human being is to reflect on one's desires with the view of justifying them to oneself. One who merely acts on first-order desires without reflecting on them is a "wanton." Lyotard too speaks of the need to adopt a reflective attitude. As we have seen, he wants us to reflect on the games we play and to hear in a moment of reflection the unpresentable voice of the other. Both Korsgaard and Lyotard regard reflection as an essential pre-ethical attitude. However, it is doubtful whether Korsgaard's kind of reflection will lead to the adoption of universal moral laws. She argues that it does, on the grounds that reflection takes place in the framework of human reason which is universal. The trouble is that thieves, murderers and terrorists too can and do reflect on their desires. Indeed, the most dangerous among them are the most reflective. As another of Korsgaard's critics has put it, the "Serbs have what I can see are quite good reasons *for them* to act as they do . . . [and we] understand perfectly well why certain groups of Muslims might want to kill Rushdie . . ." (Geuss 1996: 197). Clearly then, reflection alone is not sufficient. This comparison with Korsgaard points to the fact that there is a weaker but no less urgent skeptical normative question, namely, why should I be moral in a way expected by others? The answer to the normative question is not complete unless we can answer this question as well. Unlike Korsgaard's position, there are resources in Lyotard's postmodern ethics, as I constructed it, to provide the complete answer.

As we saw earlier, Lyotard's ethics has a rule against behavior that denies others the "pragmatics of obligation," or behavior that prevents others from playing their games, such as terroristic and murderous behavior. The question is how we can justify this rule. Again as we saw earlier, Lyotard is content to rest the case for such a rule on the regulative idea of maximum game playing. However, we still have to justify this regulative idea. For it is open to terrorists and murderers to claim that they do not see the desirability of maximum game playing, or the undesirability of preventing some people from playing their games. What Lyotard needs is an argument to show that the rule of just gaming is binding on all game players. I think a plausible one can be constructed. Notice that instead of relying on human reason and placing one's hope on its universal ability to lead us all into the Kingdom of Ends, postmodern ethics stresses the connection between game playing and observing the rules of a game. The source of normativity is not located in some mysterious and sacred place, such as autonomous human rationality. Rather, it is located right there in the very games that we are playing. Instead of the Kingdom of Ends, what we have is a community of game players. With this in mind, it is possible to show that the binding force of the rule of just gaming, its normativity, lies in the very idea of game playing itself, and that for there to be game playing at all, certain games must be ruled out and certain other games should be encouraged.

In arguing for the rules of just gaming, what we need is to establish the claim that the rules of just gaming are the *necessary* meta-rules of game playing itself. In other words, the rules of just gaming guarantee the conditions of possibility of game playing. Put this way, the claim establishes itself insofar as to play any game is to be committed to the possibility of game playing. A murderer, in playing the murderous game, is already committed to the possibility of game playing. The more terrorists and murderers insist on playing their games, the more they show their commitment to game playing. What is it to be committed to game playing? At the very least, it is to accept the conditions that make game playing itself possible, or in other words to accept the rules of just gaming. To put the matter differently, it can be said that to be a game player at all is to play the game, or meta-game, of game playing, the rules of which are none other than the rules of just gaming. A game player is committed to observing these rules by virtue of being a game player. If this is so then certain games must be ruled out because playing them breaks the rules of just gaming. Such games are impossible games in the context of game playing. What games break the rules of just gaming? Arguably they are, as

Lyotard puts it in *Just Gaming*, the games that prohibit "that the whole of reasonable beings could continue to exist," games that place "the whole of reasonable beings . . . in a position where the pragmatics of obligation [is] forbidden them" (Lyotard and Thébaud 1985: 70), in other words, games that prevent others from being game players, such as terroristic and murderous games. We have seen that a murderer cannot complain that the rules of just gaming are inconsistent because they prevent him or her from playing the murderous game. This is so because such rules do not prevent the murderer from being a game player as such, only from being a murderer, whereas by contrast the murderous game prevents others from being game players insofar as it prohibits that others "could continue to exist."

If it is accepted that to be a game player at all is to play the meta-game of game playing then it also follows that Lyotard's "presenting the unpresentable" is a postmodern moral imperative. This is so because not presenting the unpresentable, not bearing witness to it, just is to privilege one's own discourse, to accept that it alone has authority, that it constitutes the totality. It is to ignore the possibility of there being claims intelligible only in different rules of discourse, thus effectively preventing "reasonable beings" from being game players. It is worse than marginalizing them: it is placing them "in a position where the pragmatics of obligation [is] forbidden them." To be a game player is to be committed to the rules of just gaming, and this means to have a pragmatic obligation to game playing generally. This obligation translates into the obligation to bear witness and to present the unpresentable, to wage a "war on totality." One could go further and say that there is an obligation to be a virtuous game player in making every effort to entrench the conditions of possibility of game playing, in strengthening one's commitment to the rules of just gaming. Deepening one's sensitivity to the unpresentable is one way of becoming a virtuous game player. Becoming less dogmatic about one's own discourses is another. If I am right in my reading of Lyotard, his postmodern ethics can be said to provide a plausible answer to the normative question. In summary, the answer goes something like this. If the skeptic who asks "Why should I be moral?" is *really* interested in the answer, then we can say that he or she is already a game player and as such should obey the rules of the game. He or she may be playing many other games and as such should obey the rules of such games. Some of the rules are moral in the traditional sense. Also, to be a game player is to be playing the game of game playing, hence to be committed to the rules of game playing, namely, the rules of just gaming. This is why one should not engage in certain acts, such as murderous and terroristic acts, and why one should cultivate certain virtues, such as being sensitive to the unpresentable. The alternative is not to be a game player at all, which is equivalent to not existing. As for those skeptics who are not really interested in our answer, who are like

Pontius Pilate who asked "What is truth?" and then turned his back and walked away, our answer will not have any effect. But then, their question is not really a question at all.

I have argued that Lyotard has a coherent ethics. From his postmodern ethics, important moral lessons, as well as practical lessons for moral education, can be drawn. If I am right, Lyotard is a moral educator.

Notes

1 Habermas compares postmodernists such as Lyotard with avant-gardists who revolt "against the normalizing functions of tradition, . . . rebelling against all that is normative" (Habermas 1984b: 5).
2 For details see Nuyen 1998a.

6 The sublime face of just education

Pradeep A. Dhillon

> And so, when the question of what justice consists in is raised, the answer is: "It remains to be seen in each case," and always in humor, but also in worry, because one is never certain that one has been just, or that one can ever be just.
>
> (Lyotard and Thébaud 1985: 99)

I choose this sentence as a sketch of justice drawn by lines of skepticism and romanticism. The realm of education demands our awareness, as teachers and students, of the need to judge while remembering the unevenness of lives and fortunes, in order that the hopes of others should not wither. Such awareness is to be played out in a world where our knowledge of all possible situations and events, and of those we share that knowledge with, is vital to the success of our own endeavors and those for whom we are responsible. Yet such knowing is plagued with uncertainty. We are called on to judge blind: in darkness. Laughter and worry haunt our judgments.

Jean-François Lyotard's discussions of justice present nodal points at which seemingly benign assumptions underlying practices of fairness, or more subtle forms of contractual justice, emerge darkly and impose strains on liberal theory. Like that of John Rawls, Lyotard's thinking on justice requires paying attention to the institutional practices, and social interactions, that structure the experience of justice. In other words, the focus is on the rule-governed activities, "the offices and roles, the rights and duties, penalties and defenses, which give educational activities their structure" (Rawls 1999a: 190).

Explications of those occasions when we are called on to act justly reveal a dilemma between theory and practice. If we accept that there are no universal rules or principles of justice we sacrifice consistency. Giving priority to consistency we might be unjust by refusing the particularities of moral experience in favor of the ambitions of deliberative authority. Either choice imposes large costs. The broad question here can be framed thus: not only are we called on to live in an uncertain world, how are we to live in a groundless world? This question, raised within the context of just education, is about being concerned not only about how to be just in an uncertain world, but rather about how to judge in decency at all. In this essay I suggest that such questioning leads us to take up just education in a manner which respects the rigor of philosophical discourse but is alert to its demands on aesthetic sensibilities. I turn our attention to the ways in which Lyotard's emphasis on the analytic of narrativity persuades us to look again at justice in relation to liberal education. This is the central concern of this essay.

I

Modern theories of justice, particularly those informed by liberalism, assume the following shared values. First, there exist conditions of equality between persons acting within institutions. Second, societies are well-ordered to the extent they share a public sense of justice, but this need not necessarily exist under conditions of social harmony. Third, the procedures of justice are formulated and universally accepted by those who agree to exercise their liberties within these procedural limits. Fourth, individuals are educated to develop a sense of justice, such that they possess a moral and rational disposition which helps them consider a just society as a value. Fifth, individuals are educated to know the laws which govern them; and finally, sixth, individuals are educated to possess the understanding necessary for their full and free participation in such a system. The procedures of justice are enacted through institutional practices. As examples of practices, Rawls offers us "games and rituals, trials and punishment, markets and systems of property" (1999a: 190).

Lyotard shares Rawls's sense of the need to develop an institutional theory of justice in capitalist contexts not marked by social harmony. For all their differences they are arguably both thinkers within the tradition of liberalism. Nevertheless, they stand apart on important points. The central problem of our times as posed by Lyotard is to be understood in terms of:

> 1) the impossibility of avoiding conflicts (the impossibility of indifference) and 2) the absence of a universal genre of discourse to regulate them (or, if you prefer, the inevitable partiality of the judge) to find, if not what can legitimate judgment (the "good" linkage), then at least how to save the honor of thinking.
>
> (Lyotard 1988a: xii)

Like Rawls, Lyotard does not presume conditions of social harmony. In contrast to Rawls his focus is on the impossibility of a contractual consensus since so many – immigrants, children, Third World women – live outside the "idiom" of such a contractual process. We continue to live in a world racked by conflict from which of necessity we cannot turn away.

Like Rawls, Lyotard, preserves a certain metaphysics of persons. In his view, we do not live in a world of Hobbesian self-interested prudence – such prudence would be undermined by our inability to remain indifferent. Furthermore, it is not the Kantian Idea of freedom based in Reason, the practical-moral realm, which informs the Rawlsian idea of the republican social contract, that motivates Lyotard's thinking on justice. Rather, it is the Kant of the Third Critique in which aesthetic judgment, especially as it moves through the sublime, directly presents a glimpse of universality. This requirement for intersubjectivity that Kant places on aesthetic judgment makes possible decent, if not truly just, pedagogy. It is this presupposition of human goodness, of the ability to imagine ourselves in a world we share with others in conjunction with the will to power within us, that creates lived situations of continual conflict and yet, because we are sentient ("the impossibility of indifference"), obligations. This condition is exacerbated by this historical moment which refuses appeals to some overarching value as a reflex of historical structures of authority, even as it presents conditions of necessary contact through globalization and the durable structures of the state. Lyotard is not offering nihilism or some kind of passivity in activity. Through a turn to reflective judgment, he points out the responsibilities we have as teachers to attend to our acts of thinking. Such a pedagogical move presupposes thinking as action. In other words, in these times, thinking itself must become reflexively ethical. Such thinking is not in opposition to action, as we shall see, but is itself a form of action.

In "Justice as Fairness: Political Not Metaphysical" (1999b) John Rawls defends his position against criticisms regarding the metaphysical presuppositions which yield a perhaps indefensible view of persons. In Michael Sandel's view, Rawls's theory does entail an imaginary metaphysics of persons:

> The conditions of the original position cannot be so immune from actual human circumstances that just any assumptions producing attractive principles of justice would do. Unless the premises of such principles bear some resemblance to the condition of creatures discernibly human, the success of the equilibrium is, to that extent, undermined. If we could match our convictions about justice only by appealing to premises that struck us as eccentric or outlandish or metaphysically extreme, we would rightly be led to question the convictions those principles happened to fit.
>
> (Sandel 1982: 43)

As already discussed, and as also pointed out by Charles Altieri (1989) among others, Lyotard's views can be shown to share many of the concerns and features of the more subtle contractual theory of justice provided by John Rawls. He stands apart from Rawls on two key issues: first, by taking the linguistic turn, and second, by making obligation – a moral response to suffering that rests in feeling, often regarded as foreign to liberal theories of justice – the key concern. The first turn provides the fulcrum which raises the literary, aesthetic dimension of just education. The second helps us make sense of the significance of the Kantian sublime for Lyotard's thinking on justice. In so doing, he shows the significance of aesthetics in the practice of decent judgment in educational practice.

While neither Sandel nor Rawls attends to the literary in their debate, narrativity lies at its heart. Sandel's criticism turns on two kinds of narrativity: the imaginary, or the fictional, and the anthropological. That is, Rawls lays out a theory of justice which is circular – since his theory requires that we imagine a just original position in order to develop a theory of justice – and removed from the ways in which people are and the conditions within which they live their lives. Nevertheless, in making this criticism Sandel himself presupposes an idealized relation between how the world is and what we can say about it. This turn to language in thinking about justice – a turn to inhabiting a world of representations which is prefigured in Kant and made explicit in Wittgenstein – is the fulcrum on which Lyotard's philosophy turns. The choice then seems to lie not between the real and the ideal, but rather between one kind of narrative and another.

In the *Philosophical Investigations* Wittgenstein writes this:

> It was true to say that our considerations could not be scientific ones. . . . And we may not advance any kind of theory. There must not be anything hypothetical in our considerations. We must do away with all *explanation*, and description alone must take its place.
>
> (Wittgenstein 1997: para. 109)

I do not wish to enter the considerable debate, the contours of which are well presented by David Pears (1995) and Howard Wettstein (1995), around the turn to naturalism suggested in this passage. However, it is not so controversial to read this passage such that description is seen as the proffering of examples, or cases. The doing of philosophy through examples is offered as an alternative to theory building. Literature, as experiential narrative, is useful in making explicit the tension between the need for principles or rules and the demands particular experience places on the moral practice of judgment. More importantly, literature, like ethnography, offers one way of determining validity in educational discourse. Lyotard clearly suggests such an approach. It allows us to make the ostensive gesture, offer the case, against which philosophical claims can be tested (Lyotard 1988a: 29). Furthermore, to follow Wittgenstein through on this: it is not enough to say that we, as philosophers of education, should argue through example. The examples themselves must be carefully chosen – they must be accurate.

Shakespeare's description of the adjudication between Shylock, "the

Jew" – the outsider – and Antonio, a member of the dominant group in the *polis* of Venice, serves well for taking up the philosophical question of just education. *The Merchant of Venice* offers narrative particularity even as the details of its case are widely familiar. It provides a shared ground against which to explicate and evaluate Lyotard's discussion of justice: especially the turn to Kantian aesthetics and the sublime.

II

Lyotard's Wittgensteinian turn to language, like that of Stanley Cavell (1990), brings the dramaturgical nature of justice in practice into sharp relief. Disputes, even the differend, can take place only within a space that has enough shared properties to permit an encounter. The court-room, as Idea, is this theatrical space. The legal universe is prior to the encounter between the phrases of the participants in the particular encounter. It is the condition which permits the encounter of the phrases in dispute. It, too, is presented in language, as I have already shown: transcendental, within the context, and not empirical. Within dominant liberal discourse, this universe is presented as protected space: protected from the power relations which define interaction within the wider *polis*. It is also presented in the moment such that its location in the temporal, its narrative, is frozen. It is suggested that this carving-out and setting apart from broader spatio-temporal social rhythms and relations, following contractual protocols of jurisdiction, enables fair judgments. Thus, courts of law stand above the individuals who live within the institutions of the city.

Antonio's pleas for mercy fall on Shylock's deaf ears. Salerio, a friend of Antonio, suggests Antonio request the Duke of Venice to intervene in his behalf. Antonio responds:

> The duke cannot deny the course of law:
> For the commodity that strangers have
> With us in Venice, if it be denied,
> Will much impeach the justice of the state,
> Since that the trade and profit of the city
> Consisteth of all nations.
> (Shakespeare, *The Merchant of Venice.* Act III, sc. iii, 26–30)

Shylock is well aware of his rights and claims to the courts of Venice, and cognizant too of his vulnerability since he is an "outsider," a Jew. It is to this end, as Salerio informs Bassanio and Portia at Belmont, that,

> He plies the duke, at morning and at night,
> And doth impeach the freedom of the state
> If they deny him justice.
> (Ibid.: Act III, sc. ii, 289–91)

In other words, both the Duke and Shylock depend on the court-room as a place within which power is neutralized and only the protocols of judgment, mutually agreed upon, are practiced rigorously to adjudicate the case. And so we learn that the courts of Venice are set up to mete out justice to all. Everyone, regardless of his or her social position, has ways of addressing and redressing wrongs. And Shylock expects nothing more nor less than the assurance that such will be the practice. The Duke by refusing to intervene, thus putting himself above the law, though it means the death of his friend, honors the law of the city since not to do so would be to curtail the "freedom of the state." Antonio knows of the Duke's efforts in his behalf, but accepts that "no lawful means" can carry him out of the situation in which he stands to lose his life. Therefore, he expresses his willingness "To suffer with a quietness of spirit/ The very tyranny and rage" (ibid.: Act IV, sc. i, 13–14) of Shylock. Thus have all three submitted to the process of contractual justice which ensures civic freedom in the *polis*.

The Duke pleads with Shylock one last time asking for a "gentle answer." Shylock's response invokes the proprieties of personal property: freedom to use his property in any way he chooses and to use it in a manner which is no different from that of other members of the *polis*.

> You'll ask me why I rather choose to have
> A weight of carrion flesh than to receive
> Three thousand ducats. I'll not answer that,
> But say it is my humor, Is't answered?
>
> (Ibid.: Act IV, sc. i, 41–4)

He will use his money any way he wants; he could, if he so fancied, pay ten thousand ducats to have a rat banished from his house! That is, Shylock does not feel compelled in any way to give a reason for his continuing to pursue a suit in which he will certainly lose money – three thousand ducats. It is his to lose. He will have his bond.

Furthermore, Shylock insists on the use of his personal property following the same norms, the proprieties, of use that apply to all the inhabitants of Venice. In making the case for equality in use of personal property, Shylock invokes an excellent and subtle example. It is excellent since it is so accurate to the logic of the argument, and subtle since it brings into focus the unequal regard with which different forms of human life are held within the Venetian *polis*. He cries,

> You have among you many a purchased slave,
> Which like your asses and your dogs and your mules,
> you use in abject and in slavish parts.
>
> (Ibid.: Act IV, sc. i, 91–3)

It is the institution of private property and rules of trade – "because you bought them" – which permits such treatment of humans. He, Shylock, could certainly not say

> Let them be free! Marry them to your heirs!
> Why sweat they under burdens? Let their beds
> Be made soft as yours, and let their palates
> Be seasoned with such viands.
>
> (Ibid.: Act IV, sc. 1, 95–9)

And if he did make such a request more than likely the response would be: "The slaves are ours" (Act IV, sc.i, 100). That is, the Christian members of the Venetian city would invoke the rights of ownership. He too has bought human flesh, owns it, and will have it and do with it as he sees fit. In so doing Shylock exposes the nature of the normative dimension which lurks beneath Rawls's seemingly neutral description of "systems of property" as constitutive of the practices that are the basis of our institutions. If Shylock is denied what he has paid for,

> fie upon your law, There is no force in the decrees of Venice.
> I stand for judgment. Answer: Shall I have it?
>
> (Ibid.: Act IV, sc. i, 102–4)

That is, he puts Venice, the free and equal state, itself on trial. Shylock fears no judgment; he has done no wrong. He is merely asking to receive what he has paid for.

During the trial itself Bassanio turns to the Duke and beseeches him to wrest the law to his authority: "to do a great right, do a little wrong" (ibid.: Act IV, sc.i, 225). But Portia, as the lawyer, sternly rebukes Bassanio thus:

> It must not be. There is no power in Venice
> Can alter a decree established;
> 'Twill be recorded for a precedent
> And many an error by the same example
> Will rush into the state. It cannot be.
>
> (Ibid.: Act IV, sc. i, 226–30)

In other words, Portia invokes the criterion of consistency in the practice of justice. This runs contrary to the case-by-case approach advanced by Lyotard, through pointing to the linking of justice to morality which goes back to Wittgenstein and Aristotle within the western tradition. In Lyotard's words, "But if he [the judge] can and indeed must (he has no choice), judge case by case, it is precisely because each situation is singular, something Aristotle is very sensitive to" (Lyotard and Thébaud 1985: 27).

At every stage of the trial there is a call for mercy. But the law, as it stands, would honor the bond by which Antonio forfeits a pound of his flesh, "nearest his heart." Shylock, refuses each appeal to mercy, sharpening his knife on the sole of his shoe and keeping the balance ready to receive the pound of flesh. In the name of mercy, Portia calls on Shylock to have a surgeon ready to stop Antonio's wounds, "lest he bleed to death" (Shakespeare, *The Merchant of Venice*: Act IV, sc. i, 225). Shylock asks if such charity is mentioned in the bond. It is not. And so Antonio prepares to die, bidding farewell to his friends, and Portia declares judgment:

> A pound of that same merchant's flesh is thine:
> The law allows it and the court awards it.
>
> (Ibid.: Act IV, sc.i, 225)

But wait. The bond does not give Shylock "a jot of blood." The bond expressly says " a pound of flesh."

> Take then thy bond, take thou thy pound of flesh,
> But in the cutting it, if thou dost shed
> One drop of Christian blood, thy lands and goods
> Are by the laws of Venice confiscate
> Unto the state of Venice.
>
> (Ibid.: Act IV, sc.i, 325)

Thus Portia, through a maneuver which might be thought brilliant within the game of law but falls far from the idea of justice, uses his refusal to respond to the repeated calls for mercy and the law, now one that protects Christians from the attacks of aliens, against Shylock. Mercy is no longer a transcendent value: it has become hostage to the legal game of the Christian majority of Venice. This is a game whose rules have been learned by Shylock, but in a language that is not his.

The Jew's plaint, a call to the court for a resolution of difference, is become differend. He is to become victim. As we follow this turn of events, Shakespeare shows us how the state of affairs which lies outside the space of law now creeps in, making this space contiguous with, and not apart from, the social relations which obtain within the wider *polis*. We are reminded through the device of personal asides that the lawyer, the judge, in this scene is Portia, betrothed to Bassanio. In Belmont where she first heard of the case it was made quite clear that, were Antonio to lose his life in forfeit to the bond he had signed to procure funds, this would permit Bassanio to pursue his courtship of Portia. Portia is aware of the deep love Bassanio bears Antonio, and that theirs would be a hollow marriage if Shylock were successful in pushing the case to its bitter end. Her case is well prepared. Sternly, she reminds Antonio,

For as thou urgest justice, be assured
Thou shalt have more justice than thou desir'st.

(Ibid.: Act IV, sc.i, 330)

Thus, through a close and literal reading of the law, following a narrow and hard hermeneutics, it is Shylock who is now put on trial defending his life.

It is enacted in the laws of Venice,
If it be proved against an alien
That by direct or indirect attempts
He seek the life of any citizen
The party 'gainst the which he doth contrive
Shall seize one half his goods; the other half
Comes to the privy coffer of the state,
And the offender's life lies in the mercy
Of the Duke only, 'gainst all other voice.

(Ibid.: Act IV, sc.i, 362–72)

Now judgment stands against Shylock: "Thou hast contrived against the very life of the defendant, and thou hast incurred the danger formerly by me rehearsed" (ibid.: Act IV, sc.i, 375–8). "Portia," as the arbiter of justice within this space so carefully protected from the power networks of the wider social system, now turns into "Portia," close party to Antonio, Bassanio and Gratiano – the defendant and his friends – and inscribes the dominant phrase within the drama of the court.

If Shylock's obdurate stand against mercy brought cruelty and suffering to the drama, Portia's turn ushers in tyranny. Mercy is no longer the shining transcendental value which would soften the violence: in this courtroom it is rendered base coin. Violence is not averted. Portia has ensured that the violence turns against the figure of the outsider: Shylock is utterly defeated. He loses everything but his life, which is not his as natural right but given him through the morality of the Duke. The gravest loss, that of property, renders him completely defenseless as a Jew within the Christian Venetian state. In other words, through the trial scene and the inversions within it Shakespeare not only shows the need for having a rule or principle-based approach to justice, but also marks the way it can be used to the ends of those who have the power and intention to turn it so. For Shakespeare, judgment is contextual. As Portia remarks to Nerrissa on their return to the harmony of the gardens of Belmont:

The crow doth sing as sweetly as the lark
When neither is attended, and I think
The nightingale, if she should sing by day
When every goose is cackling, would be thought

No better a musician than a wren,
How many things by season seasoned are
To their right praise and true perfection.

(Ibid.: Act V, sc.i, 110–5)

Shylock is as noble a character as Antonio. If Antonio stands as an exemplar for friendship, it is through Shylock's character that we are shown how hatred is socially constructed. Furthermore, it is Shylock who gives us the most moving plea for human rights within the Western literary tradition.

I am a Jew. Hath not a Jew eyes? Hath not a Jew hands, organs, dimensions, senses, affections, passions? – fed with the same food, hurt with the same weapons, subject to the same diseases, healed by the same means, warmed and cooled by the same winter and summer as a Christian is? If you prick us do we not bleed? If you tickle us, do we not laugh? If you poison us, shall we not revenge? If we are like you in the rest, we will resemble you in that.

(Act 3, sc.i, 57–66)

The universal humanity Shylock invokes has its dark side which we see within the trial where none of the characters appears unflawed. Even the Duke, magnanimous in Shylock's defeat, is given the chance to exercise that gesture by Portia's legal inversions. Furthermore, the Duke exercises this right of office in Shylock's case but not in Antonio's case. Arguably, the Duke places his interest in having the law of Venice appear fair and just over and above all other concerns, including those of friendship. This is the terror of the majority remarked on by Lyotard (1996: 99). "This is what a wrong would be: a damage (*dommage*) accompanied by the loss of the means to prove the damage" (Lyotard 1988a: 5).

Lyotard uses the term "victim" to describe a whole range of situations. The term refers to those cases where the victim is deprived of life, or of all his or her liberties, or of the freedom to make his or her ideas public. The Kantian call to the "free and public use of reason," as a way to resist tyranny while obeying the laws of the state, is vitiated for the victim. The right to testify to the damage, or even more simply the testifying phrase, is itself deprived of authority. The Jew, spat upon, mocked and ridiculed, calls for revenge, as a way to even out the years of humiliation, and shuffles out of the court. Laughter follows him: laughter which turns bitter when the audience reflects how far we are from justice, and that the drama is not noble as tragedy, but has been made into farce.

III

There have been several readings of *The Merchant of Venice* in a manner that is sympathetic to the character of Shylock and points to

Shakespeare's anti-semitism; as, for example, James Shapiro's investigation of "the Jewish question" in *Shakespeare and the Jews* (1996). There have been some attempts, however, to show that the many inconsistencies in the play serve to resist the charge of an unmitigated anti-Semitism. These cover the range from investigating the difficulties presented to an actor by the character of Shylock, as undertaken by John Barton (1984), to arguing for his humanity, as does John Cooper (1970). The entire terrain of positions, however, rests on a liberal-individualist approach to the play. The characters can be read one way or another. Following Lyotard's social approach to the philosophy of language, I have suggested a more complex view. The social bond is "the multiplicity of games" which position people in precise places in order to have them play their parts. The characters cannot be read individually. While Shylock's position is arguably real though limited, (following Lyotard) power relations drag terror through the social bond, even into the courtroom, and turn the question of the social bond into a political issue. In this view, Venice, the city, can never be properly just. Furthermore, virtuous individuals do not make for good judges. Rather,

> virtue will manifest itself in the fact that judgments pronounced outside of critieria are judgments that are just. This is how one will know that a judge is a good judge. It is not because a judge is virtuous that he will judge justly, but if he does judge justly one will be able to say that he is virtuous.
>
> (Lyotard and Thébaud 1985: 20)

Stanley Cavell would agree. In his reading of Rawls's "drama of consent," Cavell raises concerns quite similar to those raised by Lyotard, as for example the place of silence in the practice of justice (Cavell 1990: 108). Chief among these is that when the Rawlsian veil of ignorance is lifted it discloses the scene of our lives.

> The public circumstances in which I live, in which I participate, and from which I profit, are ones I consent to. They are ones with an uncertain measure of injustice, of inequalities, of liberties and of goods that are not minimal, of delays in reform that are not inevitable.
>
> (Cavell 1990: 108)

Redemption for Cavell and Shakespeare is offered through domestic harmony and nature as pastoral. Shakespeare offers us the harmony of the gardens of Belmont in opposition to the strife of "the city of words" (ibid.: 7). Furthermore, this harmony is based on domestic relations where the women, Portia and Nerrissa, are made equal to the men through learning and property. Cavell, through a turn to Emerson and Thoreau, both of whom rely on the romanticism of nature to write their philosophical lesson books, offers us a model of moral perfectionism and remarriage: an unequal relationship made harmonious through a commitment to conversation and moral growth. Thus Cavell does not present himself in opposition to Rawls, but rather draws out the conversational aspect of justice which he sees in attenuated form in *A Theory of Justice*. He takes conversation to be the key to living within constantly negotiated democratic institutions.

Like Cavell, Lyotard does not give up on justice and is concerned with the presuppositional conditions which mark judgments making the practices of justice difficult. Unlike Cavell, however, Lyotard does not think we can find redemption through conversation. Lyotard sees the social bond so completely traversed by relations of power, hence politics, that he does not see how language, which positions in the social realm with precision, would allow an enabling conversation.

Lyotard turns instead to a Kantian romanticism (which is present even if ever so faintly) by arguing for aesthetic judgment as an analogy for the resolution of the differend. Such a resolution cannot come through an appeal to reason and therefore cannot be a moral judgment which would flow from rules. Rather, this judgment is to come from the feeling of terror with which infinity overwhelms us. The Kantian sublime is not presentable, for we do not have the forms that would enable its presentation, and any attempt at presentation would be limited. Furthermore, the sublime is not known through reason, but felt through the imagination.

One might well ask, with Stuart Hampshire, how the philosopher of stern oppositions "between nature on the one side and freedom on the other, of feeling and sensibility versus pure reason, of the universal moral law versus the contingent values and interest in human life" (Hampshire 1989: 145–56) could have foreshadowed German romanticism ? How could the Kant of the German idealists, who drew the lines between the theoretical and the practical, also have inspired the restrained romanticism of Schopenhauer and Wittgenstein? *The Critique of Judgment* (Kant 1964) has been received in two broad ways. There are those who see it as representing a complete break with the theoretical and practical critiques of reason, and therefore puzzling, or best read as a departure from the more serious concerns of Kant. Then there are those like Stuart Hampshire, Jean-François Lyotard, and Reinhard Brandt, who see it as the culmination of all the intellectual labor that went before. While there have been some attempts to reconcile Kantian ethics with aesthetics through *The Critique of Judgment*, it is fair to say that for Kant himself the two domains were analogous but not the same. Nevertheless, it is in *The Critique of Judgment* that we are taken away from an autonomous rational self, where concepts are placed under the regimes of reason, to one that is relational. Now we are presented with a softer, more amiable Kant. Here feeling is tied to cognition. And while the aesthetic remains tied to concepts, the play of imagination outscripts these concepts: this is the freedom of the will and the freedom of aesthetics. Lyotard sees a parallel between the Kantian Idea of reason and the Idea proper to aesthetic judgment, the aesthetic Idea. "The expression designates," he explains, "a mode of presentation of forms in which no determinate concept could be adequate to the presentation, nor could it be rendered by any intelligible language" (Lyotard 1994: 212). Another way, he suggests, of framing this would be to say that if practical reason offers us the transcendental freedom of the will, aesthetic judgment offers us freedom of the imagination. In other words, through the reflective judgment of aesthetics, the feeling of pleasure that demands it be communicated universally, Kant now sets out to give us the "passageway," as Lyotard calls it, to all the inhabitants of the world – to intersubjectivity. "Humanity on the one side indicates the universal feeling of sympathy (empathy), and on the other the faculty of being able to communicate our innermost feelings" (Kant 1964: sec. 60). Such a passage is tied deeply to issues of education under heterogeneous conditions, by introducing imagination and creativity as a guide to the kind of politics that would be rooted in a concern for those with whom we share our immediate and wider contexts, both as teachers and as students. It provides also a guide to living the ideal life.

Without rehearsing the relationship between Leibniz and Kant, it is worth reminding ourselves that like Leibniz, Kant maintains the notion of causality within his theoretical deliberations. Unlike Leibniz, however, he does not allow a metaphysical grounding such as "the First Cause." It is the relation that we, as theoretical and practical creatures, establish between means and ends which provides us with the causal relations that enable explanations about the world of which we are part and the rules and prescriptions for action. But these means and ends are chosen from a small fragment of knowledge which sets the limits and determines the possibilities of choice. This fragment of knowledge cannot be taken as that of the totality. It is this fragmentary knowing which demands that judgment be made in humor and worry. Antonio knows the uncertainty of the world and spreads his goods over several ships sailing to different places on different seas. His prudence, however, is of no avail, for the world exceeds his ability to know. Yet we must proceed as if we could know the whole, through the use of reflective judgment which is regulative and not constitutive of thought. The beautiful allows us repose in the harmony created through our efforts on natural materials. The sublime in nature – as for example when we stand on the edge of a Californian beach and look out to the Pacific ocean, or catch our first glimpse of the high ranges of the Himalayas – calls to that which exceeds the limit of what can be brought under reason. The sublime in nature is almost impossible to think unless it is linked to an orientation that resembles a moral attitude.

Kant, too, turns to the garden as an example of what is part of nature and yet apart from it through our efforts in cultivation. Thus we humanize the landscapes we inhabit, make them beautiful places of repose, even as the wilderness lies just beyond the edge of our garden, even as the plants themselves left untended turn also to wilderness. The Third Critique places us as embodied beings in the world and not as thinking ghosts. Thus we are both natural and cultivated; have determinate needs which are out of our control, and indeterminate ends, the pursuit of which grants us our freedom. Education, then, is a constant process of adjustment in learning. The idea of nature as system is now made more open: we come to think of the world as the creation of a world without closure. In other words, narrative complexity, as pointed out by Marcia Moen (1997), enters into the ways in which we think about and relate to the moral experience of individuals and that of relations between one another. We can never know the whole story of the person, nor his or her history of relations. Hence when we are called on to judge, we act in darkness. In order to judge between heterogeneous phrases the rules of reason will not suffice. The will has to be tied to imagination in order to ensure that any judgment will presuppose respect for the other, where community is the realm of ends. Thus Lyotard does not refuse the significance of rules in judgment, but shows the importance of imagination when judging under conditions of indeterminate knowledge and heterogeneity.

The *sensus communis* is interpreted variously as "common sense," as the "sense of aesthetic judgment we all share as humans," and as "our shared culture or tradition." Regardless of how widely we want to interpret this concept, it provides us with the presuppositional ground for a communicable aesthetic judgment. Heterogeneity, which cannot be brought together under the rules and precepts given by reason, is to be brought together through appeal to nature, which demands consistency. Affirming the place of the social in Kant, Hampshire argues that it is aesthetic awareness that arises as a feeling and can be communicated universally, "to humanity as a whole and across all frontiers" (Hampshire 1989: 156). Thus aesthetic education is responsible for cultivating an attention to this feeling, which provides us with a means to negotiate the differend, especially amidst processes of globalization. Just education would require not only a discussion of justice itself, but also, as I have both argued and shown, a reading and reconsideration of traditional texts for the making of a new, globally multicultural tradition.

Changing contexts change the readings we are called on to enter and teach. More than ever both our pedagogical and our literary practice – the canon of tradition – are to be evaluated not only against how our theories of knowledge and representation come to harm and limit the possibilities of those we share the world with, but also against how they remain relevant to the demands of a new context. This is the test of the classic. It is this evaluation that shows us, for example, the continuing relevance of Shakespeare in moral education. This is even more important for philosophical texts which must show their relevance not only within a tradition but also across traditions. As pointed out by Lyotard, we no longer live in a world where universality can be mandated through the legitimation of some metanarrative. Canonical texts, regardless of the tradition they represent, must be equal to the task of building non-hegemonic communication between diverse, even different contexts. That is, they must show their continuing relevance for the education of children who are called on to live peaceably and justly in a world of differing, even conflicting values. The canon has to be renegotiated, reworked, if it is to remain useful in educating for "humanity as a whole and across all frontiers, through the cultivation of aesthetic feeling for nature and through enjoyment of the open museums of the world" (Hampshire 1989). To refuse continually to rethink the tradition is to be involved in the project of a nostalgic education or that of resentment.

7   Another space

Richard Smith

> Il y a un autre espace, figural. Il faut le supposer enfoui, il ne se donne pas
> à voir, ni à penser, il s'indique de façon latérale, fugitive au sein des discours
> et des perceptions, comme ce qui les trouble. Il est l'espace propre au désir,
> l'enjeu de la lutte que les peintres et les poètes ne cessent de mener contre
> le retour de l'Ego et du texte.
>
> (Jean-François Lyotard, *Discours, Figure:* 135)

> There is another space, the figural. It must be thought of as buried, it does
> not lend itself to being seen, nor thought; it shows itself obliquely, fugitively
> at the heart of discourses and perceptions, as what disturbs them. It is the
> fitting place for desire, it is what is at stake in the struggle which painters
> and poets never cease to wage against the return of the ego and the
> textual.[1]

The figure in the text

For one particular child, at the beginning of his education, a space for his
early life to be inscribed upon:

> Ours was the marsh country, down by the river, within, as the river
> wound, twenty miles of the sea . . . the dark flat wilderness beyond the
> churchyard, intersected with dykes and mounds and gates, with scat-
> tered cattle feeding on it.
>
> (Charles Dickens, *Great Expectations* I. i)

Yet for Pip – more fully Philip Pirrip, his familiar and foreshortened
name little more than a mark, place-holder or conventional designation of
time passing or about to arrive – the world has already, in the preceding
paragraph, the second of the novel, presented itself as a system of signs.

> I give Pirrip as my father's family name, on the authority of his tomb-
> stone. . . . As I never saw my father or my mother . . . my first fancies
> regarding what they were like, were unreasonably derived from their

tombstones. The shape of the letters on my father's, gave me an odd idea that he was a square, stout, dark man, with curly black hair. From the character and turn of the inscription, "*Also Georgiana Wife of the Above*," I drew a childish conclusion that my mother was freckled and sickly. To five little stone lozenges, each about a foot and a half long, which were arranged in a neat row beside their grave, and were sacred to the memory of five little brothers of mine – who gave up trying to get a living, exceedingly early in that universal struggle – I am indebted to a belief I religiously entertained that they had all been born on their backs with their hands in their trouser-pockets, and had never taken them out in this state of existence.

(Ibid.)

We might, of course, exercise ourselves over the relative standings of texts, or signs, and putative reality, or at any rate the visible as the nearest thing to reality, in the above. *I never saw my father or my mother*: they, and the dead brothers, present themselves to Pip and to the reader first as inscriptions, and the tombstones thus inscribed carry, we are told, authority. The landscape of the second paragraph, however, while first promising a contrast ("My first most vivid and broad impression") to any system of abstract signs quickly and disturbingly threatens to be nothing other than a species of writing. The river functions essentially as a signpost to the sea; the flat landscape, "intersected with dykes and mounds and gates," seems a crude schematic map, and the river reappears as a "low leaden line" pencilled in without perspective. This is no chart to buried treasure (a child's most romantic expectation of a map) but to other burials altogether.

At such a time I found out for certain, that this bleak place overgrown with nettles was the churchyard; and that Philip Pirrip, late of this parish, and also Georgiana wife of the above, were dead and buried; and that Alexander, Bartholomew, Abraham, Tobias, and Roger, infant children of the aforesaid, were also dead and buried . . .

(Ibid.)

Thus, turning from the puzzle of the symbols on the tombstones to his sensible impression of things, the child finds only a second text which declares (especially in the identity of his father's name with his own) that all is over before it has begun. Well may he shiver and begin to cry.

This is a child who will have especial difficulty in distinguishing between what are signs and what are not. Invited by the reclusive Miss Havisham (whose entire household – the bridal cake, crawling with vermin, is still on the table – is primarily a signal of the precise time when she was jilted) to play for her amusement, and to endure the contempt of her ward and alter ego, Estella, Pip can only read meaning into the invitation when he later comes into a fortune from a mysterious benefactor. Surely Miss Havisham is his patroness, and means the beautiful Estella to be his! And those who think the world is full of signs and portents *for them* will perhaps be unusually slow to apprehend the otherness of other persons. So, to take just one example, Pip's friend Herbert Pocket is scarcely a separate person but more a second, more innocent and likeable, Pip, and Pip acts as his hidden benefactor in an echoing of the main plot of the novel. Another example: when he enters into his fortune Pip finds it increasingly hard to acknowledge Joe, the good-natured blacksmith who was like a father to him. Perhaps the problem, to put it paradoxically, is that Joe is not enough of a *sign*; at any rate, Joe comes to *mean* (as we say) less and less to him.

Most tellingly of all, on a visit to the village near his old home Pip is mocked by "Trabb's boy," the tailor's apprentice, a kind of mirror-image of the blacksmith's apprentice that Pip had been. Where Herbert Pocket was a likeable second Pip, Trabb's boy is an infuriating one: both demonstrate the nightmarish refusal of significant persons to be truly *other* to Pip. On Pip's first visit to the tailor after coming into his fortune, Trabb's boy had swept the shop violently with a broom "to express (as I understood it) equality with any blacksmith, alive or dead" (*Great Expectations* I. xix). Now this boy struts along the pavement on the opposite side of the street, wearing a blue bag to imitate Pip's great-coat, repeatedly exclaiming "Don't know yah!" to a crowd of his peers, in burlesque of the snob Pip has become.

> Words cannot state the amount of aggravation and injury wreaked upon me by Trabb's boy, when, passing abreast of me, he pulled up his shirt-collar, twined his side-hair, stuck an arm akimbo, and smirked extravagantly by, wriggling his elbows and body, and drawling to his attendants, "Don't know yah, don't know yah, pon my soul don't know yah!"
>
> (*Great Expectations* II. xi)

This scene expresses the deep sense of alienation experienced by one who brings himself into being by effort of will.[2] At the point where Pip meets himself coming the other way, runs as it were up against the mirror and its possibilities of self-knowledge, he finds, in Lyotard's terms, the *figural*: that which causes us to grasp that there is something unrepresentable beyond representation ("Words cannot state . . . "). What Pip perceives is more than unfamiliar. As the Other to representation the figural is an insistent blank ("Don't know yah, don't know yah") glimpsed at the center of psychic reality and energy ("*pon my soul* don't know yah!"), terrifying, annihilating even, to one desperate for the significations of what Lyotard calls discourse:

> But unless I had taken the life of Trabb's boy on that occasion, I really do even now not see what I could have done . . . to have exacted any

lower recompense from him than his heart's best blood, would have been futile.

(*Great Expectations* II. xi)

Pip's recourse is discursive, a desperate plunging back into the world of signs: he writes to Trabb withdrawing his custom, returns to London ("safe – but not sound, for my heart was gone") and sends Joe, whom he has failed to go to see on his visit, "a penitential cod-fish and a barrel of oysters." It is perhaps relevant to note that this episode occurs at almost the exact center or heart of the novel.

Back on the marshes at the opening of the story, Pip (and the reader-as-Pip) struggled with the opposition of world and text, two dimensions not so very opposite really since, as we have seen, each slides readily into the other. Because they are both essentially representational, each dimension presents us with nothing other than representation. Thus it is that Pip, named as if he were a purely textual mark (and entirely reversible since both "Pip" and "Pirrip" are palendromic, and "Philip" nearly so), is sensitive to the world of representations. However, when he meets what is radically other to representation, Pip's faculties serve him less well. The gap between the world of representation and the figural is less easy to bridge, being "not that of two terms placed in the same plane, inscribed on the same support, and, possibly, reversible given certain operational conditions" (Lyotard 1985: 135).[3] As Pip shivers on the marshes and begins to cry,

> "Hold your noise!" cried a terrible voice, as a man started up from among the graves at the side of the church porch. "Keep still, you little devil, or I'll cut your throat!"
>
> (*Great Expectations* I. i)

From among the graves, which are both part of the dimension of inscribed texts and part of the landscape, emerges the fugitive convict, Abel Magwitch. After Magwitch has turned him upside down twice, to emphasize his reversibility (the reversibility of Pip, now, as well as of "Pip"; on both occasions he sets him back on top of a gravestone), Pip brings him food and a file to cut off his convict's leg-iron. It is his gratitude for this that causes Magwitch later to become Pip's secret benefactor. *Great Expectations* is partly the story of this, and partly the story of Pip's desperate attempts to repress Magwitch, or the unsavory source of his fortune, or his own unconscious (these seem to be variants on one another): his attempts not to be disturbed by the figural.

Not everything can be reconciled with everything else. As we try to organize our lives we encounter *incommensurabilities*: not the incommensurability of finding we cannot do both this *and* that, cannot both deceive others and be trusted, cannot both enjoy stable personal relationships and live irresponsibly. Rather we come up against that sense of radically heterogeneous spaces blocked together, each in a "necessary and impossible encounter with its other" (Readings 1991: 22) that is the figural. Here are Pip and Herbert Pocket making the attempt, familiar enough perhaps, to reconcile spending too much and having enough to spend. Their technique is the managerial one of setting up a spread-sheet. The two friends make a formal appointment for the purpose, enjoy a good businessman's dinner to fortify themselves for the task, and of course ensure they have the use of appropriate software: "a copious supply of ink, and a goodly show of writing and blotting paper" (*Great Expectations* II. xv).

> I would then take a sheet of paper, and write across the top of it, in a neat hand, the heading, "Memorandum of Pip's debts;" with Barnard's Inn and the date very carefully added. Herbert would also take a sheet of paper, and write across it with similar formalities, "Memorandum of Herbert's debts."
>
> (Ibid.)

With such discursive, textual swords and shields we go forth to battle with our horrors. "This was the way to confront the thing, this was the way to take the foe by the throat. And I know Herbert thought so too." Thus Pip can congratulate himself on being a first-rate man of business. All has been encompassed within the discursive: debts and nameless Things are ticked off, docketed and tied into symmetrical bundles. Lest there should be any irruption into this well-managed world, even the margins of the text are carefully mapped and cleared:

> My business habits had one other bright feature, which I called "leaving a Margin." For example; supposing Herbert's debts to be one hundred and sixty-four pounds four-and-twopence, I would say, "Leave a margin, and put them down at two hundred." . . . I had the highest opinion of the wisdom of this same Margin. . .
>
> (Ibid.)

These maneuvers bring a deep sense of peace: "there was a calm, a rest, a virtuous hush, consequent on these examinations of our affairs." The figural has been reduced to figures, and there is no more radical oppo-sition than that of sums owing and bills paid, incomes and outgoings, all of course inscribed in the same plane, and perhaps even reversible given a few economies or more ingenious accountancy. But now, since Pip is beginning to grow a little, the one-dimensionality of the discursive proves less sustaining than alienating. As he sits "among the stationery" (that emblem of the textual/discursive: and the pun on immobility or "stuckness" is not a casual one) Pip feels "like a bank of some sort, rather than a private individual." At this point in the text the attuned reader senses the need for complacency to be disturbed. Promptly a black-bordered letter (as if to mock those who think margins are zones of security) drops through the door, informing Pip of the death of his sister. The next chapter (II. xxxv) begins:

> It was the first time that a grave had opened in my road of life, and the gap it made in the smooth ground was wonderful. The figure of my sister in her chair by the kitchen fire, haunted me night and day.

Unrepresentative remarks

Of formal education too, in our time, a good deal is expected. And so that all may know that it is meeting these expectations, delivering upon them, it is important that every aspect, every detail, should appear in the ledgers: that education should be represented accurately and comprehensively. A new language evolves to meet the need for a currency. Where other ledgers speak of pounds or dollars, the columns of the education books are headed "aims and objectives," "outcomes," "transferable skills." Regimes of quality assessment come into being to inspect university departments of history, biology, philosophy. They establish whether there are procedures in place to match objectives with putative outcomes and monitor the latter. Do the minutes of staff–student consultative committees show that customers' concerns were properly logged and acted upon? Have the limitations of a particular mode of teaching been noted in order to inform future planning?

The embodied encounter between teacher and taught, meanwhile, receives comparatively little attention: as if something there, embarrassingly, refused to be represented. More than embarrassment, too, meets the refusal to bow down before openness and accountability (this is a god of universal light, who will have no mysteries). "Well, I can't really say what I intend to achieve until I have met the students . . . " – a flicker of terror, here, in the eyes of those who know they must make everything transparent or disappear, be annihilated: those who draw the documentation flow diagram, set out the due procedures. At least we can agree on this, can we not: all coursework assignments to be handed in at Reception, names checked against the list and receipts issued. Handbooks for all modules to begin with aims and objectives, and expectations: what students can expect of their teachers, and what we expect of them in turn. Great expectations again: it is important to have high expectations of those you teach, which means of course you must know exactly where you intend to take them. Resisting this, you may say something to the effect that "you lend yourself willingly to this prescription: 'to go there,' without knowing there" (Lyotard 1993b: 74): this is listened to with a kind of tense weariness, and you see the flicker of terror again.

The phenomenon is now endemic to the system: the trade press gives us evidence almost weekly. In the *Times Higher Education Supplement* (27 August 1999) the front-page headline declares "Unis fail to ensure degree quality" (Unis are of course what universities, striving to become units in the discourses of assessment and quality control, have become). The article below the headline tells the reader that "some of Britain's most prestigious universities" cannot guarantee the quality of their own degrees and are refusing to be audited by the Quality Assessment Agency's team of inspectors. The connection between the alleged inability to guarantee quality and the refusal to be audited is not spelled out and should give us pause. We might easily imagine that, unable to offer guaranteed quality (no kite-mark: shoddy workmanship here), the universities are refusing to admit the auditors who will shine light on leaking gaskets and frayed wiring. But of course it is possible here that refusal to be audited is precisely and simply what "inability to guarantee quality" consists in: that the unaudited university, in the new regime, has forfeited its right to be a university at all, and is in danger of disappearing from the map of quality education provision. The Director of Institutional Review at the Quality Assessment Agency (QAA) utters a warning, quoted in this article:

> Institutions have got to know for themselves as awarding institutions that they have got everything buttoned down. But there are gaping holes.

Clearly we are to read this with some *frisson*. Not everything is buttoned down: holes, spaces, are appearing. Like some academic Chernobyl the university may begin to issue unaccredited, unguaranteed emissions. The Director's next words are revealing:

> He warned that even institutions with consistently excellent teaching quality may still fall foul. "In some cases there are bad systems but good provision."

Here the acknowledgement that quality and audit are not ontologically identical itself seems to slip out through some institutional crack, with the suggestion that what is at stake here is really power: your teaching may be splendid but we can still get you if you don't play our game. Perhaps not all is properly buttoned down at the QAA.

In the terms that Jean-François Lyotard has made familiar, where a dominating metanarrative asserts its "truths" from the perspective of an authorized discourse, other truths are excluded. Lyotard is hostile to the domination of any one language or, as he elsewhere calls it, genre: the cognitive genre, the performative genre and the economic genre in particular, which insist on the maximization of the efficiency of the economic system and of the education system as a subset of that. Where these languages or genres seize authority other claims, other voices and languages, which cannot readily be made commensurable with them, are suppressed and rendered inaudible. They can safely be consigned to the rubbish-bin marked, perhaps, "metaphysics" or "mystification."

Another example of the dominating discourse will indicate the tendency to suppression. It comes from David Reynolds, a British Professor of Education who also leads a government task-force on numeracy. Reynolds thinks that schools should become "highly reliable organizations," precisely like those nuclear plants where everything must be secured and buttoned down, in which teachers would be technicians working to exacting methodologies.

> Highly reliable organizations, Professor Reynolds said, have a small number of clear goals and recognized "bodies of knowledge" everyone is expected to be familiar with. They pay attention to performance evaluation. They use large amounts of data, they have high quality training, and they introduce methods of working that everyone can understand.
>
> (*Times Educational Supplement* 17 July 1998: 20)

What would follow for language from Reynolds's analysis: or, to be more truthful, his extended metaphor? Just as a nuclear plant requires a manual couched in wholly unambiguous language so that safety procedures can be transparent and readily understood, so teachers would operate according to manuals in which everything was defined in the same authoritative way. The language of "clear goals and recognized 'bodies of knowledge'," of "large amounts of data" and so on becomes the only real language in which education can be, not *discussed* for there would no longer be room for discussion worthy of the name, but carried out, executed, implemented. We then have an *operational* language for education in which everything significant can and must be encoded.

Here, in the terms of Lyotard's later writings, we have a dominating discourse or metanarrative. In the light of his earlier writings, especially *Discours, Figure*, we can see here the domination not of any particular discourse, but of *discours*, the discursive. And just as, according to the earlier Lyotard, the discursive or textual threatened not just to obliterate the figural but to obliterate its very obliteration, so the modern project of universal representation requires a similar act of obliteration or suppression. It requires the decisive rejection – even denial – of language that is not representative: of the rhetorical, the metaphorical: of the *figurative*, as we call it.

The modern state leaves nothing to chance. It employs those whose very job it is to lead the act of denial or elimination: to insist on the hegemony of the literal, of language connected to the world in commonsense and transparent ways. One such person, in the United Kingdom, is the man nominally employed as Her Majesty's Chief Inspector of Schools in

England and Wales, Christopher Woodhead (who better for this project than an education inspector or auditor?). Mr Woodhead gives an annual lecture, usually devoted one way or another to the denunciation of those obscurantists, intellectuals, and academics who suggest that education is anything more than a simple matter of raising standards. The following extract is from the 1998 lecture, called "Blood on the tracks: lessons from the history of education reform." The published version of the lecture is divided into numbered paragraphs, and in paragraph 25 Mr Woodhead is writing about in-service training and preparation for headship. The words repay close attention.

> Seeing is often believing in professional development. A course tutor who is teaching or leading a school himself has a credibility which is in itself very important. In-service training ought, moreover, to be rooted firmly in the practicalities of the particular task. This is not to adopt a deliberately anti-intellectual stance, it is rather to recognize both what teachers themselves want and what the inspection evidence confirms. Good training helps teachers solve the problems they face. It has an immediacy and a relevance. Bad training is strong on the academic rhetoric, the theorizing, the either/or let a thousand flowers bloom [*sic*]. . . . How many times have each of us been asked to organize ourselves into groups and share our experience? Put bluntly, do we want "reflective practitioners" or teachers who can teach children to read?
>
> (Woodhead 1998)

Note the way that one set of phrases, expressed in clichés that spring easily to the lips or echo folk wisdom, is deployed against a second set. Seeing is believing, rooted firmly, evidence confirms. There are simple realities which, in their immediacy and relevance, the common man can see for himself (the empiricist strain of Enlightenment metanarrative) if not bewildered by professional and indeed professorial mystics. Language can mirror these realities uncomplicatedly; it is at its most literal and trust-worthy where it identifies practicalities, particular tasks, the problems teachers face. On the other hand there is a language that is far from literal: academic rhetoric, theorizing. The contrast could not be more stark. Plain language reflects plain reality: the practitioner does not need to reflect, in any very reflective way, to see what is in front of her face.

Yet there are oddities here which a close reading uncovers. The opening sentence of the extract suggests that the crucial feature of training is not what it does but what it appears to do ("seeing is very often believing"). This is confirmed by the second sentence, which describes "credibility" as "very important." The function of this is to confer the authority of what "everyone knows," or finds credible, on the rest of the paragraph, and thus to validate the saws and clichés. Good training thus turns out to be whatever teachers believe good training is. Note that this is "to recognize both what teachers themselves want and what the inspection evidence confirms." The construction and function of this clause is interesting. There is of course no evidence for what teachers themselves want (perhaps we would not expect that in a document of this sort), but in any case what they want is subordinated to what the Chief Inspector *recognizes*. It is this that is important: he and his organization are, wisely and perspicaciously, recognizing what teachers want. Wants can of course be recognized easily enough. What they want, not being the point of the clause, can thus be taken as read. Similarly, there is apparently "inspection evidence" which "confirms." Now if there was such evidence about what makes for good training we might expect it to be highlighted. Instead mention of this evidence and its confirmatory power comes at the very end of the sentence, almost as a throw-away. Of course: we hardly needed it. What teachers want is self-evident, so much so as to amount to what they need. How powerful this literal language is!

We have just examined a complex passage of writing. If we were at all lost in its complexities – if we found it at all puzzling or felt inclined to ask questions – then the next two sentences come as a great relief to us. They tell us directly what is what. "Good training helps teachers solve the problems they face. It has an immediacy and a relevance." The simplicity has considerable rhetorical force after what precedes it. The next sentence is structured as that most classical of rhetorical devices, the ascending tricolon ("Friends, Romans, countrymen . . . "), but not ascending too neatly: "the academic rhetoric," "the theorizing," "the either/or let a thousand flowers bloom . . ." The paragraph finishes with two rhetorical questions.

But here is a paradox. For our reading has shown that the passage is itself not straightforward and commonsensical at all. It is, rather, highly rhetorical. It is language that displays many of the characteristic tricks of the trade of the speech-maker, the producer of verbal pyrotechnics, the manipulator of his audience. And it is not simply language that conceals its rhetoricity (we do not expect the orator to signal his tricks, after all): it actively denies it. It does this both by insisting that it speaks in the voice of simple common-sense and by asserting that it is the others – especially academics – whose discourse is rhetorical. Paragraph 14 of *Blood on the Tracks* declares: "this is a Government which *is* serious about raising educational standards. It must, therefore, probe the logic of its own rhetoric." The Chief Inspector is the man to take us beyond rhetoric. Thus he claims to speak an uncontaminated language, the Literal Language of Education, and he will speak it, loudly and bravely:

> A couple of weeks ago, the Chairman of the Select Committee, Margaret Hodge, reprimanded me for the intemperance of my

language. . . . I am unrepentant. . . . These things need saying, loudly, clearly and, at times, intemperately.

(Woodhead 1998: paras. 12, 13)

"Loudly, clearly and, at times, intemperately"; "Why do powerful voices in education peddle concepts of professionalism which are damagingly unrealistic, hopelessly romantic, and dangerously sentimental?" (ibid.: para. 25). The Chief Inspector is betrayed by his addiction to the tricolon. At his most literal, he is not.

Woodhead would have us believe that there is a real world of getting on with the job – teaching children to read, and so on – as opposed to a dangerous textual realm of theory and academic "rhetoric." The project here is *both* to marginalise academic theory or "rhetoric" in favor of the "real world" and the commonsense operational language supposed to map onto it, and to marginalise rhetoric itself, the non-literal use of language, in favor of the discursive representation that orders significations and arranges for their communication. One way of understanding the limitations of that project is to note that the attempt to prevent the intrusion into language of rhetorical figures for the sake of clarity ignores the fact that "'clarity' is itself a rhetorical figure, a metaphor for the absence of metaphor" (Readings 1991: 30). Another way is to enjoy the spectacle of those who would marginalise rhetoric and the figurative haunted by its return. Just as Magwitch disturbs the "smooth ground" of Pip's worlds, so rhetoric re-appears as the figural, the other to representation, at the heart of Woodhead's world, *fugitive au sein des discours et des perceptions*, as that which disturbs it.

Working behind the loom

No doubt we should not be dissecting the Chief Inspector's prose. We should be out in the classrooms and lecture rooms, busily helping to raise standards. So much to be done if the targets are to be met and the scores improved, but what do we find? Some of those charged with this important responsibility, the nation's educational and economic destiny in their care, playing at literary criticism. One of the hands, your Honour, was discovered under the loom, *reading a book*. Now, working the loom has its characteristic satisfactions – so many yards of cloth produced, the steady rhythm of the machinery – as well as its tedium. There are similar satisfactions in operating the machinery of education: the essays marked, lectures delivered, web pages attractively presented and kept up to date.

But productive space, the domain of efficiency and effectiveness, is not the only space, whether it is a chief source of job satisfaction or of ennui. There is another space, which Lyotard calls the secluded, *oikeion*, in which we can be free of the obsession with maximizing outcomes and meeting targets. (We might recall here Michael Oakeshott's idea of education as "a place apart.") In that space we can imagine possibilities and engagements resistant to becoming enlisted in the ranks of the representational. The language of such possibilities is one "that has not become public, that has not become communicational, that has not become systemic, and that can never become any of these things" (Lyotard 1993b: 105). It is a language that is attentive and alert to marginal voices which cannot be heard clearly. It is the language of "'literature', 'art', or 'writing' in general" (ibid.).

This is a space we must occupy and a language we must speak if we are to live up to our responsibility as thinkers, to do our proper *work*. In Lyotard's words: "our role as thinkers is to deepen what language there is, to criticize the shallow notion of information, to reveal an irremediable opacity within language itself. Language is not an 'instrument of communication'" (ibid.: 27). Perhaps our excursion into literary criticism was not so frivolous after all. In *Le Différend* Lyotard reminds us that this is moreover an ethical matter, that questions of *justice* are at stake:

> The *différend* is the unstable state and instant of language in which something which ought to be able to be phrased cannot yet be phrased. This state involves silence which is a negative sentence, but it also appeals to sentences possible in principle. What is ordinarily called sentiment signals this fact. "You can't find the words to say it," and so on. . . . It is the stake of a literature, a philosophy, perhaps of a politics, to bear witness to *différends* by finding idioms for them.
>
> In the *différend,* something "asks" to be phrased, and suffers the wrong of not being able to be phrased. So humans who thought they used language as an instrument of communication learn by this feeling of pain which accompanies silence (and of pleasure which accompanies the invention of a new idiom), that they are the object of language's demand, not that they increase to their own benefit the quantity of information which can be communicated in existing idioms.
>
> (Lyotard 1988a: 13, paras 22–3)

Demands are made on us, and our proper work, in the name of justice, is to try to respond to those demands. There are things which cannot be said in the language in which the bureaucrats and the powerful talk about education. We must "bear witness" and try to find suitable idioms for these things. Our work is not to be conceived essentially in the language of the economic and cognitive genres. Perhaps work is analogous to the figural in its capacity for resisting and disturbing those genres, as Readings (1991: 140 ff.) argues.

In *Great Expectations* work figures largely as a significant absence. As Trotter (1996: xviii) notes, the tradesmen in Pip's market town carry out their business largely by standing in their doorways and watching each other across the street. As a gentleman, when he comes into his fortune,

Pip will of course do no real work. Of his alter egos, Herbert Pocket finds nominal work in a counting-house (the economic genre *par excellence*): this actually pays him nothing, but gives him the opportunity to look about himself for an opening. "That's the grand thing. You are in a counting-house, you know, and you look about you" (II. iii). Orlick, the day-laborer at the forge run by Joe Gargery, where Pip is destined to be apprenticed until the intervention of fortune, also contrives to work without real engagement. He "never even seemed to come to his work on purpose, but would slouch in as if by mere accident," and he leaves at the end of the day "as if he had no idea where he was going and no intention of ever coming back" (I. xv).

There are two great exceptions – at least at first sight – to this lack of industry on the part of those seemingly immersed in the economic genre. First, we never see the lawyer, Jaggers, do anything but work: his being is wholly contained in his role. With "a manner expressive of knowing something secret about everyone of us that would effectively do for each individual if he chose to disclose it" (I. xviii), it is indifferent to him on which side of a case he appears; he is thus entirely reversible. As an emblem of the law, a phrase regime to which there is seemingly no alternative, Jaggers terrorizes witnesses, clients, juries, and the judiciary itself. He eats his lunch standing, and "seemed to bully his very sandwich as he ate it" (II. i).

Second, the reader senses that the forge where Joe and the laborer Orlick work, and where Pip is apprenticed, is a symbol of satisfying and harmonious work. It is "the glowing road to manhood and independence" (I. xiv), where Joe works "with a glow of health and strength upon his face" (II. xvi). It would be easy to view the forge in romantic, even pre-Raphaelite terms, as a place where craft skills are exercised by a man working for himself under conditions of his own choosing. But this would be to miss a more complex and important point. Perhaps the first thing to notice about the forge is that it too does not actually appear very productive (it does not operate significantly in the economic genre). Never, in the novel, does any manufactured article emerge from it. Our first sight of its operation is when Joe is called upon by the soldiers seeking Magwitch and another escaped convict to repair a set of hand-cuffs. The forge and the convicts, whom we have already seen as the figural, are indeed intimately linked: "the bellows seemed to roar for the fugitives, the fire to flame for them, the smoke to hurry away in pursuit of them, Joe to hammer and clink for them" (I. v).

If the forge can, as the figural, be blocked *against* the discursive, perhaps it is because its life-force comes elsewhere than from the utilitarian. When Joe refuses Jaggers' offer of money in return for the cancellation of Pip's apprenticeship it is as "the loss of the little child – what come to the forge" (I. xviii) that he experiences his bereavement. The rhythms of the forge are lyrical rather than economic or cognitive:

There was a song Joe used to hum fragments of at the forge, of which the burden was Old Clem. This was not a very ceremonious way of rendering homage to a patron saint; but, I believe Old Clem stood in that relation towards smiths. It was a song that imitated the measure of beating upon iron, and was a mere lyrical excuse for the introduction of Old Clem's respected name. Thus, you were to hammer boys round – Old Clem! With a thump and a sound – Old Clem! Beat it out, beat it out – Old Clem! With a clink for the stout – Old Clem! Blow the fire, blow the fire – Old Clem! Roaring dryer, soaring higher – Old Clem!

(I. xii)

When Miss Havisham, who has summoned Pip to play, suddenly requires him to sing, Pip is surprised into "crooning this ditty" (ibid.). In this song the conventional distinction between work and play is dissolved. We understand something about Orlick's relation to work when Pip tells us that "whenever I sang Old Clem, he came in out of time" (I. xv). Now we begin to sense why work shows itself in the novel obliquely and fugitively, not readily lending itself to being seen or thought (*il ne se donne pas à voir, ni à penser*) or conceptually represented. For work to be *represented* is for it to be reified, commodified. Dickens's evocation of a *poetics* of work, on the other hand, constitutes what Readings, in discussion of Lyotard, calls

> the transgression of the order of the concept [which] offers the possibility of a language of labor that cannot be approached by the dominant order, translated back into the language of power or of capitalist exchange. The figure of work thus evokes the irrepresentable, the possibility of a justice that is not just an effect of power.
>
> (Readings 1991: 152)

This in turn helps us to understand how work, so evoked, can be connected to delight, to *jouissance*. Joe had always told Pip that "when I was 'prentice to him regularly bound, we would have such Larks there!" (I. iii). If work can show itself to us like this, perhaps it can be transformed for us, rejecting the performativity which currently, and in education especially, supplies its meaning.

When Pip is become a gentleman, and Joe is about to come up to London, Biddy (whom Joe will later marry) writes – since Joe is illiterate – to arrange their meeting, if Pip will still talk to a humble blacksmith. In the postscript she writes:

> He wishes me most particular to write *what larks*. He says you will understand. I hope and do not doubt it will be agreeable to see him even though a gentleman, for you had ever a good heart and he is a worthy man. I have read him all, excepting only the last little sentence.
>
> (II. vii)

In that postscript (with its unread "last little sentence" testifying to Joe's worthiness) to a letter sent by one who cannot write – where ego and text finally, through the transfiguration of art, lose their battle, we seem to glimpse obliquely but with certainty the joy of work and friendship blocked against the discursive:

> ... and he wishes me most particular to write again *what larks.*
>
> (Ibid., emphasis in original)

Notes

1 Translations are my own unless otherwise indicated.
2 Trotter (1996: xii) writes that it "wonderfully catches the sheer unfamiliarity of the self created by desire."
3 "*l'écart n'est pas celui de deux termes* placés dans le même plan, inscrit sur le même support, à la limite réversibles moyennant certaines conditions opératoires" (emphasis in original).

8 *L'enfance*, education, and the politics of meaning

Paul Smeyers and Jan Masschelein

A framework for social justice?

It has become a commonplace that since the Second World War the Western world has changed dramatically: customs and traditions have been eroded; norms of behavior have broken down; society has been secularized. The old ethos and the importance of mutual trust that went with it have to a large extent been replaced by a discourse in which rights and reciprocal duties play an eminent role: how one should live one's life is no longer self-evident. This is no surprise. The accessibility of most goods and services for everyone – that is to say for those who can afford them – has been widened. And the social surveillance – the inquisitiveness and censoriousness – of small-scale traditional society has been displaced by a sweeping pluralism within the context of an ever-continuing increase in scale of the "world" in which we live. Many factors have contributed to this change. Mobility and communication have been transformed, have multiplied, and have grown explosively: the world is now our village, and the relatively closed culture in which people were once raised is under pressure.

At the same time, an "engineering" of all aspects of society and of our personal lives has taken over. With the growing availability of diverse goods and services there is the expectancy of the almost immediate satisfaction of needs. This has given rise to a culture of transgressing boundaries, of living at the limit, at the edge. There is a general cult of (sensual) pleasure-seeking – with or without drugs – and taking it to extremes: live for kicks – for ecstasy – get a kick out of . . . anything that does not cause your death. Experiment and see what happens. Have fun and feel good.

But is this, the question keeps intruding, *all* there is? As cultural embeddedness dissipates, for some it may well be so. But are we yet that far on the route to this kind of individualism? Has celebration of the other become only an extension of our enjoyment? Do we not still group together, are there not still bonds that hold us? Of course, against this there is also, we are inclined to say, more humaneness in some sense, wider solidarity with and understanding for what is deviant, at least as long as it does not get in our way.

Certainly the picture of effeteness evoked here does not reflect Lyotard's understanding of society today, but in its indication of what has fallen apart there is a resonance with his diagnosis and with the kinds of issues that preoccupy his writings. The concern with social justice, with the opposing interests of disparate groups, is potentially highly relevant to education, as must immediately be apparent. But there are points of contention here. The present chapter pursues the parallel between Lyotard's arguments concerning politics and his ideas about childhood. Towards the end of the essay, and in an attempt to take up his central claims, the potential and the problems of an interesting direction for philosophy of education are explored.

Differends: everything as political

Lyotard poses the question of justice in the context of the radical conflict between incommensurable traditions. Starting from the heterogeneous character of contemporary society, which he refers to as our postmodern condition, Lyotard articulates a fractured vision of the social world composed of a number of incommensurable language games or genres of discourse, each with its own particular stakes and rules for discursive as well as non-discursive action. When these come into conflict, there arises what he calls a differend, a case of conflict that cannot equitably be resolved for lack of a rule of judgment applicable to both parties to the dispute. Lyotard speaks of our responsibility to recognize and expose differends through the construction of frames of reference in which the claims of those who have been denied a voice may be heard. The point of departure is a Wittgensteinian insight: the heterogeneity of language games and/or of forms of life. He speaks respectively of "phrase regimes" (which may also be described as types of speech acts, such as, prescription, question and answer, narrative, argument) serving as building blocks for larger units or "genres of discourse." There is no genre of discourse that is capable of subsuming all the others under its rules; there is no meta-language that can allow or guarantee the passage from one language game to another, as a metalanguage also is a language game like any other. Therefore, the coexistence of multiple, distinct, and heterogeneous genres of discourse gives rise to conflicts and "differends." For Lyotard all action has meaning within one genre or another, and not in terms of something previous to the action. It is this right of every individual *to have a say* that is central: to be part of the social by *making phrases*. Social bonding originates precisely in this.

Differends are the result of an undecidable dispute, a conflict that cannot equitably be resolved for lack of a rule of judgment applicable to both arguments. When a differend takes place, the resulting incommensurability leads to a wrong done to one of the parties in the dispute. When both share the same genre of discourse, the case can be decided through litigation before a tribunal of unbiased arbiters. (At least an appeal to such a tribunal is possible; the judges perform roles within an agreed genre of discourse in a way that presupposes Apel's or Habermas's notion of communicative rationality.) In the case of differends the decision is necessarily postponed. Here one of the parties must join the discourse of the tribunal, otherwise no appeal can be made at all. It also means that once such an appeal is made, when in other words one party's discourse is imposed on the other, the case has already been decided: the discourse of one party is excluded from the outset. Moreover, it is not even acknowledged that someone is a victim here. The silencing of competing genres of discourse may be brutal or gentle, but it is inevitable. It is the price to pay for the possibility of operating successfully in any particular genre of discourse. Some of the harm caused is not relevant from a moral point of view: speakers may constantly change positions, and may find compensation in one genre of discourse for the loss of means of expression they have suffered in another. The situation is different, however, where a victim is not able to prove that he or she deserves restitution for a harm suffered: then the victim bears "a wrong." The moral moment comes when the harm is accompanied by the loss of the means to prove its existence. A differend is born from a wrong and is signaled by silence. In semiotic terms, as Adi Ophir puts it,

> A wrong takes place when either one's loss or suffering cannot be given a determined signified (or value) and cannot be reified in the language of exchange, or, if it can be reified, the exchange is blocked for lack of currency – the harm cannot be established.
>
> (Ophir 1997: 191)

Thus the victim's complaint has been silenced and the victimizer can be characterized as the one who has become deaf: that is, indifferent. This indifference to suffering is the limit of the ethical, in the same way as indifference to what is false is the limit of the epistemic domain. The authority of the normative, Lyotard seems also to hold, is thus enclosed within a circle of self-legitimization without which it is thrown into an infinite regress: norms legitimize victimization.

It is important to indicate that a clear distinction has to be made between the agent of the harm and the author of the wrong related to that harm. The latter is responsible not so much for the occurrence of a harm as for imposing – that is, imposing and reproducing – the discursive conditions that make it impossible to express the harm and establish it as a matter of fact. Indeed, this impossibility is the result of anonymous, often unrecognized rules of discourse. Suffering, Ophir (1997) suggests, is the only possible common space that can be shared by values and norms of different sorts. As a result of this, the idea of moral responsibility itself changes. Lyotard tries to show what it is that obliges us to recognize the injustice of silencing those who radically contest our own position, what it is that moves us to respect the integrity of their concerns, their right to voice them and have them taken into account. The description of the other within one's own frame of reference – for instance, one's conception of the good life – risks injustice to the other. We find ourselves in the midst of a differend in which alterity calls us to account for how we understand things. In a form of justice sensitive to diversity, the question of the just and the unjust must permanently remain open. We confront the imperative of a radically open form of political debate. We are obliged to recognize that our standards are incommensurable with the standards of others and so do not permit any justifiable domination of one sphere by the other. As Cecile Lindsay argues

> The I's displacement marks an immediate obligation toward the other, even though the content of the obligation is not known. The other's advent is not an event of cognition, but rather of feeling; Lyotard defines the feeling of obligation as a feeling of *respect*. Thus a new universe is instituted, that of the ethical phrase. Saying yes to the inde- cipherable obligation imposed by the advent of the other fractures the I, dispossesses it, and opens the I onto the other.
>
> (Lindsay 1992: 399)

According to Lindsay, ethical judgment itself becomes experimental since it calls on us to make judgments without criteria, according to what we anticipate or imagine of the future ends and addressees of every judgment. This is a prescription for an honorable postmodernity. For Lyotard the reality of suffering is the reality of a phrase that situates one as an addressee and addresses one with a demand. We are not looking for recovering a moral point of view but, as Ophir has it (1997: 201), for the recovery of a moral response-ability.

Thus Lyotard's version of ethics recasts the political. The political is not that genre of discourse that includes all other discourses, a general meta- language. Rather, everything is political in the sense that a radical conflict or differend can arise on the occasion of the slightest collision between different spheres. There is in his opinion no just society, but a just community might work in accordance with the imperative: live together in difference, but not indifferently, in respect for the irreducibly distinct other. The question he directs his attention to is the problem of how to act justly without pretending that one can succeed in justice. His ethics makes no appeal to any essence of the human that might provide a paradigm for judgment, no description that might provide a rule for the formulation of prescriptions. He therefore advocates an unstable state of revolutionary prudence. It consists in knowing that there is no golden rule that can allow us to subjugate engagement in events to a meta-discourse on history. Resistance thus becomes endless and no consensus can establish a new world order.

Compromise and respect for difference do not involve establishing some common identity or universal subject to serve as an arbitrating instance, a vantage point from which differences might be tolerated. Instead a number of subversive strategies – ruses or tricks – are identified. First, acts of resistance are context-specific and always singular. Second, acts of resistance occur all the time. Third, without predictable content or form, affirmations of resistance display respect for the other and cannot be seen as merely the negative finality of deceit. One is confronted here with a refusal to justify direct action in terms of a means to an end. Acts of resistance should be their own justification. The heteronomous determination (or limitation) of the will of the subject through a recognition of the other takes the concerns and interests of the other into account. One places the ends of one's actions in question through a submission to the appeal of the other. This revolutionary prudence is paralleled by an appeal to dissensus or paralogy – a support for legitimization by small narratives – instead of consensus.

Can radical incommensurability and normative discourses go together?

Lyotard confronts us with a problem. The presuppositions of his arguments seem incompatible with what he, no less than others, actually does. Seyla Benhabib recalls the observation of Stephen White that no postmodern thinker would give blanket endorsement to the explosions of violence associated with, say, the resurgence of ethnic group nationalism in the Soviet Union or the growth of street gangs in Los Angeles (White 1991). Yet, according to Benhabib, it is not at all clear that Lyotard has a normative discourse available for condemning such violence. She is not implying that theorists of difference are responsible for degenerate forms of politics, or that philosophical positions can necessarily be criticized for their imputed, real or imaginary political consequences in the hands of others, or that one should judge, evaluate, or question the commitment of theorists of difference to democratic ideals and aspirations. "What I will be arguing instead," she says,

> is that Jean-François Lyotard and, to some extent, Jacques Derrida, privilege in their writings on the political *a certain perspective, a certain angle, a certain heuristic framework*, which itself has deep and ultimately, I think, misleading consequences for understanding the rational foundations of the democratic form of government.
>
> (Benhabib 1994: 5)

Lyotard's emphasis on incommensurability between discourses informs a philosophical politics quite different from the politics of politicians. Lyotard preoccupies himself with the originary or foundational political act and with the recognition of the fact that a certain view of language is connected with a certain politics. But, Benhabib argues, the thesis of radical incommensurability of genres of discourse is no more meaningful than the thesis of the radical incommensurability of conceptual frameworks. If frameworks, linguistic, conceptual or otherwise, actually are so radically incommensurable with each other, then we could not actually know this. She reproaches Lyotard for disregarding the institutional mechanisms whereby constitutional traditions enable democracies to correct, to limit and to ameliorate moments of unbridled majority rule, exclusionary attributions of identity, and the arbitrary formation of norms.

Similar criticisms are made by Peter McLaren (1994). Because Lyotard largely disregards what the individual has in common with other human beings, the difference between people is pictured in a discourse of power. The otherness of the other has to be radicalized in Lyotard in order to safeguard a place for the other, McLaren argues. Lyotard's uncritical celebration of multiplicity and heterogeneity runs the risk of being used to underwrite a politics of multiculturalism that exoticizes otherness, that supports a regressive nativism locating difference in a primeval past of cultural authenticity. (Of course, Lyotard's later writings evince the strongest distaste for any such possibility, but this does not of itself refute McLaren's claims.) It is also troubling, McLaren suggests, that Lyotard's view of the subaltern subject repudiates all attempts to name such a subject, even provisionally, on the grounds that any form of naming is an act of appropriation and ultimately an act of violence: a position that can lead to both political and pedagogical paralysis. Lyotard's project thus lacks the substantive elements necessary for guiding our choices toward these ends.

Sara Ahmed (1996) argues that the aestheticism of paralogy – and the celebration of difference that goes with it – stands in the way of the recognition that local situations or events are overdetermined within broader structures or social relations that may be characterized by systematic inequality. Here the argument is that interest in, and celebration of, what is different obscure what is going on in society with an internal form of apparent legitimization. They provide even a rationalization for the perpetuation of particular power interests. Thus, paralogy might then be thought to function similarly to the free market, where antagonistic and competing interests are defined as the only basis for human relations within an unstructured and undetermined context. All of this is the consequence of Lyotard's identification of "naming something as . . ." with "the unavoidable injustice" that is done by this naming itself. The question once again is, therefore, whether injustice can simply be identified with a violence against radical indifference, or whether we need positive terms to prevent other kinds of injustices. If this is correct, then the identification of "justice" and "radical otherness" may turn out to be a logical impossibility. The criticism here then is that we need a more pragmatic, cautious, and sensitive model of how different ethical practices deal with "the other" in cases of conflict or dispute.

In realizing that we are never members of single communities and identifying ourselves sometimes as members of marginalized communities, however, we can find tools to imagine a world other than that of liberalism. Recognizing ourselves as potentially radically plural makes alternative discourses an open possibility, but requires no reference to some unrepresentable core that makes us who we are, a fiction that overlooks the possibility of infinite redescriptions made possible by identifying new communities. Even if there is no single description of the human condition, taking the law of difference as our guiding principle and treating contingency as an absolute does not leave us necessarily impotent or speechless.

Meaning and event

These matters raise, therefore, the important issue of whether Lyotard's position rests on either an epistemological mistake or a more general error over the nature of meaning. Both interpretations of Lyotard's work are common. Notwithstanding the distance between meaning (*quid*) and event (*quod*) which will later be introduced, Lyotard confronts us with the philosophical choice between language as subjectless – the unrepresentable core (see earlier) – and self-transparent Cartesian subjectivity, which seems to be unhelpful. It is particularly unhelpful if we want to account for the creation of new meaning, the escape from cliché, and to articulate new modes of saying and doings things, all so essential in reconfiguring the social world. While we can agree that any and all structures of meaning may be deconstructed and reshaped, it is difficult to accept that we should view conceptual structure as hopelessly unjust or terroristic in itself. The law of difference can allow that any narrative constructions or stories we tell about ourselves, the world, and others are always open to redescription: the self is never bound within a single or even necessarily coherent narrative. The tools of narrative are not the property of an individual but the product of history, culture, and community, which are themselves not homogeneous. Unremitting deconstruction of any and all topics will produce an ethical paralysis. So it is the prioritization of difference that seems problematic, along with the potential problem that individual uniqueness opens us all to commodification – discovering "the real you" – and to exploitation, and sets us necessarily against each other.[1]

If the subject is characterized only by the mark of difference, the Lyotardian postmodernist loses the political game: there are no grounds for urging that this or that action is unjust. The goal of the politics of difference must rather be to encourage self-respect and self-knowledge among individuals whose identity has previously been silenced, devalued, or erased because they belong to some group devalued in the ruling ideology. Individuals can then work as members of various communities and pursue their interests within the larger social structure, undermining the complacency of the existing social and political "we." Politics seems as much in need of sameness and unity as of difference as a basis for group identification. There is nothing progressive in itself about change, particularly if it obstructs oppositional politics by repudiating the formation of community and of coherent subjects, both of which are necessary for the identity formation of otherness.

Before dealing with what follows from this for education and educational theory, we will now turn to some of Lyotard's work explicitly related to education, specifically to his thoughts on childhood. To understand him correctly there is one final issue that needs to be dealt with first.

Lyotard distinguishes meaning in general from the *event*. Meaning necessarily invokes concepts that are shared and not particular to individuals. To understand something does not necessarily mean to be moved by it, to act on the basis of it. At the level of meaning indicated by concepts one is always using an already-existing apparatus to express what is particular. Radical newness is limited by the use of already-shared concepts. In the *event* it is the singularity of what happens to us that is at the forefront: we may be struck by this or that and be moved to do particular things, perhaps to see things in a radically new light. Meaning relates to *what* is happening, the *event* to the fact *that* something is happening . . . *and to me*! When I speak of the ethical, the aesthetic, the religious, about what appeals to me (meaning for a subject), clearly this is not exhausted by the dimension of meaning in terms of "what." What I say operates on multiple levels; conversely, it is also clear that it is only through words – through a shared language – and thus through concepts and meanings, that I am able to speak about what moves me. And as there is no meaning outside of the realm of my language, what touches me precedes what is put into words (and this can never exhaustively be expressed by particular words). There is the chair we can speak of and the chair we can sit on, and in some sense the latter can surprise us in a way that the former cannot. Hence, in the following this distinction between meaning (as dealt with by concepts) and event (meaning for a subject) will be used to focus on what may be the crux of Lyotard's insights as far as education is concerned.

The crisis of representation

It is questionable whether the celebration of what is different, of heterogeneity, really is what can most usefully be derived from Lyotard's critique for education. He is often thought to identify difference with the representation of a preferable (societal) state of affairs to which education must contribute, in terms either of its preservation or of its realization. In contrast to this preoccupation, perhaps the more important question

Lyotard confronts us with is whether a critical educational theory can find its starting-point in representations of what is desirable. It seems to be argued recurrently that such representations are necessary for educational theory to get off the ground. But what is left out of the picture is the fact that the coherence of our representations (or phrases) makes us forget the groundlessness or emptiness from which the event irrupts. Acting and thinking are identified with the realization or accomplishment of representation. Lyotard wants to sensitize us to this identification, and this amounts to a fundamental repudiation of educational theory and practice, understood as governed by representations and rules without remainder.

The recognition of the crisis of representation, the experience that knowing and judging in the end are groundless, lies at the basis of his search for different points of departure. In ethics the Law cannot be represented. More precisely, Lyotard looks for a point of departure that recognizes the problem that representation of the Law is unjust. The injustice has to be challenged from a *non lieu*, a non-place: that is, neither from a particular (perhaps universal) point of view, nor from a particular belief. Hence there is no representation or idea that can ultimately – exhaustively and definitively – enlighten educational theory, nor can educational theory amount merely to a representation. It is the metaphysics of representation that is the problem.

It is the nature of ethical experience, unconnected with representable commands (precepts) and manifesting itself as an affect of the unrepresentable Law, that provides the different point of departure of a Lyotardian critique. This is an affect from which one cannot liberate oneself, of which one is not the user as one might conceivably be of language. This affect, which has profound implications for the logic of action and the categories of representation, refers to an event without a cause: manifesting itself as pain or suffering, it disrupts each and every particular order. It has no place (*non lieu*) in this order but rather refers to an *ou-topia* that is older than the order of representation and that expresses a non-linguistic relation. Language is not its manner of relation. What is at issue here is not a matter of reference, neither of truth, nor whether or not a particular representation expresses the affect. What is at stake is a transcendence that surpasses all intentional objects and all representation. We are dispossessed, occupied by something we cannot fathom or understand, but only obey. Lyotard appeals to a sensitivity towards the unpredictable (yet strangely unattributable) moment in which the injustice happens. Being educated here means being able to lend one's ear to this non-representability.

Lyotard, thus, offers us the means to criticize a theoretical tradition in education aimed at the realization of certain aims or the accomplishment of particular theories and ideas. In that still very dominant tradition, courses and curricula are subordinated to a particular project. Acting is the accomplishment or realization of a representation (an ideal or aim).

Educational theories also characteristically accept that they need a representation of what is possible (conceived in utopian or ideal terms which can serve as a touchstone of criticism).[2] Yet, as we have seen, this would not only amount to an injustice but would also – what is worse – forget the injustice, affirming the logic of the "system." As a consequence it would neutralize resistance as well. The late modern system that Lyotard is looking to resist (and that he has distinguished from postmodern thinking, Lyotard 1988b, 1993b) interweaves science, technology, and economy. The ordering of this system is one of a development without finality. He uses terms such as "complexification," "flexibility," "differentiation." Communication and discussion, these mainstays of Habermas's thought, moreover, do not interrupt the system so much as provide the most effective means for it to sustain itself. This "inhumanity" crucially involves a "forgetting of (the forgetting of) the injustice."

L'enfance and education: a different departure

Against the inhumanity of the system, there is, according to Lyotard, only one possible source of resistance: namely, the inhumanity of the childhood "of which the soul is the hostage," of the child who lives permanently in the human being (Lyotard 1988b: 9–10). The inhumanity of the system that "perpetuates itself under the denominator of development" is responsible for forgetting the inhumanity of childhood (ibid.). Hope and utopia and criticism and change remain possible precisely because this inhumanity (of the child properly understood) never completely adapts in the human. Childhood refers neither to a particular age nor to a transient stage of development. Rather it points to a never-ending indeterminacy, unmanageability or wildness, a trans-conceptual silence which Lyotard interprets in two ways. Childhood or *infantia*, the speech-less (*ce qui ne se parle pas*, Lyotard 1991a: 9), is the generic term for all that does not let itself be incorporated or regulated: the non-effective, the not-being-able-to, the non-representable affect, the receptiveness or experience without words. It cannot be understood or learned, but is, according to Lyotard, a source of resistance and sensitivity. Childhood prompts us "not to forget in order to resist and possibly not to be unjust" (Lyotard 1988b: 16). Guilt is the hopeful indeterminacy out of which the child continues to be born: this resistance announces and promises the *possible*. But it is not the indeterminacy of ideas on which one relies in judging; it is the material indeterminacy of the *event*.

To clarify this further Lyotard makes an important distinction, as we saw, between the *quod*, the meaning of something as event (Lyotard refers in this context to the uttering of a phrase as an *event*), and the *quid*, the meaning of something as such (the concept). The *quod* is the event before it is given particular "meaning": before it is, as it were, labeled or named by a particular concept:

That something happens always "precedes", as it were, the question about the what of what happens. More precisely, the question itself precedes. As "that something happens" is the question about the *event*, "next" it asks about the *event* that has taken place. The *event* comes as a question mark "before" it presents itself as a question."

(Lyotard 1988b: 94)

The question which asks for a filling-in of the "what" (the *quid*) makes us forget about the question mark: "the 'that something arrives' is always guarded from what comes in, is always incorporated in a conceptual frame and outlook which is unavoidably biased" (Lyotard 1988a: 43). The *quod* has a meaning (significance) that does not dissolve in a particular concept. The event has no need for words, for meaning, for language, in order to happen.

Lyotard's distinction, as Cris Van der Hoek suggests (1995: 61), can be illuminated by Hannah Arendt's differentiation between the "who" and the "what:" the "who" cannot be grasped in words, and the relationship to this "who" does not evaporate in a question of meaning (or any other linguistic relationship). Our own relationship towards our parents or children, for example, cannot in its singularity be understood, but it is something to which we are nevertheless not indifferent. Reduce the "who" to a particular meaning to try to say "who someone is" and we are left with a "what" in which the "who" has been forgotten. The manifestation of the "who" is an *event*, a birth, with no ground or reason, without place in any already demarcated context. It is singular and yet bears witness to meaningfulness. It is an event that goes from person to person, from "eye to eye," that cannot be seized by a particular concept. Although it escapes the user of concepts, the flashing past of the event leaves the person unpreparedly touched. The event is not something one can call to mind. It is forgotten at the moment that it is present in our memory, as soon as it is there through representation, meaning. And although we cannot dispose of this forgetting, although we cannot undo it, we can nevertheless orientate ourselves in its light.

The unpresentability that is implied by this indeterminacy implies a transcendence. But to realize transcendence of this kind is to neutralize; it must instead be allowed to be. What must be sustained is a sensitivity to this indeterminacy. For Lyotard it is no less than this that characterizes the educated human being: the person inhabited by a discomfort, by disquietude, restlessness that makes him or her think. The educated person is a distressed human being; the agony of the event marks genuine thinking. The indeterminate, not-thought, "hurts because one feels good in what has already been thought" (Lyotard 1988b: 31–2). In genuine thinking

the mind is not "led," but deferred . . . this thinking does not resemble combining symbols on the basis of particular rules. But if such combining is prepared to wait and look for its rules, it may have many similarities with this kind of thinking.

(Lyotard 1988b: 31–2)

It is, however, by way of a double concept of childhood that Lyotard adumbrates this indeterminacy: on the one hand *l'enfance du corps*, on the other *l'enfance de la liberté* (Lyotard 1991a: 38f.). The former derives in part from Freud, the latter from Kant and Arendt. Both *enfances* cut across linear conceptions of time, they cut across those cause–effect connections so characteristic of educational thought with its categorizations in unambiguous chronology, with its suppositions of causal influence, with its subsumption of these in chains of reasoning. This doubled concept disrupts the typical dynamics of educational theory that stifles the event in a thinking and action governed by representations.

For *L'enfance du corps*,

Aesthetic being is being there, here and now, exposed in the space-time and to the space-time of something that touches us *before* any concept or representation. This *before*, evidently we don't know it, as it is there before we *are*. It is like birth and childhood, which are there before we are. Evidently we don't know this before, it is there before we are. It is like birth and childhood. They are there before we are. The there in question is called body. I am not born, made child. I will be born later, with language, precisely on leaving childhood. . . . The aesthetic concerns that first touch that touched me when I was not yet there.[3]

(Lyotard 1991a: 39)

The time of *l'enfance du corps* is the time which has never started nor ended (ibid.: 50). The body is subjected to an irrevocable heteronomy, to being touched before it has been informed. But even this way of putting things may still be ambiguous. The heteronomy of the body is no part of the time-logic of cause and effect. Nor, moreover, is it part of that other unexpected causality without a cause, the causality characteristic of ethics and the time of freedom.

The heteronomy of the body knows nothing of physical time nor of ethical time because the *aisthesis* that rules it is neither concatenated-shackling (in the sense of intelligibility) nor unshakled-shakling (in the sense of responsibility). It is the paradox of the time of the body, constituted out of its not belonging to itself, out of its primary ungraspability – it is the paradox of time that it is not to be taken up in any chain. . . . But time is also *stase*.[4]

(Lyotard 1991a: 50–1)

This *aisthesis* is not amenable for change by duration. It is neither permanent nor primary because that would mean that there already is a chain of time. Being touched takes place when there is not yet a chain of time.

The time of *l'enfance de la liberté*, on the other hand, is the time of the judgment that interrupts the chain of cause and effect and the logic of a system that develops only according to its own survival. It is the time of natality (in the sense of Arendt, to whom Lyotard refers, albeit with some reservation); of birth or the radical irruption through which the riddle of life, the riddle of the beginning, comes into sight. It can only be understood and represented through the mode of the "as if," which can never do away with unmanageability and indeterminacy. With "natality" no reference is made to birth as an event that can be expected, part of a totality of desires (desire for children) insinuating itself, painfully perhaps, into our world. Natality refers to the emergence of what is different, difference emerging out of itself, and not as a result of what we see in it. This being different cannot be perceived with the objective eye, nor experienced conceptually. The child is the absolute beginning, a moment that cannot be situated in a chronology. "Birth" guarantees the possibility of renewal and the discontinuity of time, the possibility of interrupting the eternal return of the same: "Childhood is the name of this faculty insofar as it brings to the world of what is an astonishment at something which, in an instant, is no more. Astonishment at what is *already* and yet is not *something*" (Lyotard 1991a: 70).[5]

A mode of being that is not nothing, but not something either. Birth is an event that does not allow itself to be incorporated into the temporality that accustomed us to a homogenous and empty framework, a framework in which facts succeeded facts according to certain laws of cause and effect. Childhood introduces us into a time in which the future is not the consequence of a past, and where what comes into the world cannot be inferred from what is already in the world. To be able to answer to such a future requires the capacity radically to expose oneself to question. It requires something different from a permanent movement of renewal, in which case it is immediately put to use and reinforces rather than interrupts the continuity. Childhood stands not for what is possible, but for what is impossible. It cannot be realized, but its truth can manifest itself. Confrontation with its truth, sensitivity to its truth do not *teach* us: they change us.

Philosophy of education: the reality of the child

Lyotard shows us the way to a philosophy of education that starts from what may be called the reality of the child, a reality that is strange insofar as it cannot be represented or laid down, neither fact nor datum. Generally educational theory has nothing to say about this reality of the child. It is ignorant of the reality of what passes between this child and me, "eye to eye," which makes crying and laughing possible and remains invisible to objective thinking (Desmond 1995: 27–54). The reality of the child cannot become a part of the world of means and ends, of representations, of what is replaceable and repeatable. It effaces those categories of cause and effect, necessity and contingency, irreversibility and publicity, that are characteristic of the theory of education and of acting and thinking understood in terms of representations.

Educational theory cannot forget the reality of "facts." The reality of the child escapes the language of theory. Of course, there is child psychology (studying children's needs and children's thinking); of course, there is sociology (studying children's loneliness or the violence they are subjected to); of course, educational theory concerns itself with matters of practical policy: for the educators, teachers, therapists, psychologists, counselors, and inspectors who evaluate and intervene, this goes without saying. Childhood is something incorporated into our practices and institutions. It is explained, understood, and given a place: we know childhood only too well (Larrosa 1998: 149–61). But for Lyotard there is more, something that surpasses each attempt to give it place. It upsets the certainty of our knowledge and questions the power and the capability of our practices. And *this* childhood has no place in our language. Our language cannot grasp the infant any more than it can speak our language. This lack is not a deficiency of knowledge. It is not about what we do not yet know or cannot manipulate or understand. It is not only a question of time, of more research, more measures, more institutions. The reality of the child is not an object of knowledge or of understanding, but what escapes all objectification, not the anchorage of our power to govern, but that which marks its impotence. The reality of the child is its absolute heterogeneity towards our world of representations (knowledge) and power (what we are capable of), an enigmatic reality that escapes us, manifesting itself as affect, disquietude, emptiness, yet laying its claims on us.

Lyotard's writing disturbs us because, among other things, it seems not to direct us but to gesture towards what cannot be said. It leaves us as orphans abandoned. It does not direct us, yet it demands that the unspoken be heard.

If this is unclarity or paradox, is it deficiency of language that is responsible? Are his words just *Spielerei*, idle talk? Neither phrase, we think, does justice to the motivation here, and an example may help to advert to what language can and what it cannot do. When losing a beloved one, we grieve. The experience of the loss of a friend, a partner, a parent, a child, overwhelms us. We speak about it to those who are dear to us; we say that we express what we feel. And yet it seems that in our words we come to realize more and more what someone meant for us. Here language cannot be characterized merely as a vehicle for our thoughts; it shapes what we think so much that we may later say that a particular phrasing was indeed the right way to put it. In the beginning we could not find the words, but after having spoken the words we recognize in what we said what we felt. The referential function in which we use shared meanings or general concepts for particular situations and things is to be distinguished from what language does in itself. The latter is performative (in Austin's sense). An excuse, a promise transgresses as it were the inner boundary of language, of spoken words, though it remains however in another sense referential. When we use language performatively, we particularize, yet in some sense all the expression's meaning is fully available beforehand. Though there is particularization, there is no singularization. Precisely here one finds Lyotard's central argument. It focuses, on the one hand, on the difference between "saying something" (the experiences that go with it, the *event* of the saying itself) and "what is said" (the conceptual content); on the other hand, it highlights the singularity.

Loss of a loved one cannot be grasped exhaustively in a particular meaning, neither can it be recovered by it. It is characterized by uniqueness, irrevocability, and unrepeatability. What is lost is irreplaceable as it is typified by a relative absoluteness. No conceptual framework contains the loss of one's child. What escapes from the shared meanings, the symbolic system, the referential use, is for Lyotard the transcendent. The transcendent provides the possibility of something that is radically new. It can be experienced but not thought of beforehand. That something happens cannot be reduced to its meaning. The transcendent escapes a definitive, exhaustive meaning.

Because of its relation with (shared) meaning(s) – we talk, of course, about something – there is always the (mistaken) suggestion that the conceptual dimension recovers the meaning of what happens. But the referential cannot do justice to the transcendent; the evocative is required. The poetic can surpass the conceptual and give it voice. Plainly this cannot be the subject of scientific research (though narrative research may aspire to something of this kind). Where science is directed towards what is general, here it is the personal and particular that are at issue: which is (only) accessible to the individual. And although this is highly subjective in one sense, it is far from being a product of whim or fantasy.

It is respect that calls on us to judge without criteria, to attend to the voice of the other, which was not heard because we silenced it. The political legacy of Lyotard's position requires us to cast off our indifference to this appeal; it requires us to be moved, touched by what is transcendent to ourselves, and affected by its truth, its resistance for fruitful education. And this calls for painstaking study. Though childhood never is what we know, it is nevertheless the bearer of a truth to which we have to listen. And we should not forget that the reality of the child can and will only be spoken of on the basis of what moves us. Thus speaking of childhood as an *event* may be a task for philosophy of education: counteracting among other things that compulsion to classify, to measure, categorize, and pigeonhole childhood, a danger particularly threatening wherever education is institutionalized. In the story that can then be told, the corresponding despair of those involved in education may be shared. Maybe the really important implication for education in Lyotard's work is, therefore, not the issue of the injustice as such but rather the reminder of the way things can be kept open, so that newness is allowed to emerge. Childhood is not an object amenable to the exercise of our power, but rather calls upon our response. It is not reducible to the place we allot, but demands our hospitality. With an ear for this paradox we can perhaps realize that we cannot be led by representations alone, representations without remainder. The rest – that which asks for our attention and responsibility – the rest, we must accept, is silence.[6]

Notes

1 It is important also to indicate another problem, which is in some sense technical in kind. Wittgenstein's private-language argument has made clear that meaning can never be exclusively and in principle singular; others must be able to understand what is expressed. But at the same time he makes it abundantly clear that in using language, in using words or concepts for particular purposes, the subject may express something singular. Such singular usage changes to some extent the palette of available meanings for a particular concept. The metaphor of family resemblance helps us to understand how this is possible, how in other words the subject can make him- or herself understood through the shared meanings, while at the same time being able to express something that until then is only seen by the subject.

Moreover, language games have their own rules, their own point, but they are embedded within a form of life. To see language games as mutually exclusive can only partly be right. Games depend not only on more technical rules (the rules of chess) but also on rules about playing (the object is to win). Inevitably social, both require an initiation. Hence it is too extreme to hold that genres of discourse and the aims they envisage somehow exclude one another. Clearly, Wittgenstein is not seeking an analysis of concepts in terms of necessary and sufficient conditions. He is not offering an "objective" account of meaning, or aiming to provide one in which intention is primary. Not only does he hold that such an approach is wrong-headed (meaning as use); his position is altogether more subtle, balancing the subjective and the intersubjective.

In the light of this Lyotard may be wrong to suggest that his own thinking here develops from a Wittgensteinian idea. If so, it may be that a number of consequences follow for his position in matters of politics. On the other hand, it is questionable how far this perhaps largely technical confusion is indeed a serious threat to the political position, whether it is crucial for what he really wants to argue for.

2 For a more detailed analysis see Masschelein 1998.

3 In the original:

> Être esthétiquement . . . c'est être là, ici et maintenant, exposé dans l'espace-temps et à l'espace-temps d'un quelque chose qui touche *avant* tout concept et même toute représentation. Cet *avant*, évidemment, on ne le connaît pas, puisqu'il y est avant qu'on y soit. Il est comme la naissance et l'enfance, qui y sont avant qu'on y soit. Le y en question s'appelle corps. Ce n'est pas moi qui nais, qui suis enfanté. Moi, je naîtrai après, avec le langage, en sortant de l'enfance, précisément. . . . L'esthétique concerne cette touche première qui m'a touché quand je n'y étais pas.
>
> (Lyotard 1991a, 39)

4   L'hétéronomie du corps n'entend rien au temps physique ni au temps
        éthique parce que l'*aisthesis* qui la commande n'est ni enchaînée-enchaî-
        nante (au sens de l'intelligibilité), ni déchaînée-enchaînante (au sens de
        la responsabilité). C'est le paradoxe du temps du corps, selon qu'il est
        constitué de sa non-appartenance à soi-même, de son désaisissement pri-
        maire – c'est le paradoxe de ce temps qu'il n'est du mode d'aucune
        chaîne. . . . Mais le temps est aussi *stase*.

                                                            (Lyotard 1991a: 50–1)

5   L'enfance est le nom de cette faculté, autant qu'elle apporte, au monde
        de ce qui est, l'étonnement de ce qui, un instant, n'est rien encore. De ce
        qui est *déjà* sans encore être *quelque chose* pourtant.

                                                                    (Ibid.: 70).

6 Translations are mainly our own, though we would like to thank James
   Williams for advice. For their help with the correct English wording of our
   thoughts we would like to thank Richard Smith and particularly Paul Standish.

9   In freedom's grip

Paul Standish

> Christians and Jews are in agreement on this point, that emancipation is
> listening to the true *manceps*, and that modernity breaks this agreement.
> Modernity tries to imagine and carry out an emancipation in the absence
> of any other.
>
> (Lyotard, "The Grip (Mainmise)")

In *The Postmodern Condition* (1984a) Lyotard examines two versions of the
narrative of legitimation of knowledge. In the first, the spread of
knowledge is held to extend freedom: it is to the narrative of freedom that
the State resorts when it needs to justify the training it imposes on its
people. The child is compulsorily schooled for the sake of his or her own,
and the larger society's, freedom. Humanity is cast as the hero of liberty, all
peoples having a right to knowledge. Education is a means to individual
freedom and the free society. In the second (Humboldtian) version, there
is a threefold aspiration whereby commitments both to science and to an
ideal of ethical and social practice are brought together by a third unifying
element, that ensures a coincidence between the scientific search for true
causes and the pursuit of just ends in moral and political life. Three in one:
education realizes a certain ideal of freedom. Lyotard connects the first of
these legitimations with primary, the second with higher education. At a
later stage, in "The Grip," he describes the modern western ideal of emancipation as involving the full possession of knowledge, will, feeling, where
one *provides oneself* with the rule of law, the law of willing, and the control
of the emotions (Lyotard 1993b: 150).

There are other intervening, or perhaps simply different, possibilities
here, and a brief sketch of some of these is germane to this chapter.
Education has offered the promise of emancipation in a number of ways that
are loosely spoken of in terms of "liberal education." An education is liberal
if, above all, it is not primarily concerned with the training of the workforce,
that is, it is not instrumentalized. But the term is a source of some confusion,
especially in view of its more stipulative usage by thinkers in the British Isles.
The widely influential idea of a liberal education developed in the 1960s by

R. S. Peters, P. H. Hirst, and R. F. Dearden, with its most obvious roots in the philosophy of Michael Oakeshott, was an attempt to restate a conception of education with ancient origins, not only in the face of instrumentalism but against the then-rapid growth of progressive or child-centered education. While, in the United States, Israel Scheffler was at the same time developing a similar line of thought, the parallel is broken when the massive influence of John Dewey in the American scene is considered: in the united Kingdom the early Dewey was a guiding light for the progressivism that liberal education opposed. In common with its classical counterpart, this modern liberal education foregrounds initiation into intellectual pursuits that are intrinsically worthwhile. But while the central preoccupation in the former is with a freeing from illusion, that of the latter is rather with the development of rational autonomy: a characteristically modern concern with obvious Kantian roots. Liberal education sees the child as lacking the development of mind. Emancipation from this condition is to be achieved only through initiation into public forms of thought, exemplified in traditional academic disciplines.

Progressivism also has emphasised the importance of autonomy, but here it has been allied more closely to notions of authenticity. There is an oscillation between a more or less horticultural picture of the unfolding essential self and a more existentialist emphasis on creativity. Where the former is dominant, Rousseau's complex account of the development of Emile through the proper education of *amour-propre* is blithely forgotten in favour of the easy slogan that man is born free. Where the tendency is towards the latter, there has been less melancholy and more defiance in the face of the prevailing norms and values of society. Insofar as progressive education regards the child as already whole or already free and merely threatened by society, any idea of lack internal to the child fades from view, and the connection with liberal education recedes. Education involves the provision of conditions that maximize the possibility of growth. The child must be emancipated from environments that lack stimulation and from constraints on growth imposed by society (including those imposed by traditional schooling).

The development of adult, further, and higher education during the 1980s and 1990s has in certain respects revived this earlier child-centeredness (even as the latter has generally been reviled), while the liberation pedagogy of Paolo Freire and the psychotherapy of Carl Rogers have been more or less immediate influences. More decisive, however, has been the hijacking of those ideas by managerialism: eagerly "listening" to its customers, late capitalism constructs its life-long learners as autonomous, discerning, authentic. The revival of the language of learner-centeredness and experiential learning should not be allowed to obscure the extent to which such principles have been distorted. In certain respects these developments have revealed problems that were latent in the earlier progressivism: in the tension between its creatively enabling aspects and the drift towards conceptualizing and providing for these systematically, especially in conditions of greater complexification. Emancipation, too fully programmed, holds us in its grip.

Perhaps the crux of the difficulty here has to do with different orientations to time, differences that Lyotard's words capture well:

> it is one thing to project human emancipation, and another to programme the future as such. Liberty is not security. What some people have called the postmodern perhaps merely designates a break, or at least a splitting, between one pro- and the other – between project and programme. The latter seems today much better able than the former to meet the challenge thrown down to humanity by the process of complexification. But among the events which the programme attempts to neutralize as much as it can one must, alas, also count the unforeseeable effects engendered by the contingency and freedom proper to the human project.
>
> (Lyotard 1991c: 68–9)

A related programmatic possibility of emancipation has been promoted in recent years with the advent of new technology. The massive effort to remove barriers to access to post-compulsory education – barriers such as physical disability, parental responsibilities, the location of classes and their timing – has been aided and partly propelled by information technology. Many of these barriers are thought to be surmountable through the overcoming of constraints of space and time, and information technology has a crucial role to play in this. The accompanying rhetoric of facilitation, entitlement, ownership, and empowerment underlines the ways in which education so reconceived can enable students to take hold of and direct their own learning. Often juxtaposed against what is in fact a heavy caricature of didactic teaching and the pointless learning of facts, its emphasis on procedures of information access promises a pure exchangeability and emancipation from the substantive and particular demands of knowledge itself.

For all their undoubted importance, however, the ideals of autonomy and authenticity are subject to a degeneration with broad cultural and educational manifestations. Autonomy becomes allied to consumerist conceptions of free choice while authenticity is subject to a sentimentalized idealization of the self and a theatricalization of the real: media images enframe us with hyperbolic images of "the real thing." The kind of mastery celebrated in autonomy correlates with an expectation of explicitness and transparency (and with self-management and presentation). With the advent of new technology especially, it takes the form of an overriding of time and space. All these forms of emancipation involve a liberation from constraints in such a way that one's hands are free, to reach out and seize: one is emancipated from the *manceps,* the one who takes hold, in order to take hold oneself (Lyotard 1993b: 144–58). This freedom is in important respects a freedom from the other (and from the need to acknowledge the other). It is a denial of lack.

The Postmodern Condition is rightly celebrated for its anticipation and exposure of the performativity that has increasingly characterized our education systems. What has been less widely understood, especially in educational theory, is the way in which Lyotard's work reveals the limitations and problems of ideals of autonomy and authenticity, and the bearing this has on education. In many respects these ideals have seemed to offer the best hope of resistance against the encroachments of performativity, yet they are partly complicit with its harms. To show why this is the case it is necessary to explore some of the contemporary ills that Lyotard identifies. The present chapter attempts this especially by taking up the themes in Lyotard's writings of childhood and "the jews."

I

It is a certain conception of the *telos* of mature freedom and fullness of being, Lyotard suggests, that leads us to think of childhood in terms of lack. Dewey saw immaturity as a strength, the power to grow, but Lyotard's point is different. Regardless of any *telos,* lack is internal to our experience of our own childhood. It is not so much that as children we lack reason. It is rather that we are

> *affected* at a time when we do not have the means – linguistic and representational – to name, identify, reproduce, and recognize what it is that is affecting us. By children, I mean the fact that we are born before we are born to ourselves.
>
> (Lyotard 1993b: 149)

The infant cannot speak for itself, cannot represent itself. Once childhood is brought to consciousness, it becomes progressively less like childhood. Our childhood exists as something that starts before we are aware of it: a necessary unrecoverable background, like the inevitable background there must be to all our knowledge and understanding. This background seems deficient in the light of our ideals of fullness of knowledge and self-awareness. It is seen as lack, and education tries in its different ways to replenish this.

The lack that is childhood is paralleled in the apparently political sphere – in fact, much more than political – by the lack that characterises "the jews." Lyotard's provocative phrase does not refer to any religious, political, or philosophical figure or subject, nor simply to real jewish people. Yet there is something in Europe's history of anti-Semitism that is apposite here. Anti-Semitism is different from racism or xenophobia in that the Jews represent *something that Europe does not want to or cannot know anything about*. Even when they are dead, it abolishes their memory and refuses them burial in its land. All of this takes place in the unconscious and has no right to speak.

(Ibid.: 159)

"The jews" suggests first those on the margins of the western world, who cannot be incorporated into it without risking their own destruction. The significance is broader than this still-political characterization might suggest, however: "the jews" are radically other to western thought, with its urge to conceptualize and encompass; "the jews" can be neither the enemy nor existentialist "outsiders." This is not a matter of nationality or nature. It is rather that representation is anathema to them: they cannot speak for themselves. So to speak, for them, would be to cease to be who they are:

"Jew" is the name of that which resists the principle of self-assertion, "jew" is that which laughs at the will to power and criticizes blind narcissism of the community (including the Jewish community) haunted by the desire of its own subjectivity. Under the epithet "jew" is denounced the conviction that dependence is constitutive, that there is the Other, and that wanting to eliminate that Other in some universal project for autonomy is an error and leads to crime.

(Lyotard 1997: 109)

The objects of alienation here are multiple. The words allude to the grotesque self-assertion of the German university hailed in Heidegger's Rectoral Address in 1933 (Heidegger 1985), where self-assertion is seen as the guarantee of the meta-knowledge of the triptych of services of labor, defense, and knowledge crucial to German identity. Lyotard's words not only resist nostalgic or complacent conceptions of community but undermine the self-consciousness and self-confidence of the politics of identity itself. And they react also to the more formal commitments of civic liberalism: the principle of social inclusion comes to seem sentimental and surreptitiously authoritarian (not least in the burgeoning requirements of "life-long learning"). National identity politics, with its obsessive recreation of origin (or destiny) stories, has its counterpart in the ideal of personal authenticity. Assertions of community and of individual identity through autonomy alike are manifestations of the *manceps*. (Western metaphysics cannot entertain the idea that something is not to be grasped.) The tendency to override the other is implicated in a forgetting.

Both childhood and "the jews" are necessarily *forgotten*, and the only justice to them is the acknowledgement of this forgetting. The danger is that this forgotten is imagined to be recoverable: this illusion amounts to a forgetting of the forgetting. The familiar failure of Holocaust films, the anthropomorphism of recollections of childhood in poetry or analysis, unwittingly point to an impossibility: "One betrays misery, infancy by presenting them" (Lyotard 1990a: 28). And these are not discrete: the political has its echo in the personal, and the personal reverberates through the political. The sections that follow examine the consequences of the denial of forgetting that Lyotard exposes in the (post)modern world.

The New Republic

Childhood and "the jews" are to be understood in terms of lacks that are purportedly to be overcome, respectively by the promise of an emancipatory education and by the presumption of an inclusionary politics. Overcoming the lack that is childhood entails coming towards full consciousness of oneself, in autonomy or authenticity. For many thinkers who have influenced the development of educational practice, this has coincided with the recognition of a human nature in which individual difference is allowed to flourish. The *telos* typically combines authentic singularity with the common measure of a universal human nature in a politics based on relationships between individuals and the state. Moreover, such a conception of human relationships is the basis of republican democracy, the mode of political organization that promises a self-realization for the individual in a way that seems to enshrine humanist ideals. As Lyotard argues in *The Differend* (1988a), the notion of a unversal human nature connects in the political sphere with the assertion of the republican "we, the people."

Capitalism becomes fine-tuned to allow individual difference to flourish within its market-place of life-styles and identities, stimulated by the artificial creation of desire. Conversely, the substance of policy is shaped increasingly by the growing reliance on focus groups. Responsiveness to desire then extends across the realm of the political, imposing requirements of its own: "Through inquiries, interviews, polls, roundtables, 'series,' 'case files,' we see ourselves in the media as humans busy fulfilling the duty to assert our rights" (Lyotard 1997: 120). What is striking is that, with their prominence in contemporary politics, rights become duties, duties to exercise choice. This is a pre-emptive move, determining the type of person that is required and the fuzzy conception of community within which that person is to see him- or herself:

> Express yourselves freely, have the courage of your ideas, of your opinions, communicate them, enrich the community, enrich yourselves, set yourselves to it, converse, there is nothing but good in making use of your rights since it takes place in respecting the rights of others, circulate, everything is possible within the limits fixed by laws or rules. And besides, these rules can themselves be revised. . . . For the exercise of one's rights and the vigilance over their being respected to be required as forms of duty, therein lies a kind of self-

evidence, as infallible as a totalitarian disposition can be. Infallible as for the ruin of self-containment. Why didn't you do this, say that, you had the right!

(Ibid.: 118–9)

In *The Third Way* Anthony Giddens calls for the "positive welfare society": unlike the negative freedoms of the welfare state, with which, in the United Kingdom, the Beveridge Report was concerned, it is now the positive freedoms of autonomy and the development of the self that must be stressed:

> Positive welfare would replace each of Beveridge's negatives with a positive: in place of want, autonomy; not Disease but active health; instead of Ignorance, education, as a continuing part of life; rather than Squalor, well-being; and in place of Idleness, initiative.

(Giddens 1998: 128)

This may be a benign liberal face of emancipation with its current "big idea" of social inclusion. There is, after all, no denying that social inclusion can encompass an obvious alleviation of harms: reduction of poverty, enfranchisement, more equal distribution of goods, harmonization of cultural difference. The globalizing of culture, on the face of it, makes all this all the more realizable. Social tension has been generated where historically and geographically contextual practices have been uprooted and juxtaposed. With information technology, however, traditionally located practices are partially superseded by the global exchange of information and cultural products. Education in the new republic expands to reach out to the deprived, the neglected, and the disenfranchised, and to overcome the barriers to a full participation in its life. "Access," "ownership," and "empowerment" have become its vocabulary within a skills-laden ethos of self-expression. Self-evaluation feeds into examination practices. Personal education extends to the *therapy* of the self, harnessing what is past in the name of better mastery and control. The requirement to take responsibility for developing all aspects of one's life is supported by a veritable magazine industry of programmes of self-improvement: makeovers for houses, gardens, and the swelling middle-aged and middle-classed. Circulate, assert yourself, *participate*: this is an aestheticized sociability. And aestheticization, loaded as it is with this suffix, is no immersion in beauty and sensuality, but rather a distancing and disengagement from content, the self-conscious voyeurism of representations.

A whole metaphysical picture is at stake here. Representation is metaphysical: in the political realm its apotheosis is found in public democratic systems; analogically, in thinking it requires a bringing before consciousness by way of retention in the memory. And increasingly computer memory is no longer merely the substitute, but rather the model for what memory is taken to be. Characteristically orientated towards the future, the aim is always more complete information (more research projects are needed, of course), information whose capacities of prediction and planning can neutralize events and manage risk, stocking the future and controlling the present (Lyotard 1991c: 65). It is not just that the will of the people is brought to full consciousness and presented in the parliament or the tribunal; it is that everything is available through the touch of a key, in the archive and the database: presentation becomes the mark of authenticity and of the real.

The republic, which articulates itself with "we, the people," must realize a maturity that can, so it imagines, put behind itself its own childhood. From what childhood has this republic come? What is the violence before the republic (for there is always violence before the established order comes into being)? So also the a-rationality behind mature self-mastery is an *ancien régime* of the soul: "Intimate Terror exerts itself without respite" (Lyotard 1997: 212). The republic and mature self-mastery alike require an assertion of rationality as sovereign that must exterminate whatever is beyond human grasp. Denial of the unknown reduces it to the exotic, gods of an archaic world now captured in reference books and museums (hence thoroughly superseded), sentimentally contained in developmental psychologies and child-care manuals. Republican politics must, it takes it as read, eradicate the irrationality of the past, its non-presence at the court of enquiry, its tyranny and subjection. It is unable to think beyond its own institution. So, then, the educated person comes to see as merely contingent the lack of reason from which reason (imagined to be sovereign) necessarily emerges. There is the denial that reason can be only the viceroy of something that is not (wholly) reason, and to which reason might otherwise bear witness.

The universal principle, and its political legacy of rights, liberty, equality: the secular thrust of these principles coincides with the "death of god." The rational autonomy, self-mastery, self-awareness promised by education deny what is other (and the need to acknowledge the other). Von Humboldt's ideal denies god in its overriding of lack. Deicide is effected through a progressive overcoming of lack and the requirement of transparency. The therapy of self-awareness that calls the self to account, that tries to haul everything from the forgotten, destroys the silent and secret part of the soul. "In the republican principle, humanity and its autonomy blur, under the guise of laws and rights, the traces of an immemorial independence" (ibid.: 193).

Megalopolis

The republic coincides with the development of a world increasingly changed by new technology in which these dichotomies –

inclusion/exclusion, public/private – dissolve. And so the new republic differs from the old in that it has no outside, no other. It is realized with the erosion of other spaces and other times and the horizons that these confer. The city, with its suburbs and surrounding countryside, the city as ancient figure of the *polis*, is displaced by the megalopolis in which all must be represented:

> If the *Urbs* becomes the *Orbs* and if the zone becomes a whole city, then the megalopolis has no outside. And consequently no inside. Nature is under cosmological, geological, meteorological, touristic. and ecological control. Under control or in reserve, reserved. You no longer *enter* into the megalopolis. It is no longer a city that needs to be rebegun. The former "outside," provinces, Africa, Asia, are part of it, mixed in with indigenous Westerners in a variety of ways. Everything is foreign, and nothing is.
>
> The last bolt in the wild propagation of the megalopolis will be sprung loose when one's "real" presence at work becomes superfluous. The body as producer is already an archaism, as are the time clock and the means of transportation. Telecommunication and teleproduction have no need of well-built cities. The megalopolis girds the planet from Singapore to Los Angeles to Milan. Wholly a zone between nothing and nothing, it is separate from lived durations and distances. And every habitat becomes a habitation where life consists in sending and receiving messages.
>
> (Lyotard 1997: 21–2)

The unimpeded flow of messages dissolves the dichotomy of presence and absence, and identity is reconfigured in the exchanges of electronic mail. Containing the other, the megalopolis colonizes inner lives with a denial of nature more total than exclusion:

> It's when the general life seeks to take hold of the secret life that things go bad. The human right to separation, which governs our declared rights, is thus violated. There is no need for a totalitarian power, or a libelous rumour, no need to expel, incarcerate, torture, no need to starve, to prohibit from working or having a home, to censor, occupy, isolate, or take hostage, in order to violate the right to separation.
>
> (Ibid.: 118)

Silence and secrecy are taboo. The private is eroded by the pervasiveness of the political demand that we be represented. In confessional television, more generally in the cult of therapy, we connive with politicians, bureaucrats, media tycoons, in forces that commandeer this "second existence," fomenting a kind of paranoia about whatever may be outside this surveillance and control. The forces that would take a grip on this, outside or within ourselves, "are thus haunted by the suspicion that there is something that escapes them, that might plot against them. They need the whole soul, and they need this soul to surrender unconditionally" (Lyotard 1997: 118). Childhood becomes an object of this fear, the other in oneself (the object precisely of recovery and control in therapy); yet this is a necessary other, always ineradicable behind the development of maturity, always acknowledged in any maturity worth its name. This second existence, silent and secret, is what we must listen to in order to find out how to say what we do not yet know how to say. It is the exception to the exchanges of rights and communication but at the same time their legitimation (ibid.: 121–2).

Denying this "second existence," the ideal of presence is the blasphemous fantasy of a timeless ubiquity, blasphemous in its denial of the other. The very possibility of criticism, of thought itself, is dulled and neutralized. The city's limits are overcome by the megalopolis; so also

> metaphysics, which was urbanizaton through concepts of something exterior to thought, appears to lose its motive when that outside, nature, reality, God, man, is dissolved through the effects of criticism. The negation at work within question and argument turns back on itself. Nihilism cannot remain an object for thought or a theme, it affects the dialectical mode that was the nerve of philosophical discourse. Nothingness requires its inscription by thought not as a product of its critical argument but as a style of its reflexive writing
>
> (Ibid.: 24).

On the pivot of this point of style rationality changes: ethics is formalized as moral reasoning (ibid.: 173). Yet the narcissism that is at work here covers over this emptiness: explanations become lures in the face of nothingness. Even the prominence of development is a product of the preoccupation with making things present. With its unwavering attention to presentation, the west diffuses its nihilism:

> There remains the way of presenting. The difference between nature and art falls apart: for lack of nature, everything is art or artifice. Development is an abstract idea, a ruler's word, that rules nothing, except decimal points. As for existence, the megalopolis views itself aesthetically.
>
> (Ibid.: 22)

Whatever problems burgeoning development throws up are, above all, to be managed. Managing is inexhaustible, it is axiomatic that everything can be managed, the presentation of its signs is self-propelling, and the criterion of efficient management is speed. The perfect exchange of performativity is quintessentially a saving of time, a denial of time, with an anxiety to have everything present – an anxiety to have everything spread out in front of us, commodities to be consumed and thrown up – that is the bulimia of Western thought (ibid.: 168).

What is forgotten

With ever more data to be binged, machines redefine (the role of) memory. Knowledge, we are surely tired of saying, is reduced to information, so that computer memory adds and subtracts: it does not forget but deletes. This denies that some people, and something in all of us, cannot be presented but must be acknowledged precisely as what is necessarily forgotten. It removes the depth of understanding that otherwise is realized precisely in virtue of its intimation of what is not represented: because it is forgotten, because it is secluded in the act of selection, or because it is unspeakable. In the megalopolis there is no other space or other time, and education and communication become just the exchange of information and skills. If, however, there is to be understanding, there must remain this sense of what is forgotten (what is gotten before), intimation of the ineffable background to our lives. Our position is always of having come after, from a background we can never fully know.

The aim must be to preserve the remainder, the remainder that cannot, without some radical distortion or fatal compromise, be recalled. Auschwitz cannot be recalled, and there is a duty to remember it as unrepresentable in this way. Make a film of Auschwitz, write a novel, and it is inscribed and hence erasable or deletable. It must remain "the unforgettable forgotten." It has "no place in the space nor in the time of domination, in the geography and the diachrony of the self-assured spirit, because it is not synthesizable" (Lyotard 1990: 26). Yet while it must be remembered as an absence, this memory must not be the Romantic melancholy of the haunting or felt absence; this is not the politics of identity (ibid.: 11) nor the cathartic work of Freud's *Trauerarbeit*. It involves the "singular debt of an interminable anamnesis" (ibid.: 94) and requires a mourning to be repeated over and over, not in an erasable inscription but in a "[w]riting and rewriting according to this mourning" (ibid.: 93). Such a writing does not impose, rather it frustrates, an interpretation of events. It does not recollect but acknowledges absence.

Sometimes almost approaching the thought of "the jews," Heidegger dreamed of an original place, but his thought is inclined to coalesce around this thought in a way that that of "the jews" cannot. Early in *Being and Time* the subject-object dichotomy is dismantled, but there is a later underwriting of community (*Volk*) as subject. Lyotard's preoccupation with "the jews," in contrast, is not a concern with the politics of cultural identity, for that very idea depends on a possibility of representing: the retrieval motivating origin or destiny stories. Plainly resisting Heidegger, he is calling not for the "fashioning" of a people but rather, in terms increasingly, irresistibly religious, for the banning or ridiculing of the longing to represent the holy, with all its graven imagery. "The people" must be delivered from

> their burden of blood and earth, from their fleshly habitat, from their bread and wine, as from so many fetishes in which, supposedly their destination as the guardian of Being was exclusively signified. This disaster presents an "occasion" – which in the pagan-Christian tradition is still called the death of God – to rethink the guardianship in an entirely different "fashion," namely, as a regard: the "people" dispersed in the desert, refusing to fashion themselves into a "people," or to project themselves according to what is proper to them alone, having learned that both unity and properness are neither in their power nor in their duty, that even the pretension to be the guardian of the Forgotten lacks consideration for it, since it is the Forgotten that holds the "people" hostage whatever their "fashion" of being-together. And that, of course, God cannot be "dead" since he is not an (aesthetic) life. He is a name of nothing, the without-name, an unapproachable law that does not signify itself in nature in figures, but is recounted in a book. Not withdrawn from the world in the world, but withdrawn and preserved in the letters that as one knows circulate, but which, on all occasions, command respect. An exteriority inside. God can, must, die (and be reborn) only in a thought of nature, a Dionysism, an Orphism, a Christianity, where the nihilistic moment of the crucifixion will be countered. In a myth, and this myth is always a geopolitics. Geophilosophy (of Germany, Greece, France) is evidently the effect of an uncontrolled "mythization" (Lacoue-Labarthe V, 132) that insists and resists in the apparently most sober thought of the late Heidegger. It remains bound to sacrality, but completely ignores the Holy.
>
> (Lyotard 1990: 80)

Cultural identity becomes a people's affirmation of authenticity, as much a prey to the pose as its personal counterpart. It may be that what needs to be dispersed are the very notions of commonality and consensus that are at the heart of many conceptions of community, and this in favour of a community of *dissensus*.[1]

Christians and jews are in agreement that emancipation is listening to the true *manceps*, but it is Christians who make present, represent, the very body of the god being taken into the mouth. The jewish god is not named but to be awaited. The "good news" brought by the incarnation turns the spiritual community linked by the reading of the Book into a concrete community, "first political (the empire), then economic (Protestant capitalism)" (Lyotard 1993b: 118), and a religion of brotherly love lays the way for the fraternity of free and equal citizens of the republic (ibid.: 161). There are, in consequence, two kinds of denial behind the modern world's self-assertion. First, there is the secular denial of the all-powerful and unfathomable god who presents himself in the world. Second, there is the preceding denial of the unknowable and unnameable god, who, unlike God-in-Christ, cannot be made present, is still to be awaited: "Emancipation seeks to undo the grip of history itself, the grip of the postponed time of the promise, since there is no history without the promise" (ibid.: 153). Thus, the longing for the god-made-present, nostalgia for the authentic, no less, must be displaced by the promise of no-thing. The different relation to the forgotten that is required turns attention to the debt that is not to be settled, to a salvation that is perpetually deferred, and to a politics without redemption. It points to "a religion that reveals that the veil does not rise" (ibid.: 160) and to the impossibility of a full transparency and scrutiny.

That there is something that cannot be spelled out is seen in the unrecoverability of childhood, the incapacity of community to incorporate "the jews," and the unsharability of our common mortality. In "The Grip" Lyotard's tone is dark and sardonic: "The emancipated ones are the persons or things that owe nothing to anyone but themselves: Freed from all debts to the other" (ibid.: 150).

The background, the second existence, cannot be named. There is then a debt to that which we cannot know but from which we come, irretrievable and other to our rational grasp of things. We must live with the ghost of childhood, and this is a work of mourning that neither culminates in catharsis nor dwells in nostalgia, but must continue. Wordsworth's childhood has come too late. Lyotard's is something more wholly other and less fully recoverable in language: it requires the art of the avant-garde.[2] Mourning must be an acknowledgement of this non-presentability in the manner of the avant-garde, an art that resists the naturalization through sense-perception of its object and in so doing bears witness to that impossibility. This is no place for emotion recollected in tranquillity.

This *anaisthesis* that the avant-garde effects releases us from the aestheticization that has extended through the fields of desire and the exercise of rights, manifested in multiple forms in education through performativity. There is a latent nihilism, moreover, where autonomy narrows to the formal elegance of moral reasoning and authenticity becomes marketable as "the real thing": "Nihilism is combated only by its interiorization as a fabulous aesthetic." (Lyotard 1997: 26) The broad narratives of autonomy and authenticity that have been prominent in educational theory and practice are exposed in this discussion to their aporias.

II

There is no need here to rehearse accounts of performativity in education, though its problems also have echoed through this chapter. It is time to ask more directly what in education is lost where the new republic and the megalopolis are dominant, what Lyotard's accounts of childhood and "the jews" require us to restore. There is, it is true, a certain melancholy here, and it involves hearing a hollowness in calls to autonomy, authenticity, and life-long learning, in liberation pedagogies, and in vapid exhortations to "progress," "standards," quality," "excellence." All account for everything and take hold. There is a melancholy and the suggestion of a negative education, resistant to performativity but at odds also with the affirmation of intensities of *Libidinal Economy*: exuberance and energy are compromised by the emphasis on the immemorial, on childhood and "the jews." The final section of this chapter, however, points to a different releasing of energy, to a *novatio* integrally related to this negativity. But, first, what happens to education in the era of the megalopolis?

It has its own new democracy of subjects, with transparency to help potential students and other "stakeholders," and to facilitate scrutiny and accountability. Emphasis shifts from substance to procedure: in the university especially, what counts in a course is that formal criteria are met (this is what makes a degree); the content of the course can be . . . well, anything, so it seems.[3] This shift is evident also in the characterization of what is to be learned in terms of competencies and skills, especially where a check-list of outcomes purports to characterize the essence of mastery of a subject. This is the curriculum of sufficient reason: nothing educates without accounting. And, of course, a curriculum devised along these lines carries its own message regarding what being educated is all about, surreptitiously crowding out other possibilities. This is the very definition of economic knowledge, and it rules out the soul:

> The understanding, which figures and counts (even if only approximately), imposes its rule on to all objects, even aesthetic ones. This requires a time and a space under control. It ignores what is not an object or what has no object – and thus the soul, if "soul" means a spirit disturbed by a host that it ignores, nonobjectal, nonobjective.
>
> (Lyotard 1990: 41)

What is needed, it should be clear, is a renunciation of the attempt fully to specify what is to be taught and learned – an emancipation from emancipation itself, from the paranoia of inspection and accountability. (Recall the place of the figural in Lyotard's early work: see Chapter 7 in this volume.) This is no call for "freedom" of content or the abandonment of traditional subject matter. On the contrary, great works of thought – before they are entered in the cultural stockpile – harbor some excess beyond all possible discourse; they preserve a kind of solitude into which the learner enters; they are irreducible to the usages and mentalities of the community (Lyotard 1997: 206–7). Reading such works, indeed reading itself, is exemplary of what is at stake here:

> Nothing is as slow, difficult, and unprofitable as learning to read,

which is an endless activity. In a society avid for performance, profit, and speed, it is an exercise that has lost its value, along with the institution that trains people for it.

(Lyotard 1993b: 160)

Avid for performance, the institution reaches out to all parts, schooling the whole child, progressively schooling the home. The system of education extends through the training and public-relations arms of companies and corporations, and back into the initial nurturing of the child. In the transparent total education of the megalopolis there is no *domus* with its domesticated rhythms and its concealing of the undominated and untamed, with its housing of childhood, with its secret places and prodigal sons. The economy of the *domus* must give way to one in which

> everything is taken and nothing received. And so necessarily, an illiteracy. The respect and lack of respect of severe and serene reading of the text, of writing with regard to language, this vast and still unexplored house, the indispensable comings and goings in the maze of its inhabited, always deserted rooms – the big monad doesn't give a damn about all this. It just goes and builds. Promotion. That's what it demands of humans.
>
> (Lyotard 1991c: 199–200)

Personal and social education promotes citizenship, and the skills-acquisition, assertiveness, and autonomy that enhance self-esteem. But there is something too glossily reasonable about an education in universal rights and responsibilities, with its overriding of that second existence. It occupies those deserted rooms. Therapies then take hold of the self. Am I together as a person? Am I the architect of my own life? Do I have *ownership* of my learning? Have I clarified my values? Is this the *real* me? These are phony questions born of the big monad's labor of colonization and normalization through its surrogate, the oppressive ego. For Lyotard, the politics for which we must prepare children is not the mainland of a universal human nature, nor is it a communal solidarity (Rorty), nor a communicational pragmatics (Habermas), but the wider dispensation of archipelagos, of "games" and "genres" of discourse, an archipelago bathed by the secret ocean of the language of reflection (Lyotard 1997: 146–7). To have freedom and to hold rights are alike forms of the *manceps*. In contrast, an openness to the irruption of the *event* undoes what Iris Murdoch has called the anxious avaricious tentacles of the self: "The event makes the self incapable of taking possession and control of what it is. It testifies that the self is essentially passible to a recurrent alterity" (Lyotard 1991c: 59). This is a basis for other-regarding virtue that escapes the frame of rights, responsibilities, and vacuous self-knowledge, but is capable of bearing witness to differends. It is not a matter of skills and procedural reasoning; rather it requires the development of the imagination in an engagement with what is outside oneself (as, in children's fiction, another world breaks through). Literacy requires readiness for what is always still to be received. Literacy, properly understood, *is* personal and social education, moral education.

Pedagogy takes control with its mastery of teaching and learning "methods," which too often it takes to be its *raison d'être*, the predictable dominance once again of procedure over substance. General transferable skills of teaching and learning are efficient uses of time. Good management, it is axiomatic, requires the explicit and precise formulation of outcomes. Good learning is a matter of finding "the learning style that suits you best." Of course, if performativity is education's capitalism, it is not surprising that this comes with its own characteristic energy, with the frenetic enthusiasms of its managerial classes, and with the predictable tyranny of its purges. Absurd optimism and excitement over the development of data-rich "high reliability organizations" are accompanied by a literature that is at once evangelical and unremittingly bland.[4] "Complete information," Lyotard tells us, "means neutralizing more events" (Lyotard 1991c: 65): the increasing ability of the technology to make everything present has its concomitant effects in planning and programming. The tidy specification of learning outcomes stifles the irruption of the event.

The token learner-centeredness of the individually tailored curriculum, of choice and ownership, is complicit with managerial values in terms of efficient throughput and electronic accounting. Whatever cannot be made explicit is suppressed, differends disappearing in the guise of litigations (see Chapter 4). A pallid communicational transparency is promoted through communication and interpersonal "skills" and, of course, through the skills of information access. Writing – the writing that can make the silence heard (Lyotard 1990: 48), that labours to silence that learned eloquence (Lyotard 1997: 215) – writing is consigned to the ghetto. "The jews" of the curriculum are not to be represented in curriculum statements (objectives and outcomes), nor in the portfolio of skills.

In such a climate, can we even imagine a J. H. Newman writing about the university today? The best to be hoped for is *The University in Ruins* (Readings 1996). Grand theory becomes more obviously outmoded, and the impossibility of the visionary text regarding education seems ever more evident. Arguments for liberal education come to seem like heritage themes, while the grander gestures of Allan Bloom have their impact less in policy and practice than in book sales to the middle-aged, educated in a different regime.

Instead, the dominant discourse of power in education is the summary report, with its numbered paragraphs, lists, and bullet points. These presentational features – in mission statements, prospectuses, and reports – are dimensions of the aestheticization of education. So also with the total mobilization of life-long learning, the learner finds him- or herself represented on the learner's skills card or record of achievement. The aestheticized *signs* of education and of performativity themselves become values that are taken up and used by performativity, stimuli to excite the new class of educational managers and entrepreneurs.

Research in education is itself colonized by this voyeurism, especially now that we know, so it is blithely claimed, that the aims of education are settled.[5] Improve performance, technologize, collect data, keep things moving. There is an abdication of responsibility here: a responsibility not to be discharged in the assembling of formulaic answers, whatever virtues of "clarity" these apparently have. In the wake of the grand narratives, thinking about education takes shelter in this technicism. To resist this, it must recognize the opportunity that the exposure of totalizing conceptions affords:

> The decline, perhaps the ruin, of the universal idea can free thought and life from totalizing obsessions. The multiplicity of responsibilities, and their independence (their incompatibility), oblige and will oblige those who take on those responsibilities, small or great, to be flexible, tolerant, and svelte. These qualities will cease to be the contrary of rigor, honesty, and force; they will be their signs. Intelligences do not fall silent, they do not withdraw into their beloved work, they try to live up to this new responsibility, which renders the "intellectuals" troublesome, impossible: the responsibility to distinguish intelligence from the paranoia that gave rise to "modernity."
>
> (Lyotard 1993b: 7)

These troublesome "intellectuals" imply something about how intelligence and responsibility themselves might be developed. For educators to be flexible, tolerant, and svelte there must be a renunciation of that intention to grasp and take control, however much this may present itself as the best path to emancipation. A renunciation, that is, not merely of control in the banal sense of domination in the classroom, but at the level of constantly holding fast to tidy objectives (behavioral outcomes) or to lofty aims (autonomy, authenticity).

III

There is no doubt an ambivalence in the tenor of these remarks: on the one hand, nostalgic for the best traditions of education, on the other, challenging and avant-garde. What of the negativity that is implicated here?

What is at stake in life and thought for Lyotard, as A. T. Nuyen puts it, is the question of presenting the unpresentable, and it is the postmodern condition that gives rise to this question:

> It follows that postmodern education is about *sublimation*. It is about intensifying the *différend* between reason and imagination. This can be

done, on the one hand, by making the demand of reason more and more outrageous, that is, by thinking up ideas that are ever more challenging to the imagination, thus spurring the imagination. On the other hand, the student needs to cultivate the power of the imagination to learn to operate with a wide variety of "stylistic operators and narratives," to learn to create new regimens of phrases, that is, to invent new ways of talking.

(Nuyen 1996b: 100)

To educate is then to enthuse the subject, encouraging the soaring of the imagination towards ever more challenging ideas. But it is not that the unbounded imagination is to be released or to be realized by an education that is simply spontaneous and anarchic. For Lyotard, Nuyen claims, the student must first learn *how*. Postmodern education must also "instruct the student about the basics of society and about progress towards the better" (ibid.: 102), without which the differend cannot come into view. Lyotard describes the intensification of feeling of the sublime as enthusiasm, the imagination so extended as to provide the means of bearing witness to the incommensurability between, on the one hand, the infinite import of ideas and, on the other, presentation. It is precisely this that yields an intimation of the destination of the human subject: to supply a presentation of the unpresentable and thus to exceed everything that can be presented (Lyotard 1988a: 166).

There are resonances here with a perfectionist education, with the longing for an impossible wholeness. And certainly the sublime scarcely makes sense without the experience of lack; this is clearly something different from a libidinal education (see chapter 12). But this lack can be given a negative or a positive cast. As Lyotard puts this in "Answering the question: what is postmodernism?" within the sublime relation between the presentable and the conceivable it is possible to distinguish two modes: in *melancholia* the emphasis is placed on the powerlessness of the faculty of presentation, on nostalgia for presence; in *novatio* it is on the increase of being and jubilation that arise from the invention of new rules for the game (Lyotard 1984b: 79–80).

Nuyen's interpretation helps to fend off those more anarchic readings of Lyotard that ally the work to liberation pedagogy or to a radical progressivism. But there is a frustrating inadequacy in the suggestion that what the student needs is a kind of know-how supplemented by (propositional) knowledge of "the basics of society," with all the baggage these phrases have acquired. (Could not this be provided, someone will say, by knowledge of the relevant facts and a course in thinking skills?) First, Richard Rorty says, there is socialization, then, roughly post-nineteen, there is education, and it is in the latter that criticism plays its role: "Socialization has to come before individuation, and education for freedom cannot begin before some constraints have been imposed" (Rorty

1996: 210). This is, it should be clear, too trite by far, yet it does seem that there must be this general pattern. A wholly anarchistic education would begin with Year Zero; criticism needs something to purchase on. Before differends can appear it is necessary to initiate the learner into particular ways of thinking that have been developed with their distinctive rules and litigations. Only against this background can the disquiet of the sublime make sense. Art and writing make the silence heard (Lyotard 1990: 48), but they do this against the background of a schooling of thought.

The problem here is how to give a clearer account of "socialization" or "the basics." To do this, something of that idea of a liberal education sketched briefly at the beginning of this chapter needs to be recalled: its key principle is that the learner must be initiated into public forms of thought, exemplified typically in traditional academic disciplines. But whereas such forms of thought are considered there in terms of the logic of their reasoning, the idea of a tradition here needs to be understood more in terms of a sustained practice of addressing particular series of problems and, most importantly, of reading certain texts. The continuity in such a tradition is sustained through the shared preoccupation with sets of texts, and the passing-on of this from generation to generation. Of course, there is no fixed canon here: the texts that are taken to be important are matters of disagreement and change. But there is sufficient continuity for there to be a sustained conversation. Tradition, so understood, essentially incorporates not only forms of criticism but the emergence of disparate paradigms and schools of thought, with their sometimes bitter rivalries and ruptures, with their filial disloyalties and strong misreadings. Literacy, in these terms, requires an attention to the text, to the substantive nature of these different products of study and practice in the way that they have developed over time. Metonymically it evokes a receptive-responsiveness: in reflection, writing, conversation, and practice. Critical thought in the absence of this attention is kicking in mid-air.

If socialization must precede education, the challenge for the teacher is in part to explore the ways in which education can infiltrate piecemeal these necessary processes, in which the prospect of an incipient criticality can gradually be made apparent to learners. Progressively, as learning advances, it will be in the vibration between such ways of thinking and between disciplines themselves that the space of the differend will open up. This is a liberal education then in which the *telos* of rational autonomy is dispersed through the acknowledgement of childhood and "the jews." The "respect and lack of respect of severe and serene reading of the text, of writing with regard to language" (Lyotard 1991c: 199–200) not only points to an education adequate to postmodernity; it celebrates what has always been part of the best realizations of those liberal traditions.

In the new republic and the megalopolis the aestheticization of education covers over difference in the sensationalism of a spurious representation. It is necessary to destabilise through a kind of *anaisthesis*.

These are the conditions for the generation of a *novatio* properly sensitive to the political demands of postmodernity. This is an enthusiasm that in its imaginative and inventive thinking most fully extends human beings. Beyond freedom's grip, childhood and "the jews" call for the preservation of a politics of the differend, and the preservation of an education that remains open to what it cannot fully comprehend, or contain or represent or name.[6]

Notes

1 In contrast to *Selbstbehauptung* Lyotard speaks approvingly in this respect of Jean-Luc Nancy's conception of the community of singularities who can share only the impossibility of sharing (shown most clearly by death, which cannot be shared).

2 Lyotard's conception of the avant-garde artist, supreme witness to the sublime, points to a necessary indirectness and refraction in thinking today:

> Célan "after" Kafka, Joyce "after" Proust, Nono "after" Mahler, Beckett "after" Brecht, Rothko and Newman "after" Matisse, these second in line, incapable of the achievements of the first in line . . . but capable because of their very incapacity; they are enough and have been enough to bear negative witness to the fact that both the "prayer" and the history of the prayer are imposssible [*sic*], and that to bear witness to this impossibility remains possible.
>
> (Lyotard 1990: 47)

The repetition of "after" here, and the naming of the first in line, imply a lack that differs from the more Derridean negative theology that is never far from the preoccupations of this chapter. It points to the way that the real hides in conditions of postmodernity, and to something epochal in Lyotard's sublime.

3 Degrees in Golf Green Studies are available, for example, at Buckinghamshire Chilterns University College. A degree course in Surf Science and Technology (Surfing and Sailboarding) is available at Cornwall College, validated by the University of Plymouth.

4 A high reliability organization is one where failure cannot be tolerated, such as nuclear power or air traffic control. There is a current movement to adapt schools so that they run on similar principles. Recent estimates of the costs of school failure in the United States are estimated as being equivalent to a plane crash every week (Reynolds 1997: 106).

5 As an example:

> Everyone is convinced of the need for change, the proof being the demise of the major ideological disputes on the objectives of education. The central question now is how to move towards greater flexibility in education and training systems, taking take [*sic*] account of the diversity of people's demands. Debate within the union must now focus on this priority issue.
>
> (European Commission 1995: 21)

6 I should like to thank Gordon Bearn, Pradeep Dhillon, Paul Smeyers, and Richard Smith for helpful comments on a draft of this chapter.

10 Exploring "Lyotard's women"

The unpresentable, ambivalence, and feminist possibility

Lynda Stone

Introduction

The title phrase, "Lyotard's women," is a tropical stand-in for a project to interpret and assess the possibility of feminism within the late French philosopher's writings. Its texts are a framing interview, a set of texts by him that are directly pertinent, feminist responses to his general project, other writings by women that are not "feminist" but assist the analysis, and related texts from him that are not about women or feminism directly. This designation "directly" is significant since to make sense of Lyotard's position on women and feminist theory, I believe, one needs to consider both texts about the topic specifically and some less directly connected. The thesis of the chapter is this: arising out of Lyotard's "basic" theoretical notion of the unpresentable is an accompanying feeling of ambivalence, ambiguity. This feeling, in an ironic way, characterizes Lyotard's view of women, since overall he works toward an ethic, a politics for social life in which all live in justice. Rhetorically as frame, given ambivalence, are women "unpresentable"? Moreover, from his work, is a feminist "philosophy" (better yet a feminist "writing") possible?[1]

A note to begin about the chapter's logic. Texts utilized are not offered herein in a chronological order. Actually to do this is difficult with Lyotard's writings, given important differences in text order of those translated into English from the French. This lack of "official" chronology, however, is not problematic except in one important respect. As indicated subsequently, English-speaking feminists have not read his work *in general* appropriately: they have missed early writings that are significant to his position on women and on a possible feminist theory. One notes, also, that Lyotard has himself played with chronology, as this chapter does, in a late text, his "fictional biography" of André Malraux in which historical women figure strongly.

An equivocation

What follows is an initial exploration into Lyotard's relationship with feminism.[2] What this is not is a thoroughgoing, specifically focused, textual analysis as in the genre of literary criticism – and this is desirable. What should be evident from this study is the potential of further inquiry. If for its complex ambivalence alone, Lyotard's philosophy is surely worthy of feminist attention that has not been forthcoming thus far.

An interview

A clue to Lyotard's position toward women and feminism appears in a rare interview (in English) conducted by Gary A. Olson for *JAC – A Journal of Composition Theory*, published in 1995. Several key sections are worth quoting at length in which, as in a central essay on "One of the things at stake in women's struggles" (Lyotard 1978), the basis is writing in the postmodern condition. The condition, Lyotard poses, is one of competitive systems originating in patriarchy. Interviewer Olson asks, "[Isn't] it patriarchy itself that is the primary operating force in the subjugation of women? That is, do you think it is possible to envision a non-patriarchal or even feminist capitalist society?" (Olson 1995: 402). Lyotard answers:

> It's not so simple historically speaking. Patriarchy is clearly the basis of the Roman theory of law, which is the basis of our society (in France), even as these rules have changed. And it was clearly patriarchal. But . . . [it is more complex]. Your question assumes that women are in possession of a feminine principle and that men are inhabited by a male way of thinking and doing. This is a prejudice. That's why I have no clear relationship with feminists.
>
> (Lyotard 1995a (in Olson): 402–3).[3]

Excepting himself from distinct feminine and masculine principles, and thus from what he takes to be the basis for French feminist thought, Lyotard then offers his most pointed statement, one in which ambivalence appears:

> Useful certainly. Cixous must be; *it* [feminist theory] must be. In fact, I've known both of them a long time. I admire certain books written by Hélène. And I had a strong discussion, even dispute with Luce [Irigaray]. . . . She gave a paper, and I was horrified. The paper was truly feminist, but in a sense I can't accept at all. . . . I have good relations with them as persons, but it's true I've not made real use of their works. I don't know why, frankly. Perhaps it was too late for me. I don't know.
>
> (Ibid.: 408–9)

One way to read this is as strongly dismissive, a negative statement with a Gallic shrug; another is to suggest this chapter's thesis, an ambiguity toward women and feminist theory that Lyotard "cannot" acknowledge. In his poststructuralist writings and here in personal attribution, what cannot be known, acknowledged, is that which is "unpresentable."

The unpresentable

"What cannot be known" is basic to Lyotard's writings, as it is to those of French counterparts such as Kristeva, Foucault, Derrida, and Cixous. The roots clearly are in Marx's excess of exchange and Freud's unconscious, as well as in various contributions from a strong literary tradition.[4]

Expressing or presenting the unpresentable is undertaken (ironically) through various namings and designations: absent presence, aporia and lacunae, lack or gap, negation, in-between, radical alterity: other of other. Basic to all of these formulations is difference, again expressed in various ways but with an important root in Saussurean structuralist linguistics. Here difference is acknowledged (and cannot be resolved) in a central formulation between the signifier and the signified. This openness of language then helps explain what is always an openness: in the unpresentable, in a "non-pinning down" of relations of center to margin, within oppositional hierarchies in which reversals only repeat "structural" inequalities. The point of all of this, it seems, is a significant undermining of knowledge, again of what can be known and from that, what can be done. The move is away from epistemology and toward ethics, for the latter especially in positions toward justice for the other. Ethics "of course" is a politics.

Lyotard "approaches" this unknown in various ways throughout his writings in a continual thread that is assumed and reintroduced and reinterpreted. While it appeared in texts written earlier but not translated, English-speaking audiences most often first encounter his unpresentable in the appendix to *The Postmodern Condition*, "Answering the question: what is postmodernism?" (1984b). For Lyotard the unpresentable is integral; he writes:

> The postmodern would be that which, in the modern, puts forward *the unpresentable* in presentation itself; that which denies itself the solace of good forms, the consensus of a taste that would make it possible to share collectively the nostalgia; that which searches for new presentations not in order to enjoy them but in order to present a stronger sense of the unpresentable.
>
> (Lyotard 1984b: 81, emphasis added)

For illustrative and elaborative purposes, two other examples introduce Lyotard's continual reworking of this "radical alterity."[5] One is "the differend," within which, commentator Bill Readings explains, "the phrase," as the subtitle of Lyotard's important book attests, is in dispute with any other phrase and their grouping.[6] It is, writes Readings, "simply the empty singularity of an event . . . of the event as pure happening" (Readings 1991: 114–5). Phrases link with other phrases, one at a time as a pragmatics of language usage in which one phrase calls forth many possible successive phrases from multiple genres (ibid.: 117). When one linkage is made, others are suppressed through a conflict that Lyotard names as "the differend." Here is his initiating definition: "[A] differend [*différend*] would be a case of conflict, between at least two parties (phrases from different language games) that cannot be equitably resolved for lack of a rule of judgment applicable to both" (Lyotard 1988a: xi). One of Lyotard's striking examples is "Auschwitz," not a concept but an unnameable feeling that results from its naming (ibid.: 104, 56–8, 88).

The second example, reminding us of a post-colonial tradition out of poststructuralism, is found in Lyotard's text *Le Mur du Pacifique,* of which translated sections were published in 1983. Within these "passages," white imperialism and the west are critiqued in attempts "to evoke what is ungraspable"(Lyotard 1983b: 90). Here as illustration is Lyotard about the continual shift of center and margin:

> Whenever a culture starts to harden . . . when anything like an organic attachment between people and institutions develops, this island then stops being the West. . . . [This] narrative recounts the expansion of the white Empire towards the East; but this East is never anything but an abandoned West, an ancient center for taking one's bearings, a darkened whiteness. . . . [This] imperial expansion . . . is power.
>
> (Lyotard 1983b: 95)

> [At] the impossible center of the Empire . . . there is no supreme authority, there is a joining of surfaces, white, ephemeral, labyrinthine, purposeless.
>
> (Ibid.)

This text demonstrates in general Lyotard's aesthetic of evocation (always attempts to evoke, attempts to name) that is most characteristic of his "philosophy."

"Presentation" of the ungraspable indeed is often taken up by Lyotard through the arts, for example painting and photography, and all along in his career, through writing and writing about it. Importantly, the unpresentable calls forth feeling, "unnameable" as well. Clearly there is uncertainty, but merely as cognitive undecidability or indecisiveness this is not sufficiently visceral: "it" is equivocality, ambiguity, even ambiloquy, analogue to "double-speaking" (*Oxford English Dictionary* 1986: 386) as a kind of "double-feeling." As will be seen, Lyotard theorizes this feeling as the sublime. For present purposes, those that concern Lyotard's women, this feeling is ambivalence about women as part of sexual difference: simultaneously love and hate, admiration and fear, seduction and detachment, along with desire to be feminine and remain masculine. Perhaps too it is a desire to deny that which is "feminine" or "masculine," in the reaching for justice. One might posit this ambivalence in the fable of "Marie."

First woman

Two years prior to the publication of the 1995 interview above, a set of essays from Lyotard appeared in French that were then translated into English as *Postmodern Fables* (Lyotard 1997). Here is part of the preface:

> Today, life is fast. It vaporizes morals. Futility suits the postmodern, for words as well as things. But that doesn't keep us from asking questions: how to live, and why? The answers are deferred. . . . But . . . there is a semblance of knowing: that life is going every which way. But do we know this? We represent it to ourselves rather. Every which way of life is flaunted, exhibited, enjoyed for the love of variety. The moral of all morals would be that of "aesthetic" pleasure. . . . [The fables are] notes on postmodern aestheticization. And against it! You're not done living because you chalk it up to artifice.
>
> (Lyotard 1997: vii).[7]

The heroine of the first fable is Marie, an academic who travels to Japan to present a lecture. The tale is a critique of the superficiality of academic life, as Marie ruminates through various "voices" about being a bit of cultural capital for sale, an archival contribution. But there is more, in an initial feminist notice of the narrative forms that shift throughout the short essay: multiple voices of Marie that Lyotard as writer undertakes. She speaks of herself to herself in the third person, she "thinks" in the first person, she is referred to by an absent other: these voices sometimes blend together within a single paragraph. Here are two examples which also connect to key themes about women. In one, Marie talks about cultural capital and alterity. She says,

> My prof, he reminded us of Kant: think for yourself, and according to yourself. Today they say, that's logocentric, not *politically correct.* The streams must all go in the right direction. . . . About what, then? About alterity. Unanimity on the principle that unanimity is suspect. If you are a woman, and Irish, and still *presentable*, and some kind of a professor in Brazil, and a lesbian, and writing non-academic books, then you are a good little stream. . . . But if you bring out for them a moderately intricate analysis . . . and its relation to death, then you're really out of it. It's commonplace. In what way does it express your difference? Where did your alterity go?
>
> (Lyotard 1997: 6–7, second emphasis added)

In the other illustration, Marie gives her lecture, and then there is this stream of consciousness:

The lights go on, applause. Enough? It's OK. We move on to the question and answer game. That part of the cultural . . . no passivity, animation, interaction. The test of a good performance. Marie, now is not the time to show that you could care less and that you've had enough. . . . Otherwise they won't invite you back. Have I been "other" enough? . . . Go on, show that your own little stream is like no other. . . . And not too long, OK? There's still dinner.

(Ibid.: 12)

Capital and performance, well-known Lyotardian themes are included as are significant others: alterity, marking, death. As Lyotard's first woman, who is Marie and how does he characterize – and feel about – her? Lyotard chooses to speak as a woman, indeed as "other" on otherness. Given his acknowledged "failure" to use feminist theory, may he unproblematically do this? From this "first" text, there appears ambivalence in his writing as and for Marie.

Feminist responses

The interview and fable published in the 1990s "begin" to suggest Lyotard's position toward women. Feminists have not to date responded to Marie or to his more "direct" writings. To begin consideration of feminist responses, two other general aspects (in my view) are pertinent. First, perusal of the *oeuvre* about Lyotard does not reveal attention to his work by French feminists: surely there is some, but it is not apparent in texts from major figures now available in English.[8] Second, citations and connections from English-speaking feminists are almost exclusively to *The Postmodern Condition* taken out of the context of his other writings; and, more saliently, there is no specific reference to the unpresentable. Thus, within English feminist theory, what results is a stilted, even incomplete, view of possibilities.

Background

The Postmodern Condition was published in English in 1984, and with it "postmodernism," reductively, is identified with Lyotard: *He* has become a trope and the "peculiar American adaptation" (Huyssen 1990: 237) based on the historical circulation of the term from the US to Europe and back. Postmodernism – with textual "representations" that range from a contemporary artistic movement to an epochal world-view – has become synonymous in many writings with Lyotard's critique of the legitimation of particular forms of knowledge relative to their "meta-narratives" (see Lyotard 1984a).

In the US scene, response to Lyotard by feminists is situated in a larger theoretical response to his postmodernism, beginning, as Mark

Poster well explains, and continuing from the late 1970s (Poster 1992: 567). Often symbolically identified as the debate between Habermas and Lyotard, it is framed in the linguistic turn of this century with "critical theory" continuing both modernity and the project of the Enlightenment through rational consensual egalitarian "speech acts," and "French theory" opposing/proposing postmodernity through an undercutting of rationality as itself "to blame." Richard Rorty puts the latter via Lyotard thus in the proposition that science (as postmodern knowledge) be "[concerned with] *undecidables,* the limits of precise control, conflicts characterized by incomplete information . . . catastrophes, and pragmatic paradoxes" (Rorty 1985: 163, emphasis added). In a word, the debate concerns "foundation" of a politics that Seyla Benhabib names as "post-Marxist radical . . . and democratic" (Benhabib 1984: 123). Among those whose marginalization has historically denied them the fruits of Western democracy, both in the ideal and the real, are women.[9]

Responses

There is a small English literature of feminist responses to Lyotard, mostly working from *The Postmodern Condition.* Illustrating what might be termed a weak affinity for feminism from 1992, T. A. Klimenkova names him along with Baudrillard, Jameson, and De Man (despite their important differences) as source for a new cultural style to which feminists can lay claim (Klimenkova 1992: 277). Her aim, along with that of noted literary critic, Linda Hutcheon, is to highlight a parallelism between feminism and the postmodern critique of universal cultural principles and practices, as caution against perpetuating sexist-based cultural binaries – and a historical hierarchy – of men and women, the feminine and the masculine. Klimenkova's approach, out of a generic feminism, is to begin by taking into account the diverse experiences of women, even as painful analysis indicates their own violence to each other. Hutcheon concurs, affirms experience, and lauds a postmodern "de-doxifying. . . [of universals as cast in] the separation between the private and the public, the personal and the political" (Hutcheon 1996: 265). For her, there is also possibility in working with potential undermining of dominant metanarratives, as long as there is no reductive conflation of feminism and postmodernism. This is because incredulity, from Lyotard, means giving up contestation of patriarchy itself and the agency required to act politically (ibid.: 266).

Feminist agency receives two other pertinent treatments – and herein affinity is strongest in calls for both a general "postmodern feminism" and specific identity-based feminisms. Taking the latter first, an identity "standpoint" is developed by Judith Roof in a detailed consideration of Lyotard for a lesbian feminism. Her tactic is this one:

[The] lesbian is legitimated both through a knowledge of identity and by being located in the most "legitimate" place in culture: the place of knowing, the place of naming, the place of controlling any unknowing. . . . [Posed is a lesbian metanarrative that] brings together the epistemological certainties . . . (and uncertainties) of real experience revealing the postmodern (and lesbian) stake not in knowledge, but in legitimating the position from which one sees it.

(Roof 1994: 62)

Her contribution is a reformulation that opens up identities, locations, texts, and the like to a freeing of irrelevance.

The second reconceptualization is by Nancy Fraser and Linda Nicholson, who work from some roots in common with Roof in feminist psychoanalytic theory. They add neo-pragmatism for a postmodern feminism that is pragmatic and fallibilistic with methods tailored to feminist needs. They summarize that such a feminism "[would underlie practices] that are interlaced with differences, even with conflicts . . . [in working toward a] complex, multilayered feminist solidarity" (Fraser and Nicholson 1988a: 391).

Thus far, feminist responses to a general Lyotardian postmodernism have suggested broad approaches to culture in new kinds of narratives and practices. One other response requires mention: from Craig Owens in an English text published prior to the English translation of *The Postmodern Condition*. Significantly his focus is aesthetic representation of sexual difference. Overall here is strong affinity, in response to the Marxist-based critique of Lyotard from Habermas and others mentioned earlier. From Owens, "[for] modern man [*sic*], everything that exists does so only in and through representation . . . [in a world that] exists only in and through a *subject* who believes that he is producing the world in producing its representations" (Owens 1983: 66). Owens offers exemplars of such representation from feminist postmodern art: in film, photography, and text that disrupt the modern connection of vision with sexual privilege.

Second "women"

Across several decades, Lyotard writes about women both directly and indirectly. This work includes the central text connecting women's lives to feminism and to writing: "One of the things at stake in women's struggles" (Lyotard 1978). Here is his initial and programmatic assertion:

It may be that you are forced to be a man from the moment that you write. Maybe writing is a fact of virility. . . . Perhaps what we call feminine writing is only a variation on a genre that is masculine and remains so: the essay. It is said that the femininty of writing depends on content. Writing is feminine . . . if it operates by *seduction* rather than conviction. But the opposition . . . [and the claim to neutrality as well is] probably masculine.

(Lyotard 1978: 9, emphasis in original)

Self-consciously, Lyotard writes here as a philosopher who attempts to escape "what is masculine," but he cannot do so since philosophical – and political methods – are themselves male. Importantly, from within male method, woman is defined. To the adult male, she is "the little girl" who as "savage" cannot write because she is created and judged by him, a creation that, as Lyotard explains, is "of the jealousy he feels for something he is forbidden to be" (ibid.: 9).

How does this state of sexual difference arise? Lyotard's answer is to recount a story from sixth-century China when a king desires to make soldiers of his women. They laugh and disobey until, that is, the two favorites are beheaded, and the rest silently obey. From this, virility and order are masculine, and "aimless humor" and disorder are feminine as a succumbing to the masculine out of a fear of death. Lyotard explains that in this tale "reason *makes use of* death," as it "shows the way to language, to order, to the consideration of lack, to meaning, to culture" (ibid.: 10, emphasis in original). From Freud and Lacan, the standard account is that the threat of death is tied both to the body and to language, to libido which is masculine intelligence and to the phallus as primary signifier. Relative to these theorizings, sexual difference is established as the little boy overcomes the threat of castration and becomes virile while the little girl merely receives and does not identify with the father. Lyotard writes that the result is this:

a woman is to become a man; let her confront death, or castration, the law of the signifier. Otherwise she will always lack the sense of lack. She thinks herself eternal for this reason and is deprived of sexuality as well as the activity constituting the body's language.

(Ibid.: 11)

Virility however has a price since the body that is man can die.

Significantly, Lyotard questions this account, especially from Lacan. First, women are not so easily mastered, and imperialistic men struggle ceaselessly with control, even as women are excluded to the border, to exteriority. But this struggle implies something more, the activity rather than passivity of women: Is there not a secret reversal of roles? asks Lyotard: "Doesn't he discover his 'origin' there? And isn't it necessary that this origin be woman: Isn't the mother the originary woman?" (ibid.: 12). But, as it might be put, man does not see this, perhaps at all and certainly not in a positive light. As a result, down through Western culture that importantly includes the time of capital, man does not honor woman and can only honor her as she becomes man.

In this analysis, enter Freud again as well as modernity. Historically, what Lyotard recognizes as a modern "unisexism" indicates that women and men have not been and are not the same: differences remain in "culture." In a positive way, Freud describes individual differences across bodies, "displacements" that posit "another sexual space" (Lyotard 1978: 13), one that traverses the basic male–female opposition. This is then related to possibilities of feminism. Here now is Lyotard's most direct assertion about women and their political (philosophical) movement:

> [It (feminism)] could be tempted to resist the assimilation of women to men by insisting on this difference, by claiming for themselves the intuition . . . [pathos, irresponsibility . . . other weaknesses attributed to them] by making them weapons in their insurrection against phallocentrism. [An] anti-masculine world . . . [could be] established, to be explored only by the voices, cries, whispers and conspiracies of feminine writing.
>
> (ibid.: 14)

At first glance, Lyotard does not equivocate here; he is not ambiguous. But a real danger exists in reversal, in a principle that can only be a complement. Still he does not give up, and posits further: "[Let] us then propose . . . a kind of theory-fiction. Let us work forging fictions rather than hypotheses and theories . . . [as] the best way for the speaker to become 'feminine'" (ibid.).

Other responses

Mention of "struggles" is found in responses to Lyotard that are not primarily feminist but that note a positive affinity. Several also indicate considerations that have implications for women and feminist theory. In a first, Maureen Turim (in the era of *The Postmodern Condition* but prior to much English publication) mentions that Lyotard refuses male authority because he "sees women as the 'Empire's limits,' the exteriority that could resist male imperialism" (Turim 1984: 92). While this is her only comment about feminism, the writing on Lyotard's aesthetics contributes significantly. To this effort, three others offer insights that lead to several key writings from Lyotard: they are Debra Jacobs, Elizabeth Flynn, and especially Cecile Lindsay.

First, Turim identifies four elements across Lyotardian texts that demonstrate desire's integration into art and politics: these four are the figural, libidinal economy, political theory, and artistic experimentation. Of these, the first two are especially significant. The first, the figural, returns attention in the chapter to presentation of the unpresentable through art. She writes,

[It] is not the figuration of representational art . . . [but] instead the elements of visual form that create illusive, yet suggestive phenomena that affect the viewer. . . . [Such art] places . . . [formal devices outside the restricted view of formalism] in the realm of desire and the unconscious.

(Turim 1984: 94)

For Lyotard, moreover, figural and discursive elements, importantly in art and writing, exist in oppositional tension as they are "simultaneously" modes within language and image.

The second element is libidinal economy that interprets desire's impact through the body. While Turim provides initial definition, writings by Lindsay in the early 1990s make this element most accessible. Given what is a resistive value of art, it is not surprising that Lyotard envisions bodily forces, what Turim identifies as "creative possibilities of the mobility of investments in the unconscious; primary processes . . . as a continuous, atemporal flow of unbounded energy" (ibid.: 97). For Lyotard, this flow operates within a body, between bodies, and between bodies and objects. In art, especially, the "media" of desire are the eye and the ear (as in Freud and Lacan) and there is the influence, not surprisingly, of Marx. In the third element, political theory takes up the "tradition." As Turim puts this,

Lyotard criticizes Marxism for viewing the category of the subject uncritically . . . as a unified entity . . . within the exchange of labor. . . . He reminds . . . that the divided subject whose creativity and political awareness comes from multiple motivations and tensions can be seen positively.

(Ibid: 101)

To Turim's helpful synthesis, Jacobs recognizes Lyotard's turn to discourse: as "the in-between," as a site of resistance. She asserts, "[this] condition of discourse discloses an 'other-ness' that Lyotard recognizes as being inscribed in speech itself. . . . But for writing to be the kind of process indicated . . . the posture a writer assumes needs to be both passive and active" (Jacobs 1996: 180). According to Jacobs, Lyotard desires a posture in which "the feminine," the unconscious, the writing orientation necessarily must have consciousness of itself in order to be actively resistant (ibid.: 181). And it must necessarily be at least in part masculine. The point is this: if the mastery of the masculine remains (for Lyotard in the dominance of philosophy over writing), then there is always – and usually reinscription of – the "inferior," passive feminine.

Flynn's account, like that of Jacobs that responds specifically to the Olson interview, is more synthetic. Several points add insight at this juncture: Lyotard's insistence on being, as person and writer, both "male and female"; his assertion that the question of gender is enormous but also unanswerable; his claim that philosophy is a "repression of 'the bodily way of thinking'" (Flynn 1996: 172). Importantly, she continues, writing and not philosophy – just as women and not the feminist movement – are resistive because both philosophy and politics are part of totalities, of systems for Lyotard (ibid.: 173). Out of these insights, and Lyotard's project in general, Flynn's final comment connects to the unpresentable; significantly she is ironically unequivocal, unambiguous, and certainly not ambivalent. She says, "What we need . . . is a *new* politics that would respect the unknown, the unwritten" (ibid.: 175, emphasis added).

Possibility

Common to the responses just presented is tacit, if not explicit, attention to the body, the bodily, and with it some implication of importance for women. That this interest has been and is continuing to be central for feminist theory must now be acknowledged (Jaggar and Bordo 1989, Conboy, Medina and Stanbury 1997). Lyotard does pay implicit attention to the body in texts thus far considered: Marie is surely embodied. Recall "her" statement to herself: "If you are a woman, and Irish, and still presentable . . . then you are a good little stream" (Lyotard 1997: 6). Bodies are certainly significant in "Struggles," at least as targets for beheading, for death from resistance. Therein, Lyotard seems to be heading in his own direction for resistance, in turning women's weaknesses into strengths. But does this then entail a reversal, an undermining in an ironic promotion of a kind of universal "feminine" and the disappearance of women? Returning to this shortly, a slight digression does suggest Lyotard's own connection to "the body." His writing on the sublime entails an aesthetic base in the corporeal, and two "non-women" texts best explicate this move.

To begin, Lyotard asks: "How is one to understand the sublime . . . [as an experience] 'here and now'? On the contrary, isn't it essential of this feeling to allude to something that cannot be demonstrated or, as Kant said, presented?" (Lyotard 1984c: 36). In answer, he ponders the temporal "now," as possible exemplar in its "existential sense" (one might say) with accompanying feeling: the now is paradoxically both a part and a non-part of consciousness, able to be grasped only after its moment. Lyotard asserts that it is what dismantles and dismisses consciousness: "[It] is what consciousness cannot formulate, and even what consciousness forgets in order to compose itself" (ibid.: 37). Relative to experience, building on what has been to what might be, there are potential feelings, anticipation "fraught" with contradictory, sometimes simultaneous, affect, response "at the very least a sign of the question mark itself" (ibid.). Feeling is joy and anxiety, pleasure and pain, exaltation and depression. Significantly Lyotard means much more by the term "sublime" than a contemporary connotation of surprised admiration: he means the classical sense, as ambivalent positive/negative feeling. In these essays, through painting and photography, Lyotard offers a characterization from within "the now":

> [The] sublime is kindled by the threat that nothing further might happen. Beauty gives positive pleasure but there is another kind of pleasure that is bound to a passion far stronger than satisfaction, that is suffering and impending death. . . . [It is an] entirely spiritual passion . . . [that] is synonymous with terror. Terrors are linked to privation; privation of light, terror of darkness; privation of others, terror of solitude; privation of language, terror of silence; privation of objects, terror of emptiness; privation of life, terror of death. What is terrifying is that the *it happens* will not happen, that it will stop happening.
>
> (Lyotard 1984c: 40)

Taking his lead from Edmund Burke, Lyotard describes the sublime as feeling, as sensation. As a consideration of the unpresentable, he names the sublime as "gratification of effort." Through the visual, Lyotard writes, "[It] is impossible to represent the absolute, which is ungratifying; but one knows that one has to, that the faculty of feeling or of imagining is called upon to make the perceptible represent the ineffable" (Lyotard 1982: 68). This ineffable, this unpresentable through feeling as Lyotard asserts, turns attention to corporality.

One more response and further possibility

In her own set of two important papers, Lindsay (1991, 1992) makes explicit Lyotard's "body connection" beyond the aesthetic. Recall a non-feminist stance as she posits the centrality of the body to postmodern thought in general: "[Given] our suspicions of metadiscourses and transcendental subjects, our postmodern sensibility desires to make contact with some ground, with the physical stripped of metaphysical pretensions" (Lindsay 1991: 33). Lyotard's contribution is thus his "complication of the idea of the 'live body'" (ibid.: 34). She continues that it "is not an empirical body. Yet it is not an illusion or a pure abstraction. It is rather a critical hybrid composed of a hypothesized element and a 'pulsional' element . . . both conjectural and experiential, an imagination fired by drives"(ibid.: 35).

For Lyotard this is a libidinal body that "makes its appearance" in his text, *Libidinal Economy* (1993a). Calling it first a surface, it is a "deconstruction" of the organic body. Consider this text's beginning, a page-long sentence description, followed by others of similar length (as expression of its extension):

> Open the so-called body and spread out all its surfaces: not only the skin with each of its folds, wrinkles, scars, with its great velvety planes,

and contiguous to that, the scalp and its mane of hair, the tender pubic fur, nipples, nails . . . expose the labia majora, so also the labia minora with their blue network bathed in mucus . . . undo the mouth at its corners, pull out the tongue at its most distant roots and split it . . . dismantle and lay out the network of veins and arteries . . . and then the lymphatic network, and the fine bony pieces of the wrist, the ankle . . . the cavernous body of the penis, and extract the great muscles. . . . All of these zones are joined end to end in a band which has no back to it, a Moebius band which interests us not because it is closed, but because it is one-sided. . . . [What] the band is on, no-one knows nor will know, in the eternal turn. . . . [It is] neither exterior nor interior.

(Lyotard 1993a: 1–3)

Lyotard's point, Lindsay explains, is to undercut the organic body as manifestation of metaphysics, of the political economy; this text is a Marxist critique overall. Connecting to Lyotard's text *Le Mur du Pacifique* (1983b) cited earlier, she notes that the linkage of bodies and power extends in space. Therein Lyotard describes the body of the white woman (like the west) as "the desired object of political libido" (Lindsay 1991: 38). But in reality this body is only skin. She writes, "It has no organs, no cavities, no interiority. . . . [It is] fantasized voluminousness . . . [and] constructed frontiers" (ibid.). Significantly, the politics is to move to singularities, to undermine effects of power with "vested interest in fixing stable identities, in linking subjects with bodies" (ibid.: 37). Lindsay does continue, by the way, that from this preoccupation with corporality in the 1970s, in the 1980s Lyotard retranslates "concerns with the body, ethics, and experimentation into . . . linguistic terms" (Lindsay 1992: 390) such as those on the sublime.

Possibility and ambivalence

Exploration

In Jean-François Lyotard's "postmodern condition," explorations – such as this one – more often than not conclude with whimpers, or in this case ambiguities/ambivalence. This has been an initiating study of possible feminist affinity with Lyotard's life project "fraught" with both possibility and ambivalence in many forms: within his writings both directly and indirectly, relating to women's lives and their theorizing, and within sets of responses to them. At the outset one other text was mentioned that has not yet been considered; this is Lyotard's last published work in English, the "biography," *Signed, Malraux* (1999). It deserves brief attention at this chapter closing because of its own possible contributions to future explorations.

Final women

Signed, Malraux (in my view) is a remarkable work, a biography whose writing is a new genre for Lyotard, a biography that reads like a novel in which there is a strong presence of the writer/a kind of narrator. Thus the story seems as much about its author as about its historical characters. What is also striking about the work is the strong presence of women in the text and in Malraux's life, and – significantly – their connection with "his" obsession with death. Given a continual playing with historical chronology in the way the biography is written, this theme appears again and again. Malraux's life, Lyotard posits, is not only an expedition to escape "dominance" of women (who he strongly desires also) but as well an attempt to escape his own death (which he often risks). Much of this life story deserves a thorough Freudian/feminist analysis, as does its writing. Lyotard even denies his own Freudian rendering, but one is compelling.

As a final consideration of Lyotard's women, a couple of examples point, I think, to further ambivalence. The question is whether Malraux's feeling is also Lyotard's own stance. First, the biography opens as Malraux's mother, "Berthe – the spider," oversees the funeral of his younger brother when Malraux is just a toddler himself. The question that is part of this chapter's conclusion is what to make of the following on women and death:

> He had barely begun to walk when Maman (Berthe) placed him on the ground for a moment [and he was witness]. . . . The casket was placed atop others already inside the ample grave. Things startled by the light were moving in there: earthworms, ghastly larvae, arachnids . . .
>
> (Lyotard 1999: 2)

Unconsciously connecting death with female presence and male absence and lack (his own father's failure to appear and his own feeling of responsibility for death), Malraux's life – through Lyotard – "would remain colonized by women veiled in black . . . [waiting and weeping, yet] laughing up their sleeves" (ibid.: 2). A life result is a "bell of failure impressed upon him" with accompanying feelings.

For Malraux, the concrete results of an impressionable experience with women and death mean, first, a continual striving for "success" at cheating death – as in series of exploits – and second, a continual ambivalent response to women in his life. His response, importantly, as Lyotard puts it, is a "sole preoccupation . . . [with] style" (ibid.: 115), with surface (with skin). For her part, Malraux's "first woman," Clara, recognizes his response to her. Writing as narrator, Lyotard "recounts" as a kind of stream of consciousness: "He's no longer with her. Had he ever been? Disenchantment, suspicion, the wretched novel of everyday life. He's auditioning before her" (ibid.: 111–2). First with Clara and subsequently with lesser "characters" but still womanly presences in his life, Malraux plays out his life through "literary" and political projects that seek immortality. Not possible, of course: the search is engendered through the unpresentable, through ambivalence.

Ambivalence

Albeit too abruptly, what is now possible in the closing of this chapter is a summing indication of exploration. Jean-François Lyotard, perhaps like many of his generation, expresses ambivalence toward women and toward feminist theory. He says in the opening interview that "it is perhaps too late." Rather one might speculate that it is "perhaps too early," even for one as committed to justice as Lyotard was, to yet recognize all of the complexities in "transforming" the sexual basis of Western thought for a new politics. At the very least, he appears ambiguous, perhaps not even capitalizing well on possibility within his own "unpresentable." Unlike English-speaking feminists, French feminists have worked from this radical alterity – they do see possibility in "the other of other" – and not simply as difference. For now, what has been accomplished in this initial exploration is a summing of efforts to date to interpret Lyotard's work for feminism (especially for English-speaking readers). What remains in addition to a wonderful feminist project of interpreting *Signed, Malraux* is a reading of "Lyotard's Women" relative to his French feminist counterparts. Perhaps as an "unpresentable" in this chapter, it seduces as future desire. Overall there seems possibility for feminist theorizing in Lyotard's writings, but more needs to be done in exploring their "basic" ambivalence.[10]

Notes

1 On occasion quotation marks are used to indicate emphasis.
2 Differing from the American context in which women's issues and "gender" studies may be distinct from feminist politics and feminist theory, it appears as if women writing in the European context "are" feminist.
3 The interview is cited twice: Lyotard's statements are from Lyotard 1995a; those from Olson cited separately as Olson 1995.
4 Exemplary authors in this tradition include Flaubert and Proust.
5 'Radical alterity' reminds that there is no simple opposition or otherness since the unpresentable is not encapsulated within them but only difference.
6 It is *The Differend: Phrases in Dispute* (Lyotard 1988a).
7 I include long quotes from Lyotard because of the literary quality of much of his writing and its various genres and styles. While naming himself as philosopher, he desires to be a writer.
8 I checked texts from various important French feminists. I did find mention of Lyotard in English commentators on Kristeva. In contrast, there seems more reference overall to Derrida.
9 A distinction for feminist theorists in the Anglo-American and French traditions

is between, on the one hand, a basis in experience or lived structural life and, on the other, a basis in discourse that "represents" experience (see Dallery 1989).

10 This chapter has benefited from support and suggestion by Michael Peters (see his important book, Peters 1995); thanks very much to him and especially to Pradeep Dhillon and Paul Standish for their invitation and infinite patience. Also, Kathleen Martin contributed early research.

11 Fables and apedagogy

Lyotard's relevance for a pedagogy of the Other

David Palumbo-Liu

At first glance, Jean-François Lyotard's postmodernism would seem to offer an enormous opportunity to critical pedagogy. As this and other volumes attest, Lyotard has been enlisted widely in the effort radically to rethink pedagogical practices and values. Peter McLaren's essay, "Critical pedagogy, political agency, and the pragmatics of justice: the case of Lyotard" (1994), argues the connection between the goals of critical pedagogy and postmodernism's attack on the tenets of modernity:

> Critical pedagogy attempts to analyze and unsettle extant power configurations, to defamiliarize and make remarkable what is often passed off as the ordinary, the routine, the banal. In other words, critical pedagogy ambiguates the complacency of teaching under the sign of modernity, that is, under a sign in which knowledge is approached as ahistorical, neutral, separated from value and power.
> (McLaren 1994: 120ff.)[1]

However, even as McLaren notes Lyotard's usefulness to critical pedagogy, he also points out a major dilemma facing anyone attempting to integrate Lyotard's postmodern theory into critical pedagogical practice: "Lyotard's position betrays a discomfiting silence with respect to understanding how agency can be linked to a pedagogical project of social justice that must include some prescriptive components, even if on provisional and contingent cases" (ibid.: 327).

Indeed, Lyotard's particular views regarding subjectivity, agency, and voice all militate against prescription, predetermined value, and the logic of representation. Seeking social justice by evoking "names" becomes a suspect activity, given the social and political practices that Lyotard believes such evocations may come to underwrite: "one should be on one's guard . . . against the totalitarian character of an idea of justice, even a pluralistic one" (Lyotard 1985: 96). My essay first theoretically and historically examines the nature of Lyotard's pessimism, then asks whether and how anything might be recovered for critical pedagogy. Specifically I address the issue of multicultural pedagogy in the United States. Can we "use" Lyotard without abusing his basic tenets, can we find openings for multicultural pedagogy within even his bleakest texts, or is there little or no use to be made of Lyotard's postmodernism? Crucially, by focusing on the problematic of *narration* we can see the contours of possibility and negation.

One prominent part of Lyotard's writings centers on the notion of singularity and difference. Singularity takes one form in the idea of an "event," which is understood as an unplanned, unforeseeable moment that, for a brief instant, refuses objectification and insertion into the production of commodified knowledge. Similarly, difference refuses incorporation into a narrative which would recuperate it by arguing difference's equivalence or similarity to that narrative: whatever difference may exist is folded into and engulfed by the logic of the master narrative. Given these two starting points, I ask how the moment of "multiculturalism" can preserve critical notions of difference, and therefore be pedagogically useful, when it is confronted by both the demands of knowledge production and equivalence-making, that process which transforms the event into a commodity with its particular assignment of exchange value, and that process wherein "difference" becomes merely one story added on to the back of the modern humanist narrative. Specifically, we must confront the question: "How does the University seem to present precisely the site in which both these debilitating moves not only take place, but are in fact *called upon* to take place?" What kinds of stories are possible here? Can any form be anticipated that would be immune from such recuperation and exploitation? The connection between this narrative concern and social justice is clear. Yet, frustratingly, if the aims of critical pedagogy include a rethinking of the social formations that undergird educational practice and the ways knowledge can serve the goals of a more just society, then just as with narrative and event, Lyotard's notions of community and justice also reject any formal pedagogical practice. Here, too, the formal practice of engendering and delivering knowledge simply reflects its commodification and points out how knowledge is joined to institutional morality-enforcement and the repression of difference.

To escape (if only temporarily) from this objectification and commodification, Lyotard maps out an alternative institutional space for "apedagogy," and a different mode of narration: the fable. Lyotard's notion of the "fable," a small narrative that is unhistorical, nonteleological, and nonprescriptive, forms the crucial component of "apedagogy." Yet this double rejection of narrative and history not only leaves us with no ground to stand on for better or worse (as is commonly remarked), it also prevents Lyotard from seeing his own historical specificity and therefore the limits of his critique. The hope he leaves us is tinged with melancholic memories of Paris '68 and the repression that immediately followed. I will argue that this melancholy not only impinges inappropriately upon our reading of multiculturalism in the United States in the late twentieth and early twenty-first centuries, it also forecloses the possibilities that were indeed opened up by that moment in the US.[2]

Community, justice, and the possibility of pedagogy

Critical pedagogy has a particular stake in understanding the formation of human community and the instantiation of just social institutions and practices. Its critical aspect is deeply linked to providing a situation wherein the classroom becomes the site for articulating and testing different ideas and arguments about what constitutes society, and an individual's role in it. Furthermore, the uneven and irregular distribution of resources, privileges, and freedoms provides a central set of topics for critical pedagogy, which tries to understand the discursive practices that allow for, demand, and hide inequality, as well as those which allow us to recognize, name, and redress such grievances. There is nothing in such critical pedagogical notions in themselves that stands in direct opposition to Lyotard. Where we get into trouble is when we try to imagine how the classroom, instantiated as a state institution, can be the site for such a community.

For Lyotard, community should be constituted by "pleasure but without interest, universality but without concept, finality but without representation of an end, necessity but without argument" (Lyotard 1992b: 1). He continues,

> It's not a question of an historical and social community which people of taste or artists, any more than people of science and will, form or want to form. It's not a question of "culture" or pleasure shared in, through and for culture. And there is no progression promised to this pleasure of the beautiful, precisely because it isn't desired. . . . It is certainly not what we call a "public." Not the society of art lovers in museums, galleries, concerts, theatres, or who today look at reproductions of works . . . in their homes. The *sensus communis* must be protected from anthropologization.
>
> (Ibid.: 6, 10)

Most importantly for our discussion, "there is no assignable community of feeling, no affective consensus in fact" (ibid.: 24). It is clear how Lyotard at once opens the door for precisely a critical pedagogy that would contest the given structures and discourses of the academy, and swerves away from enforced humanistic "feelings." It is abundantly clear that he refuses equally the *teaching* of any feeling, or of any ethical notion.

Specifically, within Lyotard's community, "justice" is to be intuited, not prescribed or taught. It will involve not a conscious pedagogical effort, but rather the "movements of the imagination" (ibid.: 3) that reach "consensus" independent of any prescribed logic or sentiment. Thus, as David Ingram points out,

The Idea of community in Lyotard's philosophy testifies to an idealism that must remain desideratum. . . . Any attempt to instill it with content by identifying it with some concrete political arrangement such as social democracy would invariably result in a transcendental dialectic.

(Ingram 1987: 299)

In this light, A.T. Nuyen is absolutely right when he asserts that for Lyotard the imagination is the only area left for pedagogical activity, difficult as that claim is to think through (how does one "teach" imagination?). Lyotard's usefulness would then reside in his argument for how we might clear a space for imagination that might lead to a community. But more than "space-clearing," it will be necessary to transform the modality through and with which we communicate with each other in that newly-invented arena, how we present ourselves in it as speaking subjects, and how we represent our ideas. But before I address the classroom as the site for a specific pedagogical community, it is necessary to briefly rehearse a few key points of Lyotard's theory. Only in so doing can one appreciate the difficulty of mapping such a pedagogical locus.

Small narratives, the political, the historical

David Carroll links the importance of Lyotard's "small narratives" to a notion of community and justice usefully and succinctly:

Lyotard's postmodern disbelief in metanarrative is rooted in a confidence in the potential critical force of small narratives, at least insomuch as their conflictual multiplicity and heterogeneity resist totalization. . . . [These little narratives] also indicate the possibility of another kind of society, of another form of social relations in fact already functioning "laterally" within the totalitarian state.

(Carroll 1987: 72, 75)

Like the "imagination," the gestural aspect of these small narratives insists on not insisting, on leaving open a trajectory without anticipating an exact arrival. Their substance inheres in their very fragility as narratives. Lyotard writes:

History is made up of wisps of narratives, stories that one tells, that one invents, that one hears, that one acts out; the people does not exist as a subject but as a mass of millions of insignificant and serious little stories that sometimes let themselves be collected together to constitute big stories and sometimes disperse into digressive elements, but which in general hold more or less together in forming what is called the culture of a civil society.

(Lyotard 1977: 39)

The randomness that characterizes these "wisps of narratives" deeply informs Lyotard's notion of history, which now is to be read not as a narration of humanity, but as an occasional, unnecessary, and unpredicatable conglomerate of just as easily dispersed elements. Equally random is "the people," that is, the conglomeration of stories that may or may not constitute anything resembling a collective human identity.

Lyotard's relutance to assert any specific mode of cohering stories together, that is, of manufacturing history, stems from his reluctance to predetermine the value and meaning of any story. Crucial is the safeguarding of any and every voice. This is the basis of Lyotard's notion of justice, which, according to Stephen K. White, takes the form of a "new pluralist justice":

> The contrast with traditional views of justice can be described as one between approaches which are primarily attuned to a sense of responsibility to otherness versus ones attuned to a responsibility to act, or, . . . a responsibility to author determinate and unambiguous principles for judgment and action.
>
> (White 1987: 309)

As Anne Barron puts it,

> Postmodernity . . . must invoke an Idea of society as a non-totalizable universe of diverse language games, an Idea which has not already been made present but which "remains to be attained; it is ahead of us." There must be not only a multiplicity of justices, but a justice of multiplicities.
>
> (Barron 1992: 34, quoted material from Lyotard and Thébaud)

Given the ethical value of preserving, as long as is possible, the right of the Other to remain Other, the drawing together of "wisps" of narratives, the formation of a story, and all that this coming together implies and may enforce, become, essentially, politics: "Politics . . . is the threat of the differend. It is not a genre, it is the multiplicity of genres, the diversity of ends, and *par excellence the question of linkage*" (Lyotard 1988a: 138, my emphasis). Such linkage is thus at once the historical and the political; the "story" is produced by linking difference into similarity (one thinks of Jakobson's famous formulation); the political is the assertion or disputation of the rightness of that process, the coherence of that story.[3] And the totalizing narrative which has produced our sense of the world is exactly the narrative of "humanity." How are the diverse "wisps" of a multitude of events linked up to underwrite our sense of ourselves in time and space? And what are the politics of this representation?[4]

The "wisps" of narratives can be associated with "events." An event is

> the *sign of history* . . . [which] introduces a further degree of complexity

into 'passages' needed to phrase the historical-political. The question raised ... is whether it can be affirmed that the human race is constantly progressing toward the better, and if so, how this is possible. The difficulties proliferate: the better, progress, and the human race are objects of Ideas, with no possible direct presentation.

(Lyotard 1988a: 164)

Like the "wisps of narratives" that indicate "the people" (but not as "subject"), this event "would merely indicate (*hinweisen*) and not prove (*beweisen*) that humanity is capable of being both cause (*Ursache*) and author (*Urheber*) of its progress" (ibid.). Again, Lyotard's raising this topic as a *question* is linked to his refusal to mandate what would amount simply to another grand narrative, a narrative which would appear only with the erasure of otherness and multiplicity. Indeed, Lyotard wonders if the "defaillancy" of the modern subject "might not have to be related to resistance on the part of what I will term the multiplicity of worlds of names, on the part of the insurmountable diversity of cultures" (Lyotard 1989: 319). The transcendental "we" of "*the* human race" has been breached by a diversity of smaller, self-legitimizing narratives.

The overwhelming tendency on the part of the modern west has been to objectify that multiplicity, difference, Otherness, and integrate it negatively into its master narrative of itself. Lyotard critiques this integrative move:

A non-cosmopolitical (or "savage") narrative proceeds by phrases like *On that date, in that place, it happened that x, etc.* The question raised by cosmopolitical narrative would be the following: since this x, this date, and this place are proper names and since proper names belong by definition to worlds of names and to specific "savage" narratives, how can these narratives give rise to a single world of names and to a universal narrative?

(Lyotard 1988a: 155)

Again, "the question is one of linkage: what genre of discourse governs the linking onto the 'Cashinahua' narrative of a phrase discerning a 'human' world therein which would stem from a universal history?" (ibid.: 156). Most important, this narrativizing transforms the event from something that could instantiate quantitative change into something that merely rehearses the status quo (Bennington 1988a: 110).

Hand-in-hand with this appropriation of Otherness is the silencing of that Other voice through delegitimization, a process which Lyotard names "terror":

What is a crime is to impose that silence on another, who is then excluded from the interlocutory community. Moreover, an even greater wrong is added to this injustice, since the one who is banished, being prohibited from speaking, has no means to appeal his/her banishment. Whether political, social, or cultural, the exercise of terror is as follows: to deprive the other of the ability to respond to that deprivation. . . . It is thus taken for granted that the human community rests upon the capacity for interlocution and upon the right to inter-locution and that it's up to the republic to watch over this right and to teach that capacity.

(Lyotard 1997: 209ff.)

It is exactly this capacity that is threatened by the objectification and commodification of difference. With regard to the topics of critical pedagogy and multiculturalism, the question becomes not only the capacity of the Other to speak, but also the intensely short-livedness of that speech as Other, and the degraded form that enunciation takes upon its institutionalization.

Objectified knowledge and the role of the university

While the classroom may provide a space wherein to articulate otherness, Lyotard argues that such articulations simply become reiterated as commodified catch-words: institutionally recognized, sanctioned, and incorporated "otherness." In the face of this threat, the "retreat into local legitimacy" is seen as a move made to safeguard against such objectification:

It might be said that this retreat into local legitimacy is a reaction to and a form of resistance against the devastating effects of imperialism and its crisis are having on particular cultures. . . . Cultural differences are . . . being promoted as touristic and cultural commodities at every point on the scale.

(Lyotard 1989: 322–3)

The essential question here is: if a "retreat into local legitimacy" is required to protect against such commodification of difference on a global scale, what is left to take place in the classroom? Where is our *local* legit-imacy within the structure of the university? How can the "local" withstand the forces which embed it so firmly? And what are the political conse-quences of having history be made unavailable, for better or worse?

Parallel to this objectification of difference in the university is the objec-tification of the "event," the transformation of an event to an object of representation, a commodity:

The modern is a feeling for the event as such, impromptu, imminent, urgent, disarming knowledge and even consciousness. The event is an absolute performance: it happens. Fashion is affirmed by the desire to be an event. As soon as it happens, it ceases to be an event, it becomes a piece of information, which circulates and which loses its destablizing force.

(Lyotard 1993b: 24)[5]

The battle against such objectification is precisely the effort to negate the entry of the event into economic circulation:

> There is a dimension of *force* that escapes the logic of the signifier: an excess of energy that symbolic exchange can never regulate . . . a 'disorder' that at times shakes the capitalist system and produces events in it that are initially *unexchangeable*.
>
> (ibid.: 61)

We may thus underscore the intimate connection between different manifestations of "diversity:" the diversity of cultures and the diversity of "events." Both are to resist supersession by the dominance of History, that would neutralize and subordinate both difference of culture and diversity of events to a *telos* of "humanity." If "culture" is at all to be understood as a singular concept, it is understood as that which preserves always the capacity to listen to otherness: "Culture is lending an ear to what strives to be said, culture is giving a voice to those who do not have a voice and who seek one" (ibid.: 33). In this sense it would seem that the moment of multiculturalism would be construed as an "event," but only in its inaugural moment, before its formal integration into the system. Unfortunately, it is precisely the university that provides the site *par excellence* of the objectification and commodification of "culture." And, without having recourse to history, Otherness can only remain in the margins.

Lyotard's critique of the university begins at a very specific turning point. In 1970, he asserts that,

> Activities and institutions previously sheltered from the requirement for the increased reproduction of capital are now under orders to operate as simple moments in the circuit of this reproduction. This is especially the case for the so-called educational and teaching function.
>
> (Lyotard 1993b: 47)

Under these conditions, the function of the teacher is "to consume cultural contents in order to produce cultural contents that can be consumed by students" (ibid.: 57). Lyotard remarks that, at the point in time, "culture is no longer a practice of listening and responding to the call of fundamental situations in everyday life" in the university (ibid.: 35). Where "cultural desire is the desire to put an end to the exile of meaning as external to activities," he emphatically argues that "its instrument cannot be the university, which dwells in this very exile, and is the product of it" (ibid.: 39). Finally, Lyotard specifies the university's inextricable link to capitalism:

> Of course, capitalism also has its "policy" for culture, which is no less alienating for being more insidious. It selects the activities of the mind according to criteria of good performance: the value of a book is judged by its sales figures, the value of a curriculum by the number of students registered.
>
> (Lyotard 1993b: 12)[6]

Under these conditions, the objectification of cultural and narrative diversity becomes a key commodity in the university:

> The relationship of the suppliers and users of knowledge to the knowledge they supply and use is now tending, and will increasingly tend, to assume the form already taken by the relationship of commodity producers and consumers to the commodities they produce and consume – that is, the form of value.
>
> (Lyotard 1984a: 4ff.)

Knowledge is and will be continually produced in order to be sold, it is and will be consumed in order to be valorized in a new production. Even critique of capital and the university is "immediately digested by the system" (Lyotard 1993b: 57). It would thus appear that "critical pedagogy" and "multiculturalism" cannot exist in noncommodified form within the university, their counterhegemonic potential can never be tapped. Any resistance to such objectification would have been anticipated by the "system" and made to serve its purposes:

> It may even be said that the system can and must encourage such movement to the extent that it combats its own entropy; the novelty of an unexpected "move" with its correlative displacement of a partner or group of partners, can supply the system with that increased performativity it forever demands and consumes.
>
> (Lyotard 1984a: 15)[7]

The cumulative weight of all such pronouncements not only nullifies anything we might aspire to call "critical pedagogy," it also effectively questions the political activity that critical pedagogy might inspire. While Lyotard persists in arguing that "We must constantly reaffirm the rights of minorities, women, children, gays, the South, the Third World, the poor, the rights of citizenship, the right to culture and education, the rights of animals and the environment," he also notes that, just as all knowledge set forth in the university will be commodified and made to serve its purposes, "Society permits us, requires us to act accordingly because it needs us to contribute, in that order that is our own, to the development of the global system" (Lyotard 1997: 68–70). Hence, "critical pedagogy" in the university serves a similar purpose to that of political protest in "society": both are functional elements of academic and social systems that will, according to Lyotard, absorb, negate, and even feed off such counterdiscourses. From 1962 to the 1990s, Lyotard only sees the persistence and intensification of this objectification and commodification in the university.

Fables of apedagogy

Given all this, it is hard to imagine what we can come away with that is of use, much less what can help us overcome a sense of despair. The remainder of my essay will attempt to piece together an answer, however partial.

First, we might compare Lyotard's view of the role of the teacher with that proposed by Peter McLaren, to see the vast difference between what Lyotard saw (and continued to see) as the institutional role of teachers and what critical pedagogy envisions. McLaren writes,

> Criticalists work against the traditional role of teachers as curators of the ancestral mind. They criticize the museumization of classrooms as places where knowledge is salvaged from its "primitive" beginnings, admired in its "advanced" stages, and mounted for discursive display.
> (McLaren 1994: 321ff.)

Lyotard's view of the academy precisely argues against the possibility of such pedagogy. Although Lyotard's project includes exactly that resistance to and argument against objectification, the institutional space in which such activity is to be placed would seem to him to objectify the act of teaching itself, as it is part of the economic life of the academy. The basic tension between Lyotard and his critics in this respect is that what is a given for Lyotard is an open and urgent question for his critics.

Specifically, in the presentation of knowledge of Others, White notes that

> societal rationalization in an age of informationalization threatens otherness and the autonomy of different spheres of meaning in new and subtle ways. It does so because the dominant discourses and institutions which carry that rationalization process forward so structure public meanings that alternative discourses find critical footholds difficult to secure. ... The problem is how to develop criteria for discriminating between pre-packaged newness and newness in which one can have at least some confidence in its autonomous qualities.
> (White 1987: 310, 312)

The problem thus becomes one which links the production of knowledge within the academy to the overarching discourses of "society," and brings us back to the key notion of narrative. Whose stories reign? Whose stories may appear? And in what form does ideology take shape? Nancy Fraser provides a useful list of such discourses. The means of interpretation and communication include:

> the officially recognized vocabularies in which one can press claims; the idioms available for interpreting and communicating one's needs; the established narrative conventions available for constructing the individual and collective histories which are constitutive of social identity; the paradigm of argumentation accepted as authoritative in adjudicating conflicting claims; the ways in which various discourses constitute their respective subject matters as specific sorts of objects; the repertory of available rhetorical devices; the bodily and gestural dimension of speech which are associated in a given society with authority and conviction.
>
> (Fraser 1986: 425)

Yet the very possibility of differentiating between the two sorts of "newnesses" described by White would be for Lyotard a futile task. And as much as we might hope to access such means of communication as Fraser sets forth, and seek to retool them to narrate "otherness" and "diversity" (as Lyotard uses these terms), any such effort would for Lyotard be futile, and damaging to the "event" and "difference," those key elements which Lyotard seeks at all costs to safeguard. As Bill Readings concisely notes, for Lyotard, "instance" or "difference" "imposes a refusal of the communicational ideology of political modernity" (Readings 1993b: xxv). We come then to a grinding halt, hedged in on one side by the notion that "difference" will be commodified and homogenized as soon as it enters the university, and on the other by the belief that *any* attempt to circulate such terms according to a preset notion of their functionality, their outcome, betrays an outdated and potentially damaging trust in "communication."

So how does Lyotard, as a teacher himself, imagine the classroom? How do we avoid exactly the pitfalls outlined above and still go to work every day? First, and most important, Lyotard invents a narrative form that accommodates the values of nonprescriptivity, of non-necessity, and of nonsequentiality. This form is the fable, and at first glance it shares many of the features of the "small narrative," which for Lyotard "remains the quintessential form of imaginative invention" (Lyotard 1984a: 60). Crucially, this new variation of the "small narrative" brings forth an *ethical* dimension, conveyed not only by its truncated form, but also by its content: "After a short story, a fable or tale, sketch or *exemplum*, a moral draws out an unpretentious, localized, and provisional bit of wisdom, soon to be forgotten. Morals often, heedlessly, contradict each other. Together, they make a rustling of maxims, a cheerful lament: that's life" (Lyotard 1997: vii). Here is his most sustained description of the fable:

A fable is exposed neither to argumentation nor to falsification. It is not even a critical discourse, but merely imaginary. This is how it exploits the space of indetermination the system keeps open for hypothetical thought.

This is also how it turns itself into the most infantile expression of the crisis of thought today: the crisis of modernity, which is the state of postmodern thought. With no cognitive or ethico-political pretension, the fable grants itself a poetic or aesthetic status. It has worth only by its faithfulness to the postmodern affectation, melancholia.

(Lyotard 1997: 101f)

The claim that the fable has "no cognitive or ethico-political pretension" has to be made in order to avoid the pitfalls of prescription, and Lyotard does so by at once cutting short its linkage to a greater narrative and fore-closing its temporal dimension.[8] It is aesthetic in its affectivity and its imagination, which seek only to be present to thought but not thought of. Its melancholia is part and parcel of the postmodern's affectation of longing, of loss. Nevertheless, the question left gapingly open is how, exactly, the affective quality of the fable is to be achieved, how it will "draw out" its small bit of wisdom. And this question of course goes to the heart of the pedagogical project.

Parallel to his concern with mapping out a narrative form that would do justice to his notion of pedagogy, Lyotard attempts to think of a *space* in which such fables might be produced and protected. As much as he argues that the French university in the late 1960s has become the stage on which "culture" is detached from life and made into a commodity, and teaching and learning made part of that system, Lyotard holds out the hope that something else might happen therein, that something else may be produced. While he states, "The university will not, of course, be revolutionary; whatever we may be able to do here can and will be recuperated by the powers that be," he goes on to assert,

> Yet the task to be carried out in the faculty is not merely one of vulgar reformation. We have to impose institutions and modes of teaching and research that allow the critical comprehension of reality in all its forms and the liberation of the power of expression.
>
> (Lyotard 1993b: 44)

This particular space will become that of fable-speaking. In an intensification of his proposal for a cultural "non-policy," he suggests that the activity of teaching take place via an "apedagogy:" "What is required is an apedagogy . . . all pedagogy participates in . . . repression, including that which is implied in the internal and external relations of the 'political organizations'" (ibid.: 59). This "imposition," this one ray of hope and target for radical renovation, of course contradicts his belief that there can be an unequivocal "good" to be imposed. His later description of what, exactly, this "apedagogy" is to look like suggests how he will work around that contradiction. "Apedagogy" will involve a space-clearing venture, one which will produce a situation amenable to public discourse within the margins of the university:

> It is only in this frayed and rewoven tissue, wherever it may have been found, Penelope-like, that we have been able to "teach" – I mean: reflect publicly in common. In this dump where the thoughts of each are transplanted and placed side by side right on the table of thought. To institute, or quasi institute, this rather vague place is to give it a name that authority can tolerate, to offer credits, to become able to grant degrees, and to prove that it can train acceptable graduates.
>
> (Lyotard 1993b: 80)

This melancholic description of what Lyotard ends up advocating for teachers, the truly desperate tenor in this voice, leads us to review what leads him there. Most important for our discussion is the link between the commodification of knowledge Lyotard remarks upon in the 1960s and the postmodern production of knowledge today. Lyotard, as is well known, was a primary figure in the *Socialisme ou Barbarie* group for a decade (1954–64) wherein he was a strong voice against colonialism, and remained active in leftist politics in *Pouvoir Ouvrier* for two more years. He was also a seminal voice in the student revolts of 1968 in Nanterre, in which period many of the essays I have cited were written. However, shortly after 1968 his positions shifted away from Marxism, especially what he considered its "master narrative" (Anderson 1998: 27; Bennington 1988a: 1; Turner 1998: 32). With this disillusionment came his notion of the postmodern, and especially his distrust of political movements founded on such notions. It is in the transition between "event" and objectification that we might locate Lyotard's suspicion of a project that might attempt to lend voice to the silenced, by examining this movement. We may understand how the "event" of multiculturalism, the historical appearance of Otherness in the academy's discourse, has been a moment of both voicedness and silencing. We may note that the preserve of "apedagogy" that Lyotard maps out in the earlier period may have effectively disappeared in his later writings, displaced by skepticism into the purely private (and extra-institutional) world of fable-telling. This is because any "authentic" articulation of Otherness that might have taken place in the margins of the university, at the site of apedagogy, has been appropriated into institutionalized multiculturalism.

One of the targets for his "postmodern fables" is precisely the marketing of cultural difference. Indeed, most pernicious for Lyotard is the objectification of "difference" in the guise of multiculturalism – what he considers its packaging of difference for curricular consumption. It is crucial to note how, in this late work, Lyotard has found a specific name for the packaging of difference. It is an *American* name, with a distinctly American inflection:

> Difference, alterity, multiculturalism. It's their dada.
>
> My prof, he reminded us of Kant: think for yourself, and according to yourself. Today, they say, that's logocentric, not *politically correct*. The streams must all go in the right direction. They must converge. Why all this cultural busyness, colloquia, interviews, seminars? Just so we can be sure we're all saying the same thing. About what, then? About alterity. . . . What cultural capitalism has found is the marketplace of singularities. May we all express our singularity? Speak from your place in the sex, ethnicity, language, generation, social class, unconscious network.
>
> (Lyotard 1997: 6–7)

> Their multiculturalism, minorities, singularities had no future in the culture industry a hundred years ago. Except as the Colonial Exhibit. This obligates many strategies of capture and exploitation. Finally, it became profitable. People get bored, they have enough of snacking always on the same images, the same ideas at the cultural fast-food outlets, they need a little something, *live* and unexpected. . . . A human community who contemplates its differences. A generalized aesthetics.
>
> (Ibid.: 11)

Now the critique of multiculturalism as commodification of difference is of course not unique to Lyotard.[9] His critique makes sense, given the trajectory we have traced in his thought regarding the value of difference and singularity and the ever-present danger of absorbing and neutralizing those things under the rubric of "humanity" or other such master narratives. However, in closing I would point out two serious flaws in Lyotard's late critique of multiculturalism. First, this "critique" of multiculturalism *tout court* stops short of any account of *its* particularity, that is, of exactly that thing which is to be guarded at all cost. Instead, Lyotard assumes a lineage from the demise of the university in France as a place of cultural life to the dismal packaging of "multiculturalism" in the United States.[10] Lyotard groups together all multicultural projects, perspectives, agendas, as if there was consensus on what "multiculturalism" is or should be. While his broad focus on the debilitating operations of capital on knowledge production has several useful elements that are indeed germane to both France and the United States, this general critique obliterates the specific national ideologies that abide in these different national spaces and their institutions, as well as the particular material historical contexts which are the stages upon which national and local pedagogies are set forth.

He ignores the deep historical and social issues that inform multicultural education in the United States, and both the manifest and potential force of critical pedagogy in addressing the actual production of otherness. That is, in insisting on why the "difference" is exactly *not* organic, like a "species," but produced by structural inequities, critical pedagogy can work against the very objectification Lyotard accuses it of embodying. Indeed, such critical pedagogy presents us with a more activist model than Lyotard's. As Seyla Benhabib puts it:

> The difficulty with political liberalism, old and new, is the neglect of the structural sources of inequality, influence, resource, and power among competing groups. In the absence of radical, democratic measures redressing economic, social and cultural inequalities and forms of subordination, the pluralistic vision of groups Lyotard proposes remains naïve.
>
> (Benhabib 1984: 124)[11]

In the end, Lyotard validates only one sort of narrative for the Other to articulate: a mini-narrative that is isolated, singular, and inward-turning.

Second, Lyotard's fables end up *as* prescriptive (if only negatively), and objectifying, for he turns multiculturalism into simply an object for his moralizing. Ironically, his attack on multiculturalism has much in common with early attacks on French theory, attacks which he publicly and vociferously criticized. Lyotard responds vehemently to the uninformed criticism of new critical thought: "By condemning thought that is in any way new or difficult to repeat, a 'well known model,' [this criticism] drastically simplifies the history of ideas, and makes the task of the reader easier" (Lyotard and Rogozinski 1987: 27).[12] Nevertheless, if we examine more closely his critique of this criticism, we find that the things he finds fault with underlie his own criticism of multiculturalism. First of all, just as he accuses his critics of simply not reading the work in question ("certain of these 'rigorous' censors seem only to know the criticized works by hearsay" (ibid.: 24)), Lyotard never actually even quotes from any works. It seems rather that their very existence, in whatever form, appears problematic. That is, any appearance of "difference" named as such already betrays its contamination.

This leads to an out-of-hand dismissal of multiculturalism in the academy, without any sense of how multiculturalism may be pedagogically practiced, of the pre-existing national cultural histories and ideologies, and of the particular institutions to which they give rise. Again, what he says about Ferry and Renaut seems as well to describe his own practice:

> It cannot be said any better: for them [Ferry and Renaut], "to identify a position" comes down to reducing diverse, heterogeneous works to the abstract identity of a "model" or "ideal type." It then becomes a facile exercise to "unmask the contradictions" of this model.
>
> (Ibid.: 25)

In this case, the "contradiction" would seem to lie in multiculturalism's insistence on "diversity" even as it appears packaged and commodified in a singular, objective form. This condemns multiculturalism for promoting its novelty when in fact it rehearses the old pattern of commodification. Again, consider what he says of his critics: "After reducing the complex to the simple and the diverse to the identical, all that remains is to reduce the new to the old" (ibid.: 26). At base, one will come to question Lyotard's ability to *listen*, since he is so inclined to dismiss out of hand the corrupt quality of multicultural speech.[13]

Finally, one might interrogate the exact status of Lyotard's preferred narrative form, the "fable." Reading through *Postmodern Fables*, one cannot help but be struck by the uneven (to say the least) manner in which it conforms to Lyotard's description of a "fable." Most importantly, as we saw above, the fable should be without "cognitive or ethico-political pretension." And yet Lyotard's pronouncements on multiculturalism are nothing if not moralistic; they harbor precise ethico-political pretensions in so far as they criticize the discourse of multiculturalism based on a pretension to know the motives and agendas of the speakers. In this sense we might see the "fable" as a smokescreen, a way for Lyotard to at once appear true to his postmodern ethics and smuggle in a moralistic criticism of multiculturalism *as if* it were indeed the thing he claims it is. Although Lyotard asserts, "the fact that I myself speak of this plurality [of language games] does not imply that I am presenting myself as the occupant of a unitary vantage point upon the whole set of games" (Lyotard 1985: 51), when it comes to actually constructing a "fable" about plurality, Lyotard argues against what he *assumes* can only be a degraded form of articulation. Indeed, at worst, multiculturalism is associated with "political correctness" and seen as an example of totalitarian oppression of difference.[14] The problem is not that this charge may be totally unfounded in every instance, it is rather that Lyotard assumes it pertains to every instance, and hence his accommodation of multiple voices is suspect. Here they are all lumped into one.

Although Nuyen argues that "new discourses such as Women's Studies, Black Studies, Queer Studies, Green politics, as well as the new political order in South Africa, are testimonies to the process of finding 'new rules for forming and linking phrases that are able to express the differend disclosed by the feeling'" (Nuyen 1996a: 84; quoting Lyotard 1988a: 13), this optimistic note would quickly be squelched if one thought Lyotard would maintain such optimism upon the establishment in the university of a "Women's Studies, Black Studies, Queer Studies," etc., *department*. In short, what we have to grapple with are the effects of the *institutionalization* of pedagogical practices that take "difference" as their object of study.

The easy answer would be to assert that the battle against commodification could be fought by always destablizing the object of study, putting it under constant surveillance and critique. Yet Lyotard is clear enough when he asserts that even such "dispute" can itself be part of the machinery. The potential for resistance remains, as John Keane notes, entirely amorphous. Speaking of Lyotard's postmodernism, he remarks:

> [its] political credentials – its implications for the existing distributions and legitimacy of power crystallized in state and non-state institutions – remain wholly ambiguous. Postmodernism is said to involve the practice of resistance; challenging master narratives with the discourse of others . . . and yet phrases such as these remain highly amorphous, thereby marginalizing or repressing outright further consideration of socio-political questions.
>
> (Keane 1992: 89)

Along with these criticisms of Lyotard's neglect of the specific national and historical contexts of multicultural pedagogy and his own lapse into less than subtle moralizing, there are several other criticisms that relate importantly to the topic of critical pedagogy and multiculturalism. First, as Douglas Kellner points out, there is the need to differentiate between many different sorts of master narratives and grand narratives that may function in totalizing ways or not (Kellner 1988: 253). This links up with Manfred Frank's question: how can we assume a wrong has been done and what are the consequences? Are there different kinds? We should also consider Benhabib's difference between raising and forcing a claim:

> The rhetorics of language Lyotard espouses does not distinguish between *raising a validity claim* and *forcing* someone to believe in something, between the coordination of action among participants on the basis of conviction generated through agreement, and the manipulative influencing of the behavior of others. . . . Surely there is a distinction between agreeing and giving in; consenting and blackmailing; refusing and being obstinate.
>
> (Benhabib 1984: 113–14)

In each case, we must wonder how airtight the case is against *any* representation of difference, and by extension any attempt within the academy to do so.

The goal of this project is nothing less than to ascertain the possibilities of presenting otherness. As much as Lyotard rightly argues against objectification and commodification, Benhabib makes a case parallel to my own: the consequences of Lyotard's position equally lead to objectification, as it "condemn[s] the subjects of this episteme to ahistoricity, to deny that they inhabit the same space with us" (Benhabib 1984: 119ff.). The critical question is to imagine a way to recognize otherness as a subject that resists objectification. Lyotard's attitude borders on condescension, presuming the abject state of otherness. He cannot imagine that a critical multiculturalism can present otherness in anything other than a commodified form; he places it in such a debased institutional and cultural position that it can only be manipulative. So what can we do? "All we can do is gaze in wonderment at the diversity of discursive species, just as we do at the diversity of plant or animal species" (Lyotard 1984a: 26). Yet this distancing, this prophylactic act, ironically keeps from view precisely the specific structural inequalities that create difference in decidedly unromantic ways.

In terms of critical pedagogy then, are we left with the strictly non-interventionist stance advocated by Nuyen? "There is a sense in which one can *learn from* geniuses, though not in the sense of copying or imitating them. One can learn from them in the sense of allowing oneself to be influenced by them" (Nuyen 1997: 40). If this seems a version of a "kinder, gentler" postmodern pedagogy, Rorty provides a countermodel which offers still the possibility of action, of pedagogical *practice*. "Social purposes are served, just as Habermas says, by finding beautiful ways of harmonizing interests, rather than sublime ways of detaching oneself from others' interests" (Rorty 1985: 174). Critical pedagogy that wishes to retain both a sense of otherness and a political engagement in structural change and activism thus would seem to have to straddle these two visions to create one that would take the better part of each without slipping into either the passivity of the former or the latter's potential for either assuming "harmony" or *forcing* consensus.[15]

Nevertheless, we still have to face up to Lyotard's belief that the best pedagogy for the university is an apedagogy, one which will constantly sidestep or bypass, as best it can, the mechanisms which objectify and commodify whatever knowledge might be produced. The depressing end-product of any discussion of difference and otherness will look like the multiculturalism Lyotard lampoons, with all its glossy and avaricious packaging of difference. Are we fated to accept this as the one outcome of multiculturalism in the US academy? Is critical pedagogy unable to step outside this abysmal circle? What allows Lyotard to make such inherently conservative pronouncements but his unwillingness to consider the specific institutional and political histories of the American academy? It is as if the entire history of civil rights, equal access to education, affirmative action, and so on, were inconsequential. According to his logic, all that takes place in the academy, any academy, equally and inevitably becomes yet another commodity.

As has been noted, Lyotard does not address the historical occasion of multiculturalism in the United States, whose notion of "diversity" is truly different from the presumptions of French unity and, indeed, universality (Lacorne 1997). In France, the modern discourse of race and ethnicity is fraught with the legacy of the wars of decolonization and the effort to "integrate" the formerly colonized into the Republic (Hargreaves 1995).

The assumptions of universality there prohibit the public discussion of "ethnicity" and race, as even articulating such terms of difference is thought to be a betrayal of the founding ideology of the modern republic. Hence, speaking of race and ethnicity threatens to identify one with either the racists on the right, or liberals on the "left." There is no tradition of civil rights activism from oppressed groups which would give rise to anything like US multiculturalism, nor are French universities the sites of the same institutional battles over "national culture." In short, there are many specific historical differences between the US and France, and each contributes to different political and social contexts that cannot simply be subordinated to "capitalism." This is not at all to say that Lyotard's fear of commodification is unfounded; rather, the stakes and possibilities of the case in the United States, the specific institutional differences and the national contexts each carry more weight than Lyotard recognizes.

Unlike that of France, the ideology of the United States calls for a certain accommodation of pluralism. While I am certainly not naive about the actualization of this ideal, I would argue that it leaves open a possibility both for manipulation, denigration, and commodification, *and* for contestation and dissensus. As I have written elsewhere,

> a critical multiculturalism explores the fissures, tensions, and sometimes contradictory demands of multiple cultures, rather than (only) celebrating the plurality of cultures by passing through them appreciatively. . . . A critical multiculturalism [would be] unwilling to bypass an engagement with the historical and material effects of monoculturalist discourse, which has argued for a single normative culture to which all may subscribe voluntarily while in fact forcing a sense of consensus from those on the margins.
>
> (Palumbo-Liu 1995: 5)

This historical opening, from the early days of civil rights activism through the Third World liberation movement and its current rearticulations of anti-racist, anti-sexist, anti-classist (and other) movements, all this takes on a very different tonality and texture here from its style in France.

While Lyotard's general caution to us all about the nature of the postmodern university should be heeded attentively (and this may be one of his most important contributions to critical pedagogy), I do not think his specific closing-down of all sites of institutional resistance and change can be held to evenly. This is not at all to rearticulate some form of American "exceptionalism," but rather to suggest that Lyotard's particular portrait of the postmodern condition derives much of its power from its broad rhetorical sweep, and this in turn washes away key distinctions. Such distinctions in no way guarantee the success of critical pedagogy in the United States, but rather suggest that a critical pedagogy that builds a strategy around the contradictions of American pluralistic ideology may have a certain leverage that is unobtainable in the national context which orients Lyotard's work.

Notes

1　See also Peters 1996.
2　Now I should underscore the fact that "multiculturalism" is a disunified field; there are many varieties and forms, many contradictory. What I have in mind is a historically-centered, critically-minded effort to understand the production of difference and its political linkages and effects, not the uncritical celebration of "difference" (see Palumbo-Liu 1995).
3　For an interesting discussion of Lyotard and Jakobson see Bennington 1988a: 81, 91.
4　See Bennington 1988a: 107.
5　The date of publication here is deceptive; the collection *Political Writings* brings together essays from the early 1960s to the late 1980s. However, I will be arguing that with regard to these matters there is a certain consistency. If anything, Lyotard becomes more pessimistic.
6　Of course, Lyotard's writings are filled with remarks to this effect:

> If we accept the notion that there is an established body of knowledge, the question of its transmission, from a pragmatic point of view, can be subdivided into a series of questions: Who transmits knowledge, What is transmitted? To whom? Through what medium? In what form? With what effect? . . . The desired goal becomes the optimal contribution of higher education to the best performativity of the social system.
>
> (Lyotard 1984a: 48)

7　See also, "As for us, whatever our intervention, we know before speaking or acting that it will be taken into account by the system as a possible contribution to its perfection" (Lyotard 1997: 204).
8　See for example this discussion of narrative and history:

> Narrative is a figure of discourse that lends its form to myth and tale, and that has, like them, the function of distributing the "facts" in a necessarily instructive succession, the function of drawing a "moral," so that the story always fulfills a desire, above all a desire that temporality should make sense and history should be signifiable, a desire that it fulfills by its very form.
>
> (Lyotard 1993b: 67)

9　See my "Introduction" to *The Ethnic Canon*, (Palumbo-Liu 1995).
10　Granted, Lyotard began teaching in the United States in the 1970s, and held an appointment at the University of California, Irvine, for many years. Yet that exposure to the American university did not bring about any historical sense of the distance between the two traditions.
11　Again,

> Insisting upon the incommensurability of language games, in the name of polytheism, may generate moral and political indifference; the call for innovation, experimentation and play may be completely dissociated from social reform and institutional practice, and the activation of differences may not amount to a democratic respect of the right of the "other" to be,

but to a conservative plea to place the other, because of her otherness, outside the pale of our common humanity and mutual responsibility.

(Benhabib 1984: 122)

12 Here he is criticizing L. Ferry's and A. Renaut's book, *La Pensée 68* (Gallimard 1985), for their criticism of Lacan, Foucault, Derrida, *et al.* (Originally published as "La police de la pensée" in *L'Autre Journal* (Dec. 1985): 27–34, trans. in *Art and Text* 26 (Sept–Nov 1987): 24–31.)
13 For the connection between letting the Other speak and actually *listening*, see Turner 1998: 27.
14 Personal communication.
15 One of the fullest visions of a "Lyotardian" argument for the university comes from Bill Readings:

> Those in the University need to recognize that the dereferentialization of the University's function opens a space in which we can think the notions of community and communication differently – without recourse to the analogy of a social totality, without organicism. It seems to me that a resistance to the technological University that does not ground itself in a pious claim to know the true referent of the University, involves attention to three elements: to institutional practices, to the temporality of study, and to language as the opacity of a community that is not transparent to itself, that does not communicate – the dissensual community that has relinquished the regulatory ideal of communicational transparency.
>
> (Readings 1993a: 184)

12 For a libidinal education

James Williams

> What would be interesting would be to stay put, but quietly seize every chance to function as good intensity-conducting bodies. No need for declarations, manifestos, organizations, provocations, no need for *exemplary actions*. Set dissimulation to work on behalf of intensities. Invulnerable conspiracy, headless, homeless, with neither programme nor project, deploying a thousand cancerous tensors in the bodies of signs. We invent nothing, that's it, yes, yes, yes, yes.
>
> (Lyotard 1993a: 262)

Education and resistance

Towards the end of his 1970 essay, "Nanterre, here, now," on the student revolts at his university of Nanterre, based in a poorer suburb of Paris, Lyotard makes the following statement: "In truth, what is required is an apedagogy" (Lyotard 1970: 58). This enigmatic claim is a tardy remark in a rather disjointed and tentative work. Its placement betrays a searching and skeptical writing and, probably, frame of mind. Lyotard cares desperately about the students' struggle, he inserts its most violent moments as fragments breaking the flow of a political essay on the university and the role of teaching:

> The cops' rage expressed itself, from the beginning, in their fighting methods: horizontal firing of lance grenades, the use of special weapons – gadgets, slingshots with steel balls, chair legs, stones, chlorine grenades, probably a few attack grenades – and towards evening damaging parked cars.
>
> (Ibid.)

But the affects of love and outrage are balanced by feelings of disillusionment, not only with the conciliatory liberal university leadership, headed by his fellow philosopher Paul Ricoeur, but also in the full range of the then-contemporary revolutionary movements, from Bolshevism through Maoism to spontaneism. The aim of this essay is to begin to sketch a possible "apedagogy" that could come out of Lyotard's work, to study its background and to discuss some objections to it.

The disillusionment in "Nanterre, here, now" is similar to, but stronger than, the one that dominates the later essays from Lyotard's work on Algeria, written for the leftist militant group *Socialisme ou Barbarie*. The Algerian war of independence did not end in revolution. So he asks: "Is such a full-blown social and political revolution possible or even desirable?" "Then what can come to replace it for those in the grip of over-powering senses of injustice?" He brings these questions to the essays on the student revolts of the early 1970s. It is also there that he begins an answer to them that will only find its full expression in the 1974 book *Libidinal Economy* (Lyotard 1974b), only then to be gradually repudiated as Lyotard drifts towards the philosophy of the different.

The disillusionment explains why I have chosen to start with "Nanterre, here, now," rather than with the earlier essay "Preamble to a charter" (Lyotard 1968), despite the fact that it puts forward a clear program and set of values for higher education institutions. The problem is that this program depends upon a social revolution that rapidly disappears as a possible future in the late 1960s: "The university will not, of course, be revolutionary; whatever we may be able to do here can and will be recuperated by the powers that be, until society as a whole is reconstructed differently" (Lyotard 1968: 44). So although Lyotard continues to defend the values put forward in his preamble (freedom of expression and assembly, democracy and universal representation), this defense cannot be the central strand of a politics or education, since, as will be argued, the struggle for values that can never be realized is nihilistic.

For Lyotard, the university is an institution that ought to maintain a revolutionary independence from the political constitution of wider society. That conception is in radical crisis in "Nanterre, here, now," that is, it is not a question of when and how we shall move towards its realization, but of whether it will be possible to do so at all. The problem is a familiar one; it extends through all of Lyotard's works. We know it best as the effort, first formulated in *The Postmodern Condition*, to keep the demand for performativity at bay at least within the realms of intellectual and cultural production. Do not seek to know or to create – do not seek to teach – solely within the remit set by late-capitalism, that is: "Any task must be justified in terms of an increase in productivity measured in terms of a gain in time."

According to this remit the dominant concern of universities should be: "Does this act of imparting knowledge allow us to make things of measurable worth faster?" If it does not, then it has no place in the university understood as the sector of society that communicates and increases knowledge, where both these functions are subject to the test of productivity:

What the teachers are completely unconscious of, though the students

sometimes perceive it, is that the only value that governs the real functioning of the teaching establishments is the same that operates openly
at the surface of society: produce and consume no matter what, in
ever-increasing quantity.

(Lyotard 1968: 57)

There is no space here for any of the traditional "for its own sakes" of
education, whether cultural, scientific, individual, or collective. The
worth of art and literature, physics and biology, of personal edification or
social and moral understanding is a matter of, ultimately, financial/
chronological measure.

In "Nanterre, here, now," unlike in Lyotard's later work on the postmodern and on the differend, the scandal of the capitalist demand for
performativity does not solely reflect its ability to break down differences
through a form of terror. In the later works, this terror consists in the claim
that any difference can be ground out by reference to measures of performativity. Any claim to difference has to be countable, or it does not count
at all, hence the terror associated with exclusion from systems of
measurement. The worth of a discipline or department over another, or
the worth of a teaching method over another, or the worth of a pedagogy
over another – skill-based or knowledge-based, edifying or vocational –
becomes an issue that can be reduced to calculation. What is important is
that if a claim to injustice is to be heard, then it must be translatable and
translated into the system:

> Anything at all may be exchanged, on the condition that the time
> contained by the referent and the time required for the exchange are
> countable. . . . Under this condition, phrases can be commodities. The
> heterogeneity of their regimens as well as the heterogeneities of
> genres of discourse (stakes) finds a universal idiom in the economic
> genre, with a universal criterion, success, in having gained time.

(Lyotard 1988a: 177)

It is only acceptable to make exceptional demands on the grounds of
inaccuracy, incompleteness, or mistaken bases; for example, "this kind of
teaching reaps dividends later than accounted for in the collection of
data." It is not acceptable to claim, for example, that subject X has an
intrinsic worth that cannot be measured, but that subject X deserves to be
funded.

For example, this form of terror has become very real in the testing and
associated funding of university departments in the United Kingdom.
Under the aegis of a government search for the most efficient higher
education sector, that is, best at contributing to growth, departments are
rated as to the excellence (or not) of their teaching and research. A
proportion of an ever-decreasing funding pot is distributed in accordance

with results and the "less-is-more" circle is squared by the claim that the efficiency gains achieved by directing money to the "best" balance out an overall squeeze. The ensuing and planned-for Darwinism where those judged excellent flourish at the expense of those that sink through under-funding can lead to self-censorship and straight top-down imposition in research and teaching.

This turn away from the modern values of experimentation and inno-vation for themselves is a necessary rather than contingent result, since the system of measurement operates with a punitive lag on teaching and research, that is, the new or the different must prove itself of value to estab-lished and far from neutral judges before it can be included in the testing algorithm. If time is invested in this push into the unknown, it will be penalized, at least in its infancy. This creates a grave tension between inno-vators and the establishment at all levels, since the means for making a case for experimentation militate against it ("But if the verdict, always pronounced in favour of gained time, puts an end to litigation, it may for that very reason aggravate differends" (Lyotard 1988a: 178)).

In response to this aggravation, Lyotard's philosophy after *The Differend* seeks to testify to the paradox of a differend, a difference that cannot be bridged in fairness to both its sides. The paradox lies in the necessity to become aware of this difference, but without the means to reach awareness becoming a means to resolve the difference. There has to be a block on passing from an "I see that here lies a conflict" to "The fact that I see it is already a step to its resolution." This explains why his later works concen-trate on the way in which the feeling of the sublime destroys the illusion that certain ideas can bridge differences; in the way the cosmopolitan idea of humanity bridges racial, historical, and sexual differences, for instance. The feeling of the sublime is a compound of pleasure and pain that triggers a hovering between attraction and repulsion. We feel pleasure at the idea of a bridge – of the idea of an education system that offers equal opportunities to all, say – and pain on signs of its impossibility. This points the way towards a somewhat marginal and/or regulative function of a pedagogy based on Lyotard's philosophy of the differend and the sublime. The role of some (all?) teachers would be to trigger the feeling of the sublime against Kantian Ideas of Reason such as humanity.

The Lyotardian teacher could then be, on a soft view, the element within a curriculum that reminded us of the limits of our understanding, morality, and systems of calculation. On a hard view, this teacher would be a last and essentially uncooperative line of resistance to the hegemony of capital and of universalist ideas. The prior function is outlined as the task of preserving a zone against the demands of rational determinations of rights in Lyotard's 1990 Amnesty International essay "The General Line":

> If humanity does not preserve the inhuman region in which we can meet this or that which completely escapes the exercise of rights, we

do not merit the rights that we have been recognized. Why would we have the right to freedom of expression if we had nothing to say but the already said? And how can we have any chance of finding how to say what we know not how to say if we do not listen at all to the silence of the other within.

(Lyotard 1997: 122)

However, it is not clear that this regulative function can be based with any consistency on absolutes ("Rights and respect for rights are owed to us only because something in us exceeds every recognized right" (ibid.: 122)). The absolute nature of the excess seems to prohibit its handling within a wider structure of rights, since this would involve some judgments with respect to the "something" on which Lyotard bases his resistance. Thus, in order to remain consistent, he should resist an interpretation of his philosophy as a part of a wider order. The fact that he encourages this misinterpretation, for example in his discussion of the role of the philosophy of the differend within democratic and debate-based political systems (Lyotard 1988a: 150), is testament to the debilitating tension that exists when the will to speak for an absolute excess coexists with a will to make that excess count within a wider political frame.

Apedagogy and negation

It is not the remit of this essay to investigate the above contradiction much further, though, as with a great deal of Lyotard's work, the question is how much leeway we are prepared to give to a thought that develops from logical contradictions without seeking to eliminate them. This, in turn, rests on a debate around the question whether logical contradictions can or ought to be eliminated from a philosophy that attempts to reflect on a world where events resistant to any "common sense" are ceaselessly thrown up. Rather, I would like to contrast the difficulties of the later work with the earlier philosophy from the period of the four or five years up to and including Lyotard's *Libidinal Economy* (1993a).

The key to this contrast lies in the paradoxes apparent in the passage quoted earlier and in their relation to the problem of nihilism. Once a goal has been set to "say what cannot be said," "give voice to silence," "testify to that which completely escapes us or to the absolutely other," the role of the philosopher and teacher becomes an essentially reactive one, policing the borders of law, morality, science, political economy in order to defeat illegitimate passages into the unknowable. The reactive element is unavoidable since what has to be spoken for cannot be approached except through the feeling of the sublime ("I feel that there is something there of great value, but I also feel that its value lies in its inapproachability"). The other cannot be affirmed as such, and only a negative struggle on its behalf is possible.

It is exactly this standing against and this defining of absolute borders that the earlier Lyotard defines as nihilism. By adopting an essentially negative stance at the heart of philosophy and pedagogy, we risk a descent into valuelessness and loss of will owing to the absence of positive values or movements to affirm. Thus, for example, within structuralist theory as it is applied to semiotics, there is nihilism where the positive perception of a signifier is not affirmed for itself but instead referred to an open-ended – futile – search for its signifieds: "Thus the sign is enmeshed in nihilism, nihilism proceeds by signs; to continue to remain in semiotic thought is to languish in religious melancholy and to subordinate every intense emotion to a lack and every force to a finitude" (Lyotard 1993a: 49). The signifier, as something that must move us prior to a reflection upon its sense, is negated in favor of a search for an absolute meaning that can never be reached.

The later Lyotard falls into this trap when he aims to testify for that which lies past the limits of rational discourse and ideas, while admitting that he cannot speak of it. In this guise, either he is a rather naive element of a system that he refuses to adopt ("We need the example of our mistaken rebels and off-beat thinkers to keep us on our guard"), or he is destined to an endless repetition of gestures of resistance with no possibility of deliverance since there is nowhere to be delivered to. However, much earlier, when he coins the term "apedagogy," he tries to avoid these traps and lays down a criticism for his later philosophy. This is because he insists that an apedagogy is neither a straightforward gesture of reversal, where a failed or wrong position is simply negated, nor a promise of a pure land that escapes the mistakes and evil of past ones. In "Nanterre, here, now", these points are made against a no doubt over-simplified Marxism, defined as a simple reversal of the power structures that it seeks to oppose: "For a century the Marxist workers' movement has only *reversed* the conduct of its class adversaries. Its leaders, hierarchy, troops, schools, discourse, directives, tactics, and strategy all offered the inverted image of the bourgeois models" (Lyotard 1970: 58). The problem lies with the politics associated with a set of pure goals. According to Lyotard, the left-wing activists in Nanterre invariably replicate the repressive political structures they seek to overthrow, because they believe that the value of their goals and the difficulty of the struggles necessitate hierarchical and, to some degree, violent political structure.

So Lyotard's real fear is of the way in which political and pedagogical movements inscribe negation and the dream of a state without negation within their proposed systems and organizations ("The teacher will not be a . . .," "The inspectors will be teachers and not politicised functionaries . . .," "Teaching is for that which cannot be handled by capitalism . . .," "We shall not be capitalists"). To replace a system with another, or to advocate the total absence of systems, is ultimately nihilistic, since the moves that are meant to liberate us carry what we seek to escape. Instead, the last lines of "Nanterre, here, now" advocate a political attitude rather than a fully-developed politics:

> The "here and now" attitude breaks with spontaneism just as it does with bolshevism. It does not propose the seizure of power, but the destruction of powers. . . . This attitude itself only serves as an example of a break with the initial repression, that which made us forget to invent, decide, organize, execute. I call it apedagogy because all pedagogy participates in this repression, including that which is implied in the internal and external relations of the "political" organizations.
>
> (Lyotard 1970: 59)

This passage is one of the first manifestations of a new direction in Lyotard's work. It combines politics, a quasi-ethical position and a new practice, all thought of here in terms of education and its institutions. The direction is characterized by the following key points; the first is political, the second ethical and the third practical, though it is important to note that the position is only consistent and tenable if all three are taken together:

1   The role of the political (or of a libidinal politics) as opposed to organized politics is to work within given structures in order to loosen them. "To loosen" is understood here as allowing as much room as possible for chance occurrences that release libidinal intensities, intense feelings and desires. Intensities trigger the disturbance of established structures and encourage the formation of new ones alongside them. Later, Lyotard describes this politics as one of flight and conspiracy. The opposition drawn between seizure and destruction of power is then understood in terms of the opposition between power and force, where power is that which one can exercise through a given structure and force is the energy that runs through us when we are in the grip of intense feelings and desires: "So for the last time, stop confusing power [*pouvoir*] with force [*puissance*]. . . . Power is an ego's, it belongs to an instance, force belongs to no-one" (Lyotard 1993a: 261).

2   In terms of an ethos, in the sense of our care towards ourselves and others, we should neither expect to know the outcome of this opening-up, since it is essentially unpredictable, nor superimpose the structures of the subject and intersubjectivity on the politics of force. Instead, the libidinal Lyotard advocates a Stoic love of the event, as something beyond knowledge, in the sense of something that can be known in advance of its occurrence. His politics and "morality" involve the love of chance, understood as the search for ways of encouraging unpredictable bursts of libidinal energy. We cannot be true to either of these

loves if we maintain and even seek to strengthen the structures of the subject (responsibility, planning, self-knowledge and knowledge of others as subjects). In *Libidinal Economy*, Lyotard advocates and often enacts this violence against the subject; he is always at pains to distinguish it from the terror of structures: "That force works towards the eradication of all subjectivity is precisely its violence" (ibid.: 261).

3   In practice, Lyotard defends different kinds of breaks in apparently seamless forms of discourse in order to promote a multiplicity of opposed discourses. Thus, his practice is one of identifying points of tension within a given discourse and of seeking to intensify them by emphasizing others and the feelings and desires that occur at the tense point. We can see, therefore, that the opposition to knowledge put forward earlier is not a stance against all knowledge. Indeed, the practical part of the philosophy involves a careful study of dominant discourses, but with an irreverent eye. The point is secretly to weave off-beat discourses and accounts around the weakest points of that discourse, in order to allow for the occurrence of new intensities, and hence further tension within the structure of that discourse and in its relation to others. From the point of view of intensities, the weakest point is not where a structure can be made to collapse, in the sense of the weakest link in a chain of command, say. It is where feelings and desires can be intensified, or are already intense but difficult to handle.

The key concept in terms of this search for points propitious to subversion is that of dissimulation, that is, that all structures dissimulate – conceal and disseminate – intensities within them. Lyotard's belief in the ubiquity of dissimulation characterizes his political strategy in two ways. First, it implies that it must always take place within structures that, mistakenly, we may have thought it was simply opposed to:

> That the structure be merely something that "covers" the affect, in the sense that it acts as a cover: that it is its secret and almost its dissimulation. This is why we must dearly love the semioticians, the structuralists, our enemies, they are our accomplices, in their light lies our obscurity.
>
> (Lyotard 1993a: 52)

This does not mean that Lyotard's practice has to be associated with specific structures; rather, it means that libidinal economists must always work with the structures into which they are necessarily thrown. Second, the ubiquity of dissimulation implies that the political strategy of libidinal economy is always possible. There is no final, solid structure that could resist change through its dependence on intensities and openness to change through new intensities:

Let us be content to recognise in dissimulation all that we have been seeking, difference within identity, the chance event within the foresight of composition, passion within reason – between each, so absolutely foreign to each other, the strictest unity: dissimulation.

(Lyotard 1993a: 52)

These last points allows us to understand further what Lyotard means by intensities. They are the degrees of intensity of feelings and desires, but oddly, they have to be thought of as prior to and independent of them. Intensity is something that occurs within the feeling and desire, it is their condition, rather than the other way round. This is because to have a well-defined account of given desires and feelings prior to intensities is to depend on and give priority to a given discourse and a given set of identities within a given structure:

The demand for clarity must be strongly denounced; it requires the power of he who loves, or who speaks, over his intensities. It demands: have power, define the intense. No, we must receive this demand in terror; flee from it, that's all we can do; it is the first imprint of power on the libidinal band. We say we are incapable of guaranteeing the link between our words, our deeds, our looks, and pulsional sweeps. Hence no clarity: sometimes it works, sometimes not.

(Lyotard 1993a.: 258)

Intensities, on Lyotard's account, have to be able to pass through anything, they are a non-identifiable force. As such, they set the scene for Lyotard's proper stance with respect to the unknowable, in his libidinal philosophy. What we cannot know – hope for, promise to ourselves – is that a given practical work of secreting tensions within a given discourse will succeed in triggering intensities.

There is no escaping the abstraction and metaphysical tenor revealed at a first scan of the main points of Lyotard's libidinal philosophy, where both terms must be given their fullest negative connotations of lofty cruelty and irresponsible fancy. However, the main aims of the remainder of this essay will be to respond to this initial reading with arguments for the consistency and sensitivity of Lyotard's metaphysics and for the justifiability and practicality of his political and educational strategies. His metaphysics is a way of binding the three views outlined earlier without allowing the political, the ethical, or the practical to dominate. But there will be no final justification of each of the views, they are put forward with a passionate wisdom that is explicitly skeptical of the dream of reducing wisdom and passion to final logical arguments. Voltaire's disdainful reaction to Pascal's sentimentalism and metaphysical reconstruction of Christianity is a good starting point for a critique of this appeal to a higher wisdom: "'All our reasoning is reduced to a yielding to sentiment.' [Pascal] Our reasoning is reduced to a yielding to sentiment in matters of taste, not in scientific fact" (Voltaire 1943: 118).

The necessity and the cunning of libidinal economics

The first essay where Lyotard develops his libidinal political attitude is slightly later than "Nanterre, here, now." "March 23" (Lyotard 1973c) claims to be an introduction to an unwritten book on the student March 23 movement started at the University of Nanterre in 1968 at the arrest of six members of the National Vietnam Committee on March 22. The movement is related to the creative spontaneity and mobility of situationism as it is outlined in Guy Debord's *La Societé du Spectacle* (1967). It was active up to and during the student revolts at Nanterre in the early 1970s. Even in the introduction, Lyotard's book does not come across as a straight work of history. Instead, he attempts to sketch the metaphysical background necessary to explain the movement as anti-political and anti-systematic, that is, as refusing demands for well-organized political structures and for a political program of plans, actions, goals, hopes. In addition, Lyotard gives an excellent example of the practice of libidinal economics in its infancy, in reflections on what he understands by history.

Against Voltaire's ironic *bon mot*, in the *Dictionnaire philosophique*, that metaphysics is wonderful because it allows us to know everything having learnt nothing, Lyotard's sketch of a libidinal energetics in "March 23" and his development of it in *Libidinal Economy* is founded on two suppositions. The first is that we can never know anything for certain due to the unpredictable occurrence of disturbing events. The second is that it is necessary to base all knowledge on an account that allows for it to develop, but that reminds it of its transitory and competitive situation. Any system of knowledge and subsequent set of practices is slave to events in two senses. First, it may be overthrown by new occurrences that are completely beyond its predictive capacity (thus not in the sense of new data that demand alterations in a theory, but in the sense of new events that render the theory as a whole redundant). Second, it does not have dominion over any given field; instead it is in an unregulated competition with other systems (actual and virtual) in terms of claims to validity. The role of a metaphysics then is to be a fictional ground (not wholly knowledge-based), that does not allow for fixed truths to emerge, but instead directs us to conflicts between structures and systems and to the emergence of events that disturb and alter that conflict. Metaphysics is wonderful when it allows us to feel that we always know nothing and have everything to experiment with.

So in "The system and the event" section of "March 23," Lyotard claims that we can *imagine* any society "as an ensemble of persons ruled by a system whose function would be to regulate the entry, the distribution, and the elimination of the *energy* that this ensemble spends in order to exist" (Lyotard 1973c: 63). This fictional energetics – inspired by scientific ideas and by Freud, but not grounded on them or dependent on them for its validity – is one possible way of insisting that systems depend on something beyond their ken: in this case, libidinal intensities defined as energy. Knowledge, in the service of power, binds libidinal energy into structures that can exploit it and that resist its capacity to invest other competing structures through points of tension:

> In the division of scientific labour, the task of constructing the system of regulation falls to political economy, social anthropology, linguistics and so on. If history were included, it would take the role of considering the event. One could call the event the impact, on the system, of floods of energy such that the system does not manage to bind and channel this energy; the event would be the traumatic encounter of energy with the regulating institution.
>
> (Lyotard 1973c: 64)

Thus, in the late 1960s the education institutions and the scientific and philosophical theories that uphold the system encounter student desires and feelings that they cannot handle.

For Lyotard, this is an entirely good thing for the institution and for the students, so long as we do not confuse good with harmless. New influxes of energy are necessary, since structures tend towards a death through over-regulation, that is, through the elimination of libidinal energy (where there is nothing really new to desire and there are no new opportunities of intense feelings). Lyotard's sense of the political, as opposed to well-structured politics, and of a libidinal education, an apedagogy as opposed to a systematized pedagogy, is directed to strategies that encourage these libidinal occurrences. These strategies reinvigorate systems, but only at the price of forcing them to change and interact with new ones:

> However, the qualitative event occurs when the very forms through which energy is rendered circulable [the institutions] . . . cease to be able to harness the energy – they become obsolete. The relation between energy and its regulation undergoes a mutation. This enigma is thus the only event worthy of the name, when the regulator encounters energy that it cannot bind.
>
> (Ibid.: 65)

For example, in his approach to the history of the March 23 movement, Lyotard is critical of history as a systematic subject, that is, one that seeks to offer a narrative explaining events and their relation to one another. Instead, history as he envisages it ought to be an opportunity for the release of unforeseen and uncontrolled intensities. Thus the historian or the teacher, while working within a given system, must look for places where it may be opened up. This is an active passivity, in a double sense.

First, it actively seeks to find points where the narrative built up by the historian or teacher may be made to quake, but without prejudicing what specific form that quake may take. Second, it is an activity that tries to conduct intensity into a system, to allow it to pass through. Knowledge must give way to intensity:

> Writing a history book always aims to produce a *historian's knowledge* as its content, that is, a discourse that is at once consistent and complete, in which the non-sense of the event will be rendered intelligible, fully signified, and thus in principle predictable. It is to seek to institution-alise something that appeared at the time as foundationless, anarchic.
>
> (Lyotard 1973c: 67)

Those who try to subvert knowledge must do so at the price of refusing to fix future outcomes, or even hope for them in specific forms, since this would put system and structure above and against the event of intensity. ("It is time to get rid of the illusion that universal history provides the universal tribunal, that some last judgement is prepared and fulfilled in history.")

In the case of Lyotard's history, the turn against knowledge is to be achieved by avoiding interpretation and concentrating on the presen-tation of unpublished documents, so that readers may be able to "take on most of the responsibility for constructing an understanding of the facts for themselves" (ibid.: 66). But more importantly, these facts must be material events as much as discursive documents. In addition to spoken and written testimony, priority must be given to

> acts, gestures, situations, silences, or even intonations, to all the traces of a sense that is transmitted in spite of discourse rather than by it, a sense that for this reason is usually considered a non-sense and is therefore not taken in consideration by the historian.
>
> (Lyotard 1973c: 66)

This does mean, however, that structure can be escaped. It is necessary for the occurrence of intensities, since they are expressed in feelings and desires that are given an identity within a given structure. There is a quite traditional detailed diagnostic work in libidinal economics. (What struc-tures are at work here? Where are the tense points within them – the tensors, as defined by Lyotard – where other structures clash with them and where intensities may occur and loosen things still further?) But then there is an apedagogical work as well, since the strategy is passively to encourage intensities to untie, disturb and renew, with no commitment as to how this will take place.

So Lyotard's active passivity, as it is can be understood as apedagogy, is an effort to write and to teach with an objective, neutral eye for the structures in place. It is also, though, an effort to introduce fissures and cracks in those structures by multiplying them in a rude and destabilizing manner, not allowing one to take precedence. It is an aesthetic effort in its commitment to the material and ideal points likely to give rise to desires and feelings: to the occurrence of intensities. This strategy finds its high point in the style of *Libidinal Economy* (it could not simply be a method without contra-diction). The book eschews academic coldness in favor of passionate descriptions; it refuses hierarchy (theory over practice or universals over particular cases and examples).

Even though *Libidinal Economy* is an instructive book about Marx, capi-talism, structuralism, and so on, it forces the reader to approach these in a shocking and tendentious context. The book is resistant to a reading in terms of for and against (Marx or capital; intensities as such or structure). Instead, the reader has to fray a way through a maze of competing theories and ideas while being buffeted by opportunities for passionate diversions (desire, hate, shock, curiosity, love, sensual attraction, anger, exasper-ation). It is therefore a strange book that fulfills the main anti-aim of active passivity: it is hard to know where it is leading us, except quite a time later, when passions are either on the wane, having quietly transformed our conscious views, or just bubbling up and emerging from an unresolved tension.

Active passivity in education

In conclusion, if we are to take Lyotard's libidinal economics as the starting point for a philosophy of education, our first step must be to take his char-acterization of it as an "apedagogy" seriously. No pedagogical program can emerge from his work in the early 1970s; instead, we are given a set of texts that are both models and provocations. So the very concept of a philosophy of education runs counter to his work, which is rather a style of thinking that seeps into others and opens them up to new possibilities. His texts are models for what I have called "active passivity" and for what Lyotard calls conductivity. This is the combination of a political attitude of subversion, an ethos that refuses to be guided by a reference to the human subject or intersubjectivity (or indeed any other transcendent idea) and that thus refuses any teleology, and a practice that seeks to multiply discourses and open them up to libidinal events, that is, to intense feelings and desires.

If this combination had to be summed up it could be done on the basis of a set of principles deduced from the last chapter of *Libidinal Economy*. The principles are: seek powerlessness in the blurring of the borders between what is discussed and the theory that discusses it; multiply prin-ciples of enunciation, that is, not only multiply theoretical discourses but also the styles of description of material events; invite failure into discourse: the Stoic love of the event; do not will as a free subject (as if your actions were either self-caused or guaranteed as to their effects); seek anonymity by abandoning analysis (abandon the lure of the self); do not believe that intensities can be chosen: the openness of libidinal economics can neither choose what desires and feelings occur, nor be assured of their occurrence.

The elements of this set have certain characteristics that invite criticism even if we accept them as principles for an apedagogy, that is, as neither for a new theory of education nor for a pure reaction against certain aspects of the old, but as guidelines to take us through our own very particular situations and impulses (to the point where some situations may only be fitted to them in a minimal way, for reasons of survival, for instance).

1   The principles will lead to an inherently difficult work, if we accept that it is harder to teach a number of incomplete positions at the same time, rather than a series one after the other.
2   They may dissipate the concentration and abstraction necessary for the learning of theories and facts because of their disrupting turn to intensities.
3   Human relations often taken as important (know yourself and others, respect others and knowledge, discover and live according to human values) are undermined at least to the extent where they are taken as fundamental. This is likely to lead to a chaotic and confusing environment, maybe even an immoral one.
4   The principles work against common-sense views of the right way to embark on a difficult task. There is a refusal to set specific aims and objectives. There is a refusal to map out a procedure, or even to accept that there are certain inherently correct procedures.

Taken together these objections are interesting, since they are also arguments for the systems that Lyotard wants to avoid, viewing them as nihilistic, in the sense of energy-sapping by endless negation and postponement. I have already explained why he is opposed to a systematic and knowledge-based approach, though this explanation cannot take the form of a definitive argument in a short introductory essay. Instead, I want to address the criticisms as practical ones, that is, not simply as wrong from the point of view of theory or commonly accepted truth and values, but as mistaken from a pragmatic point of view.

The first point to make is that active passivity is not an extremist position, since it is not subversive with the aim of bringing in a new system, but only with the aim of making space for the occurrence of intensities. To act brutally is not to act wisely with respect to Lyotard's principles, since a ground that has been simply cleared, or made uniform, or utterly chaotic is less propitious for the most varied and most rich occurrence of intensities. On the contrary, this will occur when a multiplicity of discourses and structures is allowed to flourish. *Libidinal Economy* and indeed nearly all of Lyotard's works are complex and wide-ranging rather than narrow and limited. So it is not the case that the principles lead to an iconoclastic rejection of common values and knowledge. It is rather that the context in which these are put forward is a more questioning and less reverential one, where "truths" are not set in stone, but rather constantly challenged and reinvigorated through contact with other "truths," intensities, and sensual events.

The second point is that criticisms regarding difficulty and dissipation tend to presuppose that the replication of knowledge, skills, and theories must come prior to breathing intensity into them, since that breath inhibits replication at too early a stage. But what if the danger is the other way round? What if the priority given to replication is unsubtle and unwise with regard to the relation of structure and system to feelings and desires? In Lyotard's view, that priority is likely to harden the relation into the form of for and against, action and reaction, when what is needed is a more variegated multiplicity that is not organized according to binary logic. If we accept his point of view, then even though there may be a loss in the straightforward ability to represent knowledge, theories and, ultimately, ourselves and our values, there may be a gain in terms of our capacity to live with them in an affirmative and libidinally rich manner.

So the last lines of *Libidinal Economy*, quoted here in the epigraph, must be taken utterly seriously. It is tempting to react to Lyotard's philosophy as if it is a barbaric and irresponsible reaction to well-recognized problems. In fact it is a wise and careful, perhaps even a modest, way of living with the nihilistic tendencies of the dominant and necessary structures of our societies.

13 Pointlessness and the University of Beauty

Gordon C. F. Bearn

To the Memory of Jean-François Lyotard:
"The time has come to philosophize."

> Philology ... has nothing but delicate, cautious work to do and achieves nothing if it does not achieve it *lento*. But for precisely this reason it is more necessary than ever today, by precisely this means does it entice and enchant us the most, in the midst of an age of "work", that is to say, of hurry, of indecent and perspiring haste, which wants to "get everything done" at once, including every old or new book: – this art does not so easily get anything done, it teaches to read *well*, that is to say, to read slowly, deeply, looking cautiously before and aft, with reservations, with doors left open with delicate eyes and fingers.
>
> (Preface to 1886 reprint of *Daybreak*, Nietzsche 1982: 5)

> Development imposes the saving of time. To go fast is to forget fast, to retain only information that is useful afterwards, as in "rapid reading." But writing and reading which advance backwards in the direction of the unknown thing "within" are slow. One loses one's time seeking time lost. Anamnesis is the other pole – not even that, there is no common axis – the other of acceleration and abbreviation.
>
> (Introduction to *The Inhuman*, Lyotard 1991d: 3)

He knew. He knew. In 1979, he knew that the shape of the university in the late twentieth century had already changed, had already become an institution, an institute whose central value was no longer knowledge ... not even usefulness ... but performativity and productivity, efficiency at any price (Lyotard 1984a: 88n.30). Universities were becoming machines for the delivery and discovery of information whose value consisted entirely in its contribution to the efficient performance of the system.'The system, the neutral name Lyotard gives to the unopposed global reach of capitalist democracy, the system, which uses its openness to all points of view to grease the gears of its operation, the system generates by polite competition not peace, but security, not progress, but development (Lyotard 1997: 199ff.).

He knew that universities were bound to rely more and more on information processing machines, and that this would put a new constraint on the forms of knowledge which could be studied in a university. If a form of knowledge could not be translated into bits of information, it was bound to become more and more invisible to the system and to those, all eyes on efficiency, who administered universities (Lyotard 1984a: 4). And universities would pride themselves on their new, pinched vision, for by concentrating on the delivery and discovery of information, they would make themselves more marketable, more attractive to their customers, students, and granting agencies alike.

He knew that research would divide into those projects which promised to be of immediate service to the system by increasing its productivity, and those projects whose contribution to increasing the system's productivity would require some initial investment. As it is with money, so it is with knowledge: there is liquid knowledge and investment knowledge (ibid.: 6). And experimentation outside the boundaries of accepted values and languages? Research unconcerned with the discovery of information? When this takes place, it will no longer necessarily take place within universities, any more than it did so during the times of Descartes and Spinoza, Marx and Darwin (ibid.: 50).

He knew that these changes could not leave the pedagogical activities of universities untouched. No longer concerned with the grand project of building new subjects for new republics, universities replaced their ideals with a hollow "excellence" and oriented their pedagogical aims to serving the system.[1] Skills immediately necessary for the efficient functioning of the current system would be taught: accounting, nursing, the law, medicine, thus producing a professional intelligentsia (ibid.: 49). Skills necessary for the growth of the system, the mastery and development of technologies and technological skills, would also be taught, thus producing a technical intelligentsia (ibid.: 49). Universities would offer a menu of these two types of skills first to the young, as a set meal, and once again, *à la carte*, to adults who found themselves no longer able to serve the central value of the system: performativity and productivity: efficiency at any price (ibid.: 49).

He knew. In 1979, he knew that universities were already becoming centers designed to improve the performance of the system by the delivery and discovery of information. The poignant dedication of his report on knowledge bears witness to the loss it describes:

> Such as it is, I dedicate this report to the Institut Polytechnique de Philosophie of the Université de Paris VIII (Vincennes) – at this very postmodern moment that finds the University nearing what may be its end, while the Institute may just be beginning.
>
> (Lyotard 1984a: xxv)

It must be a mark of how hurried we have become, of how restless we feel during slow movements, of how concerned we are with saving time, that Lyotard's description of the postmodern condition was at first so frequently taken as an endorsement of that very system. Apparently it was very difficult to resist concluding from Lyotard's pessimism about the possibility of an alternative to the system that therefore he must endorse the system entire, itself. But his philosophy is not painted in the slack, poly-chromatic colors of eclecticism: Mickie D's for lunch and Thai for dinner, driving to a late Beethoven sonata with bubblegum love on the radio (ibid.: 76). Neither is it painted the reassuring black of a glorious tragedy. Although he never suggests we should become comfortable with it, Lyotard's philosophy is painted a melancholic grey (Lyotard 1997: 120; Lyotard 1995b: 10).[2]

The system is open. Yes. It welcomes the diversity of cultures and ideas. There is no doubt. It encourages dialogue, discussion, and communication in all directions. Our universities insist on it, but we would attend anyway. Willingly we attend "training sessions," designed to make us even more sensitive to difference, training sessions led by listless young people who insist that they are not leading us at all, but only facilitating our interac-tions, listless young facilitators whose taste for diversity extends no further than the cool air of the climate control system. Disney difference. Epcot diversity. And not a bug to be seen, anywhere.

The system is open, but its central value is always what Lyotard calls performativity: a low input/output ratio (Lyotard 1984a: 54). This is often called productivity, or simply efficiency, and since it is a unique goal, I have characterized it as efficiency, at any price. It is a technical goal, not an aesthetic goal like that of enjoying the free play of the senses. And this is the first reason Lyotard's philosophy is melancholy. He distinguishes between phrase regimens and genres of discourse. The technical goal or value of performativity characterizes one genre of discourse, and it is a constraint on the linking of one phase to another (Lyotard 1988a: sect. 147). His melancholy derives in the first instance from the way the technical genre of discourse operates by silencing other genres. A brief look at this wave of novel phrases will help us understand what is happening here.

One of the nice touches of irony in Lyotard's *The Differend*, which intro-duces these phrases, is that, predicting the next century will have no time for books, Lyotard prefaces his book with a "reading dossier" which provides a piano reduction of the book, for those in a hurry (Lyotard 1988a.: xi–xvi). The "article" is the typical product of the academic in a hurry, so it is appropriate, however embarrassing, that in hurrying to my part of this article, pointlessness and the University of Beauty, I should find myself turning red and citing from the roughly ten lines that constitute what the dossier calls "Thesis."

"A phrase, even the most ordinary one, is constituted according to a set of rules (its regimen)" (ibid.: xii). But what is a phrase? Many philosophers will find it hard to proceed without a definition, hard not to proceed according to what Kant would have called determinative judgments: theory first, examples second (Kant 1987: 18ff.). But Lyotard is weary of theory (Lyotard 1988a: xiii). And this zips us right to the heart of Lyotard's philosophy, for to insist on theoretical definitions first is precisely to insist on a certain phrase regimen, the definitional one, and a certain genre of discourse, the dialogical one (ibid.: sect. 106). Thus this demand for a definition will itself silence other phrases and genres of discourse and reveal, yet again, Lyotard's melancholy. Instead of a definition, Lyotard offers examples, thus proceeding by what Kant would call reflective judgment: examples first, theoretical definitions second (Kant 1987: 18ff.). The examples of phrases range widely, including: Give me a lighter; Was she there? They fought till their last round of ammunition; $ax^2 + bx + c = 0$; Whoops!; a wink; a shrugging of the shoulder; a tapping of the foot; a fleeting blush; an attack of tachycardia; the wagging of a dog's tail; the twitching of a cat's (Lyotard 1988a, sects 109, 110, 198). It dawns on us that there might be little that could not count as a phrase, that phrases might simply be occurrences, events. And so it is (ibid.: sects 99, 132). The significance of the phrase, the situation which draws it in, is something else, something Lyotard divides into four: sense, reference, addressee, addressor (ibid.: sect. 24).[3] These all help to determine what happens, the situation, but the phrase, itself, is simply *It happens*, or rather, stressing the fact that we are leaving the significance of the phrase to one side: *Is it happening?* (ibid.: sects 131, 115).

Putting this notion of a phrase in a Cartesian context, Lyotard insists that what survives universal doubt is nothing cognitive or even significant at all, but simply the event, simply "the passage, time, and the phrase (the time in the phrase, the phrase in time)" (ibid.: sects 94, 101). What survives doubt is in the space neither of reasons nor of causes, and I find myself blushing again, this time for wanting to substitute quotation marks for thinking. I want to say the phrase is a presentation "before" the present, "before" the chronological present.[4] The chronological division of experience into past–present–future actually unties and unites at the same time, and both of these functions can be derived from the intentionality of consciousness, which I will read, somewhat crudely, in terms of its goal-directedness (Lyotard 1991d: 90).[5] Having a goal, whether large and physical, like building a bonfire, or small and visual, like observing a spear of summer grass, unties our experience dividing it into beginning–middle–end, past–present–future. But having a goal also unites these three, for it is precisely in terms of their relation to the goal that *this* past and *this* future are the past and future of *this* present. The significance of the chronological present is constituted by the way it is linked to particular pasts and futures, but more, the chronological present itself is constituted by these linkings. Thus since the phrase is "prior" to the linkings which would situate its significance, the chronological present could not possibly be the passage, the phrase, the time in the phrase, the phrase in time, which survives universal doubt.

The time beyond doubt, the time in the phrase, is a time "prior" to the linkings, linkings which link to other occurrences, events: other phrases. Each phrase, therefore, exists "before" significance, therefore "before" before, "before" past–present–future, and that is why the scare quotes are unavoidable. There is no way to understand phrases, neat. Their being understood presupposes their being linked, fore and aft. Their being understood, or misunderstood, presupposes that they have been situated as a what happens, no longer simply an *It happens* or an *Is it happening?* Lyotard:

> Joined to the preceding one by and, a phrase arises out of nothingness to link up with it. Paratax thus connotes the abyss of Not-Being which opens between phrases, it stresses the surprise that something begins when what is said is said.
>
> (Lyotard 1988a: sect. 100)

This is what a phrase is, an event "before" the linkings which would situate its significance: an *insignificant event.* "Not a major event in the media sense, not even a small event. Just an occurrence" (Lyotard 1991d: 90). *It happens,* or leaving significance farther to one side, *Is it happening?* The phrase thus tamed, we can return to the reading dossier provided for those in a hurry.

"A phrase, even the most ordinary one, is constituted according to a set of rules (its regimen). There are a number of phrase regimens: reasoning, knowing, describing, recounting, questioning, showing, ordering, etc." (Lyotard 1988a: xii). Different regimens are constituted by different rules for linking phrases together, throwing a chain from one to the other across the abyss of Not-Being which opens between phrases. The question is, how to link, how to cross the abyss? This is one way of reading the question *Is it happening?* surprised by something else on the glass table, *Link me.* To do so according to one phrase regimen situates the phrase in one way; to do so according to another will situate it another way. The answer to this question is provided by genres of discourse which determine "what is at stake in linking phrases," the end or goal of linking: "to persuade, to convince, to vanquish, to make laugh, to make cry, etc." (ibid.: sect. 147). Genres of discourse, like strategies, guide particular moves, particular linkings across the abyss (ibid.: sect. 185). And to link one way is not to link another. "And because several linkages are possible does that necessarily imply that there is a differend between them? – Yes it does, because only one of them can happen (be 'actualized') at a time" (ibid.: sect. 40).

A Differend. The dossier informs us: "As distinguished from a litigation, a differend would be a case of conflict between (at least) two parties, that cannot be equitably resolved for lack of a rule of judgment applicable to both arguments" (ibid.: xi). Whenever we link according to one phrase regimen, we are not linking according to another, and there is therefore an inevitable differend whenever we link.

> No matter what its regimen, every phrase is in principle what is at stake between genres of discourse. This differend proceeds from the question, which accompanies any phrase, of how to link onto it. And this question proceeds from the nothingness that "separates" one phrase from the "following." There are differends because, or like, there is *Ereignis* [an event, an occurrence].[6] But that's forgotten as much as possible: genres of discourse are modes of forgetting the nothingness or of forgetting the occurrence, they fill the void between phrases.
>
> (Lyotard 1988a: sect. 188)

Genres of discourse hide the abyss of Not-Being which opens between phrases, making it appear that the finality of genres of discourse is not the finality of an absence supplemented, but the finality of a necessary, final causality (ibid.: sect. 188). And with that we can return to the postmodern condition of the university.

The first reason Lyotard writes of universities in a melancholic grey is that universities, like the system itself, are guided by a unique genre of discourse, a technical one whose end is performativity. This means that the openness of universities is a sham. Everyone is welcome, but only if the stakes of their phrasing are those of the technical genre of the system: performativity. All genres of discourse and all phrase regimens are welcome but there is only one way to link on to them, namely, according to the technical genre of discourse dear to the system. So literature, for instance, is welcome but situated technically, it becomes – however enjoyable – a waste of time. At best a pastime. History is welcome, but situated technically, it shows itself to be – however insightful – of only historical interest. A pastime. The same will be said of philosophy and all the arts; although it will be said less of philosophy which the system can put to immediate use, applied ethics, and it will be said least of all of the most famous of all postmodern arts, the most obviously useful art, architecture.[7] The second reason Lyotard writes in grey is that there is no way out. Even if we are successful in turning one differend into a litigation, there will always be another differend. "The differend is reborn from the very resolutions of supposed litigations" (Lyotard 1988a: sect. 263). There can be no phrasing without exclusion, so no phrasing without differends.

In 1979, Lyotard had one hope. He thought that the results of recent scientific investigations had pulled the rug out from under the performative imperative of the system. The system requires that we use a genre of discourse that aims at performativity: lowering the input/output ratio.

This presupposes that the system itself is relatively stable so that what lowered that ratio in the past will be able to lower it again (Lyotard 1984a: 54). Citing Mandelbrot on fractals and Thom on catastrophe theory, Lyotard suggested that the presupposition of the system's commitment to a technical genre of discourse, that the system is stable, was empirically false (ibid.: 54–61). Thus deprived of its legitimation through performativity, Lyotard predicted that the system would soon be recognized as receiving its legitimation from the opposite of efficient performance, from the rough ground of paralogy, paralogical investigations which produce not the known but the unknown, not consensus but dissensus, not efficiency but catastrophe (ibid.: 60).

Lyotard's paralogy is an extension of the Kantian idea of a transcendental paralogism in which there is a "transcendental ground constraining us to draw a formally invalid conclusion" (Kant 1961: 328). The idea is that the system is not stable, that it inevitably throws off words and deeds which exceed the system, which do not quite make sense, and that therefore these inevitable paralogical effects express the inventive plasticity which is the essence of the system. The system might then receive something like a legitimation from little narratives of invention which tell how what is taken for granted as known can become, once again, unknown: the rough ground of dissensus, and then how these barely meaningful, paralogical effects, could recrystalize as a new shape of knowledge (Lyotard 1984a: 100, n.207). In this case, the legitimation of the system would come not primarily from lofty goals of liberation, emancipation, or even from performativity – whose empirical presuppositions are bankrupt – but from these little narratives revealing the paralogical effects of the system. In a certain sense Lyotard's hope was not so much for legitimation as for critique, in the sense Greenberg extracts from Kant, that is, using the characteristic methods of the system – here, paralogical invention – not to legitimate the system, as it were from outside, but to entrench the system more firmly within its proper limits. (See Greenberg 1993: 85.) That is, to make manifest the necessary, not to say transcendental, conditions for the life of the system: paralogical invention. In this way he hoped at one and the same time to acknowledge the inevitability of the system's power and the ethical importance of what escapes, if only for a moment, the system's grasp.

In 1979, this was Lyotard's hope. But it evaporated (Lyotard 1991d: 2). Paralogical investigations do indeed make space for what escapes the system, but Lyotard came to believe that this could never muscle performativity out of the system's center: "the system rather has the consequence of causing the forgetting of what escapes it" (ibid.: 2). Which leaves us painting the university a melancholy grey.

Mark this point.

At this point, for reasons I will consider in a moment, Lyotard puts his resistance to the system in terms not of paralogy but of the sublime.

Lyotard never, so far as I know, brought his interest in the sublime together with his work on education, but his writings about the sublime project a Lyotardian vision of the university as concerned with both performativity (he never lost his mature belief that there was no alternative to the system) and a sublime resistance to the current shape of the system. This is a resistance whose presence within the university would be explained *not* by its legitimating the system, but simply by its service to the system. The system *is* served by smoothing over anxieties and hatreds, for example, between races and religions, because such hatreds interfere with the unimpeded pursuit of performativity: efficiency at any price. But mark this point, for we will be returning to it again. I will argue that at this point, Lyotard mistakenly turns to a version of the sublime – projecting an ideal University of the Sublime – when he should have turned to the beautiful, projecting an ideal University of Beauty. The difference is the difference between double negation and full fledged affirmation. The difference is the difference between No and Yes.[8]

It is worth considering why paralogy was a failure. I have just cited the reason Lyotard gives (Lyotard 1991d: 2). But there is a more fundamental, and equally Lyotardian reason. What escapes the system is the bare phrase "before" it is linked on to, while it is "still" surrounded by an abyss of not-being. Paralogy was to legitimate the system by inventing "new statements" (Lyotard 1984a: 65). But whatever genre of discourse we use to guide our linking to that phrase, we will exclude other genres and start further differends. That is why the paralogical imperative to make "new statements" can neither remove the differends nor legitimate the system.

Lyotard's turn from paralogy to the sublime is a turn from simply making new statements to what the reading dossier describes as the "stakes" of the book it abbreviates: "to bear witness to the differend" (Lyotard 1988a: xiii). To bear witness to the differend is to bear witness to the bare phrase lying in the abyss of not-being (ibid.: sect. 100). This could not mean simply linking on to the isolated phrase according to this or that genre of discourse, for to do so would simply be to "fill the void between phrases" (ibid.: sect. 188). Thus to bear witness to the differend, we must not link according to any genre of discourse at all. But how can we bear witness to the differend without acknowledging a genre of discourse? The arts are not genres of discourse, neither is (philosophical) thinking, neither is philosophical politics (Lyotard 1991d: 88, 73–4; Lyotard 1988a: xiii, sect. 190). Thus Lyotard could write: "What is at stake in a literature, in a philosophy, in a politics perhaps, is to bear witness to differends by finding idioms for them" (Lyotard 1988a: sect. 22). Now, how do we do that?

One bears witness to the differend by bearing witness to the event, the occurrence, the *It happens* or *Is it happening?* And we know already that the time of the event is a *now* which is, in some sense, "before" chronological time, "before" the chronological *now* in the series past–present–future, before–now–after. It is the bare phrase in an abyss of not-being that is offended by linking according to any genre of discourse. Every differend starts from this offense. So bearing witness to the differend – the highest calling of the arts, philosophy, and politics – is bearing witness to *now*, this *now* before chronology. In the case of thinking, what this comes to is this:

> To think is to question everything, including thought, and question, and the process. To question requires that something happen that reason has not yet known. In thinking, one accepts the occurrence for what it is: "not yet" determined. One does not prejudge it, and there is no security. Peregrinations in the desert. One cannot write without bearing witness to the abyss of time in its coming.
>
> (Lyotard 1991d: 74)

And as Barnett Newman might have said, this *now* is sublime: "The Sublime is Now" (O'Neill 1990: 170ff. Lyotard 1991d: 89ff.).

What makes it sublime is the alternation or vibration between two moments, which Lyotard, when writing about Kant's notion of the sublime, refers to as "an affective 'no' and 'yes'" (Lyotard 1994: 68). In a moment, I will argue that while No and Yes may be the way to describe the sublime in Kant, the sublime in Lyotard is better expressed as a double negation No, No. Kant had described the feeling of the sublime as "a pleasure that arises only indirectly: it is produced by a feeling of momentary inhibition of the vital forces followed immediately by an outpouring of them that is all the stronger" (Kant 1987: sect. 23). In Kant's case a first failure of the faculty of imagination, for example, our inability from a certain place to present a single intuition of a tremendously large building, is followed second by the discovery that reason can, indeed, think the infinite as a totality, even if it could never be presented as such in an intuition (ibid.: sect. 26). First No, then Yes.

Something analogous occurs when we bear witness to a differend. First is the painful feeling of the differend itself. Second, is the attempt to turn the differend into a litigation, to find idioms to present what in the differend escapes presentation. Here is Lyotard:

> In the differend something "asks" to be put into phrases, and suffers from the wrong of not being able to be put into phrases right away. This is when human beings who thought they could use language as an instrument of communication learn through the feeling of pain which accompanies silence (and of pleasure which accompanies the invention of a new idiom), that they are summoned by language, not to augment to their profit the quantity of information communicable through existing idioms, but to recognize that what remains to be phrased exceeds what they can presently phrase, and that they must be allowed to institute idioms which do not yet exist.
>
> (Lyotard 1988a: sect. 23)

First is the pain of silence and the feeling that we are being called to put something for the first time into phrases. Second is the actual invention of a new idiom to do just that. Sometimes Lyotard distinguished two different ways in which we can feel the differend's pain as the demand to bear witness. He figures this demand as deriving from a doubled other of representation: "The *thing* which, without asking anything, commands the work, and the inaudible *voice*, which obliges your act to rectitude and your judgment to justice" (Lyotard 1995b: 8).[9] The invisible thing demands work: literary, philosophical, artistic work; the inaudible voice demands action: justice in action.[10] But in either case, bearing witness to the differend runs on the same alternating current as the sublime: first No, then Yes.

According to Lyotard, one paradigmatic artistic effort to bear witness to the differend arrives in the solo work of Arakawa and also in his joint work with Madeline Gins. Lyotard tells us that

> The Differend (1983) tries to give an ontological and linguistic (or better yet, "sentential" "phrastic") status to what Arakawa calls the "blank." . . . It's the emptiness, the nothingness in which the universe presented by a phrase is exposed and which explodes at the moment the phrase occurs and then disappears with it.
>
> (Lyotard 1988e: 31–2)

The blank is very closely related to the sublime *now* prior to the series of chronological *nows*; indeed, Lyotard tells us that "blank is nothing other than the passage from now to now," which I read as the passage from one chronological *now* to another (Lyotard 1984d: 10). But in spite of Lyotard's championing, which we would expect to bring Arakawa's blank together with the sublime, Arakawa's work, even as Lyotard presents it, does not seem to run on alternating current: first No, then Yes.

Lyotard pointedly draws our attention to the subtitle of the Arakawa and Gins project *The Mechanism of Meaning* (1979), namely "work in progress" (Lyotard 1984d: 5).[11] And his point is that it is not possible to bear witness to a differend. Any presentation of blank, even one that resists romantic nostalgia (Lyotard 1991d: 92–3), even one that resists representation altogether, contenting itself with the bare witness of the brute painting, itself (ibid.: 93), even then, there will still be a differend. For however incommunicable (ibid.: 77), however unlike a bit of information, any attempt to bear witness to the blank, to what exceeds representation, must betray the blank by putting it into some idiom or other, an idiom of color, sounds, words, actions, an idiom, a link, a phrase. Bearing witness will always be a work in progress.

This feature of bearing witness to the blank shows that Lyotard's philosophy does not run on the same alternating current as the Kantian sublime: first No, then Yes. In Kant's story, although imagination cannot present the infinite (No), reason does indeed have a full fledged Idea of the infinite (Yes). But Lyotard's story never finds its Yes. Although the differend does cause a painful feeling, a painful demand by the thing or the voice to bear witness to what cannot be represented (No), the bearing witness can never be successful (No). The bearing witness is, itself, another failure. Not a true Yes, it simulates Yes by double negation, by negating the sources of the first negation. This can clearly be seen in Lyotard's interpretation of Arakawa, for there we can see him slowly moving in on the blank by negating those features of our linking life that fill the void, that obliviate the event, the phrase, the blank. And what are those features? Linking itself, in all its forms.

The first doubled negation negates representation, for whether we represent one or many, real or fictional objects, representation situates the phrase that comes along, the blank, within an articulated universe of significance. Describing one of Arakawa's watercolors Lyotard notes that it "offers nothing to look at but itself . . . not representing any 'genre scene,' any landscape or still life, I can only describe to you its plastic disposition, and that is all its 'content'" (Lyotard 1984d: 10). Lyotard's figure for the way representation occludes the blank is derived from Duchamp's *The Bride Stripped Bare by her Bachelors, Even* (1915–23). He figures the occlusion of the blank as painting on glass, rendering the transparent opaque, and he suggests that the blank itself could be figured as the gap between focusing on the glass as an object and focusing on the objects beyond the glass (ibid.: 4). The blank, therefore, is figured as transparency, itself. Blank. So the first of the double negations is the negation of representation, representational form. Thus the blank is to be presented neither as this nor as that, neither as one nor as many, but formlessly, blank. Moreover, as formlessness is the characteristic source of sublime feelings, we are approaching both the blank and the sublime together, by negation (Kant 1987: sect. 23).

The second doubled negation turns against the chronological *now* to "neutralize the diachronic illusion," to negate "clock time" (Lyotard 1984d: 13, 6). This is an approach to the sublime *now*, and it requires a subsidiary negation, the negation of desires, goals, purposes, the various points of action. Goals and purposes are what divide our temporal experience into past–present–future, so to leave clock time, to approach the sublime *now*, we must negate or eliminate our desires and goals. Lyotard has a voice ask: "You don't want to want, you want not to want?" (ibid.: 4).[12] The goals of our activity, the point of existence will have to be removed, and with it, another subsidiary negation, we will negate or eliminate a creature we can call the desiring self. Or if desire is constitutive of the self, we would be negating the self, itself. Lyotard says as much: "But I would like to efface my presence as Arakawa tries to efface his, to untie the knot of the three 'I's where blank misapprehends itself, and to let blank happen (ibid.: 4).[13] A "theater of the end of the I" (ibid.: 22–3).

And with desires and the self removed, we can take another step, by multiply doubled negations, to the sublime *now*, beyond chronological time, to the blank.

It is not very surprising, therefore, that Lyotard figures Arakawa's blank negatively, as not being any of the things which occlude the blank. The blank is to explain how meaning is possible, but it is described in exclusively negative terms: "to link, some emptiness is necessary" (ibid.: 23). But since linking is the way to sense and to non-sense, blank must be a different kind of non-sense: "Blank is what permits these intermittences, the non-sense in which meaning is decided by forgetting non-sense" (ibid.: 13). The blank is figured in terms of transparency and as the desert: "Juxtaposition [paratax] destroys the architecture of meaning. It discovers the desert on which meaning constructs itself" (ibid.: 15). If this is the way to the sublime then the sublime may be, as Newman told us, *now*, but it might have been more apt to enter the idea that the sublime is *No*.

There is, however, something very unsatisfying about this account of the possibility of meaning, the possibility of linking. It is unsatisfying because it is conducted entirely in negative terms. Consider, for example: "to link some emptiness is necessary" (ibid.: 23). What is to be explained is that there is a multiplicity of different ways to link, different phrase regimens, different genres of discourse. Emptiness, blank, the void, each explain the possibility of these different ways of linking by clearing away the idea that the linkages were somehow necessary so that there would always be only one right way to link, one right way guaranteed by some special semantical object or other. This clearing away of special semantical objects is fine, so far as it goes. What it leaves completely out of account is why anything would ever arrive or occur within this emptiness, blank, void. That is why Lyotard finds himself writing a sentence like: "paratax thus connotes the abyss of Not-Being which opens between phrases, it stresses the surprise that something begins when what is said is said" (Lyotard 1988a: sect. 100). Approaching this explanatory problem only negatively, the positive arrival of one or another phrase must, can only ever, remain a mystery, a surprise. It is therefore understandable that in writing of the sublime *now* in Newman's work, and consistent with Newman's own interests, Lyotard gives this surprise a frankly religious tone.

> It is chromatic matter alone, and its relationship with the material . . . and the lay-out . . . which must inspire the wonderful surprise, the wonder that there is something rather than nothing. Chaos threatens, but the flash of the Tzim-tzum, the zip, takes place, divides the shadows, breaks down the light into colors like a prism, and arranges them across the surface like a universe. Newman said that he was primarily a draughtsman. There is something holy about the line in itself.
>
> (Lyotard 1991c: 85–6)

When you approach the other side of representation with your feet squarely planted on this side, then nihilism and holiness will be your only options. Representation represents "groundlessness as a completely undifferentiated abyss, a universal lack of difference, an indifferent black nothingness" (Deleuze 1994: 276). From the side of representation the other side can only look like nothingness, and if something arrives out of this nothing it will, of necessity, be incomprehensible: as terrifying as dread or as wonderful as grace.[14] But why should we settle for this? Isn't this a failure of philosophical imagination? Isn't this mysterious holiness cousin to that dubious approach to the deity which asks the deity to plug all the holes in our understanding?

Lyotard has discovered a limitation of representational thinking and stops, right there, before the mystery that there is something rather than nothing. This is a familiar philosophical response to a discovery of the limitation of some representational faculty: making some kind of peace with skepticism, whether Wittgensteinian, Kantian, Humean, Pyrrhonian, or something. I want to turn this around: "every time we find ourselves confronted or bound by a limitation or an opposition, we should ask what such a situation presupposes" (Deleuze 1994: 50). Rather than asking how to make peace with the limits of our knowledge, I want to ask: what must the world, the world as it is in itself, be like for our representational knowledge to be in this way limited? The world beyond representation cannot be *one* thing, or it could be represented as such, nor can it be *many* things, or they too would be able to be represented. Neither one nor many, the world beyond representation is "a swarm of differences, a pluralism of free, wild or untamed differences" (ibid.: 50). The University of Beauty will make its goal the release of these swarms of differences, this "world *without identity*," this "world of intensity" (ibid.: 241). Not to bear witness to the nothingness between phrases, the goal of the University of Beauty is to break on through (to the other side).

Return to your mark.

The University of the Sublime would have been a university painted a melancholy grey, a university whose highest ideals would have been those of bearing witness to the differend: devoted to presenting the unpresentable. This is a serious project, and Lyotard writes with a moral seriousness that is at once attractive and chastening, but it is nevertheless subject to two criticisms. First, the attempt to bear witness to the differend, to present the unpresentable, must fail. But as somber as this result is, it is still no reason to stop. Rather, by itself, it is yet another reason to respect the ethical trajectory of the man and the work named Lyotard. But we have also met a more fundamental criticism. The whole problematic of bearing witness to the differend is derived by double negation from the system: the system fills the void surrounding each phrase with linkages governed by the strategic goal of increasing efficiency, at any price. Bearing witness to the differend is an attempt to pare back the system's linkages to reveal the bare phrase, the blank, the sublime *now,* the abyss of Not-Being which opens up between phrases. The second criticism of Lyotard's project is that this negative account of the other side of representation needs to be supplemented by a positive, affirmative, account of what is beyond representation. And it is this positive account which projects an alternative ideal of a University of Beauty, a university devoted to breaking on through (to the other side).

Lyotard is not very attracted to Kant's account of beauty. On the one hand it comes with the demand that everyone agree, although they will never actually agree, and this brings the beautiful closer to the Habermasian ideal of consensus than Lyotard would ever come. He mocks Kant's account by telling us that its unanimous republic of taste should really be called The United Tastes (Lyotard 1988e: 38). But the main reason Lyotard ignores the beautiful is that, in spite of his deep respect for and knowledge of Kant, he tends to think of beauty in classical terms, as copying a perfect form. Commenting on Arakawa's panels he notes: "The work is a sumptuous artifact, entirely subject to the sober rules of beauty, and this is how it *pleases.* It is also by this perfection that it deceives" (Lyotard 1984d: 17). Lyotard seems to think of the beautiful in clear contrast with the sublime: the sublime, a negative pleasure taken in the formless; the beautiful, a positive pleasure taken in the perfectly formed.

This notion of perfection is not absent from Kant's account of taste (Kant 1987: sect. 15). But the notion of beauty I want to invoke is that of free beauty. Kant gives a few famous examples:

> Thus designs *à la grecque,* the foliage on borders or on wallpaper, etc. mean nothing on their own: they represent nothing, no object under a determinate concept, and are free beauties. What we call fantasias in music (namely music without a topic), indeed all music not set to words, may also be included in the same class.
>
> (Kant 1987: sect. 16)

These examples have the right feature for our purposes, they do not represent anything. This brings Kant's characterization of free beauties close to Lyotard's characterization of what it would take to bear witness to the sublime *now;* but with one essential difference. The non-representational quality that Lyotard finds in Newman and Arakawa is construed negatively: according to Lyotard, these two artists simply subtract representationality from their work. On the other hand, free beauties are non-representational not by negation but by affirmation, not by subtracting representations but by indeterminately increasing them. Let us begin our approach to the University of Beauty by returning to the two steps Lyotard took backwards in his effort to bear witness to the blank: the stepping-back from representation and stepping-back from chronological time. Non-representationality, pointlessness, escaping the chronological *now*, the loss of the self: each of these notions is fundamentally equivocal. They come in two flavors: negative and positive.

First, what would it be to become non-representational, but *not* by subtraction? Wallpaper. Patterns on the wall which don't represent anything and which are not simply recognizable geometrical shapes. Curving lines that suggest this representation, but then again another, and another, and so on. Representing many different objects, but not in some crazy one-man-band sum. This multiplicity of representational suggestions does not simply add a man's torso to a horse's body; rather, one finds and loses the representational powers of the wallpaper lines, undulating up and down the wall. A pleasing conceptual tease. Neither one representational form, nor many representational forms, free beauties suggest an indeterminate multiplicity of forms. Lyotard's sublime *now* was formless in a negative sense – it was *without* form – but free beauties are formless in a positive sense. They suggest an indeterminate multiplicity of forms, initiating the playful activity of the mind-seeking forms which slip and slide away, again. Formlessness construed negatively can stimulate the agitated, serious, negative pleasure of the sublime. Formlessness construed positively can stimulate the playful positive pleasure of the beautiful. To enjoy this formlessness is rather like enjoying caresses. It is almost as if we were allowing our minds to caress the indeterminate multiplicity of forms in the wallpaper. And like the delicate eyes and fingers mentioned in my motto from Nietzsche, the tempo of these conceptual caresses is likely to be *lento*. Caressing is not for lovers in a hurry. There is nothing efficient about it.

Someone will be wondering how the experience of wallpaper can possibly be paradigmatic of intense enjoyment of the beautiful. If this is not a worry that comes from the shock that anyone could take wallpaper seriously, the shock that one might actually feel the wallpaper entering into the life of a room and our lives within it, if it is not that shock, it is the shock of repetition.[15] After all, wallpaper is made of repeating patterns. However playfully indeterminate, however positively formless the pattern, the pattern repeats. And we naturally think that repetition is bad for meaning, repetition draining the authentic meaning out of our words and actions. But this is a mistake, a version of the same mistake we are mapping all along the difference between the Universities of the Sublime and Beautiful: the difference between No and Yes. Repetition can seem to drain significance from our words and the patterns on the wallpaper, but only if we insist on looking at the other side of representation from this side. Then repetition reduces significance to nothing. But repetition can also be a way of discovering differences between things that we had thought identical. Take wallpaper itself. The repeating patterns don't repeat perfectly, and caressing the shapes on the wall discovers swarms of differences where those living comfortably in the hurried land of representation can only see dumb repetition. The way down is the same as the way up, and just as repetition can drain simple univocal significance from the wallpaper patterns, so it can discover indeterminate multiplicities of differences: whether we are talking about taking the same drive, again and again, or reading the same poem, again and again, or caressing the patterns on the wall, the crease down your lover's back, again and again. Repetition releases differences.

Second, we might try to see if we could recharacterize the escape from chronological time in an analogously positive direction. This will be slightly more complicated, but only because the escape from chronological time involved Lyotard in some subsidiary negations, namely, of our purposes and of either our desiring selves or our selves, themselves. Lyotard subtracted desires, purposes, the point of action, because it is the goals of human action which divide our experience into past–present–future, into a series of chronological *nows*. The sublime *now*, approached by the sublime *No*: subtracting purposes, the remainder is pointlessness. This negative sense of pointlessness is precisely the one appealed to by Hardy when he insisted that the "great bulk of higher mathematics is useless" (Hardy 1973: 135). This is not the sense of pointlessness that I am interested in. Pointlessness, like non-representationality, can be approached positively. Think of this in terms of what happens in the middle of a purposive trip. In the middle of a walk to the store, we are not just setting out, and we are not coming to the end: in the middle of a trip we can be lost in a swarm of different thoughts, ideas, feelings, worries, enjoyments. These are activities which are pointless in much the way that caressing the patterns in the wallpaper was the enjoyment of formlessness. Not one point, not many points in some strange one-man-band existence, but an indeterminate multiplicity of points. And again the caress can be our model. In order to caress we have to leave behind the instrumental glory of the opposable thumb of the human hand. When we use our hands to do one thing, say typing, then we turn off all their sensations except that necessary to stay on top of the QWERTY world. A speeding typist may dance across the keys, but it is a dance from key to key. The instrumental use of our hands says No; No to the spaces between. But to caress we let the hand dangle as if it were a thing, but a very special kind of thing: a sensation machine. Dragging the hand, backwards and upside down, up the forearm of your lover. Unlike the typing fingers, the caressing hand welcomes every sensation. It can only say Yes. The caressing hand aims at no particular sensation. It welcomes an indeterminate multiplicity of sensations. Caressing is pointless not because it has no point but because it is involved in myriad points. There is a good kind of pointlessness.[16]

Giving up goals, in a negative sense, was linked by Lyotard to the loss of the desiring self, even the self, as such. And this good kind of pointlessness is also a way of losing the self, for a self pulled in myriad ways is not a self with any specific identity. It is as indeterminately identified as the positive kinds of formlessness and pointlessness which I have just sketched. Moreover the chronological *now* is overcome at the same time. For there are no longer any specific goals with which to define it, not however because there are no goals, but because in this world without identity, the "self" is stretched left and right, up and down, fore and aft.

When Lyotard was moving in on Arakawa's blank by following negative versions of non-representationality and pointlessness, the trajectory of his project was towards blank emptiness. Tracking the same series of concepts, but now positively construed, we find ourselves moving in the direction not of emptiness but of *intensity*. Think of graph paper. Each of the intersecting lines can be imagined pulling against each other, so putting tension on each intersection along two dimensions, x and y. A three-dimensional graph is a space of lines pulling their intersections along three dimensions, a twenty-dimensional graph along twenty dimensions. And an n-dimensional graph is a space of lines putting tension on each intersection along an indeterminate multiplicity of dimensions. Formlessness and pointlessness move us in this direction not towards emptiness, but towards a beauteous intensity. This is what the other side of representation is: swarms of differences, swarms of intensities, a world without identity. And in its pointlessness, beauty will recover its autonomy, but this time, not by negation. This time beauty's autonomy derives not from its lack of connection, but from the myriad lines connecting it from here to everywhere.

A maximally intense, maximally beautiful work of art would materialize this graphic image. The thought here is that every thing in the world of representation is, in reality, such a swarm of intense differences, but that our representational practices, our genres of discourse and phrase regimens, regiment this intensity, tying the lines of this graph in a knot. To break on through to the other side of representation is to untie these knots, to release the swarms of intensities. A more famous image for this other side can be found in Leonardo's studies of water, vortices, and deluges. For we can imagine a maximally intense, maximally beautiful work of art, in terms of these drawings. In one water study, water from a single source pours into a turbulent pool producing a swarm of swirls ejecting flows in all directions (Pedretti 1980: plate 29A).[17] We can imagine maximally intense activities in terms of water pouring in from all directions producing swarms of almost Cartesian vortices, then ejecting flows in all directions, to begin the cycle again. The University of Beauty is dedicated to the cause of releasing the lines of that intense graph, the powerful turbulent flows which Leonardo depicts, sometimes even breaking apart mountains (ibid.: plate 42).

There is, however, no reason to segregate the University of Beauty from the vocational activities which take place in universities today. It is now widely recognized that over the course of a life, the importance of technical training fades, and the importance of an independent, inventive imagination grows greater and greater. For the sake of our students and their employers, no less than for the sake of the dynamism of universities themselves, we should encourage those features of higher education (in whichever field) that ignite the fires of the imagination, radiating "light without heat," burning with a fire that does not consume (Freeman 1999). The positive pointlessness which I have been describing can be the secret to intensifying the life of the imagination, in any field. For an intensity machine must be a connection machine constrained neither by a stuffy respect for disciplinary boundaries nor by the mock wisdom of gruff practicality.

The University of Beauty will not relinquish the training of a professional and a technical intelligentsia (Lyotard 1984d: 49). There is, in any case, a sense in which such training will take care of itself. There is no need to fear that universities will relinquish that job any more than there is to fear that they will unplug from the world wide web. This is not to deny that some people can announce a commitment to technical training and the world wide web as if it were a breathtaking insight. The training of these two kinds of intelligentsia will continue in the University of Beauty, but like the consumption of food on a date, this training will not be the primary idea governing the university. The primary idea will be intensity, intensity achieved through pointless investigations, investigations which are pointless because of their many connections to an indeterminate number of points. For it is through achieving pointlessness that one breaks through the frame of representation releasing swarms of intensities, and it is this experience which is the source of breakthroughs which may sometimes actually even increase performativity but which, even if they do not, teach students what real thinking is like: not calculating within a representational frame, but experiencing the joy and ecstasy of breaking through.

The University of Beauty is dedicated to releasing these swarming intensities. That is its way of breaking through representation, not by negation to emptiness, but by proceeding pointlessly towards maximal intensity. The central focus of a University of Beauty would be the production of intellectual and emotional intensity. This is meant to be a description adequate to the best of what I see in universities, but it is more clearly a normative ideal of what a good university, of whatever size or focus, might reach for. A university might make its goal the production of energetic minds. A series of well-trained, graduating engineers and historians would be a beginning, but engineers and historians so energized by their life in the university that they could make things a little difficult for their first employers: that would be the end, the goal. An energized mind is a little unruly, but a university could do worse than produce physicists and biologists, computer scientists and Chaucerians who have been made a little unruly. This was the effect of the "preliminary course" at the Bauhaus, especially that of Albers, and it remains a tremendous technique for inciting innovation and discovery (Dearstyne 1986: 90–4).

Albers focused on playing with the materials to discover the more or less essential properties of the medium. Playing is a natural way to break free of the received representational framework, for thinking, especially rational thinking, tends to follow the ruts of the past. Albers's course had two moments that characterize almost any breaking through (to the other side), namely, a moment of free flight (play) and a moment of settling down again (inventing a new representation). But it is the first moment which increases intensity, and it is the first moment which made the Bauhaus ideal a little unruly. But universities at their best, have always been a little unruly. The Bauhaus is, in addition, a great model for how to insert the University of Beauty into the system, for the Bauhaus worked together with local industries to market the imaginative constructions that it stimulated. There is therefore no reason to think that the system would not be well served by Universities of Beauty, in both the long and the short term. But the goal of a University of Beauty is not to serve the system but to break through the frameworks with which problems are approached in each field that it includes under its roofs.

How do you break on through to the other side of representation? Here I take my cue from Deleuze and Guattari: I do not think it can be done alone. It takes at least two, perhaps not two persons, but it takes two (Deleuze and Guattari 1987: 243–4). And it must be beautiful. We begin to break on through by contagion, catching it, like a virus, from the intense, beauteous particles emitted by something or somebody else, inhaling beauteous particles deep inside our bodies, allowing them to take over our organs and cells, disorganizing them, releasing more particles, becoming imperceptible as self and as other, camouflaged by swarms of beauteous particles (ibid.: 280). Beauty: Deleuze rarely mentions it.[18] He speaks of the anomalous (ibid.: 243–4). But the anomalous is very close to what free beauty is for Kant: the wild play of sensations untamed by this concept or that, eluding the frame of representation, extending play to infinity. The anomalous can be a person, but it can also be a book, or a problem, or the light in the trees some afternoon, or a puzzle, or a surprise in the library or laboratory. It is whatever doesn't resolve itself when we approach the anomalous with routinized, received representations. Moreover the anomalous is attractive, it has the energy to draw us out. That is what teachers in the University of Beauty would be doing. Drawing students out, untying the representational knots that have inhibited the maximal intensity of the n-dimensional graph. Permitting Leonardo's swarming turbulent swirls to break through the frame of representation: releasing energizing joyful intensities.

In broad terms there are two ways or methods of intensifying, energizing the intellectual and emotional life within universities. The two methods can be construed as two aspects in the vignette by Leonardo that I imagined above: first, the arrival, from all directions, of flows of water to the turbulent pool, and second, the dispersal of such fluids, again in all directions. One can think of the first moment as the moment of compression or concentration, and the second as the moment of connection or extension. We should think of the targets of intensification, by either method, not as problems or fields or disciplines but as sites. The model is the archeological site which cries out to be studied by ecologists, economists, specialists in religion, architecture, pottery, farming, art, and so on. What we want to learn about is, in the first instance, such a site, not a discipline or a problem. Only if we lose sight of this important fact, will university research decay into empty scholasticism, but it is very easy to lose sight of.

The first method of intensification, the method of compression for increasing intensity of our engagement with a site operates by finding more and more within one site of investigation – a World in a Grain of Sand – for example, one text, perhaps one of Plato's dialogues, or one problem, perhaps Fermat's last theorem. By the method of compression we learn to see how endlessly much can be dug out of one site of investigation. The second method of intensification, the method of connection or extension, intensifies our engagement with a site by revealing its connections to other sites, other cares, other projects, so that, for example, a small move on the page or in the ground is shown to be relevant to many apparently distantly-related goals and concerns. Engineering projects can be intensified in this way, of course, because interdisciplinarity is a constant feature of engineering problems, but art-historical or philosophical research can be intensified in structurally similar ways. But as the figure inspired by Leonardo's drawings indicates, these two methods of intensification are abstracted from a complex turbulence, and thus the distinction between the two methods is somewhat artificial: each one reaches to the other.

The University of Beauty will be able to house the intensity of compression and the intensity of connection. These two kinds of intensity can be made accessible to undergraduates and graduates alike, and a University of Beauty might make it part of its mission to provide its students with an experience of both. But the demands these two techniques of intensification place on a university are quite different: where one needs easy access to the world, the other needs a quiet place apart. They both need a place where pointlessness can flower into intensities: the University of Beauty.

I will bring these abstract thoughts to an end by starting again, by reconsidering the distance between the University of Beauty and the current condition of the university. Again, I will be beginning with Lyotard, but this time, at one remove. In his posthumously published *The University in Ruins* (1996), an excellent interpreter of Lyotard, Bill Readings, sketched the possible shape of a university within which one might, here and there, occasionally, manage to bear witness to the differend. He does not really imagine a University of the Sublime, but rather a university within which the sublime *now* could *occur*. Readings characterizes the postmodern condition of the university in terms of the word university administrators use for performativity: excellence. Using only shades and shadows of grey, he paints a very Lyotardian picture of what he calls the University of Excellence. However, towards the end of his book, his account takes a slightly upward turn. But only slightly.

In the classroom, he suggests, there should be respect for the other, in two senses: not just in the sense of respecting the voices of this or that generally silenced group, but also in the sense of respecting the philosophical other, the blank, the differend. In the strict terms of Lyotard's philosophy we are told that "thought names a differend, it is a name over which arguments take place, arguments that occur in heterogeneous idioms," and he describes the aims of education in terms of remaining open to thought in this sense: "education is this drawing out of the otherness of thought that undoes the pretension to self-presence that always demands further study" (Readings 1996: 161–3). Readings takes his final task to be that of finding some way of folding this Lyotardian sublime into the University of Excellence.

His solution is intended to be neither pessimistic nor optimistic, but pragmatic, where "pragmatic" means no longer justifying the practices of the university in terms of some grand idea, but simply turning the activities of a university, here and there, to the demands of justice: bearing witness to the differend (ibid.: 129). This is what he calls dwelling in the ruins of the university, without nostalgia: not to turn the University of Excellence into the University of the Sublime, but to find a way "to think in an institution whose development tends to make Thought more and more difficult, less and less necessary" (ibid.: 175). He imagines the future shape of the University of Excellence as "an increasingly interdisciplinary general humanities department amid a cluster of vocational schools" (ibid.: 174). In Readings's vision, it will be in that domain of interdisciplinary, general humanities, that thought, here and there, might take place.

The institutionalization of a commitment to thought would, of course, kill it. Readings therefore suggests an opportunistic strategy. To bear witness to the abyss of Not-Being which lies behind every representation of a site of research, he would encourage self-conscious novel representations of such sites. In this way, accountability and judgment might be returned to the obsession with accounting that characterizes the University of Excellence (ibid.: 154). Accounting practices take a representation of a site for granted and simply determine efficiency within that frame of representation. The obsession with accounting is part of a concern with truth, for the truth of representations. Readings therefore turns away from truth to justice, away from calculation within a frame of representation to what escapes representations:

> My aim, then, is an anti-modernist rephrasing of teaching and learning as sites of *obligation*, as loci of *ethical practices*, rather than as means for the transmission of scientific knowledge. Teaching thus becomes

answerable to *the question of justice*, rather than to the criteria of truth. We must seek to do justice to teaching rather than to know what it is. A belief that we know what teaching is or should be is actually a major impediment to just teaching.

(Readings 1996: 154)

Readings imagines that just teaching will occur whenever teachers feature the blank which lies behind any representation and so he favors the formation of "short-term collaborative projects of both teaching and research (to speak in familiar terms) which would be disbanded after a certain period, whatever their success," thus avoiding institutionalization and departmentalization (ibid.: 176). These short term collaborative projects would, in Readings's picture, take place in the open area of generalized humanities, not in the vocational schools floating through those fluid collaborative projects. And they would, in their own way, here and there, bear witness to the sublime *now* even within the boundaries of the University of Excellence.

Readings's is a somber Lyotardian vision of a university dedicated to performativity and the forgetting of the differend, which nevertheless, here and there, can acknowledge that there is something which escapes the technical genre of discourse aimed at performativity. But the University of Beauty is rather more affirmative and polychromatic than this somber portrait of Readings in the Ruins. It is a matter of rhythm. A rhythm method which, like the other one, is designed to forestall what some conceive to be the point of all this (educational) activity. Designed to incite the intense joys of pointlessness. The rhythm to which I refer is that defined by Messiaen in the following terms:

Schematically, rhythmic music is music that scorns repetition, straightforwardness and equal divisions. In short it's music inspired by the movements of nature, movements of free and unequal durations.

(Messiaen quoted in Samuel 1976: 33)[19]

Elaborating, Messiaen tells his interviewer that military marches are not rhythmic because marches divide time into equal units repeating for as long as the march lasts. Even syncopated rhythms are not rhythmic: they feel off-beat only because of the regular repeated beat that we feel underneath the syncopation. Messiaen insists that rhythmic music in his sense, unlike either marches or syncopations, is music that does not have "an identical note-value interminably repeated" (ibid.: 39). Messiaen identifies three rhythmic characters, those with note-values that expand or extend, those that contract or compress, and those that never change: active, passive, and immobile characters (ibid.: 37).[20] The first two characters are cousins of the two methods of intensification that I have already discriminated: the flows arriving in Leonardo's pool are compressing, the flows leaving the pool are connecting or extending.[21] The pool itself suggests something like the immobile character, the terrain on which the University of Beauty will seek to stimulate intensities of compression and connection. Designing the University of Beauty is designing that pool.

Rhythm in the sense of Messiaen keeps us off balance in a far more profound way than even syncopation, and it is this aspect of Messiaen's notion of rhythm that can help us imagine a University of Beauty. For the sense of beauty at play in the university is the pleasing conceptual tease, curving lines that suggest one representation, but then also another, and again a third, and so on. Free beauties keep the mind in playful motion ever off-balance, not sure and stable, one solid informational bit after another. Off-balanced. If one is interested in increasing intensity either by compression or connection then one might make an effort to keep one's audience off-balance, and either of Messiaen's two irregularly changing rhythmic characters – the active or the passive – could be enlisted to this end. A work of art, a work of literature, a course, a seminar, a university, could each become an intensifying machine by learning from the rhythmic studies of Messiaen. Even textbooks. They would each, in their different ways, thereby become difficult, because nothing is easier than identical note-values interminably repeated, nothing is easier or more efficient than filling in a received representation, bit by informational bit. Painting by numbers. Whitehead was here before us:

> Whenever a text-book is written of real educational worth, you may be quite certain that some reviewer will say that it will be difficult to teach from it. Of course it will be difficult to teach from it. If it were easy, the book ought to be burned; for it cannot be educational. In education, as elsewhere, the broad primrose path leads to a nasty place. This evil path is represented by a book or a set of lectures which will practically enable the student to learn by heart all the questions likely to be asked at the next external examination.
>
> (Whitehead 1949: 16)

An excellent university devoted to the smooth and easy delivery of information, class by comfortable class, should be burned too. A good textbook, like a good university, keeps those it addresses off-balance. Not to bear witness to the differend, but to bring more and more different aspects of a site of investigation into play. Insensibly, increasing the number of conflicting directions in which the student is pulled as if becoming n-dimensional graph paper. Caressing the site, one curvilinear line of study turning imperceptibly into another, and another, and so on. To what end? To stimulate the enjoyment of pointlessness, intensities of compression and connection. Not the sublime. The beautiful. With this change of direction, we can learn from Readings's sketch of a university within which it would be possible, here and there, to bear witness to the sublime.

A University of Beauty would share Readings's turn from truth, for the truth is the truth of a representation. But beauty comes from breaking through (to the other side). Whether in Readings's formulation or my own, this can be shocking. But truth by itself matters very little to us. There are hoards of truths, the investigation of which would be a sign of insanity: whether the dust balls in houses on the left side of the street weigh more or less than those on the right side of the street.[22] In spite of what they all say, nobody really cares about truth, just truth. Indeed, if falsehoods, such as Newton's mechanics, give us what we want, for example reliable bridges, then nobody, except philosophers, cares much about the falsity of the effective falsehoods. A University of Beauty will allow truth to be trumped, not by efficiency, not by the sublime, but by intensity, intensities of compression and connection. To this end a University of Beauty will use a (Messiaenic) rhythm method to keep its inhabitants off-balance, folding the multiplicities of their cares and interests together. At the limit, nothing would be kept separate from anything else.

A University of Beauty would also share Readings's thought that to believe that we know what teaching is or should be is actually an impediment to teaching. Many universities today fund programs of faculty *development*, a name which would not surprise Lyotard, which are, in part, concerned with increasing the effectiveness, performativity, efficiency of teaching. This familiar goal – to increase the number of grades given by each teacher in a unit time – is sought in at least three ways. First, teachers are being encouraged to use the Internet to increase the reach of their lectures. Second, teachers are being encouraged to ask their students to work or learn *on their own* so that each student takes fewer minutes of a teacher's time. Finally, teachers are being encouraged to increase the efficiency of each of the decreasing number of minutes they spend physically or electrically with their students by learning from the sociological studies of learning methods: some learn best from lectures, some from discussion, some are visual, some are aural, some in groups, some alone, and so on. Each of these three ways of increasing efficiency presumes that when students go to university, they are there to be filled up with information, and each of these is a way of increasing the efficiency of the delivery of information.

In their postmodern condition, universities of excellence are sure they know what teaching is – the delivery of information – and they therefore take an otherwise surprising interest in teaching. Many are mislead by this blunt concern with pedagogical performativity into thinking that universities, by their concern with teaching, are becoming more humane. As if it is more humane to classify students into seven types representing seven learning styles and then sort them like eggs into bins designed for each type. But the worst of it is that this concern with teaching will, there is no doubt, pump information more efficiently into more students, and the university will have increased its productivity, its production of bags of bits of information. Neither the sublime nor the beautiful will be served. And there will be no reason to read Melville, for as packed with facts as his descriptions of life on the Pequod are, there are far more efficient ways of learning about whaling than reading *Moby Dick*. And what are the learning styles appropriate for the teaching of the sublime or the beautiful? What is the most efficient way to produce a powerful work of art? The most efficient way of falling in love? Somebody in a hurry may actually be conducting such research right now.

In a University of Beauty, teaching would not be smooth and efficient but rough and rhythmic, inspired both by rhythm's active character to connect otherwise disparate sites of intellectual activity, and by rhythm's passive character to find more and more stimulation from the energy compressed into a single site. Although the thought is familiar, it is still worth asserting that being a person well trained to deliver information as efficiently as possible has almost nothing to do with being a good teacher. Good teachers are passionate about something and that passion will keep them and their lectures, seminars, and classes off-balance, because the rhythm of passion is unpredictable. If it were not, it would not be a passion. And there is no technological substitute for passion. With passion, a teacher can excite students using any pedagogical technology; without passion, even most sophisticated technology is just wires. But in the age of the system, passion's rhythmic unpredictability looks like waste.

A University of Beauty would, a third time, share Readings's commitment to short-term collaborative interdisciplinary activities of teaching and research. Not however for the reason that such activities would, by featuring the invention of a new representation of a site of investigation, help bear witness to the differend. A University of Beauty would encourage short-term collaborative projects as a way of unsettling disciplinary comfort and bringing more forces to bear on a site of investigation than would otherwise be possible. Collaborators with different interests, sometimes even if they are technically from the same discipline, can disrupt the regimented rhythm of research which is so important to those who seek performativity, efficiency at any price.

But a University of Beauty would *not* be willing to restrict the activities I have been sketching to the generalized humanities department, ignoring the vocational schools which cluster around it. Apart from the difference in the aims of education, this is the largest difference between the University of Beauty and the university Readings imagines. For beauty and pointlessness are not only important for the humanities. There is no bigger mistake in thinking about the University of Beauty than that of thinking that beauty is only of value *outside* the vocational schools where one is free to be pointless; because there are no jobs there anyway. Energizing thinking about any subject depends on intensity. It may be the intensity of compression, or it may be the intensity of connection, but it always depends on intensity. Even the learning of Japanese grammar depends on relating that grammar to situations where language can show its power. Otherwise learning is like memorizing a dictionary. Of course I am not suggesting that we should use textbooks which have the bit where you explain it and then the bit where it is employed in an insipid little conversation. To learn a language is for the language to enter into your life, your body. Intensifying by connection. The same can be said for the learning of basic mathematics. Nothing kills intensity faster than being told that for these two months we will be sharpening our skills so that we can employ them in the third month. The intensity, pleasure, and joy must be there from the very first. If the mind is not a trunk to be filled with inert bits of information, neither is it a tool to be sharpened and honed with no attention to its use (Whitehead 1949: 42, 17–18).

It is true that from the perspective of performativity, the narrow channels of professionalized education have increased the rate of change: but always within defined channels. The problem is that the major changes, the breakthroughs as they are called, depend on breaking out of the ruts, breaking through the received frame of representation, and this task cannot be set aside as only needing to be attended to once a century. A freedom from the security of comfortable dogma, a playful attitude to the dogmas of our teachers, is an essential ingredient of turbulent intensity – not to say progress – in each of the narrowed professionalized fields. This is why vocational schools should *not* be spared the joys of intensity: compression and connection. Vocational schooling, as I intimated before, is even the ripest field for the intensities derived from pointlessness in the University of Beauty. Vocational schooling – already, and without changing anything – involves theory, practice, pleasure, function, and economy. Think for example of what is at stake in building a road or a bridge connecting two communities. Such a site of investigation might be approached from the side of population flows or bridge construction or the chemistry of concrete or the aesthetics of bridge design or the costs to the communities involved in terms of money or loss of independence and so on. It is simply a matter of not hiding this multiplicity of purposes behind the desire to seem either gruff and practical or sophisticated and theoretical. Unveiled, this multiplicity is a fine example of positive pointlessness, of beauty. Pointlessness is not to be restricted to the humanities, generalized or otherwise, it is the key to progress and excitement in every field. The University of Beauty is not mourning anything; it is a place where the intrinsic and extrinsic values of a university education are both ordered by the quest for the positive sense of pointlessness: beauty.

The University of Beauty is a pool into which flow cares and dreams from all directions, and out of which flow further cares and dreams in equally diverse directions. How should the pool be designed? The pool should stimulate passive rhythmic characters of systolic compression and active rhythmic characters of diastolic connection. The pool should un-balance the inhabitants of the University of Beauty. The recent architectural work of

Arakawa/Gins fits these requirements almost perfectly. I am referring to the Reversible Destiny Houses in which there is not a horizontal floor to be found. (See Arakawa and Gins 1997: 258ff.). Walking across the floor of a Reversible Destiny House requires irregular changes in the rhythm of one's walking, becoming sometimes quicker sometimes slower. These houses require their inhabitants to embody Messiaen's rhythmic characters and will make it inevitable that the several parts of the lives of their inhabitants will be folded together. Pile it all disorganized in. Le Corbusier's nightmare. I am particularly taken with what Arakawa and Gins call their Infancy House, which they describe in the following terms:

> Moving through a passageway that prefigures the dining room by mimicking its features, a resident can get a sense of entering the room even before setting foot into it. Bathrooms that exist on three distinct scales at once remain, appropriately enough, tentative and unresolved. Curved walls that lead ever elsewhere and make it difficult to know where to come to rest help strip residents of the dwelling habit. Residents embrace infancy as an openness to everything. Each resident repeatedly throws herself into the arms of her own infancy – an infant once again.
>
> (Arakawa and Gins 1997: 267, 302)

The Infancy House is a fine design for the University of Beauty, helping the residents of that university to become open to everything. Like a caress that only says yes. I thus find myself returning, at the end of this essay, to familiar Lyotardian terrain. Childhood. Lyotard, naturally, wants us to bear witness to childhood, to the "childhood of an encounter, the welcome extended to the marvel that (something) is happening, the respect for the event" (Lyotard 1992a: 112). My own interest is in recovering the intense joys of pointless play. Not to build a castle, but just to play with the blocks. Pointlessly. Intensely. Beautifully. As Brancusi warned, when we are no longer children, we are already dead.

Notes

The research on this project was supported, in part, by a grant from The Sloan Foundation (Grant #B1996-03).

1 See: Bill Readings, *The University in Ruins*, for an interpretation of the new shape of the university, its postmodern condition, as a university of excellence (Readings 1996).
2 I owe this chromology to Michael Mendelson and to his unpublished 1998 manuscript *Moral Horror*.
3 See the helpful discussion of the difference between presentation and situation in Williams (1998b: esp. 74–9).
4 Lyotard does not use "chronological" in precisely this way. In fact, he can sometimes speak of the task of art as "a 'chronological task'" (Lyotard 1991d: 88).

5 Lyotard does not stress the sense of intentionality as goal-directedness in quite this way (Lyotard 1991d: 90).

6 Lyotard translates *ein Ereignis* as "an event, an occurrence," (Lyotard 1991d: 90).

7 This is postmodern architecture in Jencks's sense (1987). Lyotard makes a point of differentiating what he describes as the postmodern condition from Jencks's postmodern architecture which is rather a naive expression of the system (Lyotard 1991d: 127).

8 This way of putting the difference between the sublime (No–No) and the beautiful (Yes) recalls the concluding lines of *Libidinal Economy*, which Lyotard published in 1974, and it projects another project, namely that of assessing the distance between the University of Beauty which I describe and what might be called a Libidinal University.

9 The thing appears in Lyotard 1991d: 3, as the "unknown thing." The voice appears in Lyotard 1991d: 77. The thing also appears in Lyotard 1997, where it is sometimes described as a "non-empirical entity" (1997: 140) and sometimes as the "unmanageable thing" (ibid.: 189). In general this essay, "Sight Unseen," does for painting what "Music, Mutic" does for music, but its distinction between the thing and the voice is more vivid than elsewhere in Lyotard's writings (ibid.: 217–33).

10 When he was asked how, given that neither the voice nor the thing could be represented, he could be sure there were two sources of the differend's demands, Lyotard said that of course certainty was out of the question but the fact that one could be a great artist and have no sense of justice was a sign that it was possible to bear witness to the *thing* but not to the *voice* (Conversation at Lehigh, September 11, 1995).

11 Lyotyard 1984d is the first appearance of the article "Longitude 180° W or E", in a trilingual edition: French, Italian, and English. It is unpaginated, but I refer to page numbers I have added in such a way that the first page of text is page 3. The subtitle, "work in progress," is part of Arakawa and Gins 1979. It is not part of the title of the version of *The Mechanism of Meaning* included in Arakawa and Gins 1997: 54–111, but that work is there described as an "ongoing project" (Arakawa and Gins 1997: 110).

12 I am blushing yet again, this time because in my hurry I am not giving any weight to the fact that Lyotard's article on Arakawa's blank is conducted as a dialogue between a voice from the east and a voice from the west. The rhetorical question cited here comes from the east.

13 The three "I"s are the three tubes labeled "tube," "twisted tube," and "broken tube," which appear in a panel of "Review and self criticism" of the version of *The Mechanism of Meaning* in Arakawa and Gins (1979: 93). That panel is almost titled POINT BLANK. (Compare the panel in Lyotard 1984d: 12, and the discussion at 11–13.)

14 In previous work, I have argued that for analogous reasons, we should be prepared to discover something like wonder in the work of the later Wittgenstein (Bearn 1997: 193–7). The objections I am here raising to Lyotard could therefore also be directed to that interpretation of Wittgenstein.

15 Robin Dillon, in one brief conversation, encouraged my seriousness about wallpaper.

16 Remembering pointless conversations with Alison Freeman in which this approach to pointlessness surfaced in the midst of a discussion of repetition and driving.

17 As Lord Clark has repeatedly pointed out, the drawings in the present category of water studies can be considered as the forerunners of the Deluge series. Their quality of line conveys an effect of impetuous flow, but one that

can be analyzed in its minutest components – lines of force that circle around and penetrate one another to generate bubbles of escaping air, themselves recurring in a circle of glittering rings on the turbulent surface. An incredible feat in draughtmanship, which achieves an unprecedented effect of plasticity as of a volume of frozen energy reminiscent of the variegated stones of geological ascent that had so much fascination for Leonardo at this time.

(Pedretti 1980: 43)

18 Here is one place where Deleuze and Guattari do speak of beauty: "Nothing is beautiful or loving or political aside from underground stems and aerial roots, adventitious growths and rhizomes" (Deleuze and Guattari 1987: 15).
19 Messiaen's notion of rhythmic music is what Tournier would call a meteorological rather than a chronological concept (Tournier 1998: 82–3).
20 Deleuze makes use of these three characters in his interpretation of Bacon's triptychs in Deleuze 1996, and Messiaen's appearance in that book helped me to imagine what could be called a Messiaenic rhythm of education (Deleuze 1996: 1: 48–9).
21 Deleuze characterizes these two characters, active and passive, in terms of the two phases in the beating of the heart: active dilation, diastole, and passive contraction, systole (Deleuze 1996: 1.55).
22 I first came to believe in the unimportance of truth by reading Nelson Goodman.

Bibliography

Adorno, T. (1977) "Letters to Walter Benjamin" in *Aesthetics and Politics*, trans. R. Taylor (ed.), London: Verso.

Ahmed, S. (1996) "Beyond humanism and postmodernism: theorizing a feminist practice," *Hypatia* 11: 71–93.

Altieri, C. (1989) "Judgment and justice under postmodern conditions, or, how Lyotard helps us read Rawls as a postmodern thinker," in R. W. Dasenbrock (ed.), *Redrawing the Lines: Analytic Philosophy, Deconstruction, and Literary Theory*, Minneapolis: University of Minnesota Press: 61–91.

Anderson, P. (1998) *The Origins of Postmodernity*, London: Verso.

Apel, K-O. (ed.) (1976) *Sprachpragmatik und Philosophie*, Suhrkamp: Verlag.

Arakawa and Gins, M. H. (1979) *The Mechanism of Meaning: Work in progress (1963–1971, 1978), Based on the method of ARAKAWA*, New York: Harry N. Abrams.

—— (1997) *Reversible Destiny: We have Decided not to Die*, New York: Guggenheim Museum.

Austin, J. L. (1962) *How to Do Things with Words*, Oxford: Oxford University Press.

Barr, A. H. (1936) *Cubism and Abstract Art*, New York: Museum of Modern Art.

Barron, A (1992) "Lyotard and the problem of justice," in A. Benjamin (ed.), *The Lyotard Reader*, Oxford: Blackwell: 26–42.

Barton, J. (1984) *Exploring a Character: Playing Shylock*, London: Methuen.

Baynes, K., Bohman, J. and McCarthy, T. (eds) (1987) *After Philosophy: End or Transformation?* Cambridge, Mass.: MIT Press.

Bearn, G. C. F. (1997) *Waking to Wonder: Wittgenstein's Existential Investigations*, Albany: State University of New York Press.

Benhabib, S. (1984) "Epistemologies of postmodernism: a rejoinder to Jean–François Lyotard," *New German Critique* 33: 103–26.

—— (1994) "Democracy and difference: reflections on the metapolitics of Lyotard and Derrida," *Journal of Political Philosophy* 2: 1–23.

Benjamin, A. (ed.) (1989) *The Lyotard Reader*, Oxford: Blackwell.

—— (ed.) (1992) *Judging Lyotard*, London and New York: Routledge.

Bennington, G. (1988) *Lyotard: Writing the Event*, New York: Columbia University Press (a)/Manchester: University of Manchester Press (b).

Bernstein, R. J. (ed.) (1985) *Habermas and Modernity*, Cambridge, Mass.: MIT Press.

—— (1994) "Democracy and difference: reflections on the metaphysics of Lyotard and Derrida," *Journal of Political Philosophy* 2 (1): 1–23.

Best, S. and Kellner, D. (1991) *Postmodern Theory: Critical Investigations*, New York: Guilford Press.

Blake, N. (1995) "Ideal speech conditions, modern discourse and education," *Journal of Philosophy of Education* 29 (3): 355–68.

Blake, N., Smeyers, P., Smith, R. and Standish, P. (1998) *Thinking Again: Education After Postmodernism*, Westport, Conn.: Bergin and Garvey.

Bobbio, N. (1995) *The Age of Rights*, London: Polity.

Bohman, J. (1987) "Introduction," in K. Baynes, J. Bohman and T. McCarthy (eds), *After Philosophy: End or Transformation?* Cambridge, Mass.: MIT Press.

Bromley, H. (1989) "Identity politics and critical pedagogy," *Educational Theory* 39 (3): 207–23.

Brons, R. and Kunneman, H. (eds) (1995) *Lyotard lezen. Ethiek, onmenselijkheid en sensibiliteit*, Boom: Meppel.

Burbules, N. C. (1997) "A grammar of difference: some ways of rethinking difference and diversity as educational topics," *Australian Education Researcher* 24: 97–116.

Carroll, D. (1987) "Narrative, heterogeneity, and the question of the political: Bakhtin and Lyotard," in M. Krieger (ed.), *The Aims of Representation: Subject/Text/History*, New York: Columbia University Press: 69–106.

Cassidy, J. (1999) "The firm: Goldman, Sachs ends a Wall Street era," *New Yorker* (8 March): 28–36.

Castoriadis, C. (1988) *Political and Social Writings*, ed. and trans. D. A. Curtis, Minneapolis: University of Minnesota Press.

Cavell, S. (1990) *Conditions Handsome and Unhandsome*, Chicago: University of Chicago Press.

Cheah, Pheng (1997) "Given culture: rethinking cosmopolitical freedom in transnationalism," *Boundary 2* 24 (2): 158–97.

Chen, Kuan-Hsing (1997) "The decolonization effects," *Journal of Communication Inquiry* 21 (2): 79–96.

Cohen, G. A. (1996) "Reason, humanity and the moral law," in *Sources of Normativity*, Cambridge: Cambridge University Press.

Cohn-Bendit, D. and Cohn-Bendit, G. (1968) *Obsolete Communism: The Left-Wing Alternative (Gauchisme, remède à la maladie sénile du communisme)*, trans. A. Pomerans, London: Deutsch.

Conboy, K., Medina, N. and Stanbury, S. (eds) (1997) *Writing on the Body: Female Embodiment and Feminist Theory*, New York: Columbia University Press.

Constant, B. (1988) *Political Writings*, trans. B. Fontana, New York: Cambridge University Press.

Cooper, J. R. (1970) " Shylock's humanity," *Shakespeare Quarterly* 21: 117–124.

Coyote, P. (1998) *Sleeping Where I Fall*, Washington, D.C.: Counterpoint.

Cumings, B. (1998) "The Korean crisis and the end of 'late' development," *New Left Review* 231 (September/October): 43–72.

Curtis, D. A. (ed. and trans.) (1988) *Political and Social Writings*, Minneapolis: University of Minnesota Press.

Dallery, A. (1989) "The politics of writing (the) body: écriture feminine," in A. Jaggar and S. Bordo (eds), *Gender/Body/Knowledge: Feminist Reconstructions of Being and Knowing*, New Brunswick, N.J.: Rutgers University Press.

Dallmayr, F. (1997) "The politics of nonidentity: Adorno, postmodernism – and Edward Said," *Political Theory* 25: 33–56.

Dasenbrock, R. W. (ed.) (1989) *Redrawing the Lines: Analytic Philosophy, Deconstrcution, and Literary Theory*, Minneapolis: University of Minnesota Press.

Dearstyne, H. (1986) *Inside the Bauhaus*, New York: Rizzoli.

Debord, G. (1967) *La Société du spectacle*, Paris: Gallimard.

Deleuze, G. (1994) *Difference and Repetition*, London: Athlone Press.

—— (1996) *Francis Bacon: Logique de la sensation* (vol. 1: Text, vol. 2: Illustrations), Paris: Editions de la Différence.

Deleuze, G. and Guattari, F. (1987) *A Thousand Plateaus: Capitalism and Schizophrenia*, Minneapolis: University of Minnesota Press.

Denzin, N. K. (1986) "Postmodern social theory," *Sociological Theory* 4 (Fall): 194–204.

Desmond, W. (1995) *Perplexity and Ultimacy:. Metaphysical Thought from the Middle*, New York: SUNY.

Doan, L. (ed.) (1994) *The Lesbian Postmodern*, New York: Columbia University Press.

Ellsworth, E. (1989) "Why doesn't this feel empowering? Working through the repressive myths of critical pedagogy," *Harvard Educational Review* 59: 297–323.

—— (1997) *Teaching Positions: Difference, Pedagogy, and the Mode of Address*, New York: Teachers College Press.

European Commission (1995) *Teaching and Learning: Towards the Learning Society, White Paper on Education and Training*, Brussels: European Commission.

Flynn, E.(1996) "Writing as resistance," *JAC – A Journal of Composition Theory* 16 (1): 171–81.

Forster, E. (ed.) (1989) *Kant's Transcendental Deductions: The Three 'Critiques' and the 'Opus Posthumum'*, Stanford, Calif.: Stanford University Press.

Foster, H. (ed.) (1983) *The Anti-Aesthetic*, Fort Townsend, Wash.: Bay Press.

Frank, M. (1988) "Lyotard et Habermas," in *Jean-François Lyotard: Réécrire la modernité*, Lille: Les Cahiers du Philosophie: 163–83.

Frascina, F. (ed.) (1985) *Pollock and After: the Critical Debate*, London: Harper and Row.

Fraser, N. (1986) "Toward a discourse ethic of solidarity," *Praxis International* 5 (January).

Fraser, N. and Nicholson, L. (1988) "Social criticism without philosophy: an encounter between feminism and postmodernism," *Theory, Culture and Society* 5 (2–3): 373–94 (reprinted (1988b) in L. Nicholson (ed.) (1990) *Feminism/Post-modernism*, New York: Routledge).

Freeman, A. (1999) "Light without heat," *Lehigh Review* 7.

Freire, P. (1972) *Pedagogy of the Oppressed*, Harmondsworth, Penguin.

Fritzman, J. M. (1990) "Lyotard's paralogy and Rorty's pluralism: their differences and pedagogical implications," *Educational Theory* 40 (3): 371–80.

Frye, M. (1983) *The Politics of Reality*, Trumansburg, N.Y.: Crossing Press.

Geiman, K. P. (1990) "Lyotard's 'Kantian socialism'," *Philosophy and Social Criticism* 16 (1): 23–37.

Geuss, R. (1996) "Morality and identity," in *Sources of Normativity*, Cambridge: Cambridge University Press.

Giddens, A. (1998) *The Third Way: The Renewal of Social Democracy*, Oxford: Polity.

Greenberg, C. (1939) "Avant-garde and kitsch," *Partisan Review* (Fall).

—— (1993) *Collected Essays and Criticism, vol. 4: Modernism with a Vengeance 1957–1969*, Chicago: University of Chicago Press.

Greene, M. (1995) *Releasing the Imagination: Essays on Education, the Arts and Social Change*, San Francisco: Jossey Bass.

Habermas, J. (1971) *Knowledge and Human Interests*, London: Heinemann.

—— (1979) *Communication and the Evolution of Society*, London: Heinemann.

—— (1984a) *The Theory of Communicative Action ,vol. I: Reason and Rationalization of Society*, London: Polity.

—— (1984b) "Modernity versus postmodernity," *New German Critique* 22: 3–14.

—— (1987) *The Theory of Communicative Action ,vol. II,* trans. T. McCarthy, Boston: Beacon Press.

—— (1989) *Moral Consciousness and Communicative Action*, London: MIT Press.

Hampshire, S. (1989) "The social spirit of mankind," in H. Foster (ed.), *The Anti-Aesthetic*, Fort Townsend, Wash.: Bay Press.

Hardy, G. H. (1973) *A Mathematician's Apology*, Cambridge: Cambridge University Press.

Hare, W. and Portelli, J. (1996) *Philosophy of Education: Introductory Readings*, Calgary: Detselig.

Hargreaves, A. G. (1995) *Immigration, 'Race' and Ethnicity in Contemporary France*, London: Routledge.

Heidegger, M. (1962) *Being and Time*, trans. J. Macquarrie and E. Robinson, Oxford: Blackwell.

—— (1985) 'The self-assertion of the German university," trans. K. Harries, *Review of Metaphysics* 38 (3): 470–80.

Hoagland, S. L. (1982) "Femininity, resistance, and sabotage," in M. Vetterling-Braggin (ed.), *"Femininity," "Masculinity," and "Androgyny:" A Modern Philosophical Discussion*, Totowa, N.J.: *Rowman and Allanheld*: 85–98.

Hutcheon, L. (1996) "Coda, incredulity toward metanarratives: negotiating post-modernism and feminisms," in K. Mezei (ed.), *Ambiguous Discourse: Feminism Narratology and British Women Writers*, Chapel Hill, N.C.: University of North Carolina Press.

Huyssen, A. (1984, 1990) "Mapping the Postmodern," in L. Nicholson (ed.), *Feminism/Postmodernism*, New York: Routledge.

Ingram, D. (1987) "Legitimacy and the postmodern condition: the political thought of Jean-François Lyotard," *Praxis International* 7 (3/4): 286–305.

Jacobs, D. (1996) "Writing for the Other: Lyotard on writing, resistance, and potential," *JAC – A Journal of Composition Theory* 16 (1): 176–81.

Jaggar, A. and Bordo, S. (eds) (1989) *Gender/Body/Knowledge: Feminist Reconstructions of Being and Knowing*, New Brunswick, N.J.: Rutgers University Press.

Jameson, F. (1984) "Foreword," in J-F. Lyotard, *The Postmodern Condition: A Report on Knowledge*, trans. G. Bennington and B. Massumi, Minneapolis: University of Minnesota Press: vii–xxii.

Jencks, C. (1987) *The Language of Post-Modern Architecture*, New York: Rizzoli.

Kant, I. (1961) *Critique of Pure Reason*, trans. N. K. Smith, New York: St. Martin's Press.

—— (1964) *The Critique of Judgment*, trans. J. Creed Meredith, Oxford: Clarendon Press.

—— (1987) *Critique of Judgment*, trans. W. S. Pluhar, Indianapolis, Ind.: Hackett.

Keane, J. (1992) "The modern democratic revolution: reflections on Lyotard's *The Postmodern Condition*," in A. Benjamin (ed.), *Judging Lyotard*, London and New York: Routledge: 81–98.

Kellner, D. (1988) "Postmodernism as social theory: some challenges and problems," *Theory, Culture and Society* 5 (2–3): 239–70.

Kelly, M. (ed.) (1998) *Oxford Encyclopedia of Aesthetics*, Oxford: Oxford University Press.

Kiziltan, M. U., Bain, W. and Canizares, M. A. (1990) "Postmodern conditions: rethinking public education," *Educational Theory* 40 (3): 351–69.

Klein, K. L. (1995) "In search of narrative mastery: postmodernism and the people without history," *History and Theory* 34 (4): 275–99.

Klimenkova, T. (1992) "Feminism and postmodernism," *Philosophy East and West* 42 (2): 277–85.

Klinger, C. (1997) "The concepts of the sublime and the beautiful in Kant and Lyotard," in R. M. Schott (ed.), *Feminist Interpretations of Immanuel Kant*, University Park: Pennsylvania State University Press.

Korsgaard, C. (1996) *Sources of Normativity*, Cambridge: Cambridge University Press.

Krieger, M (ed.) (1987) *The Aims of Representation: Subject/Text/History*, New York: Columbia University Press.

Kuhn, T. S. (1970) *The Structure of Scientific Revolutions*, Chicago: University of Chicago, 2nd edn.

Lacorne, D. (1997) *La crise de l'identité américaine*, Paris: Fayard.

Lacoue-Labarthe, P. (1987) *La Fiction du Politique*, Paris: Christian Bourgois.

Larochelle, G. (1992) "That which resists, after all", *Philosophy Today* 36 (4): 402–17.

Larrosa, J. (1998) *Apprendre et être. Langage, littérature et expérience de formation*, Paris: ESF.

Lash, S. and Friedman, J. (eds) (1994) *Modernity and Identity*, Cambridge, Mass.: Blackwell.

Lee, D (1976) *Valuing the Self: What We Can Learn from Other Cultures*, Englewood Cliffs, N.J.: Prentice-Hall.

Levins, R. and Lewontin, R. (1985) *The Dialectical Biologist*, Cambridge, Mass.: Harvard University Press.

Levinson, M. (1998) "The world economy in turmoil," *Dissent* (Fall): 5–6.

Lindsay, C. (1991) "Lyotard and the postmodern body," *L'Espirit Créateur* 31 (1): 33–47.

—— (1992) "Corporality, ethics, experimentation: Lyotard in the eighties," *Philosophy Today* 36 (4): 389–401.

Luhmann, N. (1969) *Legitimation durch Verfahren*, Neuweid am Rhein: Luchterhand.

Lyotard, J-F. (1968) "Preamble to a charter," ("Projet pour une Charte")in *Political Writings*, trans. B. Readings and K. P. Geiman, Minneapolis: University of Minnesota Press: 41–5.

—— (1970) "Nanterre, here, now," ("Nanterre, ici, maintenant") in *Political Writings*, trans. B. Readings and K. P. Geiman, Minneapolis: University of Minnesota Press: 46–59.

—— (1971) *Discours, Figure*, Paris: Klincksieck.

—— (1973a) *Dérive à partir de Marx et Freud*, Paris: Union Générale d'Éditions.

—— (1973b) *Des dispositifs pulsionnels*, Paris: Union Générale d'Éditions.

—— (1973c) "March 23," (le 23 mars") in *Political Writings*, trans. B. Readings and K. P. Geiman, Minneapolis: University of Minnesota Press: 60–7.

—— (1974a) "Adorno as the devil," *Telos* 19 (Spring): 128–37.

—— (1974b) *Economie libidinale* (*Libidinal Economy*), Paris: Minuit.

—— (1977) *Instructions païennes*, Paris: Galilee.

—— (1978) "One of the things at stake in women's struggles," *Sub-Stance* 20: 9–17.

—— (1979) *La Condition postmoderne*, Paris: Minuit.

—— (1980) *Des Dispositifs pulsionnels*, Paris: Christian Bourgois.

—— (1982) "Presenting the unpresentable: the sublime," trans. L. Liebmann, *Artforum* 20 (8): 64–9.

—— (1983a) M*oralités postmodernes*, Paris: Galilée.

—— (1983b) "Passages from *Le Mur du Pacifique*," trans. P. Brochet, N. Royle, and K. Woodward, *Sub-Stance* 37/38: 89–99.

—— (1983c) *Le Différend*, Paris: Minuit.

—— (1984a) *The Postmodern Condition: A Report on Knowledge*, trans. G. Bennington and B. Massumi, Minneapolis: University of Minnesota Press.

—— (1984b) "Answering the question: what is postmodernism?" trans. R. Durand, in *The Postmodern Condition: A Report on Knowledge*, trans. G. Bennington and B. Massumi, Minneapolis: University of Minnesota Press.

—— (1984c) "The sublime and the avant-garde," trans. L. Liebmann, *Artforum* 22 (8): 36–43.

—— (1984d) "Longitude 180° W or E," in *Arakawa* Padiglione d'arte contemporanea, 19 gennaio–20 febbraio 1984, Milan: Padiglione d'arte contemporanea.

—— (1985) *Discours, Figure* (Paris, Klincksieck)

—— (1988a) *The Differend: Phrases in Dispute*, trans. G. Van Den Abbeele, Minneapolis: University of Minnesota Press.

—— (1988b) *Het onmenselijke* (L'inhumain), Kampen: Kok Agora.

—— (1988c) "A memorial for Marxism," in *Peregrinations: Law, Form, Event*, New York: Columbia University Press.

—— (1988d) "An interview with Jean-François Lyotard," W. van Reijen and D. Veerman, *Theory, Culture and Society* 5: 277–309.

—— (1988e) *Peregrinations: Law, Form, Event*, New York: Columbia University Press.

—— (1989) "Universal history and cultural differences," trans. D. Macey, in A. Benjamin (ed.), *The Lyotard Reader*, Oxford: Blackwell: 314–23.

—— (1990) *Heidegger and "the jews,"* trans. A. Michel and M. S. Roberts, Minneapolis: University of Minnesota Press.

—— (1991a) *Lectures d'enfance*, Paris: Galilée.

—— (1991b) *Phenomenology*, trans. by B. Beakley, New York: State University of New York.

—— (1991c) *The Inhuman: Reflections on Time*, trans. G. Bennington and R. Bowlby, Stanford, Calif.: Stanford University Press.

—— (1991d) *The Inhuman: Reflections on Time*, trans. G. Bennington and R. Bowlby, Cambridge: Polity.

—— (1992a) *The Postmodern Explained to Children: Correspondence 1982–1985*, trans. J. Pefanis and M. Thomas, Sydney: Power / London: Turnaround, The Power Institute of Fine Arts.

—— (1992b) "Sensus communis," in A. Benjamin (ed.), *The Lyotard Reader*, Oxford: Blackwell: 1–25.

—— (1993a) *Libidinal Economy*, trans. I. Grant, Bloomington: Indiana University Press.

—— (1993b) *Political Writings*, trans. B. Readings and K. P. Geiman, Minneapolis: University of Minnesota Press.

—— (1993c) "In the name of Algeria," in *Political Writings*, trans. B. Readings and K. P. Geiman, Minneapolis: University of Minnesota Press.

—— (1994) *Lessons on the Analytic of the Sublime*, trans. E. Rottenberg, Stanford, Calif.: Stanford University Press.

—— (1995a) "Resisting a discourse of mastery: a conversation with Jean-François Lyotard" (with Gary A. Olson), *JAC – A Journal of Composition Theory* 15 (3): 391–410.

—— (1995b) "Sight unseen," typescript of "Les yeux fermés," trans. P. Dailey, presented as a lecture at Lehigh University, September 11.

—— (1997) *Postmodern Fables*, trans. G. Van Den Abbeele, Minneapolis: University of Minnesota Press.

—— (1998a) "A propos du différend: entretien avec Jean-François Lyotard," *Les Cahiers de Philosophie* 5.

—— (1999) *Signed, Malraux*, trans. R. Hanvey, Minneapolis: University of Minnesota Press.

Lyotard, J-F. and Larochelle, G. (1992) "That which resists, after all," *Philosophy Today* 36 (Winter): 402–27.

Lyotard, J-F. and Rogozinski, J. (1987) "The Thought Police," *Art and Text* 26 (September–November): 24–30.

Lyotard, J-F. and Thébaud, J-L. (1985) *Just Gaming*, trans. W. Godzich; Afterword by S. Weber, Minneapolis: University of Minnesota Press.

MacIntyre, A. (1981) *After Virtue*, South Bend, Ind.: University of Notre Dame Press.

Martin, W. (1987) *Recent Theories of Narrative*, Ithaca, N.Y.: Cornell University Press.

McLaren, P. (1994) "Critical pedagogy, political agency, and the pragmatics of justice: the case of Lyotard," *Educational Theory* 44 (3): 319–40.

McNally, D. (1993) *Against the Market: Political Economy, Market Socialism, and the Marxist Critique*, London: Verso.

Masschelein, J. (1998) "How to imagine something exterior to the system: critical education as problematization," *Educational Theory* 48: 521–30.

Melas, N. (1995) "Versions of incommensurability," *World Literature Today* 69 (2): 275–81.

Mezei, K. (ed.) (1996) *Ambiguous Discourse: Feminism Narratology and British Women Writers*, Chapel Hill, N.C.: University of North Carolina Press.

Moen, M. (1997) "Feminist themes in unlikely places: re-reading Kant's *Critique of Judgment*," in R. M. Schott (ed.), *Feminist Interpretations of Immanuel Kant*, University Park: Pennsylvania State University Press.

Newton, A. Z. (1997) *Narrative Ethics*, Cambridge: Harvard University Press.

Nicholson, C. (1989) "Postmodernism, feminism, and education: the need for solidarity," *Educational Theory* 39 (3): 197–205.

Nicholson, L. (ed.) (1990) *Feminism/Postmodernism*, New York: Routledge.

Nietzsche, F. (1982) *Daybreak: Thoughts on the Prejudices of Morality*, Cambridge: Cambridge University Press.

Nussbaum, M. C. (1995) *Poetic Justice: The Literary Imagination and Public Life*, Boston: Beacon.

Nuyen, A. T. (1992) "Lyotard on the death of the professor," *Educational Theory* 42: 25–37.

—— (1996a) "Lyotard's postmodern ethics," *International Studies in Philosophy* 28 (2): 75–86.

—— (1996b) "Postmodern education as sublimation," *Educational Theory* 46: 93–103.

—— (1997) "Education for imaginative knowledge," *Journal of Thought* 32: 37–47.

—— (1998a) "Lyotard's postmodern ethics and the normative question," *Philosophy Today* 42: 411–17.

—— (1998b) "Jean-François Lyotard: education for imaginative knowledge," in M. Peters (ed.), *Naming the Multiple: Poststructuralism and Education*, Westport, Conn.: Bergin and Garvey.

Olson, G. (1995) "Resisting a discourse of mastery: a conversation with Jean-François Lyotard," *JAC – A Journal of Composition Theory* 15 (3): 391–410.

Onega, S. and Landa, J. A. G. (eds) (1996) *Narratology: An Introduction*, London and New York: Longman.

O'Neill, J. P. (1990) *Barnett Newman: Selected Writings and Interviews*, New York: Knopf.

Ophir, A. (1997) "Shifting the ground of the moral domain in Lyotard's *Le Différend*," *Constellations* 4: 189–204.

Owens, C. (1983) "The Discourse of Others: Feminists and Postmodernism," in H. Foster (ed.), *The Anti-Aesthetic*, Fort Townsend, Wash.: Bay Press.

Oxford English Dictionary, ed. J. Simpson and E. Werner, Oxford: Clarendon.

Palumbo-Liu, D (ed.) (1995a) *The Ethnic Canon: Histories, Institutions, Interventions*, Minneapolis: University of Minnesota Press.

—— (1995b) "Critical introduction," in D. Palumbo-Liu (ed.), *The Ethnic Canon: Histories, Institutions, Interventions*, Minneapolis: University of Minnesota Press: 1–30.

Pears, D. (1995) "Wittgenstein's naturalism," *Monist* 78 (4): 411–24.

Pedretti, C. (1980) *Leonardo da Vinci Nature Studies from the Royal Library at Windsor Castle*, Johnson Reprint Corporation.

Peters, M. (1989) "Techno-science, rationality, and the university: Lyotard on the 'postmodern condition'," *Educational Theory* 39 (2): 93–105.

—— (1994) "Review of Jean-François Lyotard's political writings," *Surfaces* IV, 4 (electronic journal).

—— (ed.) (1995a) *Education and the Postmodern Condition*, Westport, Conn. and London: Bergin and Garvey.

—— (1995b) "Education and the postmodern condition: revisiting Jean-François Lyotard," *Journal of Philosophy of Education* 29 (3): 387–400.

—— (1996) *Poststructuralism, Politics and Education*, Westport, Conn. and London: Bergin and Garvey.

—— (ed.) (1998) *Naming the Multiple: Poststructuralism and Education*, Westport, Conn.: Bergin and Garvey.

Plato (1991) *The Republic* trans. A. Bloom, New York: Basic Books.

Poster, M. (1992). "Postmodernity and the politics of multiculturalism: the Lyotard–Habermas debate over social theory," *Modern Fiction Studies* 38 (3): 567–80.

Rawls, J. (1999a) "Justice as reciprocity," in *John Rawls: Collected Papers*, ed. S. Freeman, Cambridge, Mass.: Harvard University Press.

—— (1999b) "Justice as fairness: political not metaphysical," in *John Rawls: Collected Papers*, ed. S. Freeman, Cambridge, Mass.: Harvard University Press.

Readings, B. (1991) *Introducing Lyotard: Art and Politics*, London and New York: Routledge.

—— (1993a) "For a heteronomous cultural politics: the university, culture, and the state," *Oxford Literary Review* 15 (1–2): 163–200.

—— (1993b) "Foreword: the end of the political," in J-F Lyotard, *Political Writings*, trans. B. Readings and K. P. Geiman, Minneapolis: University of Minnesota Press: xiii–xxvi.

—— (1995) "From emancipation to obligation: sketch for a heteronomous politics of education," in M. Peters (ed.), *Education and the Postmodern Condition*, Westport, Conn. and London: Bergin and Garvey: 193–208.

—— (1996) *The University in Ruins*, Cambridge, Mass. and London: Harvard University Press.

Reynolds, D. (1997) "School effectiveness: retrospect and prospect," *Scottish Educational Review* 29 (2): 97–113.

Rojek, C. and Turner, B. S. (eds) (1998) *The Politics of Jean-François Lyotard*, New York and London: Routledge.

Roof, J. (1994) "Lesbians and Lyotard: legitimation and the politics of the name," in L. Doan (ed.), *The Lesbian Postmodern*, New York: Columbia University Press.

Rorty, R. (1985) "Habermas and Lyotard on Postmodernity," in R. J. Bernstein (ed.), *Habermas and Modernity*, Cambridge, Mass.: MIT Press: 161–75.

—— (1989) *Contingency, Irony, Solidarity*, New York: Cambridge University Press.

—— (1991) "Cosmopolitanism without emancipation: a response to Jean-François Lyotard," in *Objectivity, Relativism, and Truth: Philosophical Papers, vol. 1*, Cambridge: Cambridge University Press.

—— (1992) "Cosmopolitanism with emancipation: a response to Lyotard," in S. Lash and J. Friedman (eds) (1994) *Modernity and Identity*, Cambridge, Mass.: Blackwell.

—— (1996) "Education without dogma: truth, freedom, and our universities," in W. Hare and J. Portelli, *Philosophy of Education: Introductory Readings*, Calgary: Detselig: 207–17.

—— (1998) *Truth and Progress: Philosophical Papers, vol. 3*, New York: Cambridge University Press.

Samuel, C. (1976) *Conversations with Olivier Messiaen*, London: Stainer and Bell (first published in French 1967).

Sandel, M. J. (1982) *Liberalism and the Limits of Justice*, Cambridge, Mass.: Cambridge University Press.

Schott, R. M. (ed.) (1997) *Feminist Interpretations of Immanuel Kant*, University Park: Pennsylvania State University Press.

Schrift, A. (1995) *Nietzsche's French Legacy: A Genealogy of Poststructuralism*, New York and London: Routledge.

Schumpeter, J. A. (1950) *Capitalism, Socialism and Democracy*, New York: Harper and Row.

Searle, J. R. (1969) *Speech Acts: An Essay in the Philosophy of Language*, Cambridge: Cambridge University Press.

Shapiro, J. (1996) *Shakespeare and the Jews*, New York: Columbia University Press.

Shakespeare, W. (1992) *The Merchant of Venice*, New York: Washington Square Press.

Smart, B. (1998) "The politics of difference and the problem of justice," in C. Rojek and B. S. Turner (eds), *The Politics of Jean-François Lyotard*, New York and London: Routledge: 43–62.

Smith, M. (1995) *The Moral Problem*, Oxford, UK and Cambridge, Mass., USA: Blackwell.

Tournier, M (1998) *The Mirror of Ideas*, Lincoln: University of Nebraska Press.

Turim, M. (1984) "Desire in art and politics: the theories of Jean-François Lyotard," *Camera Obscura* 12: 90–106.

Turner, B. (1998) "Forgetfulness and frailty: otherness and rights in contemporary social theory," in C. Rojek and B. S. Turner (eds), *The Politics of Jean-François Lyotard*, New York and London: Routledge: 25–42.

Trotter, D. (1996) Introduction to Charles Dickens, *Great Expectations*, Harmondsworth: Penguin.

Usher, R. and Edwards, R. (1994) *Postmodernism and Education*, New York: Routledge.

Van der Hoek, C. (1995) "Het overleven van Lyotard," in R. Brons and H. Kunneman (eds), *Lyotard lezen. Ethiek, onmenselijkheid en sensibiliteit*, Boom: Meppel: 50–69.

van Reijen, W. (1990) "Philosophical-political polytheism: Habermas versus Lyotard," *Theory, Culture and Society* 5: 95–103.

Veerman, D. (1988) "Introduction to Lyotard," *Theory, Culture and Society* 5: 271–5.

Vetterling-Braggin, M. (ed.) (1982) *"Femininity," "Masculinity," and "Androgyny:" A Modern Philosophical Discussion*, Totowa, N.J.: Rowman and Littlefield.

Voltaire (1943) *Lettres philosophiques*, Oxford: Blackwell.

—— (1964) *Dictionnaire philosophique*, Paris: Garnier Flammarion.

Wade, R. and Venerosa, F. (1998) "The gathering world slump and the battle over capital controls," *New Left Review* 231 (September/October): 13–42.

Wettstein, H. (1995) "Terra firma," *Monist* 78: 425–43.

White, S. K. (1987) "Justice and the postmodern problematic," *Praxis International* 7 (3/4) (Winter): 306–19.

—— (1988) *The Recent Work of Jürgen Habermas*, Cambridge: Cambridge University Press.

—— (1991) *Political Theory and Postmodernism*, Cambridge: Cambridge University Press.

Whitehead, A. N. (1949) *The Aims of Education, and Other Essays*, New York: New American Library/Mentor.

Williams, J. (1998a) "Lyotard," in M. Kelly (ed.) *Oxford Encyclopedia of Aesthetics*, Oxford: Oxford University Press.

—— (1998b) *Lyotard: Towards a Postmodern Philosophy*, Cambridge: Polity.

—— (2000) *Lyotard and the Political*, London: Routledge.

Wittgenstein, L. (1997) *Philosophical Investigations*, 2nd edn, trans. G. E. M. Anscombe, New York: Blackwell.

Woodhead, C. (1998) *Blood on the Tracks: Lessons from the History of Educational Reform*, London: Office for Standards in Education.

Žižek, S. (1989) *The Sublime Object of Ideology*, London: Verso.

Index of themes

active passivity 225–9; critique of
228–9; principles of 227–8; *see also*
apedagogy
aesthesis(an) 152, 176
aesthetic(s) 67–8, 70, 111, 112, 120,
123, 145, 146, 147, 151, 205; aestheticization 27–8, 169, 175;
freedom of 122; Kantian 114
Algeria 23–6, 34f., 216
apedagogy 17, 195, 203–6, 206–8, 211,
216, 219
architecture 235
art 67, 186, 246
Auschwitz 167
authenticity 158f., 159
autonomy 67–9, 158ff.

Bauhaus 247–8
beauty 21, 242, 246
birth 152
blank 239, 240, 241, 246
body, the 151, 189

capitalism 217–18
childhood 160f., 149, 151–2, 154–5,
160–2, 256
colonialism 4, 44, 69, 206
commodification 194, 206–10
commodity 44
community(ies) 88, 146, 167, 196, 197,
200
computers 231
consensus/dissensus 2, 4, 12, 45, 50,
51, 59, 60, 62–4, 74, 77, 143, 196
Cubism 69
cultural difference 33, 195; marketing
of 206

decolonization 213

depoliticization 25
differend(s) 6, 7, 36, 37, 43, 80, 98–100,
136, 141, 173, 218
discursive, the 125–39
dissimulation 222–3
diversity 211, 232

emancipation 24, 29, 30, 32, 157f.,
163, 159
European Commission 176
event(s) 146, 149, 171, 195, 198, 200–1

fable(s) 17, 195, 203– 5, 208, 209
feeling 121, 123
figural, the 124, 125–39
forgetting 150, 161, 167f.

genre(s) 78, 198; multiplicty of 180, 198

heterogeneity 4, 10–11, 63, 67, 75, 78,
145
heteronomy 151

identity(ies) 32, 161, 167–8, 183, 198;
logic of 28
imagination 15, 71, 75, 85, 92–3, 103,
171, 196–7
incommensurability 3, 7, 40, 43, 49,
50, 51, 64, 128, 144
incommensurable 29, 46, 49, 51, 75
indeterminacy 5, 123, 149–52
intensity(ies) 22, 224–7

"jews" ("the jews") 119–24, 160–1, 167f.
jouissance 138
judge 5, 120
judgment 2, 5, 37, 43, 112, 116, 120,
122, 123, 143, 198; moral practice
of 113, 120; reflective 122

Index of names